Hist
959.303
B788
k
v.1

7541005

DISCARD

MAIN LIBRARY
Memphis and Shelby
County Public Library and
Information Center

For the Residents
of
Memphis and Shelby County

THE
KINGDOM AND PEOPLE
OF
SIAM.

VOLUME I.

AMS PRESS
NEW YORK

S.P.P.M. Mongkut
Rex Siamensium

THE KINGDOM AND PEOPLE

OF

SIAM;

WITH

A NARRATIVE OF THE MISSION TO THAT COUNTRY
IN 1855.

By SIR JOHN BOWRING, F.R.S.

HER MAJESTY'S PLENIPOTENTIARY IN CHINA.

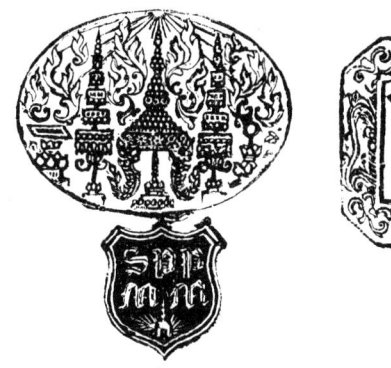

Seals of the First King of Siam.

VOLUME I.

LONDON:
JOHN W. PARKER AND SON, WEST STRAND.
1857.

Library of Congress Cataloging in Publication Data

Bowring, Sir John, 1792-1872.
   The kingdom and people of Siam.

   Reprint of the 1857 ed. published by J. W. Parker,
London.
   1. Thailand. I. Title.
DS563.5.B68 1975   915.93'03'3   70-179172
ISBN 0-404-54802-4

Reprinted from the edition of 1857, London
First AMS edition published in 1975
Manufactured in the United States of America

International Standard Book Number:
Complete Set: 0-404-54802-4
Volume I: 0-404-54882-2

AMS PRESS INC.
NEW YORK, N. Y. 10003

TO HIS MAJESTY

PHRA BARD SOMDETCH PHRA PARAMENDR MAHA MONGKUT
PHRA CHOM KLAU CHAU YU HUA,

The First King of Siam,

THESE VOLUMES

ARE RESPECTFULLY AND GRATEFULLY

DEDICATED,

BY ONE WHO HAS WITNESSED IN HIS MAJESTY THE RARE AND
ILLUSTRIOUS EXAMPLE OF A SUCCESSFUL DEVOTION OF THE TIME AND TALENT
OF A GREAT ORIENTAL SOVEREIGN
TO THE CULTIVATION OF THE LITERATURE AND THE STUDY OF
THE PHILOSOPHY OF WESTERN NATIONS;
BY ONE WHO FEELS HONOURED BY HIS MAJESTY'S CONFIDENCE AND KINDNESS
AND WHO REJOICES IN THE HOPE THAT THE EXTENSION OF
COMMERCIAL AND SOCIAL RELATIONS
WILL ASSOCIATE THE GROWING ADVANCEMENT OF SIAM WITH THE
PROSPERITY AND CORDIAL FRIENDSHIP OF THE
CIVILIZED WORLD.

GOVERNMENT HOUSE, HONG KONG,
August, 1856.

PREFACE.

IN submitting these volumes to the indulgent consideration of the public, the Author feels assured that the peculiar circumstances under which they are necessarily published (he being many thousand miles away from England, and therefore unable himself to correct the press) will not be forgotten by the reader, and that he will not appeal in vain for a lenient judgment on such errors as may be in consequence found in the Work. At the same time, he has taken every precaution in his power to ensure correctness.

The Author cannot omit this opportunity of returning his thanks to Bishop PALLEGOIX, for the permission kindly given by him to make use of the contents of his interesting work (published in 1854) entitled *Description du Royaume Thai ou Siam*. He has not failed to take advantage of this permission to a considerable extent.

The majority of the Illustrations contained in these volumes are taken from original photographs, made on the spot expressly for the Work. In this category is the portrait of the First King of Siam, the original of which his Majesty has done the Author the honour to send him.

Hongkong,
August, 1856.

CONTENTS OF THE FIRST VOLUME.

CHAPTER I.
GEOGRAPHY 1

CHAPTER II.
HISTORY 35

CHAPTER III.
POPULATION 81

CHAPTER IV.
MANNERS, CUSTOMS, SUPERSTITIONS, AMUSEMENTS 93

CHAPTER V.
LEGISLATION 170

CHAPTER VI.
NATURAL PRODUCTIONS 200

CHAPTER VII.
MANUFACTURES 237

CHAPTER VIII.
COMMERCE 241

CHAPTER IX.

Revenues 262

CHAPTER X.

Language and Literature 270

CHAPTER XI.

Religion 287

CHAPTER XII.

Christian Missions to Siam 335

CHAPTER XIII.

Bangkok 391

ILLUSTRATIONS IN THE FIRST VOLUME.

PORTRAIT OF THE FIRST KING OF SIAM . . . . *To face Title.*
FACSIMILE OF FIRST KING'S AUTOGRAPH 1
MODE OF APPROACHING SUPERIORS 129
MANDARIN IN ORDINARY COSTUME (No. 1) 130
MANDARIN IN ORDINARY COSTUME (No. 2) 132
SPECIMEN OF ANCIENT SIAMESE INSCRIPTION, ABOUT A.D. 1284 . 278
IMAGES OF BUDDHA 316
FLOATING HOUSE ON THE MEINAM 403
MONUMENT OF THE LATE KING OF SIAM 413
PRINCE IN FULL DRESS 449
PAGODA OF THE LATE SOMDETCH CHAO PHAJA 456
THE SACRED ELEPHANT OF SIAM 476

THE
KINGDOM AND PEOPLE OF SIAM.

CHAPTER I.

GEOGRAPHY.

THE kingdom of Siam is composed of forty-one provinces, each governed by a Phaja, or functionary of the highest rank. There are a considerable number of other districts under the authority of officials of lower ranks.

There are five provinces in the north—*Sang Kalôk, Phitsalôk* or *Phitsanulôk, Kamphang Phet, Phixai, Rahëng.*

In the centre, nine provinces—*Nontaburi* or *Talat-Khuan, Pak-Tret, Patummatani* or *Samkhok, Juthia* or *Krung-Kao, Ang-Thong, Muang-Phrom, Muang-In, Xainat, Nakhon-Savan.*

Ten eastern provinces — *Phetxabun, Bua-Xum, Sara-Buri, Nophaburi, Nakhon-Najok, Pachin, Kabin, Sasong-Sao* or *Petriu, Battabong,* and *Phanatsani Khom.*

Seven western provinces—*Muang-Sing, Suphan* or *Suphannaburi, Kan-chanaburi* or *Pak-Phrëk, Rapri* or *Raxaburi, Nakhon Xaisi, Sákhonburi* or *Tha-Chin, Samut-Songkhram* or *Mei-Khlong.*

Ten southern provinces—*Pakhlat* or *Nakhon-Khuen-Khan*, *Paknam* or *Sanauthaprakan*, *Bangplasoi* or *Xalaburi*, *Rajong*, *Chantabun* or *Chantaburi*, *Thung-Jai*, *Phiphri* or *Phetxaburi*, *Xumphon*, *Xaija*, *Xalang* or *Salang*.

Siam has been divided by Siamese annalists into two regions, the Northern, Muang-Nua, and the Southern, Muang-Tai; the Northern being that first occupied. The Southern annals are sometimes denominated the " Records of the Royal City " (Ayuthia), and take their date from the period when Ayuthia became the capital of Siam.*

The native name of the kingdom of Siam is Thái, meaning the Free, or Muang Thai (the Free kingdom, or kingdom of the Free). Bishop Pallegoix, a high authority in such a question, says that the modern name Siam is derived from one of the ancient titles of the country, Sajam, meaning "the dark race." In the Siamese books, according to Kämpfer, it (the name of the kingdom) is sounded with this epithet, Krom-Threp Pramma Laa Ikoon—Circuitus visitationis Deorum—" The Circle of the visitation of the Gods." This somewhat resembles the common Chinese name for their empire, Tien-hia, the " Under Heaven," meaning that celestial influences are confined to China alone.

The frontiers of the kingdom have considerably

---

* João de Barros says that nine kingdoms were in his day subject to the sovereigns of Siam, of which only two were peopled by the Siamese races; namely, the southern kingdom, of which Ayuthia was the capital, and the northern, having for its capital Chaumua. Only in these two was the Siamese language spoken.—*Decadas*, vol. v. p. 161.

varied at different periods of its history;* but on the western, northern, and eastern frontiers of Siam, the territorial line cannot be very accurately traced, as there are many tribes whose subjection is by no means complete, and border wars between the Malayan and Burmese races on one side, and the Cambodian and the Cochin Chinese on the other, are of constant occurrence; but its present boundaries extend from four to twenty or twenty-one degrees of N. lat. or nearly twelve hundred miles in its greatest length: its greatest breadth is from ninety-six to one hundred and two degrees of E. long., and may be estimated at about three hundred and fifty miles. Borgman estimates the whole area of Siam and its dependencies at two hundred and ninety thousand square miles, Crawfurd at one hundred and ninety thousand miles. The districts beyond the limits of Siam proper, to the north and east, are in a state of some dependence, and pay tribute with more or less regularity, but generally once in three years. The token of subjection is the presentation of a tree made of gold or silver, usually accompanied with gifts of the various and most valuable produce of the country. The more sub-

---

* Camoens speaks of Tavai as the beginning of the Siamese empire—
Olha Tavai cidade, onde começa
De Siâo largo o imperio tam comprido—(*Lus.* can. x. cxxiii.)
and of the subjection to Siam of Pam, Patane, and other kingdoms. The earliest accounts we possess of Siam are those given by the ancient Portuguese chroniclers. These, in all important particulars, agree with those which are to be found in other early records of travellers. João de Barros devotes one chapter of his *Decades* (Decada iii., liv. ii. cap. v.) to a description of the Grande Reyno de Siâo, which he ranks among the three great Oriental empires, subject to "poderosos principes," the first being China, the second Siam, the third Bisnaya.

stantial evidence of recognised authority is the furnishing the contingents of troops when the King of Siam is engaged in war with the neighbouring States. But the hold of the Suzerain on the vassal is as fluctuating as the political agitations which from time to time trouble the tranquillity of these regions. Siam itself pays tribute to China; the King of Siam seeks from the Emperor at Peking a special recognition of his right to reign. He sends every three years his envoy to the Chinese capital. There is no doubt that the Siamese receive in the remission of duties upon the cargoes of the tribute-bearing ships more than an equivalent for the tribute they bear, and the Government of China in no respect interferes with that of Siam, nor do the Chinese in Siam enjoy any other privileges and advantages than those which result from their superior industry, activity, aptitude for business, perseverance, and capital. Yet the external forms of vassalage continue to be observed rather out of reverence for ancient traditions and usages, than from any power which China possesses to enforce the rights of sovereignty, or any disposition on the part of Siam practically to submit to them.

The extent of submission of all dependent States is decided by the adjacency and the efficient display and exercise of civil or military authority on the part of the sovereign authority, whose influence is relaxed by distance. The sovereign governs as much and as far as he is able. He frequently (as in more civilized parts of the world) appropriates to himself titles which are shadows, mementos of a state of things that has passed away. At the present time have we not a King of Jerusalem in Italy? and it was only by the Treaty of Amiens that the title of *Rex Franciæ* was surrendered by the Sovereign of Great Britain. Sovereignty over the kingdom of Cambodia, which is on the frontiers of Siam and Cochin China, is claimed by each, and the Cambodian prince, unable to resist either of the sovereigns, pays tribute to both.

The snowy mountain ranges of the north descend from the Chinese province of Yunnan, and branch off into two great divisions, between which lies the fertile valley of Siam: another chain runs down to the western side, extending over a surface of seven hundred and fifty miles, to the Malayan peninsula. The elevation of these mountains has not been accurately ascertained, but they probably tower up to five or six thousand feet. On the eastern bank of the Tenasserim river rises the chain of the " Three Hundred Peaks," which, as their name denotes, are remarkable for their sharp and conical forms. It is said there would be little difficulty in establishing a water communication between the Bay of Bengal and the Gulf of Siam. In about lat. 11° the direct passage across the isthmus is about fifty miles. A ship canal, if practicable, would be next in importance to those which have been proposed to cross the Isthmus of Darien, in America, and that of Suez, in Egypt; and it is to be hoped that our opening relations with Siam will lead to an investigation and solution of a question so interesting to geographical and commercial inquiry.

This would, indeed, be a noble work; and, if the information I received be correct, a few miles of canalization are alone required to unite the navigable river communications which now exist. The time which would be saved in all voyages between India and Eastern Asia, by avoiding the long *détour* by the Straits of Malacca, may often be estimated, not by days, but by weeks.

The chain of mountains which divide Siam from Cambodia is little known; but where it has been seen or visited, the elevations are found to be of a moderate height, and are clothed with vegetation. Communications with Cambodia are for the most part tardy and difficult. I was informed by the Catholic Bishop, that in visiting Bangkok he has been able to traverse by water a considerable part of the distance between the Cambodian and the Siamese capitals; but the existing maps are very unsatisfactory and imperfect.

The various mountain chains which run through the Siamese territories are ramifications from the great Himala range, and descend into Cambodia on the south-east, and to the Malayan peninsula on the south-west. But Siam proper may be deemed a vast plain from which the mountains rise higher and higher as we reach the Laos dependencies. What the Nile is to Egypt is the Meinam to Siam, with the distinction that while deserts and desolation bound the green line which fringes the borders of the Nile, there is along the banks of the Meinam, wherever labour has failed to redeem the soil, a vast, fertile, and feracious jungle, which has to be reclaimed, but which when reclaimed would, no doubt, be magnificently productive. The flowing of the never-failing rivers—the fall of the periodical rains—the fervour of the tropical sun—the richness of the soil,—all invite the cares of the cultivator, and would bring the recompence of abundant harvests. The area of the valley of the Meinam has been estimated by some authorities at about 12,000 square miles, but this extent probably embraces only that alluvial portion of the soil which is visited by the annual inundations. The soil of Siam is indeed in all the prolific parts alluvial, formed of the mud or clay brought down by the rivers from the mountains. The *Meinam* (or *Menam*),* a word which means the "mother of waters," has its source in the mountains of Yunnan in China, at a distance of about 800 miles from its mouth. It receives many tributaries in its course—divides itself after receiving the waters of the Phitsalok branch, and again unites above Bangkok, where, with a depth of from six to eight fathoms, it rolls its magnificent tide into the Gulf of Siam.

The Meinam has its annual inundation. Impregnated with the rich soil which it brings from the interior, in the month of June its waters begin to rise, and in August they overflow the banks to a height sometimes exceeding six feet above the ordinary level. In the first public audience I had with the first King, he called my attention to the inundation

---

* Olha o rio Menâo que se derrama
Do grande lago que Chiamai se chama.

The Meinam now behold, whose waters take
Their sources in the great Chiamai lake.—Camoês, *Lus.* x. cxxv.

of the river, as the main source of the fertility of the soil: the rice-fields become greener and more promising as the waters spread, which generally remain till the month of November, the land having the appearance of a lake. Boats traverse it in all directions, temporary canals being formed among the rice-fields to facilitate their circulation. Pallegoix affirms that though the high lands are submerged for several months, the lower regions of the country at a distance of thirty miles from the sea are never inundated, which he attributes to the strength of the tides, which, in rising, drive back the descending waters with an irresistible force; and at the ebb they make their way by the ordinary stream to the ocean, so that they have no time to spread themselves over the adjacent lands. A failure of the inundation is perdition to a large portion of the rice-crops.

But the country sometimes suffers fearfully from these inundations. That of 1831 nearly destroyed all the sugar plantations, and three or four feet of water continuing to cover the face of the country, almost all the cattle perished. The rice-harvest was seriously affected, and the finest fruit-trees swept away, so that it was said only one durian tree was left in Siam; but fruit abounded—fruit of singular variety and excellence—in 1855, and the mischiefs of the floods appeared to have been wholly repaired.

The following note on the names of rivers in Siam is from the pen of the present king, and is one of his contributions to the Bangkok Calendar of 1850:—

"The word *Menam* in Siamese is a generic name for river, and one of the names of the Bangkok river.

But as the Siamese call all rivers 'Menam,' and the word is used by them in the same manner as river in English, and Nudi in Hindustani and Pali, it is wrong for Americans and some other nations to call the Bangkok river simply 'Menam,' for it has a specific name, same as the Amazon, Ganges, &c. It is the custom of the Siamese to call the stream nearest to them 'Menam,' and add the name of one of the principal towns or villages on its banks to it, as Menam Bangkok, Menam Koung, Menam Tachin, &c. The true name of the Bangkok river is 'Menam Chau Phya,' but it has become obsolete."

When the waters of the Meinam are supposed to have reached their highest point, the King deputes one hundred Bonzes, who are instructed to command the inundation to proceed no further. These functionaries embark on state barges, issue the royal mandate to the waters, bidding them turn back in their course; and they accompany their intervention with exorcisms, which are sometimes ineffectual, and show that the falling of the waters is no more subject to the commands of the Sovereign of Siam than were the tides on the British shores controlled by the Danish King.

The ancient annals of Siam report that, in the seventh century, Chinese junks ascended the Meinam as far as Sangkhalok, which is a distance of one hundred and twenty leagues from the sea. At the present time, the river is only navigable to a distance of about thirty leagues.

On the eastern branch of the Meinam the rapids commence at Pak Priau, where the rowers leave the boats, and drag them, as they are able, through the rocks and foaming waters; but they are often driven back by the impetuosity of the stream. There are about ten waterfalls within the space of seven or eight leagues, but none impassable, and during six months of the year the great floods cause them to disappear.

The Meinam disembogues itself through its three mouths at the head of the Gulf of Siam, after a course of nearly eight hundred miles, though by some writers estimated at one thousand miles, of which about four hundred and fifty form what is called the valley of the Meinam, with an average breadth of about fifty miles of land, constituting, according to the usually-received estimates, an area of above twenty-two thousand square miles of territory, whose fertility is not exceeded by that of any portion of the globe.

In ascending and descending the Meinam, I was amused with the novel sight of fish leaving the river —gliding over the wet banks, and losing themselves among the trees of the jungle. Pallegoix asserts that such fish will wander more than a league from the water. "Some years ago,"—I translate his words,— "a great heat had dried up all the ponds in the neighbourhood of Ayuthia: during the night torrents of rain fell. Next day, going for a walk into the country, how great was my surprise at seeing the ponds almost full, and a quantity of fish leaping about! 'Whence have these fish come?' I inquired of a labourer: 'yesterday there was not one.' He said they were come under favour of the rain. In 1831, when fish were uncommonly cheap, the Bishop of Siam thought fit to buy a supply of living fish, and he poured fifty cwt. into his ponds: but, in less than a month, nine-tenths escaped during a rain that fell in the night. There are three species of this wandering fish, called Pla-xon, pla-duk, pla-mó. The first is voracious, and about the size of a carp; salted and dried, it can be preserved for a year: it is very abundant, and exported to China, Singapore, and Java, and is a particularly wholesome and health-giving fish.

"The *dog's tongue* is a fish shaped like the sole; it attaches itself to the bottom of boats, and makes a sonorous noise, which is more musical when several are stuck to the same bank and act in concert."*

Kämpfer puts forth a theory that "were it not for the vast pains it would require to trace out its several channels through the forests and deserts, and to open a navigation, it might be possible for vessels to go from hence (Siam) to Bengal." Of the Meinam he remarks that the inundations, beginning in September, and falling in December, are the results of the dissolving of the snow in the mountainous regions, aided by the heavy rains; that the water on the land rises to the level of the river before the river swells, and inundates the banks; that the land water is nitrous, the river sweet and wholesome; that though the flow of water is naturally towards the sea, the inundations principally benefit the upper and middle regions; that the fertility of the soil is such, that the rice grows as fast as the water rises, and that the ripe ears are gathered by the reapers, and the straw, "often of

---

* Pallegoix, i. 193—4.

incredible length," left in the water; and that if the absence of the north wind prevent the return of the waters to their ordinary channel, there is a great creation of *malaria*, whose effects are most pernicious to the public health, and are sought to be warded off by imposing and costly religious ceremonies through the whole country.*

According to the reports of travellers, there are numerous towns and villages to the north of Bangkok, along the sides of the Meinam; the adjacent plains being principally dedicated to the cultivation of rice. In some of the inhabited localities, the different races, Siamese, Cochin-Chinese, Peguans, Laos, and Chinese are blended; in others a separate race is located. Between the modern and the ancient capital, Bangkok and Ayuthia, is a village called the "Sunken Ship," the houses being erected round a mast which towers above the surface at low water.

The ancient city of Ayuthia, whose pagodas and palaces were the object of so much laudation from ancient travellers, and which was called the Oriental Venice, from the abundance of its canals and the beauty of its public buildings, is now almost wholly in ruins, its towers and temples whelmed in the dust and covered with rank vegetation. Ayuthia was founded A. D. 1351, and was devastated by the Burmese in 1751, when Bangkok became the royal residence. The native name of Ayuthia was Sijon Thijan, meaning "Terrestrial Paradise."†

---

* Kämpfer, p. 44.
† The Siamese are in the habit of giving very ostentatious names to their cities, which, as La Loubere says, "do signify great things." Tian-

The general outlines of the old city so closely resemble those of Bangkok, that the map of the one might easily be mistaken for the representation of the other.

It may not be out of place here to introduce the description of Ayuthia from the pen of Mandelsloe*— one of those painstaking travellers whose contributions to geographical science have been collected in the ponderous folios of Dr. Harris (vol. i. p. 781).

"The city of Judda is built upon an island in the river Menam. It is the ordinary residence of the King of Siam, having several very fair streets, with spacious channels regularly cut. The suburbs are on both sides of the river, which, as well as the city itself, are adorned with many temples and palaces; of the first of which there are above three hundred within the city, distinguished by their gilt steeples, or rather pyramids, and afford a glorious prospect at a distance. The houses are, as all own he Indies, but indifferently built, and covered with tiles. The royal palace is equal to a large city. Ferdinando Mendez Pinto makes the number of inhabitants of this city amount, improbably, to four hundred thousand families. It is looked upon as impregnable, by

---

tong, for instance, signifies "True gold;" Canapong-pet, "Walls of diamond;" La Kongunau, "Mountain of heaven."[1] Pallegoix speaks of the ambitious titles given to Siamese towns, among which he mentions "the City of Angels," "the City of Archangels," and the "Celestial spectacle."

* Mandelsloe was born in Lower Saxony, A.D. 1615. He left Europe on his Oriental travels in 1636 to make a tour of the Indies, of which the principal object was to establish relations between the Duke of Holstein and the Shah of Persia.

[1] La Loubere, English Translation, p. 4. London, 1693.

reason of the overflowing of the river at six months' end. The King of Siam, who takes amongst his other titles that of Paecan Salsu, *i. e.*,—Sacred Member of God,—has this to boast of, that, next to the Mougul, he can deduce his descent from more kings than any other in the Indies. He is absolute, his privy councillors, called mandarins, being chosen and deposed barely at his pleasure. When he appears in public, it is done with so much pomp and magnificence as is scarce to be imagined, which draws such a veneration to his person from the common people, that, even in the streets, as he passes by, they give him godlike titles and worship. He marries no more than one wife at a time, but has an infinite number of concubines. He feeds very high; but his drink is water only, the use of strong liquors being severely prohibited, by their ecclesiastical law, to persons of quality in Siam. As the thirds of all the estates of the kingdom fall to his exchequer, so his riches must be very great; but what makes them almost immense is, that he is the chief merchant in the kingdom, having his factors in all places of trade, to sell rice, copper, lead, saltpetre, &c., to foreigners. Mendez Pinto makes his yearly revenue rise to twelve millions of ducats, the greatest part of which being laid up in his treasury, must needs swell to an infinity in process of time."

Ayuthia was formerly one of the most distinguished cities of the East. The spires of the pagodas and pyramids, blackened by time, still tower above the magnificent trees which grow amidst the masses of ruins they overshadow. The ancient city was about three leagues in circumference. Amidst the broken walls of palaces and temples are colossal statues from fifty to sixty feet high. These are mostly of brick, covered with brass of the thickness of two fingers. The annals of Siam report, that in founding one of these statues, 20,000lbs. of copper, 2000lbs. of silver, and 400lbs. of gold were employed. The walls of the city are overturned—thick and impenetrable masses of weeds, brushwood and tall trees, tenanted by bats and vultures, cover the vast desolation. In the midst of the heaps of rubbish, treasures are often discovered. The new city of Ayuthia surrounds the ancient site. It has two lines of floating bazaars. Its population is about 40,000. At a league's distance from the city, on the northern side, is a majestic edifice called the "Golden Mountain," built A.D. 1387. It is a pyramid four hundred feet high, each side having a staircase by which large galleries surrounding the building are mounted. From the third stage there is a splendid prospect; and there are four corridors by which the dome is entered, in whose centre is a gilded image of Buddha, rendered fetid by the depositions of millions of bats, which day and night are flitting in dire confusion around the altar. The dome is elevated one hundred and fifty feet above the galleries, and terminates in a gilded spire.

I have received the following account of the present condition of Ayuthia, the old capital of Siam, from a gentleman who visited it in December, 1855:—

"Ayuthia is at this time the second town of the

kingdom. Situated, as the greater part is, on a creek or canal connecting the main river with a large branch which serves as the high road to Pakpriau, Korat, and Southern Laos, travellers are apt entirely to overlook it when visiting the ruins of the various wats or temples on the island where stood the ancient city.

"The present number of inhabitants cannot be less than between twenty and thirty thousand, among which are a large number of Chinese, a few Burmese, and some natives of Laos. They are principally employed in shopkeeping, agriculture, or fishing, for there are no manufactories of importance. Floating houses are most commonly employed as dwellings, the reason for which is that the Siamese very justly consider them more healthy than houses on land.

"The soil is wonderfully fertile. The principal product is rice, which, although of excellent quality, is not so well adapted for the market as that grown nearer the sea, on account of its being much lighter and smaller. A large quantity of oil, also an astringent liquor called toddy, and sugar, is manufactured from the palm (Elaeis), extensive groves of which are to be found in the vicinity of the city. I was shown some European turnips which had sprung up, and attained a very large size. Indigenous fruits and vegetables also flourish in great plenty. The character of the vegetation is, however, different from that around Bangkok. The cocoa and areca palms become rare, and give place to the bamboo.

"The city is naturally considered one of the most important in the country, but is protected by no fortifications. It has a governor and deputy-governor, and some inferior officers appointed over it.

"The King pays commonly one visit during the year to the capital of his ancestors, which lasts a week or two. He has a palace erected on the river-side, on the site of the old palace, which, however, has little of the appearance of a royal residence, the greater part of the building being constructed of teak and bamboo.

"Most of the principal merchants of Bangkok have houses in the town, which are used either as shops or as residences wherein to pass a week or two of recreation in the hot season.

"The only visible remains of the old city are a large number of wats, in different stages of decay. They extend over an area of several miles of country, and lie hidden in the trees and jungle which have sprung up around them. As the beauty of a Siamese temple consists not in its architecture, but in the quantity of arabesque work with which the brick and stucco walls are covered, it soon yields to the power of time and weather, and becomes, if neglected, an unsightly heap of bricks and woodwork, overgrown with parasitical plants. It is thus at Ayuthia. A vast pile of bricks and earth, with here and there a spire still rearing itself to the skies, marks the spot where once stood a shrine before which thousands were wont to prostrate themselves in superstitious adoration. There stand also the formerly revered images of Guadama, once resplendent with gold and jewels, but now broken, mutilated, and without a shadow of their previous splendour. There is one sacred spire of immense height and size, which is still kept in some kind of repair, and which is sometimes visited by the king. It is situated about four miles from the town, in the centre of a plain of paddy-fields. Boats and elephants are the only means of reaching it, as there is no road whatever, except such as the creeks and swampy paddy-fields afford. It bears much celebrity among the Siamese, on account of its height, but can boast of nothing attractive to foreigners but the fine view which is obtained from the summit. This spire, like all others, is but a succession of steps from the bottom to the top; a few ill-made images affording the only relief from the monotony of the brickwork. It bears, too, none of those ornaments, constructed of broken crockery, with which the spires and temples of Bangkok are so plentifully bedecked.

"This is all that repays the traveller for his visit,— a poor remuneration though, were it the curiosity of an antiquarian that led him to the place; for the ruins have not yet attained a sufficient age to compensate for their uninteresting appearance.

" As we were furnished with a letter from the Phya Kalahom to the governor, instructing him to furnish us with everything requisite for our convenience, we waited on that official, but were unfortunate enough to find that he had gone to Bangkok. The letter was thus rendered useless; for no one dared open it in his absence. Happily, however, we were referred to a nobleman who had been sent from Bangkok to superintend the catching of elephants, and he, without demur, gave us every assistance in his power.

"After visiting the ruins, therefore, we inspected the

kraal or stockade in which the elephants are captured. This was a large quadrangular piece of ground, enclosed by a wall about six feet in thickness, having an entrance on one side, through which the elephants are made to enter the enclosure. Inside the wall is a fence of strong teak stakes driven into the ground a few inches apart. In the centre is a small house erected on poles, and strongly surrounded with stakes, wherein some men are stationed for the purpose of securing the animals. These abound in the neighbourhood of the city, but cannot exactly be called wild, as the majority of them have, at some time or other, been subjected to servitude. They are all the property of the king, and it is criminal to hurt or kill one of them. Once a year, a large number is collected together in the enclosure, and as many as are wanted of those possessing the points which the Siamese consider beautiful are captured. The fine points in an elephant are: a colour approaching to white or red, black nails on the toes (the common colour of these nails is black and white), and intact tails (for, owing to their pugnacious disposition, it is rarely that an elephant is caught which has not had its tail bitten off). On this occasion the kings, and a large concourse of nobles, assemble together to witness the proceedings; they occupy a large platform on one side of the enclosure. The wild elephants are then driven in by the aid of tame males of a very large size and great strength, and the selection takes place. If an animal which is wanted escapes from the kraal, chase is immediately made after it by a tame elephant, the driver of which throws a lasso to catch the feet of the fugitive. Having effected this, the animal on which he rides leans itself with all its power the opposite way, and thus brings the other violently to the ground. It is then strongly bound, and conducted to the stables.

"Naturally enough, accidents are of common occurrence, men being frequently killed by the infuriated animals, which are sometimes confined two or three days in the enclosure without food.

"When elephants are to be sent to Bangkok, a floating house has to be constructed for the purpose.

"As elephants were placed at our disposal, we enjoyed the opportunity of judging of their capabilities, in a long ride through places inaccessible to a lesser quadruped. Their step is slow and cautious, and the rider is subjected to a measured roll from side to side, which at first is somewhat disagreeable. In traversing marshes and soft ground, they feel their way with their trunks. They are excessively timid; horses are a great terror to them, and, unless they are well trained, the report of a fowling-piece scares them terribly."

Above Ayuthia the navigation of the Meinam is often interrupted by sand-banks, but the borders are still occupied by numerous and populous villages; their number diminishes until the marks of human presence gradually disappear—the river is crowded with crocodiles, the trees are filled with monkeys, and the noise of the elephants is heard in the impervious woods. After many days' passage up the river, one of the oldest capitals of Siam, built fifteen hundred years ago, is approached. Its present name is Phit Salok, and it contains about five thousand inhabitants, whose principal occupation is the cutting teak-wood, to be floated down the stream to Bangkok.

The account which Bishop Pallegoix gives of the interior of the country above Ayuthia is not very flattering. He visited it in the rainy season, and says, it appears little better than a desert—a few huts by the side of the stream—neither towns, nor soldiers, nor custom-houses. Rice was found cheap and abundant, everything else wanting. Some of the Bishop's adventures are characteristic. In one place, where he heard pleasant music, he found a Mandarin surrounded by his dozen wives, who were playing a family concert. The Mandarin took the opportunity to seek information about Christianity, and listened patiently and pleased enough, until the Missionary told him one wife must satisfy him if he embraced the Catholic faith, which closed the controversy, as the Siamese said *that* was an impossible condition. In some places, the many-coloured pagodas towered above the trees, and they generally possessed a gilded Buddha twenty feet in height. The Bishop observes that the influence of the Buddhist priests is everywhere paramount among the Siamese, but that they have little hold upon the Chinese, Malays, or Laos people. In one of the villages they offered a wife to one of the missionaries; but finding the present unacceptable, they replaced the lady by two youths, who continued in his service, and he speaks well of their fidelity. (*Annales de la Propagation*, vol. xxxv.)

The principal port of Siam is that of Paknam, at the mouth of the Meinam river, from which Bangkok is distant about eighteen miles in a straight line, but nearly thirty in consequence of a considerable bend in the river. There is a bar composed of hard sand on the southern, and soft sand on the northern side, which is between three and four miles in width, and which crosses the entrance of the Meinam at a distance of five to six miles. This bar has only twelve to thirteen feet of water at spring tides, and in many parts only two to three feet at the neap.

Paknam has a population of between six and seven thousand souls. It has three handsome fortresses, one on each bank of the river, and the other in its centre commanding the entrance. A tree, called the *samé*, which grows abundantly in the neighbourhood of Paknam, is much valued, because its wood being once kindled, the flame is not easily extinguished. The inhabitants are expected in case of summons immediately to man the fortresses.

A few miles above Paknam is Paklat, a town principally peopled by Peguans. The number of inhabitants is about seven thousand. It has a considerable fortress on each side of the river; attached to that on the left bank is a strong beam composed of heavy iron cables and huge spars of wood, which might be employed to prevent the passage of any hostile vessel up the Meinam to Bangkok. The number of troops on the forts appeared to be small. Paklat furnishes considerable supplies of firewood to the capital. Rice and garden-stuffs are largely cultivated, and palm-leaves for the roofs of the houses of the poor.

Independently of its main branches, the Meinam has many smaller tributaries. The western, or longest branch, called in Chinese, Nan-ting-ho (Southern Ting River) has its source in lat. 24°, and is joined in lat. 22° by the Meiprein, which is deemed the principal arm by the Siamese. The Me-Klong is sometimes called a branch of the Meinam; but though joined before it reaches the sea by one of the arms of the Meinam, it appears an independent stream running from the Kareen country from between lat. 16° and 17° N.; and though the valley which it waters is narrow, it is extremely fertile. The Ta-Chin branch of the Meinam flows between Me-Klong and Bangkok, but is only navigable for small craft. At Saphai, a distance of sixty miles from the sea, there is on the Me-Klong so strong an ebb and flow of the tide that large vessels are often left quite dry.

The capital of the province of Me-Klong bears the name of the river. It was visited by Pallegoix, who speaks of it as a populous and beautiful city, with its floating bazaars, fine pagodas and gardens, and a population of ten thousand, the largest proportion of which are Chinese. There is a considerable fortification for the defence of the place. The soil is remarkably fertile, and the salt-pits produce enough to supply the whole kingdom. Both sides of the river are peopled and cultivated. One place is called the village of the Twenty Thousand Palms, from the quantities of that noble tree which are found in the locality.

Of the Me-Klong canal and river Dr. Dean gives the following account:—" On Monday morning we went to the mouth of the Ta-Chin river, a couple of miles below the town, where our boatmen cast their net for fish. It was past mid-day on Monday, when, the tide favouring, we passed up the Ta-Chin river, some three or four miles from its mouth, when we entered the Me-Klong canal, which connects the Ta-Chin with the Me-Klong river. We reached the town of Me-Klong, at the opposite terminus of the canal, at half-past nine o'clock the next morning, having stopped an hour and a half where the tides meet, at a place called Ma-Hou (dog-howl).

" At Me-Klong we took breakfast in our boat, while anchored in front of a wat or temple. These wats are the only hotels as well as the only school-houses and colleges in the country. Here travellers find a shelter in the open sheds in front of the temples; but every traveller in this country is supposed to carry with him his bread and provisions, and cooking materials. This town has a population of ten or twelve thousand Siamese; but a short distance above, on the Me-Klong river, are villages of Chinese, with their floating houses and well-filled shops. Me-Klong is the native place of the Siamese twins, whose parents are now dead. Some of the family still reside at this place, whose chief interest about their absent brothers is that they should send home some money for their poor relations. But if, as is reported, they were sold for money, and sent away by their friends into a foreign country, they may not be under very great obligations to remit money to those who sold them.

"At six o'clock P.M. on Tuesday, we entered the canal from the Me-Klong river, which leads to the gardens of Bangchang; and at nine o'clock the same evening reached the mission-house, now occupied by Chek-Suan. On calling to him from the boat, he replied that he was 'reading for evening worship, but had not prayed.' When he had done praying, he came to the boat to receive us. Bangchang is an extensive plain of the richest soil, in many parts highly cultivated as gardens." (*Missionary Magazine*, p. 40.)

Chantaburi is of the ports of Siam probably the second in commercial importance. It is at the mouth of a river, which, though not long in its course, fertilizes a considerable district by its inundations during the rainy season.

The rocks at the entrance of Chantaburi present all the appearance of a colossal lion couchant,—to whose head, mane, throat, eyes, and ears, nothing seems wanting; but the illusion is dissipated on approaching the river, and the lion is separated into masses of rudely-shaped stones. Trees, called Kong-Kang, whose roots have the form of a tripod sustaining the trunk, are spoken of as peculiar to the banks of this stream.

There is a custom-house at the entrance of the Chantaburi river, and a considerable trade is carried on, principally with Cochin China, and by the Cochin Chinese, among whom the Catholic missionaries claim about one thousand as their converts. Chantaburi has six thousand inhabitants—Siamese, Chinese, and Cochin Chinese. There is a public market-place, a manufactory of arrack, and many pagodas. In consequence of the cheapness of wood, and the facility of conveying it down the river, the building of ships is generally in a state of activity. About a dozen junks come annually from China with the produce of that country; and they carry away pepper, cardamums, gamboge, eagle-wood, hides, ivory, sugar, wax, tobacco, salt fish, and other commodities, which are also shipped to the Straits settlements. There is much cultivation in the neighbourhood of the town, and the fruits of the field and the garden are various and excellent. The planting of coffee has lately been introduced, and the quality is said to be good.

The inhabitants of the forests of Chantaburi are accustomed to chase the wild beasts with fire-arms and nets; but they attack the rhinoceros armed with solid bamboos, of which one end has been hardened by exposure to the fire and sharpened: they invite the animal by loud cries and clapping their hands to meet them, which he is wont to do by rushing violently upon them, opening and closing his wide mouth; they attack him in front, and drive the bamboos violently into his throat with surprising dexterity, taking flight on all sides. The animal, in his agony, throws himself on the ground, and becoming exhausted by the effusion of blood and the extremity of his suffering, he soon becomes the prey of his courageous assailants. All the passages to a district are sometimes closed with nets, and fire being applied to the jungle, the wild animals are destroyed as they seek to escape.

In the north of the province of Chantaburi is an elevated mountain, called the Mountain of the Stars. Popular tradition reports, that from its peak every star is seen of the size of the sun. It is also averred that the mountain is rich in precious stones. I am not aware that any traveller has ascended it.

On the eastern side of the province is a mountain, or mountain range, extending nearly thirty miles, called Sahab. At its foot are prosperous plantations of coffee. Report speaks of its unexplored mineral riches. Various streams flow towards the plain, whose waters are conveyed by wheels constructed of bamboos for the irrigation of the plants.

The Governor of Chantaburi, and the principal authorities, dwell in a fortification near the riverside, on a hill at about two leagues from the capital. The fort is surrounded by a deep ditch. The soil at the foot of the hill is so impregnated with metallic oxides, that it is of a deep purple or blood colour, and may be used for paint.

Not far from the foot is the mountain celebrated among the Siamese as the Precious Stone Mountain. The topaz, the ruby, the sapphire, the garnet, and others are found there. Pallegoix says he himself picked up precious stones from the ground.

A little to the north of Bangplasoi, and about thirty miles to the east of Paknam, is a large navigable river, the Bangpatung, which is reported to have its source in the mountains of Cambodia.

Little is known of its exact course; but it flows through a rich and cultivated country, and sends the produce of its banks to Bangplasoi for shipment or sale.

Bangplasoi has a convenient harbour, whose waters are so abundant in fish that the price is incredibly low. There are great numbers of Chinese settlers. The town has about six thousand inhabitants. The neighbouring country is productive. There are extensive salt-pits, and boundless supplies of shells, which are burnt into lime for agricultural purposes.

The Mei-Kong is a large river flowing through the eastern side of Laos and Cambodia; it is said to be more than fifteen hundred miles long, but its navigation is much impeded by shallows and sandbanks at its mouth. This is the river of which there is a fine description in the tenth book of the *Lusiad*, at whose mouth the poet was wrecked, and into whose placid and gentle stream he speaks of flinging his luckless songs.

> See thro' Cambodia Meikon's river goes,
>   Well named the "Captain of the Waters," while
> So many a summer tributary flows
>   To spread its floods upon the sands, as Nile
> Inundates its green banks.—
>
> And shall I to this gentle river throw
>   My melancholy songs, and to its breast
> Confide the welted leaves that tell the woe
>   Of many a shipwreck, dreary and distrest,—
> Of famine, perils, and the overthrow
>   Of him, by fate's stern tyranny opprest—
> Of him whose resonant lyre is doomed to be
>   More known to fame than to felicity?

Ves passa por Cambaja Mecom rio,
  Que capitão das aguas se interpreta;
Tantas recebe d'outro sò no estio,
  Que alaga os campos largos e inquieta.
Tem as echentes quais o Nilo pio. . . . . .

Este receberà placido e brando
  No seu regaço os cantos que molhados,
Vem do naufragio triste e miserando
  Dos procellosos baixos escapados;
Das fomes, dos perigos grandes, quando
  Serà o injusto mando executado,
Naquelle cuja lira sonorosa
  Serà mais affamada que ditosa.

Lusiadas, cant. x. cxxvij. cxxviij.

There is a group of islands which form the harbour of Kosichang, near Bangplasoi, in lat. 13° 12′, long. 100° 55′, which are much visited for supplies by vessels trading to Siam; a considerable extent of land is there under maize cultivation. The edible birds'-nests are collected in considerable quantities in the vicinity. The harbour is very fine, affording complete shelter for any number of vessels, and has great facilities for watering from a fine fresh stream, which will fill one hundred casks in a day. Hamilton calls this group "The Dutch Islands;" and, it appears, vessels of that nation were formerly accustomed to wait there for their cargoes, the open roadstead opposite Paknam being much exposed and dangerous, and at a considerable distance from the shore. As a naval station, the position is important. (*Singapore Chronicle*, March 16, 1826.)

The Gulf of Siam is little exposed to the typhoons and tempests which do such damage in the Chinese seas. The Admiralty charts are full of extraordinary blunders.* Some were pointed out by Mr. Crawfurd more than a third of a century ago, but have remained uncorrected to the present hour. On board H.M.S. *Rattler*, when, according to charts, and our own accurate reckoning, we ought to have been safe in the middle of the bay, we were driving right ahead upon Cape Liant, which is placed in the charts twenty-five miles too much to the east. The anchorage at the mouth of the Menam is placed fifty-two miles too far to the eastward. Most of the islands are more or less out of their real positions. There is a gulf current, which, from October to March, flows from north to south at the rate of nearly three miles an hour. After April, its ordinary course is from south to north. Calms prevail during the months of May, June, and July.

Many of the islands in the Bay of Siam present objects of interest, and their productions might be well worthy of attention. Pallegoix speaks of the beautiful marble he found in the island of Si-Xang, polished as brightly by the waves of the sea as it could have been by the hand of man. In many of the islands are caves, in which the sea-swallow builds its glutinous nests, which are collected four times in the year, and form so large an article of commerce and consumption in China. Great are the

---

* Pulo Panjang—lat. 9° 18' N., long. 103° 36'. Placed on Admiralty chart about eighteen miles too far west.

Cape Liant—lat. 12° 34', long. 101° 11'. Placed on Admiralty chart twenty-five miles too far east, and six too far south.

Menam Bar—anchorage in four fathoms, lat. 13° 24' 50" N., long. 100° 36' 30" E. The entrance to the Menam river in four fathoms is placed on Admiralty chart fifty-two miles too far east.

perils to which the natives expose themselves in mounting or descending to collect these precious ministers to the *gourmandise* of the central Flowery Land, and many lives are lost in the adventurous pursuit. Fine specimens of rock crystal, white, yellow, and blue, and beautiful varieties of shell-fish, are among the attractions of the islands.

" The whole of the coast from Kamao, in Cambodia, quite up to what is called by the Siamese Lem Samme-san, the Cape Liant of Europeans, is an uninterrupted archipelago of beautiful islands. Pulo Uri, the most easterly, is but a small island six miles long. I had an opportunity of landing on it, and found a family of Cochin-Chinese, and two or three Chinese, who, had settled here for the purpose of procuring the sea-slug, which abounds on its coasts. Their hut was miserable, and a little cultivated ground near it, producing a few sweet potatoes, constituted the whole of their wealth. In it was a figure of a Chinese deity, and a number of tablets, containing the names of the junks which had touched at it for some time. They commonly stop here for a day or two, on their way from China to Siam, for the purpose of procuring fresh water, of which the island contains an abundant supply. Previous to their sailing, it is their custom to consult the before-mentioned deity as to whether they shall prosecute their voyage or not. This is done in the following manner:—A book is prepared, in which a number of sentences are written and numbered. A similar number of small pieces of sticks are prepared, with correspondent numbers on them. These are placed in a hollow bamboo, and shaken until one of them falls out; the number of the piece of wood is then compared with the corresponding motto, and according as this latter is favourable or otherwise, the junks pursue their voyage, or wait until they obtain a more favourable answer." (Moor's *Notices Ind. Arch.* p. 239.)

The coast of Siamese territory on the side of the Bay of Bengal has many groups of islands, among which a vessel can pass safely, the depth being seldom less than from four to five, and generally from twenty to thirty fathoms. St. Matthew's Island, in lat. 10°, is eighteen miles long and six broad, having an excellent harbour. Salanga, or Junk Ceylon, in lat. 8°, is sixteen miles in length and six in breadth; on the east side it has several harbours, as have the islands of the Lacaive group.

Our knowledge of the interior of Siam is exceedingly imperfect and fragmentary. Indeed, with large portions of the kingdom we are wholly unacquainted. The impediments to communication are no doubt in progress of removal, but some of the difficulties and embarrassment which the traveller meets with may be judged of by the following extract from a Report of Father Bruguière in the *Annales de la Foi*:—

"It would be impossible for a traveller, left to himself, not to lose himself in these dense forests. One has sure guides walking before to clear the way, who cry out from time to time, and make signals to those behind them. Recourse must frequently be had to the hatchet and fire in order to open a way. The number of sloughs, pools, and small streams which are encountered, often compelled those who were on foot to travel with bare feet, which, from the thorns and venomous insects which abound in these situations, was not without danger. Providence watched over us, and in the midst of so many perils preserved us from all accidents. From the hour of ten in the morning till four in the afternoon the heat is excessive. For shelter against the power of the sun's rays, it is customary for native travellers to cover the head with a linen cloth, which acts as a veil. This, however, does not prevent the skin of the face from blistering and peeling off. When one is forced to traverse sandy tracks in the hot season, the rays of the sun, thrown back by the sand as by a reflector, render it intolerable. The eyes, above all, are sensibly affected by it. So many inconveniences combined rendered all my party sick, with the exception of myself, and obliged me to renew a part of my escort." (*Association de la Prop. de la Foi*, No. xv. p. 254, 5.)

The climate of Siam is, for a tropical region, salubrious. During our visit we suffered somewhat from the heat, which was frequently from ninety-five to ninety-six in the shade; but the health of the members of the embassy, and of the officers and crews of Her Majesty's ships, was good; and the missionaries bore testimony to the general excellence of the climate. We expected to have been much tormented with musquitoes, which are such a pest on the Irawaddy; but though they abounded at Paknam, they troubled us little at Bangkok or its neighbourhood. The jungle fever is perilous to travellers who pass into the interior, exposed to all the inconveniences which the absence of shelter and succour brings with it. The diseases which afflict the Siamese are those common to tropical regions; fevers, diarrhœas, and dysenteries being the most fatal. The southwest monsoons generally envelop the mountains of Western Siam in clouds, which are dispersed in thunder-storms, and followed by heavy rains. The north-east monsoon, which visits Siam at the end of September, brings with it cool and refreshing weather; but as the wind veers gradually towards the south, and thence to the south-west, the change of climate from cold to heat is quiet and agreeable. In the month of March, heavy dews fall at break of day.

CHAPTER II.

HISTORY.

ANTERIOR to the establishment of Ayuthia, about the middle of the fourteenth century, the annals of Siam are made up of traditional legends and fables, such as most nations are fond of substituting in the place of veracious history. The Siamese group their early ancestors around the first disciples of Buddha (Gaudama), and begin their annals about five centuries before the Christian era. A succession of dynasties, frequently shifting their capital cities in which Buddhistical miracles and the intervention of superhuman agency are constantly exhibited, figure in the first volumes of the Siamese records. There are accounts of intermarriages with Chinese princesses, of embassies and wars with neighbouring States, all interblended with wonders and miraculous interpositions of Indra and other divinities; but from the time when the city of Ayuthia was founded by Phaja-Uthong, who took the title of Phra*-Rama-Thibodi, the succession of

---

* As the word Phra, which so frequently occurs in these volumes, here appears for the first time, I have to remark that it is probably either derived from or of common origin with the Pharaoh of antiquity. It is given in the Siamese Dictionaries as synonymous with God—ruler, priest, and teacher. It is, in fact, the word by which sovereignty and sanctity are associated in the popular mind. As the title *Divus* was appropriated by the Roman Emperor,—as in most monarchies a sort of sacredness is attached to

sovereigns and the course of events are recorded with tolerable accuracy.

The following dates, which are taken from the annals and constitute important religious epochs in the early history of Siam, may be probably deemed approximative to the truth:—

	Christian Era.	Buddhist Era.
The present ruling Buddha is said to have died on the third day of the sixth month of the year of the Serpent, corresponding with B.C.	543	
The first great Buddhist Council was assembled under Ajata Sutra (in India), the year of Buddha's death		1
The second Great Council, under Kala Sokkaraja (India) was called together in	443 —	100
The third Great Council, by Sri Dhamma Soka, in	325 —	218
The fourth Great Council, in	143 —	400
The Buddhist teacher, Phra Buddha Ghosa, introduced Buddhism into Cambodia, A.D.	422 —	965

It was in the one-thousandth year of Buddha, A. D. 457, that King Ruang, whose advent and glorious reign had been announced by a communication from Gaudama himself, and who possessed, in consequence of his "merits," a white elephant with black tusks, introduced the Thai alphabet, which was communicated to a large assemblage of Buddhist priests. The ancient annals terminate with the establish-

---

the royal person,—the Orientals have made "gods" of their kings, their heroes, and their sages, without any scruple. Image-worship is, in fact, only the materializing or incarnating of the idea of Deity.

ment of Chao Uthong, in the new city of Si Ayo Thaya (Ayuthia), but they leave the exact date of the establishment in some obscurity.

The following is the succession of Siamese monarchs from the founding of the capital of Ayuthia :*—

Siamese Era.	Christian Era.	
712	— 1350	Phra Rama Thibodi.
731	— 1369	„ Rame Suen (his son).
732	— 1370	„ Borom Raxa (his brother).
744	— 1382	„ Rame Suen (2nd).
747	— 1385	„ Phaja Ram (his son).
763	— 1401	Inthaxara.
792	— 1430	Borom Raxa Thirat.
805	— 1443	Boroma Trai Lókharat.
834	— 1472	Phra Rama Thibodi.
875	— 1513	Raxa Kuman.
876	— 1514	Xaja Raxa Thirat.
889	— 1527	Phra Jot Fa.
891	— 1529	Maha Cha Kraphat Raxa Thirat.
909	— 1547	Phra Chao Xang Phuok.
914	— 1552	Mahinthara Thirat.
926	— 1564	Phra Naret.
957	— 1595	Eka Thotsarot.
963	— 1601	Chao Fa.
964	— 1602	Phra Chao Song Tham.
989	— 1627	Phra Chao Prasat Thong.
1017	— 1655	Chao Fa Xai.
1018	— 1656	Phra Chao Xam Phuok.
1050	— 1688	Phra Phet Raxa.

---

* It will be noticed that the spelling of the names in this list is not in all cases identical with that in the detailed annals which follow. The discrepancy arises from the peculiarity of the Siamese language, and the variety of spelling employed by the different authorities cited. The same remark applies to all the similar variations in the names of individuals and places throughout these volumes

Siamese Era.	Christian Era.	
1059	— 1697	Chao Dua.
1068	— 1706	(Name of king unknown).
1120	— 1758	Chao Dok Ma Dua.
1128	— 1766	Interregnum.
1129	— 1767	Phaja Tak.
1173	— 1811	Phra Phuti Chao Luang (founder of present dynasty).
1187	— 1825	Phen din Klang.
1213	— 1851	Phra Chao Prasat Thong.

Somdetch Phra Paramendr Maha Mongkut, the reigning sovereign, succeeded to the throne in 1851.

The attempts to disentangle the facts from the fictions of Siamese chronicles would be a hopeless, and consequently a useless task, and would represent, like most of the pages of Oriental antiquity, revolutions, conspiracies, murders, changed dynasties, and events which would afford excellent materials for the novel or the drama, but often in their details of very doubtful historical authority. During the last five centuries, the ordinary vicissitudes of Oriental despotisms are exhibited in interrupted successions, losses and conquests of territory; but in the obscurity which surrounds the shifting and uncertain names of the Kings of Siam, the reigns of the different sovereigns will not always be recognised under the titles I have given, as various authorities employ various designations, and some of the terms are but vague enunciations of the royal rank. It is the Siamese theory that the name of a king is too sacred to be uttered.

What follows is a translation from the Latin, and is given by Bishop Pallegoix as a

ORIGIN OF THE SIAMESE.

Chronology of the Kingdom of Siam.

(The explanatory notes have been furnished to me in MS. by the first King.)

The annals of the Siamese are divided into two parts. The first[*] is entitled the Annals of the Northern Kingdom; it comprehends a tolerably fabulous history, from about the time of Buddha Phra-Khôdŏm to the foundation of Juthia. The later annals, however, commence from the building of Juthia, and give a sufficiently veracious narrative down to the present day.

Part I.

This is, then, the origin of the Siamese :—

There were two Brahminical recluses dwelling in the woods, named Sătxănalăi and Sîtthĭmŏngkhŏn, coeval with Phra-Khôdŏm, and one hundred and fifty years of age, who having called their numerous posterity together, counselled them to build a city having seven walls, and then departed to the woods to pass their lives as hermits.

But their posterity, under the leadership of Bathămărăt, erected the city Săvăn thevălôk, or Săngkhălôk, about the year 300 of the era of Phra-Khôdŏm (B. C. about 243).

Bathămărăt founded three other cities, over which

---

[*] "The first part of the ancient history of Northern Siam is prepared and printed by Bishop Pallegoix, according to a book which he has read from one book of an author; but there are other books of the ancient Siamese histories which are otherwise, and which the Bishop J. Pallegoix does not know, but they all full of feable, and are not in satisfaction for believe."—MS. Note of the first King of Siam.

he placed his three sons. The first he appointed ruler in the city of Hărĭpunxăi, the second in Kamphôxă năkhon, the third in Phĕtxăbun. These four sovereignties enjoyed, for five hundred years or more, the utmost peace and harmony under the rule of the monarchs of this dynasty.

About the year 960 of the era of Phra-Khôdŏm, Aphăjăkhamŭni, king of Hărĭpunxăi, having retired to a mountain for the purpose of meditation, had intercourse with a queen of the Nakhæ,* to whom he presented his ring. She conceived and brought forth a son in the same spot. Now, a certain huntsman accidentally discovered the child with the royal ring, and brought him up. The youth having one day entered the court, the whole palace trembled; the King acknowledged his son, received him, and gave him the name of Arŭnnărà̀t. When he had grown to be a man, he was made king of the city of Săt̆xănalăi, under the name Phra-Ruàng; at that time he threw off the yoke of the King of Cambodia, and reduced to his authority all the sovereigns in his vicinity. In the year 1000 of the era of Phra-Khôdŏm, Phra-Ruàng abolished the Buddhist era (phŭthăsăkkhărât), and ordained a new one, which is the era of the Siamese, and is called chŭulăsăkkărât—the lesser era. Incensed because the Emperor of China would not unite with the other kings for the purpose of abolishing the era, Phra-Ruàng, having embarked in a ship with his brother, reached, by some wonderful means, the pre-

---

* The Nakhæ are a fabulous race, dwelling under the earth.—Bishop Pallegoix.

sence of the Emperor of China, who professed himself to be his disciple, and gave him his daughter in marriage. Phra-Ruàng returned with a large retinue of Chinese, introduced the characters of the Siamese language, and appointed his brother King of Xieng-măi. Proceeding one day to the river, he disappeared; it was thought he had rejoined his mother, the Queen of the Nakhæ, and would pass the remainder of his life in the realms beneath. His brother, Sŭchărat, succeeded him in the kingdom of Sătxanalăi. Shortly after, Sithămmăkrăi pĭdŏk, King of Xieng-sén, with five other monarchs of Laos, besieged the city of Sătxănalăi; but by the mediation of a celebrated Talapoin (priest), Phra phŭthă Kôsá, Sŭchărăt surrendered his daughter to the King of Xieng-sén, and concluded peace.

Sithămmăkrăi pĭdŏk founded the city Phĭtsănŭlôk, or Phĭtsilok, formed a matrimonial alliance between his son Krăisónrăt, and the daughter of the King of Sătxănalăi, and made him ruler in Lôphăburi (otherwise Lăvô.) Sithămmăkrăi pĭdŏk died about the year 1300 of the Buddhist era, and was succeeded by his son Phra-chào xát Sákhon. At this time wars arose among the Kings of Laos, and, after seven generations, the ancient regal race was almost totally extirpated.

In the year 1600 of the Buddhist era, Khôtăthevărăt reigned in Inthăpăt, the royal city of Cambodia. At that time every one was expecting the advent (phù-mi-bŭn) of some powerful monarch. Then Phra-In (or the deity Indra) appeared to a certain paralytic lying on the highway, and presented him with a miraculous horse and trappings, and some celestial medicines; having anointed himself with which, he immediately became whole and vigorous; he mounted the horse, and, borne through the air in rapid flight, arrived at the city of Inthăpăt; seeing which, Khôtăthevărăt fled eastward with one hundred thousand men. His son Phăja Khôtăbong founded the cities Phŭchĭt and Phĭxăi. But this paralytic was made King of Cambodia, under the name Phăja Krëk, and is reported to have instituted a new era adopted by no one. The posterity of Phăja Krëk became extinct after three generations; there remained only the King's daughter, who was married to a powerful and rich man named Uthong. Phăja Uthong reigned seven years in Cambodia, but a severe pestilence having prevailed, he emigrated with his people, and proceeding to the south, founded on a certain island in the river Mĕnăm a new city, Krŭng Thèph măhá năkhon Síajŭthăja—"a great town impregnable against angels:" Siamese era 711, Christian era 1349.

There is another account of the foundation of Juthia. Phăja Uthong was reigning in Kămphing phĕt; having despatched men to inspect the southern country, they brought back intelligence that it was extremely fertile, and abounded in fish. Phăja Uthong then emigrated with all his people, and arrived at the aforesaid island, in which he erected Juthia. This latter account is more credible than the former.

Part II.*

Chŭulăsăkkărăt.		Christian Era.
712	King Uthong assumes the name Phra Rama-thĭbodi; appoints his son Phra Rame suén, King of Lŏpha-buri. At that time, the following kingdoms were subject to the King of Siam:—1, Mălaka. 2, Xa-va. 3, Tanaosi (Tenasserim). 4, Năkhon si thămărăt (Ligor). 5, Thăvai. 6, Mo-ta-mă (Martaban). 7, Mo-lămlóng (Moulmein). 8, Sŏng Khlá. 9, Chănthabun. 10, Phitsănulôk. 11, Sŭkkhôthăi. 12, Phĭxăi. 13, Săvănkha-lôk. 14, Phichĭt. 15, Kămphingphĕt. 16, Năkhon săvan. War was entered into against the Cambodians, and numerous captives were brought away.	1350

The founding of the city of Sia Yutíyá, the sacred city, commonly known by the name of Ayuthia, called Indura or Indayá by the Burmese, and sometimes spoken of in old books as India, is one of the most memorable events in Siamese annals. The Brahminical soothsayers having been consulted, they decided that in the 712th year of the Siamese era, on the sixth day of the waxing moon, the fifth month, at ten minutes before four o'clock, the foundation should be laid. Three palaces were erected in honour of the King; and vast countries, among

---

* "This part also was prepared and printed by Bishop Pallegoix according to the books written by a party of authors. There are other books and statements of old men said differently in other wise, but the reign and numbers of late kings very correct. All names of cities and place and kings are very uncorrect, as they were got from corrupted sounds of pronouncing of Sankrit of the ignorant teacher, and not accort the knowledge of literature in Siam. The teachers of the author are not persons of royal service, do not know the proper names of kings, &c."—MS. Note by the first King of Siam.

Chŭulăsăkkărât. A.D.

712 which were Malacca, Tenasserim, Java, and many 1350
others whose position cannot now be defined,
were claimed as tributary States. But it would
be idle now to inquire how far they were held
in subjection; and with respect to many of them
there is no record showing when or how, if ever
really subjected, they emancipated themselves
from the Siamese yoke.

731 Phra Rame suén succeeded his father, but 1369
reigned only one year.

732 Phra Bŏrŏmmăraxa, his brother, occupies 1370
the throne, and reigns twelve years. In the
year A.D. 1380, a gold image of Buddha is said
to have been cast in the city of Pichai, which
weighed fifty-three thousand catties, or one
hundred and forty-one thousand lbs., which
would represent the almost incredible value (at
seventy shillings per ounce) of nearly six millions sterling. The gold for the garments
weighed two hundred and eighty-six catties.

744 The King having died, is succeeded by 1382
Chao thong lăn, who, after three days, is slain
by his brother Phra Rame suén. The city of
Xieng-măi is taken, and many of the people of
Laos are made captives.

747 The King of Siam takes possession of the 1385
capital of Cambodia, and leaves but five thousand souls therein. In 749, he builds the famous
temple Phŭkhăo thong (mount of gold), and
afterwards dies. His son Phăjàramchào reigns
fourteen years.

763 Intharaxa, King of Sŭphănnăburi, takes 1401
Juthia; instals his son Chào ài, King of
Sŭphăn; Chào ji, King of Préksíraxa; Chào
sám, King of the city of Xăinât.

Chŭulăsăkkărât.		A.D.
780	At the decease of their father, Chào ài and Chào jí hasten to Juthia to seize the throne; mounted on elephants, they both meet together on a bridge; a contest ensues, and both fall, killed by each other's hands. At the death of his brothers, Chào sàm rules the kingdom under the name Bŏrŏmmăraxathïràt.	1418
792	The King conquers Xieng-măi, and leads twelve thousand of its inhabitants into captivity.	1430
796	At the King's decease, his son Bŏrŏmmătrăi lôkănàt ascends the throne.	1434
805	A great dearth prevails; one khănan or coco of rice costs one fu'ang.	1443
834	The King being dead, his son Plira Rama- thibodi succeeds to him; he cast an immense image of Buddha, in a sitting posture, from gold, silver, and copper, the height of which was fifty cubits.	1472
871	Phra Bŏrŏmmăraxa succeeds his father.	1509
875	Raxa kuman ascends the throne.	1513
876	At his father's death, Xăijă raxa thïràt rules the kingdom.	1514
887	A vast conflagration occurs in Juthia, lasting three days, and destroying one hundred thou- sand houses.	1525
889	At the decease of his father, Phra Jòt fa, aged eleven, is appointed king. But the Queen, his mother, Si sŭda chăn, proclaims a certain mandarin, her paramour, king, and murders her son; but soon after a conspiracy having been formed, the usurper and the Queen pay the penalty of their crimes; and an uncle of the	1527
891	defunct monarch ascends the throne, under the name Măhá chăkrăphăt ràxathïràt.	1529
894	The King of Siam conquers Cambodia; the	1532

Chŭulăsăkkărât.

		A.D.
894	King of Cambodia surrenders his sons, one of whom is made ruler of Săngkhălôk.	1532
905	The King of Hŏngsávădi (Pegu), with a vast army of three hundred thousand men and seven hundred elephants, advances to besiege Juthia. The King of Siam enters into single combat with the King of Pegu; but his elephant having fled, the Queen Sŭrĭjôthäi, clad in the royal robes, with manly spirit fights in her husband's stead until she expires on the elephant from the loss of an arm. Being compelled to raise the siege from want of provisions, the King of Hŏngsávădi returns to his dominions.	1543

Of this period of Siamese history Diogo de Couto gives the following account :*—A warlike expedition was fitted out by the Burmese and Peguans in 1544, to obtain possession of a white elephant belonging to the Siamese, which had excited the cupidity of the King of Ava. He attacked Siam with innumerable armies, besieged the capital, and made peace ultimately on condition that the King of Siam should become his vassal—" should give him his daughter in marriage, send every year a lady of high rank to Ava, and certain elephants for the King's service;" but, in 1548, when the Burmese ambassadors came to claim the lady, the Siamese nobles revolted, and killed the ambassadors. This led to another war, and Siam was attacked by a force which, with Oriental exaggeration, the chronicle represents to have consisted of one million five hundred thousand soldiers, four

---

* Decadas.

thousand elephants, and beasts of burthen not to be counted. The King of Pegu was accompanied by a considerable number of Portuguese for the protection of his royal person, under the command of Diogo Soares de Mello, and the account given by the Portuguese chronicler of the expedition is in the most inflated and extravagant style.

"This barbarous people," he says, "marched with majesty and greatness exceeding that of all the kings of the world; for at night they never rested, except in beautiful houses, gilded and decorated, and prepared anew every day for their reception. They brought with them from Pegu the timber, the furniture, the roofs, the doors, and every needful thing, which were sent forward on elephants, who were accompanied by more than two thousand workmen, such as blacksmiths, carpenters, locksmiths, painters, gilders, and others, who built, furnished, and adorned the habitations. They had forges too; so that, on the King's arrival, handsome palaces awaited him, with numerous apartments, verandahs, boudoirs, cooking establishment, with arrangements for his women; and the palaces were surrounded with strong fortifications, and the King was served in vessels of gold and precious stones; and he had horses and elephants for his special service, and a triumphant car worked in gold—all making an infinite machinery." When he came to a river, a branch of the Meinam, "the greatness and the display exceeded that of Xerxes when he crossed the Hellespont to the conquest of Greece." They were twenty-five days travelling over high

Chŭulăsăkkărât.

905 mountains, in order to find a passage. There were twenty-five thousand Siamese to defend the place where it was determined to cross; and the Burmese having placed thirty thousand men under the command of Soares, they forced their way across the river, and marched to the attack of the Siamese capital, which was defended by six hundred thousand men, having two years' provision within the city.

A.D. 1543

The description given by Couto of the banks of the Meinam, which, he says, is the *Doris fluvius* of Ptolemy, resembles in most respects their present condition.

The result, however, of the great expedition was calamitous. The city was bombarded on many sides; but the Siamese King had, as the Portuguese chronicler tells us, the good fortune to possess fifty brave Lusitanians, to whom he committed the defence of the weakest part of the city walls, so that neither Peguans nor Burmese could enter. Meanwhile, the waters rose; upon which attempts were made to bribe the heroic Portuguese defenders; but, to use the words of the historian, " they sent the same reply which the men of the city of Synania gave to Brutus the consul, when he besieged them; and seeing their constancy and valour, he sent to ask for a sum of money, and he would raise the siege; to which they answered, ' that their ancestors had not left them money to redeem their lives, but arms to defend them.' No other nation but the Romans, says Valerius Maximus, was worthy of using language so noble; but the privilege also belonged to the valiant knight of Portugal in Siam, who

Chŭulăsăkkărât.
905 told the invader, that all the gold in the world would not seduce them; that while they were alive he should not enter the city; and that even after they were all dead and cut to pieces, if it might be, they would still defend it."
So the undeceived Burman withdrew with his army, and, after a march of twenty days, beleaguered the great city of Campape; but all his efforts failed, which the chronicler attributes to a somewhat ignoble method of defence which the Siamese employed; for they made a great collection of human excrements in huge jars, which they flung down upon the besiegers, who, unable to bear the intolerable stench, retired with their whole army to the countries from whence they came.

A.D. 1543

909 At this time the city of Juthia was exceedingly flourishing, and was resorted to by the merchants of all nations. The King possessed seven white elephants, from which was derived the name Phra Chào Xang phuok. Having been informed of this, the King of Hŏngsávădi sent an embassy to demand two white elephants from the Siamese superfluity; on the King of Siam refusing, the King of Pegu came with an army of nine hundred thousand men, seven thousand elephants, and fifteen thousand horses, to besiege Juthia. But when the two Kings met together, the King of Juthia gave up four white elephants and his son, and the King of Pegu returned through Phïtsănŭlôk.

1547

Mendez Pinto, who is much less of a liar than he is generally held to be, speaks of an excellent King of Siam who reigned A.D. 1547, and who, returning from a successful war, was

VOL. I.   E

Chŭulăsăkkărât.

909 poisoned by the Queen to prevent his discovering that she had been faithless to him in his absence, and was then in a state of pregnancy. Once entered upon this criminal career, she murdered her son, the heir to the crown, and placed her lover on the throne, in 1548. But, in 1549, the usurper and his paramour were assassinated in a temple, and an illegitimate brother and uncle of the two last kings were called forth from a cloister and advanced to the throne.

Bishop Pallegoix' version is to the effect, that about this period the King of Siam was so fortunate that he captured no less than seven white elephants. This extraordinary good fortune excited the cupidity of the King of Pegu, who, in the year 910 (A.D. 1548), sent an embassy of five hundred persons, desiring that two of the seven might be transferred as a mark of honour to himself. After much fruitless negotiation, the King of Siam refused to accommodate his royal neighbour, on the plea that the Peguans were uninstructed in the art of managing white elephants, and had once, on that account, returned two to the King of Siam (alarmed, no doubt, at the consequence of any disaster befalling the sacred animals); while, on the other hand, the King of Siam had observed what an unwonted prosperity the possession of so many sacred quadrupeds had brought to his country. The refusal, however, was thought by the King of Pegu sufficient to justify his making war upon Siam, which he invaded with ninety thousand men, and succeeding in his attack so as to menace Ayuthia, the Siamese capital, the matter was

A.D. 1547

SIEGE OF JUTHIA.

Chŭulăsăkkărât.

909 arranged; and, in compensation for the trouble he had taken, he obtained four white elephants instead of two from the King of Siam, and then returned complacent to Pegu. — A.D. 1547

914 The King of Juthia abdicates in favour of his son Mahĭnthărathĭràt, and becomes a talapoin, to which order he is ordained the following year.* — 1552

917 The King of Hŏngsávădi advances with a formidable army of one million men, and surrounds Juthia with his forces; the siege endures for nine months. In the mean while, Phra Chào Xang phuok dies. His son, much given to pleasure, neglects the siege, and on the 26th day of the ninth moon of the year 918, by the treachery of a particular mandarin, the city was betrayed to and seized by the enemy. The King of Hŏngsávădi bore away from thence immense wealth, and innumerable captives, leaving there only a thousand men, under the government of Phra Thămmăraxa thĭràt, once King of Phĭtsĭlôk; but he led away captive the King of Juthia, who died on the way. — 1555

Bishop Pallegoix says, the heir to the Siamese throne was captured, and, falling ill, was given over to the care of ten physicians. He died, and all the physicians were put to death.

The King of Cambodia availed himself of the disasters of Siam to invade the kingdom,

---

* This withdrawal from political squabbles to the safety and sanctity of the religious profession is not an uncommon occurrence in Siam. When the late King usurped the throne, his present Majesty retired to a Buddhist temple, from whence he was brought forth to occupy the throne after the seclusion of a quarter of a century.—See chapter xiii.

52 HISTORY.

Chŭulăsăkkărât. A.D.
917 and failing to conquer the capital, he devastated 1555
the whole of the country through which he
passed.

919 The King of Lăvêk (Cambodia) fails in his 1557
siege of Juthia, but takes away many prisoners
from the country.

920 Phra Thămmăraxa thĭràt appoints his son 1558
Phra Nărèt-suen, sixteen years old, King of
Phĭtsanŭlôk.

921 The King of Cambodia again and again 1559
assaults Juthia, and depopulates the whole
country.

926 The King of Hŏngsávădi, dreading Phra 1564
Nărèt on account of his valour and warlike
exploits, insidiously invites him, wishing to
kill him; Phra Nărèt proceeded to meet him,
but, having been made acquainted with the
plot, returns, bringing away ten thousand captives from the country of Pegu; and when a
formidable army pursues him, he upsets the
general who commanded in the King's stead
from his elephant by a stroke of his gun;
upon which the enemy was thrown into confusion and put to flight.

929 Phra Nărèt subdues several cities lying 1567
westward, and leads away from them innumerable captives to Juthia; the walls and towers
of which place are restored by him.

930 Phra Nărèt is victorious over the King of 1568
Xieng măi; he then conquers the King of
Hŏngsávădi, whom he repeatedly drives back
from the boundaries of his dominions. He
subjects to his rule the kingdom of Laos, and
other adjoining States.

945 Phra Nărèt had bound himself by an oath 1583

Chŭulăsăkkărât.

945 to wash his feet in the blood of the perfidious 1583
monarch of Cambodia; so, immediately on finding himself freed from other enemies, he assailed Cambodia, and besieged the royal city of Lăvêk; having captured which, he ordered the King to be slain, and his blood having been collected in a golden ewer, he washed his feet therein amid the clang of trumpets.

949 The indefatigable warrior Phra Nărèt in- 1587
vades the kingdom of Pegu, and takes Mo-ta-ma (Martaban) and the capital of Hŏngsávădi, and appoints Siamese to govern them.

Bishop Pallegoix narrates that Phra Nărèt held Ayuthia in subjection to the King of Pegu; but being called on to march with a large contingent of troops, he was informed by a bonze of an intention to sacrifice him; upon which he invaded the Peguan territory, made ten thousand captives, and after long wars established his own authority in Siam. He attacked the King of Cambodia, accusing him of perfidy, and of his invasion of the kingdom in the moment of his adversity. He swore that he would bathe his feet in the blood of the perfidious Cambodian, who having been made prisoner, was murdered, and his blood, still warm, brought in a golden vessel to Phra Nărèt, who, in the presence of his courtiers, and to the sound of loud music, literally accomplished his vow. He died while leading an army to attack the Burmese.

955 Phra Nărèt collects an army for the invasion 1593
of Angoa (Ava), but dies on the way; his brother, Ekathŏtsărŏt, succeeds to him, and reigns peacefully for six years.

Chŭulăsăkkărăt.

955 Misunderstandings, contests, negotiations, victories, and reverses, fill the pages of Siamese, Peguan, Laos, and Cambodian history to the end of the sixteenth century. Immense armies figure on those pages,—one of a million, and another of half a million of men. Much childish narrative is mingled in the annals. It has been remarked that *guns* are referred to long before the discovery of gunpowder in Europe,* while "gunpowder" is first spoken of in the Siamese annals in the year A.D. 1584. In the same year there is mention of the capture of Portuguese vessels which had taken part with the Cambodians against the Siamese. The phraseology found in some of the records is amusingly characteristic. One of the Siamese kings, in answer to the menaces of the Peguans, says, "As well may a white ant endeavour to overthrow Mount Meru."† A Peguan asks, "Are the Peguans only posts, to which the Siamese elephants are to be tied?" — 1593

963 At the death of Ekathŏtsărŏt, his son, Chaò Fa, "the one-eyed," ascends the throne, and is murdered by conspirators in the following year. Then Phra Sí sín is exalted to the regal dignity, under the name of Phra Chaò Sŏng thăm. In his reign was discovered and consecrated the celebrated footstep of Buddha, Phra Bât, at the base of a famous mountain to the eastward of Juthia. — 1601

Of the political relations of Siam in the beginning of the seventeenth century, the

---

* *Chinese Repository*, vi. p. 397.
† The Central Mountain of Earth, reported in Buddhist books to be 798,000 miles high.

Chŭulăsăkkărât.

963 following account is given by Peter Will Floris (Thevenot, vol. i. p. 21) :—

"The King of Siam fortified himself by the destruction of the kingdom of Pegu, and has since conquered the kingdom of Cambaya, Laniaugh, Zayomay, Leegor, Parava, Thenasarim, and several others. This conqueror, called by the Portuguese the Black King of Siam, died in 1605, and left his kingdom to his brother, whom they designated as the White King. He was a prince who only desired to reign in peace. He died in 1610, leaving several children. Thence arose great troubles in the State; for the King, on his deathbed, caused his eldest son, a youth of great promise, to be put to death; the murder being committed at the suggestion of one of the nobles, who, being very rich and powerful, aspired to the throne. The present King is the second son of the White King, and soon caused the traitorous noble to be put to death. Among his slaves there were two hundred and eighty Japanese, who, on the report of his death, rushed to the palace, gained possession of the gates and the King's person, making him promise to put to death four of the principal nobles, signing the promise with his blood;—and, not content with this, they retained as hostages four principal palipas, or priests, as a security for the fulfilment of his promise. These slaves, satisfied with their vengeance, and loaded with booty, returned home, leaving traces of their cruelty in every direction, while none of the country people dared to appear before them. This mark of weakness brought about

A.D. 1601

Chŭulăsăkkărât.		A.D.
963	a revolt in the kingdoms of Cambaya and of Laniaugh. A Peguan, named Banga-de-lau, raised a faction in that State; and in the following year the King of Laniaugh entered the kingdom of Siam, hoping to find it in disorder from the revolt of the Japanese, but they had already left the country; and the King of Siam having taken the field, the Laniaugh King retired, not daring to encounter him. It is reported that the neighbouring princes have formed a league, and are to enter the country with a large army; an attempt which is not likely to succeed, unless they have established some private understanding."	1601
989	Phra Chaò Song thăm is killed by a mandarin named Sŭrĭvŏng, who seizes the throne under the name Phra Chaò Präsât thong. He had a son named Phra Năraі, so called from his appearing at his birth to have four arms.	1627
1017	Phra Chaò Präsât thong dies, bequeathing his sceptre to his son, Chaò Fa xăi, who is soon afterwards slain by Phra Năraі, and his uncle, Sĭ Sŭthămmăraxa. His uncle reigns some months; but having attempted to violate the sister of Phra Năraі, he is vanquished and killed by the enraged brother.	1655
1018	Phra Năraі is made king, under the name Phra Chaò Xang phuok. He kills his two brothers for engaging in a conspiracy against him. Phra Năraі is the sovereign who became afterwards famous in European history in consequence of his political relations with Louis XIV., and the nomination of the celebrated Greek Constantine Phaulcon (or Falcon) to be his prime minister.	1656

Chŭulasŭkkărât.   A.D.
1019   Constantine Falco arrives at Juthia; he   1657
       makes himself most acceptable to the King,
       who raises him by degrees to the rank of Phăja
       Vixaïen. Phra Chaò Xang phuok sends am-
       bassadors to France.
1023   He despatches an army to besiege Ava, which   1661
       he is unable to conquer: proceeding thence, he
       overcomes Xieng măi.
       Constantine Falco is raised to the first dignity
       of the State, Chaò phăja Sămŭkă najŏk; he
       compels many talapoins to withdraw from the
       temples and execute works, and thus excites the
       hatred and indignation of the mandarins against
       himself, who, under the generalship of Chaò
       Dû'a, attempt to accomplish his death. Phra
       Nărai was then sick at Lŏphăburi.
1044   Chaò Dû'a and Phra Phĕtraxa conspire   1682
       against the King; they assassinate Constantine,
       and, the King being deceased, usurp the king-
       dom.
       The intimate union of Phaulcon with the
       French no doubt led to his own destruction, and
       that of his master. There are sufficient grounds
       for believing that Phaulcon was desirous of
       handing over the sovereignty of Siam to the
       French King, of which the advent of consider-
       able bodies of French soldiers is unmistakeable
       evidence. Chaò Dû'a, a natural son of Phra
       Nărai, associated himself with a leading noble,
       Phra Phet Raxa, and the most influential
       bonzes, to preserve the religion and the inde-
       pendence of Siam. It is said that, on Phet
       Raxa's succession, he sent an embassy to Paris
       to conciliate the exasperated *Grand Monarque*.
       This sovereign is harshly spoken of by the

58 HISTORY.

Chŭulăsăkkărât. A.D.

1044 Catholic missionaries,—as is his successor, 1682 Chaò Dŭ'a, whom they call a cruel, barbarous, and debauched monarch. The resistance and persecution they experienced at this period may well account for the severity of their strictures.

1050 Phra Phĕtraxa again sends ambassadors to France. 1688

1059 At the decease of Phra Phĕtraxa, Chaò Dŭ'a 1697 takes possession of the throne; he delighted in angling and hunting, and was notorious for his debauchery and cruelty.

1068 The son of Chaò Dû'a succeeds his father. 1706 He drives out the Anamese from Cambodia, which he makes tributary to him.

1094 At the King's death, a civil war arises; 1732 Upărât, or the Viceroy, kills the King's sons, and usurps the kingdom. During his reign, gold mines were opened in Bangtaphan.

1120 The King being dead, Chaò Dôk Mădû'a 1758 reigns but one year; he resigns the sceptre to his brother, and becomes a talapoin. The King of Ava besieges Juthia, but, being seized by a malady, retreats and dies on his way home.

1128 The King of the Burmans depopulates the 1766 whole country, and besieges Juthia for two years; and, having taken it, sets it on fire, and almost totally destroys it. But the King of Juthia escaped from the country, and, wandering about, soon afterwards died, wasted away by famine.

1129 The Burmans being still in possession of 1767 Juthia, there arose a powerful man named Phăja Tăk, who had been governor of one of the northern provinces of Siam, whose father was a

Chŭulăsăkkărât.   A.D.

1129 Chinese, and his mother a Siamese. He, fore- 1767
seeing the destruction of the city, gathered
together about a thousand brave men, and with
them he routed the Burman troops, and advan-
cing to Bangplasòi, Rajong, Chănthăbun, Phŭ-
thăimàt (Cancao), reduced under his rule not
only the maritime provinces, but even Cambodia; and, hearing of the destruction of Juthia,
furnished a hundred ships with arms and fighting men, hastened to the yet smoking ruins of
the city, assaulted the Burmans, routed and
dispersed them, and established the seat of a
new government at Thănă Buri (Bangkok).
Then occurred a distressful famine; Phăja Tâk
imported rice from foreign lands, and liberally
distributed it to the people.

1131 Phăja Tâk conquers Korât (Ligor), Phĭtsănŭ- 1769
lók and Cambodia.

1136 Phăja Tâk seizes Xieng măi, to which he 1774
appoints a new ruler. The Burman hordes
having made an incursion, he surrounds them
with his forces until the enemy, reduced by
famine, surrender themselves prisoners.

1139 He conquers the kingdom of Sătănakhănăhŭt 1777
(Vieng Chăn), from whence he carries off a
most precious image of Phra Kèo, formed of
an immense emerald.*

1142 The King, seized with insanity, wishes to be 1780
equally adored with Buddha, exacts money
from the rich, and treats the mandarins harshly.

1143 This occasions sedition; the populace attacks 1781
him in his palace; the terrified monarch flies
to a temple, and is ordained a talapoin.

---

* See chapter xiii.

Chŭulăsăkkărât. A.D.
1144   But, soon after, Phăja chăkkri, returning from 1782 the war against the Anamese, ordered him to be dragged from the temple and slain, and occupied the throne in his place, under the name Phra Phŭttŭchaò lúang (Phën dĭn tŏn). At this time he transferred the city and palace from the west to the east bank of the river. During his reign the Burmans made frequent incursions into the Siamese territories, but were always strongly repulsed.

Of this sovereign (Phăja Tâk) Bishop Pallegoix gives the following account:—He came forth from the mountain retreats of Makhon Najok, defeating again and again the Burmese troops. Descending to Bangplasoi, he was there proclaimed king; and being joined by multitudes of the people, he took Chantabun, constructed a hundred ships of war, seized upon Phuthaimat or Kankao on the confines of Cochin China, reduced Cambodia, drove from Ayuthia and the rest of the kingdom all the Burmese invaders, and established his royal residence at Bangkok, to which he gave the name of Thanaburi. He conquered Ligor, Phitanulok, and afterwards Vieng Chan, the capital of the Laos kingdom, whence he brought what is called the Emerald Buddha (Phra Keo), which is the pride and glory of Bangkok at the present day. His exactions are said to have been greater than his conquests. The bonzes averred that he aspired to the divine honour of Buddha. A revolt took place in the city, and the King escaped to a neighbouring pagoda, and declared himself to have become a member of the priest-

Chŭulăsăkkărât. A.D.

1144 hood; but the prime minister who succeeded 1782
him caused him to be driven from the pagoda,
and he was executed in 1782, under the plea
that he would trouble the public peace.

1173 His successor reigned twenty-nine years, and 1811
was succeeded by his son, who carried on the
administration peacefully for fourteen years.
His common name among the people is Phën-
dĭn-klang.

1187 At his death, his son, the late monarch, 1825
ascended the throne, under the name Bŏrŏm-
măthăm-mĭkăraxathĭràt Phra Chaò Prăsât
Thong.

The two principal events which distinguished the reign of Chao Prasat Thong, were the burning of the royal palace, and his war upon the Laos country, in 1828. Of the results of that war an account is given by a writer obviously well informed; and the picture of manners is so graphic and characteristic, that I transfer it to these pages.* The invasion of Cochin China by sea and by land had no other result than the capture of a number of Guannanites, (the Chinese name for Cochin China is Guan-nan, usually written Annan or Annam,) who were, according to custom, condemned to slavery in Siam.

"The expedition against Laos was successful. As usual in Siamese warfare, they laid waste the country, plundered the inhabitants, brought them to Bangkok, sold and gave them away as slaves. The

---

* The whole paper is entitled "Notes on Siam," taken in 1833, from Moor's *Notices of the Indian Archipelago*, p. 199, 200; Singapore, 1837.

prince Vun Chow and family made their escape into Cochin China; but instead of meeting with a friendly reception, they were seized by the King of that country, and delivered as prisoners to the Siamese. The King arrived in Bangkok about the latter end of 1828, and underwent there the greatest cruelties barbarians could invent. He was confined in a large iron cage, exposed to a burning sun, and obliged to proclaim to every one that the King of Siam was great and merciful, that he himself had committed a great error and deserved his present punishment. In this cage were placed with the prisoner, a large mortar to pound him in, a large boiler to boil him in, a hook to hang him by, and a sword to decapitate him; also a sharp-pointed spike for him to sit on. His children were sometimes put in along with him. He was a mild, respectable-looking, old grey-headed man, and did not live long to gratify his tormentors, death having put an end to his sufferings. His body was taken and hung in chains on the bank of the river, about two or three miles below Bangkok. The conditions on which the Cochin Chinese gave up Chow Vun Chan were, that the King of Siam would appoint a new prince to govern the Laos country, who should be approved of by the Cochin Chinese, and that the court of Siam should deliver up the persons belonging to the Siamese army who attacked and killed some Cochin Chinese during the Laos war."

I requested the King to favour me with an account of his own dynasty, and received the following reply:—

"*His Excellency Sir John Bowring, Knighted Doctor of Laws, the Governor of Hong Kong, &c. &c. &c. &c.*

"RESPECTED SIR,—In regard to the particular narrative or ancient true occurrance of the present royal dynasity reigning upon Siam, I beg to say what I knew from statement of our parents and ancestors, and other tolerable and corresponding families whom I have been present of in considerable space of time when they have been living or alive.

"The first family of our parternal ancistors, it is said, have been inhabitants of the city of Hanswatty (proper Sanskrit name), the capital of Pegu, written by Bishop Pallegoix in corupted sound or pronouncing of Sanskrit name 'Hongsawadi,' upon the time of reign the King of that city Pegu named Jumna ti cho by Peguen name, and 'Dusadi sawijay' by Sanskrit name (marked in book of the Bishop Pallegoix with figure 1). This family became officers of state; employed as a part of military service of that King who has conquered Ayudia on about Christian era 1552, have placed the Siamese King of Northern Siam, who has been alliayed to him, upon the throne of whole Siam, at Ayudia, in name of 'Phra Maha Dharmmarajatdhiraj' (marked 2 in the book in which the corrupted name printed); and the King marked 1 has taken the son of the Siamese King, marked 2, to Pegu for security. As Siamese King promised to be dependant of the Pegu on that time, the royal son accompanied the King, marked 1, named Phra Naresr (printed in book Phra Narit, and marked 3), who has been or was at Pegu during the living time or reign of the conqueror, in demise of whom he observed the governments of Pegu, being in great distress in complex opinion to establish the successor of the expired King for about half a month, has concilliated many families of the inhabitants of that city in his power, and took them with him, flied from thence, returned to his native land, Siam, and proclaimed independancy to the Pegu again, the aforesaid family or party of military officers of state then have alliayed with King Phra Naresr, marked 3; on his returning to Siam has accompanied him, and took their residence at Ayudia, which was bestowed them by that King.

" A large Buddh's image was constructed at a place of worship near of their residence, remained until the present day with some ancient inscription.

" After the time of the King Phra Naresr, marked 3, the particular narrative statement of this family is now disappeared to us until the time of reign of Phra Narayu, printed in book Phra Narai, marked 4, reigned at Ayudia and Lawoh about the Christian year 1656 to 1682. On the reign of this king, two brother, extraordinary persons, have been descendants of the said family; became most pleased to the king, who has appointed the older brother in place or office of the lord of the foreign affair, in name or title of 'Chau Phya Phra Khlang,' who has been at presence of the receipt of the French embassy visited Siam upon that time, and the younger brother of his Excellency Phya Phra Khlang, named Mr. Pal, was appointed head of Siamese embassy to France, of return of friendship with the French Government, and met with the being wrecked, lost of the ship at Cape of Good Hope, where he with his suit remained during considerable while, and afterward became to France, met with favourable treatment of the French Government upon that time, and returned to Siam, when his older brother was died. The King Phra Narayu has appointed him (Mr. Pal) the head of embassy in the office of his elder brother, the lord of foreign affair, 'Chau Phya Phra Khlang :' from this person extraordinary our ancestors were said to be descendants ; but their office and affairs in royal service were not continued in generations during a few reign of their Majesties Siamese King, who succeeded his Majesty the King Phra Narayu, until the time of his Majesty Bhumindr Rajatdhiraj, marked 5, reigned upon Siam since the Christian year 1706 to 1732, in which the first person being father of the first king, and grandfather of the royal father of the present king (myself), and late king (my late brother) of Siam, was an extraordinary son of a family descended from aforesaid lords of foreign affairs, who removed their situation at Ayudia for happiness of lives, and situated their place at ' Sakutrang,' a port in small river, being branch of great river, at the connected realms of Northern and Southern Siams, at about latitude N. 13° 15′ 30″ more little, and long. 99° 90′ E. : the said extraordinary person was born there, and became man of skill and knowledge and ability of royal service, came from ' Saketrang' to Ayudia, where he was introduced to the royal service, and became married with a beautiful daughter of a Chinese richest family at Chinese compound or situation within wall of city and in south-eastern corner of Ayudia, and became pleased by the kings marked 5 and 6, and appointed in office of the preparer of royal letters and communication for northern direction (*i. e.* for all states or regions of both dependencies, and in dependency to Siam at northern direction), and protector of the great royal seal for that purpose being ; his title was His Excellency ' Phra Acksom Sundom Smiantra.' He has five children ; his first wife, who afterward was died, and has, secondly, married with the younger sister of his late wife, with whom he has a single daughter.

"In particular of the aforesaid five children, the first was a son became man in service of the second King upon the time of the King of Siam marked 6, and leaving a sole daughter only was died before Ayudia was conquered by Burman Army; the second and third were the daughters their descendants, many remained until the present day (the royal mother of the present Major and second Kings of Siam (myself and my younger brother) was a daughter, being third child of the latter). The fourth was an extraordinary son, became the first King of Siam in the present dynasity marked in the book 8, who was born in March 1736, of Christian era, and of whom the present and late Kings of Siam (myself and my late brother) are grandchildren, and the fiveth was the person who was born in September 1743 of the Christian era, and who became finally the second King upon the reign of his elder brother here, and died before his brother's death 6 years. The firstly said ancestor His Excellency 'Phra Acksom Sundom Smiantra,' has also another illegitimate son, being youngest born from a maid-servant whom he (H. E. our ancestor) has take with him, went to Northern Siam upon the time of the Ayudia being seighed by Burman army, on the Christian years 1765 and 1766, to obtain new situation or station for refuge, leaving here all above said legitimate sons and daughters who were married, and live with their own families, for the consequences of difficulty in going with large party in very hurricane and hindering manner of journey.

"He, on his arrival at 'Phitsanulok,' the great city at Northern Siam, became regent or superintendent of supreme governor of that city, who proclaimed King of Siam after burning of Ayudia was in hand of Burman army, and who died by structing of fever after a few month of the royal proclamation. In this destress H. E., our ancestor, took refuge at a town out of that city, where he was died of fiver, and burn by his maid-servant, wife, and the son born of her. His relicks were brought here by them, and were delivered to his legitimate children here, and remained in our royal house of worship of royal ancestors until the present day.

"And his two extraordinary son, on lossing of Ayudia, took refuge at various places, and afterward became combined with the King Phya Tarksing, first of Bangkokese kings, marked 7 in book: finally, the elder was appointed the supreme general Chau Phya Chukkry, the lord regent of country, and afterward styled in name or title and dignity of 'Maha Krasute suk,' *id est*, 'the King of war,' who has resisted Burman armies came to take station of Siam every year upon that time.

"The younger was appointed the King of Northern Siam, governing at Phisnuloke, where his father has been and died; he bore the name of Chau Phya 'Surasint.' So, upon that time, there were three kings presented in Siam, viz., Supreme King 'Phya Tark,' King of war, our grandfather, and the latter said King of Northern Siam.

"On the year of Christian era 1781, when two brother kings were sent to tranquel Cambodia, which was in distress or disturbance of rebellion, the King Phya Tarsing, marked 7, remained here. He came mad or furious, saying he is Buddh, &c., and put many persons of innocents to death, more than 10,000 men, and compeled the people to pay various amounts of money to royal treasure, with any lawful taxes and reasonable causes; so here great insurgents took place, who apprehended the mad king and put to death, and sent their mission to Cambodia, and invited two Kings of war and of Northern Siam to return here for the crown and throne of whole Siam and its dependancy.

"Our grandfather was enthroned and crowned in May, 1782, in name of 'Phra Budhyot fa chulatoke,' marked in book 8; his reign continued 27 years; his demise took place on the year 1809, in which our father has succeeded him. His coronation took place on August, 1809; his reign continued happily 15 years; his expiration took place in the year 1824, in month of July. His royal name, 'Phra Budh Lord

Luh nobhaluy,' marked 9 (names of these two kings were printed in book, by Bishop Pallegoix, 'Pheen din ton' and 'Pheen din Klang'). These names, improper as they were very popular and vulgar, are 'Pheen din ton,' *i. e.*, former or first reign; 'Pheen din Klang,' *i. e.*, middle or next reign only, not royal tittle.

"Our elder brother, the late king, succeeded our royal father ; his coronation took place on August, 1824. His name was Param Dharwik rajahdhiraj (proper Sanskrit), and in Siamese name Phra Nangklau chau yu Acca. His reign continued 26 year ; his demise took place on 2nd April, 1851 ; then my succession of him concluded, and I was crowned on May 15th of that year. My name in Siam is Phra Chomklau chau yu hua, and I bear the Sanskrit name as ever signed in my several letters—

" S. P. P. M. MONGKUT.
" incontract that are
" SOMDETCH PHRA PARAMENDR MAHA MONGKUT,
" Rex Siamensium."

I have inserted in the Appendix some brief notices of the history of Siam, which were written by the King, and have been prepared for the press by Dr. Dean; also the account sent to me by the King of the results of the last attack by the Siamese on the Burman city of Chiantoong.

Mr. Wade, the acting Chinese Secretary to the Superintendency in China, has kindly furnished me with the following account, extracted from sundry Chinese authors, of the relations, past and present, existing between Siam and the empire of China.

These notices take us back into periods far more remote than any authentic records derivable from other sources, and I have introduced them as a valuable contribution to historical knowledge.

Notices of Siam are to be found in

1. The Urh-shih-yih-Shih, chronicles of China, compiled by the Imperial historiographers of succeeding dynasties.

2. The Ta Ming Hwui Tien. Statutes of the Ming dynasty.

3. The Ta Tsing Hwui Tien. Statutes of the present dynasty.

4. The Yih Tung Chi. Cyclopædia of the statistics of the present dynasty.

5. The Tien-Hia Kiun Kwoh Li-ping Shu. Discriminative notice of the excellence and defects of the states of the world.

6. The Hai Kwoh T'u chi. Notice of foreign countries, illustrated with maps and engravings, a work based on one compiled under the direction of Commissioner Lin.

7. The Ying hwan chi hoh. A general geography by Sü Ki yu, at the time governor of Fuh kien.

There is no great variety in the earlier details furnished by these several works, and the total of the information collected is scarcely sufficient to repay the trouble of research.

Allusion is first made to Siam in the chronicle of the Eastern Tsin dynasty (A. D. 303—416,) as a country named Fu-nan, or Fu-nam,* lying about one

---

* The Canton pronunciation seems to me to be more probably that used in approximating the names of these southern countries. Some remarks

thousand miles west of Lin, that is, the city of a district called, under the Han, Siang Lin, "elephant forest," (which must have been in modern Anam,) in a large bay.

The chronicle of the Liang (536—552) places it at the same distance south-west of Lin, and double that distance south of the province of Jih-nan, or Yat-nam (Anam).

In the chronicle of the Lin (584—622) it is stated that Fu-nam is also called Chih-tu (Chik tu, or chikdu), red earth, and that it is one hundred days' sail to its capital.

The "discriminative notice, &c." states that it was also called Polosha, and that in the reign of Ta-nie (608—21) of the Sui dynasty, a Chinese officer of the Board of Works made a voyage to Siam.

We hear no more of it in the chronicle until the days of the Yuen, the Mongol dynasty (1281—1366). In the second reign of this, tribute was sent to the Emperor of China, the accompanying document being in letters of gold (probably on silk).

The Siamese had been long at war with the Maliyi, or Maliurh (Malays?) but both nations laid aside their feud and submitted to China.

The chronicles of the Ming speak of the country by its present Chinese name, Lien Lo, or Tsien Lo, or in Cantonese, Tsim-Lo. The name Siam is doubtless to be found in the first syllable; the presence of the second will be explained presently. It lies, says

---

of Mr. Edkins in the fourth volume of the Transactions of the Chinese branch of the Asiatic Society, on the ancient pronunciation of Chinese words, are worthy of notice.

the same authority, south-west of the Chains (of Cochin China), and may be reached in ten days from China if the wind be fair.

The country known to the T'áng (620—900), and Sin, as Chikdu, was subsequently divided into Lo-fo and Sien (or Tsim), and the latter becoming sufficiently powerful to absorb the former, the composite State was named Sien Lo-fo. Sien (says the discriminative notice) was less fertile than Lo-fo, and drew its supplies from it.

From the foundation of the Ming by Hung-wu, in 1367, the relation of Siam to China as a friendly tributary, but perfectly dependent State, seems never to have been materially affected.

In 1369, the third year of Hung-wu, we find that sovereign bestowing upon the Court of Siam a present of some silk, and a copy of the Imperial Almanac of China.

The following year comes a mission from the then king, Cham lit chiu piya, with a tribute of Siamese produce, and an address* written on gold leaf; and next year, an offering of black bears, white apes, and other produce of the country. In 1373, the king's sister sent a present to the Empress. Hung-wei wrote a despatch declining it. It was again tendered, and again declined; but the envoy was publicly entertained, and, in gratitude, a map of Siam was sent to the Emperor as a supplementary tribute.

The regular tribute of this or the preceding year had been damaged in a storm, which drove the tri-

---

* Address—of vassal to suzerain. That of the King to the Emperor was a *piaou*; the one here spoken of, a *tsien*.

bute vessel on Hainan Islands. The authorities of that place behaved well to the crew, and the envoy Shalipa came on to Canton, to tender the residue of the original quantity of manufactures and spices. The officials of Canton were instructed not to receive these, as there was no address with them, and it was decreed that tribute should be brought once in three years. An address* to the heir-apparent of China was received this year from the Crown Prince of Siam, and in 1376 the Prince was sent to do homage to the Emperor, who desired the Board of Ceremonies to provide him with a court dress; also to make a state seal, for the use of the Court of Siam; which State was for the future to be called Sien-Lo.

Tribute was now brought annually, and sometimes twice a year. In 1382, China accorded the envoys a state passport,† and sent a return of figured silk and porcelain.

In 1386, a Chinese envoy was sent to Siam with special thanks for one hundred piculs of pepper and one hundred piculs of Sapan wood. In 1387, Siam sent thirty elephants, with two attendants to each; and the following year, the Crown Prince gave notice of his father's death, and prayed to be invested as his successor. A eunuch, high in office, was sent to perform the ceremony after he should have duly mourned and sacrificed to the late King. In 1389, a tribute of seventeen hundred piculs of Sapan wood was sent; and, two years later, Siam applied for the standard weights and measures of China, which were granted.

* See note above. † A paper tally with a docket.

In 1402, the first year of Yung Loh, that emperor conferred on Siam a silver-gilt seal, with a handle shaped like a camel. In the following year, a Siamese trader was driven on the coast of Fuh kien, and the authorities proposed to turn her cargo to account as tribute, but were forbidden by the Emperor. Siam sent to thank his Majesty, and to pray again for the standard weights and measures of China. The Emperor sent these, and also one hundred copies of the History of the Eminent Women of China—a well-known work of the Han dynasty.

In 1408, the Emperor died, and Siamese envoys came to mourn. The Court farther propitiated that of China by surrendering some criminals who had escaped to Siam, and was commended accordingly.

In 1415, another King of Siam was, at his own request, installed by the patron State; and the latter, in 1418, farther manifested his sense of its importance by directing both Siam and Malacca to forego the animosity which kept them constantly at war, and to live at peace with one another. We have other evidence of this sense, and of the title of China to entertain it a few years later.

In 1456, the Siamese envoy Naisando was sent to complain of the Chams (of Cochin-China) who had plundered a Siamese vessel. China commanded them to make good the loss sustained: the Chams, however, retorted, that what had been done was only in retaliation for former acts of a like character on the part of the Siamese.

In 1472, application was made for a new passport, that granted in 1382 having been destroyed by the worms. In the tenth year of Hung-chi (1496) orders were sent to Canton to procure interpreters versed in written and spoken Siamese; there being no one in the interpretorial* establishment at Peking who knew anything of the language. We do not learn that they succeeded; and in 1514, when the address on gold-leaf was presented by the tribute-bearers, the Emperor Ching Teh ordered some of the suite to be detained to teach Siamese.

In 1508, the eunuch superintending the customs at Canton, and the local authorities, had levied duties on the cargo of a Siamese vessel driven into port by stress of weather, to assist, as it was alleged, in defraying the expenses of the suppression of piracy. The levy was disapproved by the Emperor Ching Teh, then on the throne.

The laws at this time against foreign trade were extremely strict. In 1520, the collector of Canton allowed one of his retinue to trade with a Siamese vessel, and the offender was decapitated.

This was in the reign of Kia Tsing, memorable for the Japanese piracies on the eastern coast, and naturally for dread of dealings with outside people. In 1552, white elephants formed part of the tribute, and we have then no record of any being transmitted for several years. Siam, in the mean time, suffered severely in a war with Tung man ngau, a neighbouring State. The capital fell into the enemy's hands;

---

* The Sz' i Kwan, or hall of the four barbarians or divisions of barbarian peoples, originally distinguished as Tih the northern, I the eastern, Jung the western, and Mwan the southern. I became, and is, with a few exceptions, still, a generic for all races not within the pale of Chinese civilization.

the King hung himself, his son was taken prisoner, and the state seal given by China was lost. In the reign of Lung King (1565-71), the son having regained his liberty, prayed that emperor to invest him, and grant him a fresh seal; and, vowing vengeance against Tung man ngau, commenced a war against Chan-lap; dethroned its king, and appropriated his territory down to the south-west coast. In the seventh year of the long and chequered reign of Wan-lih (1578) the tribute sent consisted of elephants, ivory in the tusk, rhinoceros' horns, peacocks' tails, feathers of the blue swallow, shells of the tortoise in rolls or entire, six-footed tortoises, precious stones, gold rings, common camphor, camphor in large crystals, and various kinds of spices, drugs, and manufactures.

Later in the same reign (1593) the Japanese invaded Corea, and Siam offered to co-operate with Wan-lih in an invasion of Japan. She appears subsequently to have backed out of the engagement. In 1643, the last year but one of the Ming, it is recorded that tribute was sent from Siam; and since the tenth year of Shun Chi, the first monarch of the present dynasty, it has come without interruption.

The statutes show that, in 1667, Kang-Hi limited the tribute-ships to three; two regular and one supernumerary; to contain not more than one hundred men each, only twenty-two of whom, including officers, were to escort the tribute to Peking; the rest were to remain at Canton, at the charge of the Chinese Government; and vessels, which appear to have been sent supplementarily, to ascertain whether the tribute-ships had reached China or not, were not to be admitted into port.

In 1673, King Shănlitpaklapchiukulungpimahulu-kwansz' sent tribute by way of Tagapuoi, and prayed that an officer should be deputed to invest him; also that he should be supplied with a new seal. A silver-gilt seal, with a camel handle, was accordingly bestowed on him. Siam, at this time, was divided into nine takusz', provinces (?); fourteen fu, prefectures; and seventy-two hien, districts. In 1684, the envoy applied to be allowed to beach the vessels at Canton, so as to lose no time in unloading and shipping, and that the local authorities of Canton might be directed to settle the purchase of all articles bought for Siam. The Emperor agreed, and the following year added a present of fifty pieces of silk, and decreed, a few years later, that all produce brought by the envoy should be exempted from duty.

Towards the close of his reign, the Emperor's attention was attracted by the envoy's report that rice was to be obtained in Siam for two or three mace a picul; and in 1722, the last year of his reign, we find a decree commanding the importation of three hundred thousand piculs by ship into Kwang-Tung, Fuh-Kien, and Chik-Kiang. The rice paid no duty. Supplies continued to be sent; and in the second year of Yung Ching, ninety-six Chinese sailors who had been sent to Siam for rice were so satisfied with that country, that they requested and obtained permission not to return to China. This, under the most exclusive and severe of the sovereigns of the present dynasty, is remarkable. But Siam seems to have been in high favour; and in 1729, Yung Ching presented the King with a tablet, on which he had written with his own hand, " *tien nan loh kwah,*"—the happy state of the south.

In 1735, Kien Lung commenced his reign, and was immediately addressed by the Board of Ceremonies, to whom Siam had applied to replace a Court dress, presented some years before by the Court of China, and which had been destroyed by time. The application was for one or two dresses accordingly; also for some copper to make the character *Fuh*—happiness, which it was an annual custom to place in the temple or temples. Farther, it was prayed that the restrictions on the export of copper should be relaxed. This was all negatived by the Board; but the Emperor added to a present of silk eight piculs of copper, with a warning at the same time that this liberality was not to be looked on as a precedent.

Rice was now regularly brought to Fuh-Kien; cargoes over ten thousand piculs paying half duty; five thousand piculs three-tenths, and under five thousand piculs two-tenths duties. Wood, too, was found to be cheap in Siam; and, by a decree of 1744, Chinese were allowed to build vessels there, and to bring them to be registered in China. In 1751, Chinese traders bringing up more than two thousand piculs of rice were recommended to the throne, and rewarded with a mandarin button; that is to say, an official grade.

In 1753, Siam preferred a singular request, viz. for some ginseng, some long-haired oxen (yaks ?), some good horses, and some eunuchs conversant with the ceremonial of the Court and household. A present of ginseng was made, but the rest of the request appears to have been negatived.

In 1781, tribute was sent, and the address stated that the country had been suffering much from the depredations of the Burmese; but that the territory lost had been recovered, and vengeance duly taken. There was, however, no heir to the throne, and the assembled magnates of Siam, having elected the memorialist, by name Ching, to be *Kwoh-Chang* (senior of the State), he prayed the Emperor to invest him regularly. He presently died, and his son Ching-hwa was made king in 1786, by letters patent forwarded from Peking.

It was desired in 1790 that the tribute received of the *wai-fan*—outer foreigners—was to be disposed of as follows:—That from Corea, as heretofore by the Board of Ceremonies; that from Anam and Siam, by the Court of the Household.

There are two more notices of tribute-bearing, one in 1802, one shortly afterwards; the former remarkable for the name of its envoy, who figured in Chinese as *Pi wo mun sun mun to a pa tee*. He died at Canton, and the Emperor ordered three hundred taels to be sent home to his family. In the latter case the vessel was wrecked off Hiang-shan, the Macao district, and all the tribute lost. The Emperor's rescript says it was a case beyond the reach of human means, and that no blame being attributable to the envoy, he is not to be called on to make good the articles missing.

There had been a formal attempt made in 1748, the thirteenth of Kien-Lung, to establish a college of interpreters, Siamese and others, at Peking. Eight offices were formed, with ninety-six officers or students; Siam, Burmah, Papih or Patpak, and Pih or Pak, belonging to the eastern department; and the Mahometans, Kan-chang, Sifan (western foreigners, commonly believed to be savage tribes beyond Sz'chuen) and Si-tien, being included in the western department. Of the success of this scheme we are not informed.

CHAPTER III.

POPULATION.

PALLEGOIX estimates the population of Siam at six millions, which can at best be only approximative to the truth. In the uncertainties of Oriental statistics, with the small acquaintance we possess respecting the inhabitants of the interior, and amidst various opinions which fluctuate between three and seven millions, I am disposed to consider the real population of Siam as composed of from four millions five hundred thousand to five millions of souls. The elements of which Pallegoix makes up his total are the following:—

Siamese proper (the T'hai race)	1,900,000
Chinese	1,500,000
Laos	1,000,000
Malays	1,000,000
Cambodians	500,000
Peguans	50,000
Kareens, Xongs, &c.	50,000
Total	6,000,000

With reference to the official census, Pallegoix says, that in speaking of the population, neither old men, nor women, nor children are ever spoken of by the Siamese. To all questions as to the number of inhabitants, the reply is, so many *men*. He estimates the number generally at five times the amount of the record; but though the records of the census are regularly made to one of the high functionaries, he is restrained from communicating the particulars to any but the King and the ministers.

La Loubère says that in his time the Siamese population was estimated at one million nine hundred thousand; but he thinks from this some retrenchment is to be made "for the vanity and lying essential to Orientals," though, on the other hand, the fugitives who have sought sanctuary in the woods against the Government ought to be added.

Siam may, with its dependencies, be considered as occupied by the dominant race, or T'hai, a vast but for the most part migratory Chinese population, the Laos people, the Cambodians in such parts of Cambodia as recognise the Siamese authority, the Peguans in a part of the Mon or Pegu territory, numerous Malayan tribes, with a variety of mountain races in a state of greater or less subjection to the Government of Bangkok.

The Siamese are located principally on the two banks of the Meinam, and on those of the tributary streams which flow into that great river from the latitude of 13° to about 20° N. They also occupy the gulf from the head of the peninsula down to latitude 7°, where the Malayan races are settled. To the east of the British possession on the Tenasserim coast, in lat. 11° up to lat. 16° 30′, about two-thirds of the peninsula is peopled by Siamese races.

The bulk of the Laos people are spread over the great valley through which the Meikong, or principal river of Cambodia flows, between the latitudes

13° and 21° N. The country is reported to be thickly peopled, except in the mountainous parts contiguous to Tonquin and Cambodia. Though the limits of Laos are not accurately laid down in the maps, and the country is but little known, it is said to contain more square miles than Siam itself. All its princes are tributary to Siam.

The Cambodians occupy the southern districts of the Meikong down to the frontiers of Cochin China. Up to the latitudes 12° to 13° N. tribute is said to be regularly paid, especially by the fertile province of Batabang.

About fifty thousand Mons or Peguans pay tribute; and between latitudes 3° and 7° N. the Malays in the principalities of Patani, Calantan, and Tringanu on the east, and on the west those of Quedah and Perak, are subjected through the Governor of Ligor to the Siamese sovereignty; but that sovereignty is by no means undisputed by the inhabitants in the less accessible parts.

Among the mountain tribes the most remarkable are the Kareens, the Lawa, the Ka, and the Xong. The Kareens inhabit the mountain ranges on the Burmese frontier up to lat. 21°; the Lawa, a more numerous people, the same regions farther south; the Ka, the mountainous district between the Meinam and the Meikong. The Xong dwell on the hilly region in the N. E. angle of the Gulf of Siam, from the latitude of about 11° 30′ to 13° N.

The population of Siam is probably nearly stationary. The number of the bonzes condemned to celibacy, the multitudes of men who, being slaves, are unable to marry—the prodigious proportion of women who are childless in consequence of the practice of polygamy,—all seem to check the generally prolific character of tropical regions. The annual influx of Chinese being confined to males, does not bring with it the ordinary augmentations of a vast emigration; nor is there an adequate supply of women for the demand produced by the constant flow of men from China, who are brought down by every north-east monsoon.

Chinese.—The extraordinary diffusion of the Chinese emigrants over all the regions from the most western of the islands of the Indian archipelago,—in the Straits settlements, in Siam and Cochin China, and now extending over a considerable portion of Western America, particularly in California, and reaching even Australia and Polynesia,—is one of the most remarkable of the events of modern history, and is likely to exercise a great influence on the future condition of man: for the Chinese do not migrate to mingle with and be absorbed among other tribes and peoples; they preserve their own language, their own nationality, their own costume and religious usages—their own traditions, habits, and social organization. Though they intermarry with the races among whom they dwell, the Chinese type becomes predominant, and the children are almost invariably educated on the father's model, the influence of the mother seeming almost annihilated. And though the Chinese frequently acquire large fortunes, great influence and sometimes high rank as a consequence of their prosperity, the ties that bind them to their country seem never to be broken; and the tides of population flow Chinaward with every south-western monsoon, to be replaced by a stronger stream when the monsoon of the north-east sends the junks on their wonted way towards the south. It is estimated that in the kingdom of Siam there are more than a million and a half of Chinese settlers; in the city of Bangkok alone there are supposed to be two hundred thousand. In fact, all the active business appears to be in their hands. Nine out of ten of the floating bazaars which cover for miles the two banks of the Meinam are occupied by Chinamen; very many of them are married to Siamese women, for a Chinawoman scarcely ever leaves her country; but the children are invariably educated to the Chinese type: the tail is cultivated if it be a boy, and the father alone seems to model the child's nature and education. Yet, that strong parental affection which has been remarked as one of the characteristic virtues of the Chinese is almost invariably exhibited. Fathers are constantly playing with and carrying about their children; encouraging their gambols, teaching them to observe, pleased when they are noticed by strangers, and generally deeming their children objects of pride and pleasure. With rare exceptions, the Siamese women are well treated by their Chinese husbands. They seem to be inspired with a greater love of labour, occupy themselves more busily with domestic concerns, and generally appear to improve under the influence of the foreign element. The Chinese not only occupy the busiest and the largest bazaars, but their trading habits descend to the very lowest articles of barter; and hundreds of Chinese boats are vibrating up and down the river, calling at every house, penetrating every creek, supplying all articles of food, raiment, and whatever ministers to the daily wants of life. They penetrate to and traffic with the interior wherever profits are to be realized. As a community they are nearly isolated from the Siamese, though professing, for the most part, the same religion. They have their own temples, and carry on their worship of Buddha, not according to the usages of the priests of Siam, but following the customs and traditions of China; and their Buddhism, as in China itself, is held in subservience to their reverence for the teachings and writings of the Chinese sages,— Confucius, Mencius, Sze mat ze, and the ancient teachers of their native land. The signs over their warehouses, shops, and houses are all written in Chinese,—in the Chinese language they carry on all their correspondence; nor do I remember an example of a Chinaman being able to write, though they almost all speak, the Siamese language. Over their doors are the same inscriptions one is accustomed to see in China, such as, "May the five felicities dwell in this abode." The moral aphorisms, the fragments of poetry which are suspended on the walls in China, written on scrolls or tablets, always in pairs, decorate the houses of the Chinese established in Siam. But the Siamese keep the Chinese in absolute subjection; and while I was in Bangkok, I saw no instance of resistance to the native authority. In 1847, however, a serious insurrection of the Chinese population menaced the Government, but the insurrection was soon suppressed.* A Chinese merchant of enormous wealth, who held the opium monopoly, with, I was informed, more than ninety other monopolies, has been raised to the ranks of nobility, and was present among the multitude of prostrate nobles, dressed in the distinction of mandarin costume, when that article of the treaty was read to them which abolished the whole system of monopoly, and established free trade from the month of April, 1856. Certainly, he bowed his head in silence, but looked as if a hundred thunderstorms were concentrated in that proud, scornful, yet resigned expression. He had been told his doom at a conference with the principal ministers; but, as the opium monopoly, the most precious and profitable of all, was preserved to him, he had the sagacity to feign a willing resignation, and to say he would employ his capital for the future in legitimate instead of privileged commerce. Though a small number of the Chinese profited by

---

* The Siamese have managed to keep the Chinese in tolerable subjection, though not without serious controversies and tumults. The insurrection which took place in the year 1847 had its origin in the imposition of a new or an augmented tax, to be levied on the sugar-boilers. The Governor visited the malcontents at Petriu, was seized and decapitated by the Chinese labourers; after which the Chinese dispersed themselves in the neighbouring districts; but at Leukonchesi they not only killed the Governor, but took possession of the fort. The Siamese troops sent to subjugate the insurgents exhibited great poltroonery against the besieged, who had only beans to fire from the guns of the fort, and who were wholly ignorant of the art of war; but, notwithstanding, the gates of the city were finally destroyed. Elephants were sent out, and a general massacre of unresisting men, women, and children took place. It was supposed that a general rising of the Chinese was intended; and it is very doubtful whether the Siamese Government could have maintained itself against any extensive combination.

the farms, the enormous majority expressed their great delight at the emancipation which the treaty provided. The China trade has suffered seriously from the interruption to which it has been exposed from the pirates who swarm along the coast from Canton to the Gulf of Siam; and, at the time we visited Bangkok, where in more prosperous times a hundred junks would have arrived from China, only five or six had entered the waters of the Meinam, and three or four were anchored outside waiting for the spring-tides to cross the bar. The majority of these junks are the property of Chinamen settled in Bangkok, many of whom have their partners or branch establishments in the principal ports of China. The trade is mostly with the ports of Kwantung, Fookien, and the Island of Hainan, from which regions almost all the settlers come; but junks sometimes arrive from the Yang tze Kiang, from Shantung, and even from the Tien tsin river, in Pecheli.

Laos.—I felt great interest in the Laos people from the first. Often I heard sweet music and sweet voices as I passed along the streets, or floated upon the waters of the Meinam; and, on inquiry, I learnt that the sweetest was the music of Laos. Once, calling on the second King, I found him playing on a singularly harmonious instrument, composed of reeds of the bamboo, an instrument nearly eight feet in length: it was, he said, a gift from the Prince of Laos, and he gratified me by presenting it for my acceptance. On visiting the houses of the high nobility, I have been often asked, " Will you see the dances? will you hear the singing? will you listen to the music of

Laos?" and groups of meek-eyed, gentle, prostrate people have been introduced, to exhibit the movements, which rather resemble the graceful positions of the ancient *minuet* than the friskiness of the European "light fantastic toe." Sometimes they hold garlands of flowers, which they present in graceful varieties of attitude. Sometimes, torches or candles are moved about in centric, or eccentric orbits. The songs—they are generally tales of love—are often pathetic and pleasing. They are sometimes accompanied by music; at others, the songs and the music are heard alone. Bishop Pallegoix, who is well acquainted with the Laos people, speaks of their music as very sweet, harmonious, and sentimental. Three persons will form a melodious concert: one plays the bamboo organ, another sings romances with the voice of inspiration, and the third strikes in cadence the suspended tongues of sonorous woods. The Laos organ is a collection of sixteen fine and long bamboos, bound by a circle of ebony, where there is an opening for the aspiration and inspiration of the breath, which causes the vibration of a number of small silver tonguelets, placed near a hole made in each bamboo, over which the fingers run with great dexterity. I have seen the Laos women of the highest ranks sent for by their lords to gratify my curiosity. They have crawled into the presence, and, with bowed head, waited tremblingly for the commands of their husband. Their dress is more graceful than that of the Siamese women, especially their mode of arranging and adorning their hair, which was sometimes ornamented with fragrant white flowers. They wore the *pagne*, which is the universal costume of Siam: a sort of light scarf passed over the shoulders and covered the breast, and a handsome silk tissue encircled the waist; no shoe or sandal was on the feet, and the legs were uncovered to the knees, though there seemed an anxiety to conceal the feet beneath their garments when they crouched down. Almost all the opulent nobles have wives from Laos, many of whom would be considered pretty. They are of diminutive stature, singularly meek expression, liquid eyes, and graceful movement. They have the art of obtruding the elbow forwards, which is deemed an aristocratic accomplishment among the Siamese ladies, who frequently take occasion to exhibit the subtile action of their arms, and which could only be produced by very early training.

The Malayans are a migratory race, and being among the best of sailors from their nautical habits, they are spread widely throughout the East, and perhaps rank next to the Chinese in the spirit of adventure. Though they are very numerous, I should doubt the accuracy of Bishop Pallegoix' estimate, which reckons them at a million in the kingdom of Siam. They are mostly Mahomedans, and, like all the followers of the Prophet, very devoutly attached to their faith. There is little of the spirit of proselytism among the Mussulmans, though they sometimes receive large accessions of converts from barbarous tribes. This may be safely attributed to the simplicity of their teachings, which consist merely in the formula, "There is no God but God, and Mahomet is His prophet,"—for doubtless the creed, that there is one supreme, undivided, spiritual unity, whose commands have been communicated to the world by a succession of prophets, of whom Mahomet was the greatest and the last, conveys nothing of a repulsive character likely to stagger reason, or to make great demands upon confiding faith. I observed few evidences either in the shape of mosques or minarets, or public exhibitions of Islamism, in the city of Bangkok; but, no doubt, the Malay races would be more thickly scattered in the regions adjacent to the Burmese and Tenasserim frontier. The usages of the Malays more closely resemble and more readily accommodate themselves to those of the Siamese than do those of the Chinese settlers. Like the Siamese, they are constantly chewing *betel* and the areca nut. Their ordinary food is rice, sago, fish, ox and buffalo flesh, sweet potatoes, and fruits. They are little given to agriculture, and their cultivation seldom goes beyond a few plantain trees, sugar-canes, sometimes pepper or coffee bushes, and the commoner fruits of the country; but energetic or persevering enterprise forms no part of their character. Their language is widely spread, and one of the most valuable instruments of intercourse through ultra-India. It is simple in construction, harmonious in sound, and easy of acquirement. They preserve a sort of social organization, under the authority of a supreme chief. The sarong and loose trousers, with a turban covering their shorn head, are the universal vestments. They almost invariably carry a kris, or bent poignard, in their belt; and, though not a quarrelsome race, are, when excited or exasperated, disposed to take the wildest revenge upon their adversaries. When engaged in a lawless career, there seems no bound to the reckless ferocity and bloodthirstiness of the Malay.

As regards the Cambodians, the estimate of half a million requires verification, even were the whole population of Cambodia more accurately estimated than it is; and of these the number in a state of absolute subjection to Siam remains to be ascertained. In Siam proper there are many Cambodians in a state of vassalage, and others who are mixed with the general population of the country.

Pretty much the same may be said of the less populous races,—the Kareens, Xongs, and others. These, who still occupy their native haunts, are more or less tributary to the Siamese; and many of them who have been captured in war are in a state of slavery in the capital and provinces of Siam.

CHAPTER IV.

MANNERS, CUSTOMS, SUPERSTITIONS, AMUSEMENTS.

I HAVE collected some extracts from the writings of the earlier historians and travellers in Siam, whose narratives still retain much of their interest from the fact that the habits and customs of the Siamese have undergone few changes from the time of the first intercourse of Europeans down to the present hour.

Van Schenten, who lived, as he says, eight years in Siam, and wrote his memoirs in 1636, gives the following account of the King and the Government at that time existing:—

"The King of Siam is quite absolute in his States; he is of an ancient and noble family, which has long ruled over the country. On important state occasions, it is customary for him to communicate his intentions to some of the higher nobility, called mandarins : these mandarins assemble other officers, to whom they communicate the propositions made by the King, and all unite to consider the answer or remonstrance they shall send. Much respect is paid to the sovereign ; he disposes of all the offices of the State, without regard to the birth of those on whom he bestows them: as, however, he takes places away for the smallest fault, his subjects serve him with the submission of slaves.

"His train is magnificent; he seldom appears in public, and even the highest nobles see him but seldom, and on certain appointed days. Upon the days of audience, his palace is richly adorned: the King seated on his throne, and all the nobility of the country kneeling before him with crossed hands and bowed heads: his guard is composed of three hundred men; his answers are received as oracles, and his orders exactly obeyed. Besides the Queen, he has a number of concubines chosen from among the most beautiful maidens of the country. He keeps a good table, but his religion forbids him to take wine, brandy, and strong potations, so that his ordinary beverage is water or cocoa-nut milk: the people would be greatly scandalized did their sovereign or his chief officers fail to observe this law.

"Sometimes he goes upon the river in barges, each of which has from eighty to one hundred rowers, besides the praos of the King, of which there are seven or eight. He is followed by three or four hundred others, holding the nobles: in the midst of each boat is a gilded pavilion, in which one may sit; and in this manner the King is frequently followed by fourteen or fifteen hundred persons. When he goes by land, it is in a gilded chair carried on men's shoulders: his guard, and those who compose the Court, follow in order, keeping entire silence, and all who meet them in the way are obliged to fall prostrate before them. Every year, during the month of October, he shows himself to his people—one day in a procession by water, another by land, when he repairs to the principal temples, followed by his whole Court; two hundred elephants lead the procession, each having three armed men, and followed by a band playing on musical instruments, trumpeters, and a thousand foot-soldiers well armed. The nobles follow, some among them having as many as eighty or one hundred followers; after them follow two hundred Japanese soldiers, the King's body-guard, his riding-horses and his elephants; then the officials of the Court, who carry fruit or other offerings to the idols; after them, the highest nobility, some of whom are even crowned: one of them bears the royal standard, another a sword, which is the emblem of justice. His Majesty then appears on a throne placed upon an elephant's back, surrounded by persons carrying parasols, and followed by the heir-apparent. His ladies follow upon elephants, but in closed chairs, which screen them from sight: six hundred men close the procession, which usually consists of fifteen or sixteen thousand. When the King goes by water, two hundred nobles head the procession, each in his own barge, with from sixty to eighty rowers; four boats filled with musicians follow, and fifty richly-ornamented royal barges. After these come ten very magnificent barges, covered with gold even to the oars. The King is seated on a throne in the most splendid of the barges; on the fore part of the vessel one of the nobles bears the royal standard: the Prince and the King's ladies follow, with their suite: I reckoned four hundred and fifty boats in all. The people repair to the banks of the river, with joined hands and drooping heads, showing the utmost respect and veneration for their sovereign. His revenue is several millions, drawn principally from the rice (which grows abundantly in this country), sapan wood (used as a red dye), tin, saltpetre, and lead; only the royal factors being allowed to sell these productions to foreigners, as also the gold, which they wash from the sand, and that which they procure from the mines. There are taxes upon foreign merchandize, governors and vassal princes paying tribute. He has also large profits from commerce with China and the Coromandel coast, which gives him at least two hundred catties of silver annually. There are many officials who collect these taxes, and the profits are usually applied to the building of idol temples, the surplus being put into the treasury of the Prince, who is supposed to be very rich. On the death of the King, his eldest brother succeeds; when he has no brothers, his eldest son: should he have several brothers, they succeed one another according to seniority. Women do not succeed. The established rule is frequently set aside; the Princes who are most popular frequently rendering themselves masters of the State.

"The reigning King has thus usurped the throne, and has put to death his competitors, the better to secure to himself the possession of the empire. There is a written law, and a council of twelve judges, over which a thirteenth presides, regulates all civil and criminal affairs. There are other jurisdictions subordinate to the council, whose affairs are directed by attorneys and advocates, in the lengthy way which is customary in Holland: when an affair has been investigated, it is written as a *procès verbal* or narration, and sealed up, to be opened in the Council of Twelve. In criminal cases, when the crime is not fully proved, there are many ways of discovering the truth: sometimes the informer is obliged to plunge into the water and remain there; others are forced to walk barefoot over burning coals, to wash their hands in boiling oil, or to eat charmed rice. Sometimes two poles are fixed in the water; the two parties plunge in, and the one who remains longest between the poles gains his law-suit. When forced to walk over burning coals, a man presses their shoulders: if they get across without being burned, their innocence is considered proved. As to the charmed rice, it is prepared by the law doctors, who also give it to the counsel: if he can swallow it, he is pronounced innocent, and his friends bring him back in triumph, his accuser being punished severely: the last proof is the most usual of all. This prince has Mahometan and Malay soldiers in his service; but the Japanese are the most esteemed for their courage, and the Kings of Siam have always employed them as their principal force.

"The present King had become jealous of them, and put to death all of that nation who were found in his kingdom; but they have again settled there for some time. The Siamese were in the army without pay: a twentieth or a hundredth part of the people accorded to the King's wants; he provides officers to command them: besides this, the nobles maintain a number of soldiers who serve them in time of war. The King can put under arms one hundred thousand men, with two or three thousand elephants, who serve both to carry soldiers and baggage; nevertheless, his armed troops do not exceed fifty thousand. These troops retain their rank and military discipline, but are poorly armed with bows and pikes, few knowing how to use the musket. The cavalry is not better armed, having but the shield, the bow, and the lance. The principal force of their army consists in a number of war elephants, each ridden by three armed men. They have pretty good artillery, but are not skilled in using it; still less can they manage that which is placed on their galleys and ships of war: they are not good mariners. They have a number of small galleys in their rivers badly armed, and quite unable to resist European vessels; but they are much feared by the neighbouring nations. The Kings of Siam have often made great conquests with these bad soldiers, and formed a large State in that part of Asia, of which they are considered emperors.

"The Kings of Pegu and Ava have frequently made war upon him; for, finding themselves of equal strength, they dispute the empire with him: so that the frontiers of the two kingdoms, which are never in repose for two or three successive years, are quite ruined and desert. Almost every year the King of Siam sends an army of twenty-three or thirty thousand men during the six months of the dry monsoon, as it is called, that is to say, when the land is not flooded, to the frontiers of the kingdoms of Iangoma, Tangan, and Langhs-iangs: and lately he has made war upon his vassal, the King of Cambodia, who revolted against him; but he is defending himself and making head against him. From the time of the Cambodian war the kingdom has remained in peace till the King's death.

"His son succeeded contrary to the custom of the country, which decrees that the King's brothers should succeed to the throne: all the princes of the blood who could pretend to it were put to death, and the kingdom came into the possession of a usurping prince of his race, who put him to death, and who, after long civil and foreign wars, ruled with much reputation and authority. He is now at war with the Kings of Ava and Pegu, as well as the Cambodian rebels."

Kämpfer landed on the shores of Siam on the 7th of June, 1690. His account may still be read with interest, as of course the broad geographical outlines of the country remain unchanged; nor, as I have before remarked, have the customs of the people or the character of the government undergone any considerable modifications. He amused himself, as travellers might still amuse themselves, by shooting monkeys on the banks of the Meinam; he admired the beauty of the forests, but was somewhat afraid of "the tygers and other voracious beasts," who interfered with his "simpling:" and he tells us, on one occasion, how the director of the Dutch factory had ordered all his people to keep within doors, as the King intended to go out; and "if any happens by chance to meet the King or his wives, or the Princess Royal, in the open fields, he must prostrate himself with his face flat to the ground, turning his back to the company till they are out of sight."

A Siamese funeral among the high nobility, as

described by Kämpfer, scarcely differs from the present usages in any respect; the same processions, the same accompaniments of bonzes and music, the same costly cremation, the same gathering together of the ashes, the same pyramidical erections on the spot where they are finally deposited. There seem to have been a greater proportion of Moors, Mahometans and Indians occupying high places at the Court, than are now to be found. Their influence has been superseded by the greater influx of the Chinese races.

Some of Kämpfer's details regarding events nearly contemporaneous are curious, and no doubt authentic. He speaks of the protection and favour the Dutch enjoyed, while the French were persecuted on account of Phaulcon's intrigues. He mentions that two of the King's brothers, in consequence of being Phaulcon's associates, were " carried out of the city of Livo to a neighbouring temple, where they were beaten to death with clubs made of sandal-wood; the respect for the royal blood forbidding the shedding of it." The same mode of execution prevails to the present time, and was practised only a few years ago, in the reign of the late King. He represents the King, who patronised Phaulcon, to have died of grief two days after the murder of his brothers. And as to the uncertainty of succession, Kämpfer says,—"By virtue of the ancient laws of Siam, upon the demise of the King, the crown devolves on his brother; and upon the brother's death, or if there be none, on the eldest son. But this rule hath been so often broken through, and the right of succession brought into such a confusion, that at present, upon the death of the King, he puts up for the crown who is the most powerful of the royal family, and so it seldom happens that the next and lawful heir ascends the throne, or is able to maintain the peaceable possession of it." (P. 24.)

Diogo de Couto's* description of the festivities connected with the turn of the inundations would serve for the present day as well as for those centuries ago:—

" The King comes out of the city, accompanied by the whole of the nobility, in barges richly gilded and covered with ornaments, with great display and noise of musical instruments. They proclaim that the King is about to order the waters to disperse; and this is the great festival of the year. A mast is raised in the middle of the stream, adorned with silken flags, and a prize suspended for the best rower. All the contending boats put themselves in trim, and at a given signal start, with such cries, and shouting, and tumults, as if the world was being destroyed; the first who arrives carrying off the prize. But in the contest there is terrible confusion—boats running against and swamping one another, oars tangled and disentangled in a disorder admirable to look at from around. So that the people are not so barbarous, but that they imitate the ancient Trojans (as in the same manner, Eneas, when he arrived in Sicily, had the festival of his galleys, giving precious prizes to the most alert); and when these Siamese have won the prize, they return to the city with such rejoicings, shoutings, and tumultuous music, that the noise shakes both the waters and the land. Then the

---

* Diogo de Couto, the continuator of the *Decades* of João de Barros, was born in 1542, and died in 1616.

King having returned to the city, the people say he has driven back the waters, because these heathens attribute to their Kings all the attributes of God, and believe they are the source of all good."

Generalizations as to national character are among the great defects of writers on foreign countries, and, when examined, will in most cases be discovered to be the result of impressions early and hastily formed, or of some solitary examples of individual experience, from which all-embracing deductions are drawn. Mr. Abeel says,—" Those who have commercial dealings with the Siamese declare that, with the fewest exceptions, dishonesty and deceit are characteristic of the nation: they will buy and frequently endeavour to cheat the seller out of the stipulated sum; they will borrow and never return; and unless they desire your society as amusement, when they can get nothing more from you, they will never come near you." (P. 220, 221.) Other missionaries endorse and confirm the general correctness of this picture; and vastly more knowledge than is attainable by casual visitors is needful for a just appreciation of the whole.

Father Le Blanc gives, in the *Annals of the Propaganda*, a very unfavourable portraiture of the Siamese character. He says,—" They never employ open force against their enemies when they have any hope of succeeding by fraud or surprise—no artifice is too low or too shameful for them. As for the point of honour, they know not what it means; and good faith is equally an unknown word among them. One and the same word expresses in their language roguery, wit, wisdom, address, treachery, and prudence." This must be only a form of speech, or the Dictionary is deceitful. "This," he continues, "has given rise to a proverb which prevails throughout Siam—Trade must be left to the Dutch, arts and manufactures to the Chinese, war to the French, but wit to the Siamese." The truth is, Father Le Blanc wrote under the influence of the exasperation which Phaulcon's death, and the banishment of the French, and the disappointment of the hopes of the Jesuits, had naturally enough produced. The reports of the Siamese were far more favourable while they continued in amicable alliance with the French; and the Dutch, who established their influence upon the unpopularity of the missionaries, are disposed to give a different account of the Siamese.

"The Siamese character," says another and more modern Catholic missionary, "is gentle, light, inconsiderate, timid, and gay; and they are fond of cheerful persons. They avoid disputes, and whatever produces anger or impatience. I refer especially to scientific disquisitions; for they sometimes quarrel, and the surrounding spectators take an active part. They are idle, inconstant, fond of amusement; a nothing excites, a nothing distracts their attention; they are great supplicants—everything attracts them, and they unhesitatingly ask either for trifles or articles of value. This characterizes all classes: a prince of the blood will ask for snuff, for a pencil, a watch, a jug; but they are quite willing to be supplicated in turn."[*] Our experience certainly did not

---

[*] Lettre de Mons. Bruguière, Bishop of Capu, Coadjutor of the Vicar Apostolic of Siam. *Annales de la Foi*, xxvi., p. 159, 160.

confirm the latter part of this statement of the reverend father; I never witnessed so little exigency among Orientals. Perhaps this was the result either of superior orders, or of the general deference with which the Mission was treated. On receiving their courtesies, we had frequently to inquire what objects would be most welcome to the givers in return for their gifts; but we were scarcely ever annoyed by any clamorous supplications.

Siam, in Murray's *Historical Account of Discoveries and Travels in Asia*, occupies only ten pages of the three volumes. His *résumé* of the Siamese character is the only passage which appears worthy of quotation. " In general, the Siamese character appears to be such as despotism usually forms. They are mild, polite, courteous,—but artful, deceitful, timid, avaricious, incurious, proud to such as they think in their power, and cringing to those who treat them with haughtiness; honest in their dealings, and so kind to their relations that beggary and pauperism are scarcely known."* The lines in this description are too strongly drawn: want of sincerity is no part of the Siamese nature; and the absence of pauperism is attributable to the extraordinary fertility of the climate, the cheapness of living, and the general habit of almsgiving, which is among "the merits" of Buddhism.

La Loubère bears emphatic testimony to the strength of the parental and filial affections in Siam: —" Parents," he says, " know how to make themselves

---

* Vol. iii., p. 241.

extremely beloved and respected, and Siamese children have great docility and sweetness. Parents answer to princes for the conduct of their children; they share in their chastisements, and deliver them up when they have offended. If the son takes flight, he never fails to surrender himself when the prince apprehends his father or his mother, or his other collateral relations older than himself to whom he owes respect." (P. 54.)

And of the affection of parents for children, and the deference paid by the young to the old, we saw abundant evidence in all classes of society. Fathers were constantly observed carrying about their offspring in their arms, and mothers engaged in adorning them. The King was never seen in public by us without some of his younger children near him; and we had no intercourse with the nobles where numbers of little ones were not on the carpets, grouped around their elders, and frequently receiving attentions from them.

According to my experience, the mendacity so characteristic of Orientals is not a national defect among the Siamese. Lying, no doubt, is often resorted to as a protection against injustice and oppression, but the chances are greatly in favour of truth when evidence is sought. My experience in China, and many other parts of the East, predisposes me to receive with doubt and distrust any statement of a native, when any the smallest interest would be possibly promoted by falsehood. Nay, I have often observed there is a fear of truth, *as* truth, lest its discovery should lead to consequences of which the inquirer never dreams, but which are present to the mind of the person under interrogation. Little moral disgrace attaches to insincerity and untruthfulness; their detection leads to a loss of reputation for sagacity and cunning, but goes no further. In Siam I was struck with the unusual frankness as to matters of fact.

Dishonesty, too, is repugnant to Siamese habits. There is much extortion practised by the ruling few upon the subject many, and there are many persons without means of honest existence who, as elsewhere, live by their wits; but organized robberies and brigandage are almost confined to the wilder parts of the country.

Suicide is rare. Now and then, a fanatic is known to cover his body with resin and oil, and offer himself to be burnt as a living sacrifice to Buddha. It is said that in the last instance that occurred, the unhappy wretch, after inviting the people to witness his public execution, sprung in agony from the funeral pile, and rushed into the Meinam to be drowned. One such example must be potent to prevent the repetition of the folly.

Pallegoix, than whom no writer is better entitled to speak from experience, gives on the whole a favourable description of the moral qualities of the Siamese. "They are," he says, "gentle, cheerful, timid, careless, and almost passionless. They are disposed to idleness, inconstancy, and exaction; they are liberal almsgivers, severe in enforcing decorum in the relations between the sexes: They are fond of sports, and lose half their time in amusements. They are sharp and even witty in conversation, and resemble the Chinese in their aptitude for imitation."

Serious disputes are of rare occurrence, and murders are very rare,—not one on an average in a year. In their reception of strangers they are eminently hospitable. Buildings are erected for the convenience of travellers, and women spontaneously bring to them jars of water to appease the thirst of those who are journeying. Their religion teaches humanity to animals; in fact, the tameness of many living creatures which in Europe fly from the presence of man is observed by all strangers. I heard of more than one instance in which Siamese had quitted the service of Europeans because they were unwilling to destroy reptiles and vermin. The gardener of the French Mission was commissioned to kill the serpents he should find among the shrubs; he refused, saying, " I cannot commit murder to gain my wages." It is a not uncommon practice for rich men to buy live fish, to have " the merit " of restoring them to the sea; and on certain days, especially the 8th and 15th of the month, which are deemed holy, fishing and hunting are absolutely prohibited.

The dwellings of the Siamese represent far more than I have seen in any other part of the world the grades of their social condition. From the beautiful stone palaces of the Kings, crowded with every European comfort and luxury, and ornamented with every decoration which either the eastern or western world can supply, to the shaking bamboo, palm-covered hut of the peasant, whose furniture consists only of a few vessels of coarse earthenware or wicker-work, and a mat or two spread upon the floor, the difference of position upwards or downwards may be distinctly traced. Removed from the very lowest ranks, in the Siamese houses will be found carpenters' tools, a moveable oven, various cooking utensils both in copper and clay, spoons of mother-of-pearl, plates and dishes in metal and earthenware, a large porcelain jar, and another of copper for fresh water. There is also a tea-set, and all the appliances for betel-chewing and tobacco-smoking, some stock of provisions and condiments for food.

A sauce called *nam-phrik* is used by all classes in Siam. It is prepared by bruising a quantity of red pepper in a mortar, to which are added *kapi* (paste of shrimps or prawns), black pepper, garlic, and onions. These being thoroughly mixed, a small quantity of brine and citron-juice is added. Ginger, tamarinds, and gourd seeds are also employed. The *nam-phrik* is one of the most appetite-exciting condiments.

The Siamese prepare considerable quantities of *curry* as their habitual food. These are generally so hot that they burn the mouth of a European. I recollect one of the Regents complaining bitterly that a sore mouth deprived him of the pleasures of the table: the wonder to me was that a sound mouth could tolerate such ardent comestibles as he habitually used. One of the eel tribe furnishes a material for fish curry which is specially esteemed—an eel said to be singularly sagacious, for it opens its mouth near holes where the currents of water pass, which convey to its gullet without other care or concern,—it being among the privileged who "while waiting *are* served,"—a supply all-sufficient for its appetite.

Fish, in the early stages of putridity, is mixed with a variety of exciting substances, such as capsicums and chillies, mynth, sprouts of the mango, the orange and citron trees, cocoa-nut milk, sugar: lard and pork fat are used to modify the stronger flavours.

The Siamese have learnt from the Chinese the art of salting and preserving eggs, which, in their estimate, rather improve than deteriorate by time. The egg is covered with a thick paste of ashes and lime. Eggs so prepared may be sent on long voyages, and have become a considerable article of export to California and other places.

The tables of the opulent are crowded with a succession of dishes. In our intercourse with the high authorities, it was their purpose to entertain us in European style—and wonderfully well did they succeed. On one occasion, however, I requested the Krom Hluang (King's brother) to give us a genuine Siamese repast. On arriving, we found the table spread in the accustomed and approved European-Oriental style, with an abundance of plate, glasses, wines, soups, fish, roasted and boiled meat, *hors-d'œuvres*, with a variety of pastry, jellies, &c.; but, apart, the Prince had provided what he called a Siamese dinner for *one*, and I imagine the succession of dishes could have been scarcely less than sixty or seventy. He said he wished to gratify my curiosity, but that courtesy required him to entertain me according to the usages of *my* country, and *not* of Siam.

The ordinary meals of the Siamese are at 7 A.M. and 5½ P.M., but the more opulent classes have a repast at mid-day. The guests help themselves out of a common dish with spoons or with their fingers, using or not small earthenware plates which are before them.

Of the meals of the Siamese, Bishop Pallegoix says, " The Thai take their repasts seated on a mat or carpet. The dishes are in great brazen vases with a cover, over which a red cloth is placed; the meat is cut into small pieces, and the rice is kept apart in a large deep porringer on one side of the floor, while a great basin of water is on the other, having in it a drinking-cup. The guests have neither knives nor forks, but use a mother-of-pearl spoon to dip into the various dishes, of which after having eaten a sufficiency, they drink pure water or tea. To help themselves one after another from the same plate, to drink one after another from the same cup, has nothing strange. The husband is served at table by his wife. Social repasts are always silent, and seldom last more than a quarter of an hour. But no interruptions are permitted during meals, even in the case of dependents or slaves."*

Tea is nearly as generally used as in China. Coffee has made its way among the opulent classes. Arak is manufactured by the Chinese, and consumed *furtively* by the Siamese, though sobriety is certainly one of the virtues of the national character: but where a passion for strong drinks once takes pos-

---

* Pallegoix, i. 217—8.

session of a Siamese, it becomes irresistible, and almost invariably leads to his own perdition and the impoverishment of his family.

The Siamese, in cooking their rice, wash it four or five times, and place it in a pot or kettle filled with water: after boiling about three minutes, the water is poured out, the pot is placed upon a slow fire, where the rice is steamed without being burnt; its flavour is preserved; the different grains do not adhere to one another, or stick to the fingers when eaten. Rice is used by the poor as the main aliment of life; by the opulent, as an accompaniment to their meals, as bread in Europe. Glutinous rice is employed either in flour or grains; a favourite cake is thus prepared:—the rice is cooked without water or steam; it is then sprinkled with condiments consisting of ginger and other spices; it is divided into small parcels, which are wrapped up in plantain leaves, and in twenty-four hours a sweet and vinous liquor exudes, when the cake is fit for eating: if kept longer they become intoxicating, and if distilled produce arak, which, subject to re-distillation, gives a strong and fragrant drink.

The use of opium has greatly extended in Siam during the last thirty years. Its consumption among the Siamese has been prohibited by a severe edict of the King,* imposing heavy fines and degrading punishments on those who indulge in so pernicious a practice. It is farmed by a Chinese of great opulence, who has been raised to the rank of nobility;

---

* See Appendix.

and the annual importation is now about twelve hundred chests, most of which is smoked by the Chinese settlers. The fatal consequences of the habitual use of this drug is a frequent subject of representation from the Siamese priests, and the Catholic and Protestant missionaries; but to prevent its introduction and its consumption would seem to be beyond the powers of legislation, and perhaps the legalization of its import is a lesser evil than to allow an unlawful and irrepressible trade to extend itself, as it has done in China, where the native cultivation of the poppy must be allowed to afford strong evidence that the repeated injunctions against the dealers in and smokers of opium are not to be attributed wholly to a desire to prevent its use. The strong argument against the abolition of the opium farm is, that it is better that the trade should be *under* than beyond the control of the Government.

The seeds and leaves of the hemp are used as in India[*] and Arabia,[†] and produce effects of exhilaration and depression resembling those caused by opium-smoking.

A nobleman never moves about without the bearer of his areca-box—the box called a xrob. Some of these are of solid gold, ornamented with jewels, and are among the customary presents of the King to the higher nobles. When a Siamese sits down, the xrob-bearer deposits it on the ground, so near that his master can conveniently reach it. It is in constant requisition.

On all state, ceremonial, or official occasions, a

---

[*] Bang.   [†] Khashish.

slave carries a sword (dab) upon his right shoulder, standing at a respectful distance from his master.

The consumption of the areca and the betel nut is enormous throughout Siam. A Siamese who is tolerably well off is scarcely ever seen without the nut in his mouth; and he is invariably attended by servants who carry a supply of the material, with all the needful paraphernalia, whose costliness depends upon the opulence and rank of the possessor. Among the nobles the boxes are almost invariably of gold; and in the case of the very highest ranks, they are covered with diamonds or other precious stones, and are constantly in a state of passage from the hands of the servants to their masters, and back again when the want of the moment has been supplied. These boxes hold the fresh leaves of the betel, the areca-nut, and the pink chunam, or quicklime coloured with curcuma. The nut and the lime are wrapped in betel leaves, and the whole, in the shape of a cigar, transferred to the mouth for mastication. The betel (*betel piper*) is a creeping plant, producing a long and somewhat fleshy leaf, nearly resembling a heart in shape, of a sharp and aromatic flavour. The areca is a palm-tree, whose stem is straight, growing sometimes to the height of fifty or sixty feet, having leaves only at the top, where it produces two or three enormous bunches, each bearing two or three hundred nuts, which are at first green and ripen to a reddish colour. These nuts contain a hard, bitter, and astringent pulp. It is usual first to rub the teeth with tobacco. The chewing the areca produces a large quantity of blood-coloured saliva, which is spit into spittoons of earthenware, brass, silver, or gold, according to the rank of the party. It is said the use of the betel diffuses a sort of gay tranquillity; and when the areca has lost its flavour in the mouth, water is used, and the operation of chewing is recommenced, though generally interrupted by the smoking of cigars or cheroots from Manila, or of native tobacco wrapped in palm-leaves, somewhat resembling the *pajetos* used in Spain, though larger in size. Betel-chewing blackens the teeth, which is considered a recommendation in Siam; it purifies the breath, and is said to be a preservative of the tooth's enamel when used moderately and without an undue quantity of quicklime. The betel is such a necessary of life in Siam, that were the choice offered to a hungry Siamese of food, or his favourite betel, there is no doubt he would reject the first, and ask for the second in preference.

Tobacco may be said to be universally used in Siam. Boys of five or six years old begin to smoke. Women chew the weed with the areca-nut. The common mode of preparing tobacco for use is to envelop finely-cut shreds in a covering of plantain or palm leaves. Some of the opulent smoke the long pipe. The use of snuff is not general among the Siamese.

The habit of bathing is almost a necessary result of the heat of the climate, and the adjacency of the river, into which the Siamese often wade and swim many times a day. They are fond of ablutions, and their bodies are thus kept quite free from vermin. They must be deemed a cleanly people: they pluck out the hairs of their beard as soon as they appear;

clean their teeth, so that foul breath is scarcely known among them; they constantly change their garments, exposing them to the action of the sun's rays.

I have nowhere in the tropics tasted *fruits* comparable in their excellence with those of Siam, except perhaps in the Island of Java; but the Siamese durians, mangoes, mangosteens, and some others, appeared to me of unparalleled size and flavour. Almost every day furnished a new variety. We had mangoes which in their greatest girth measured above nineteen inches. Sometimes the King would send fruit, gathered in the jungle, which none of us had before seen. The sweet tamarind was also a novelty to us; and there were very many to us unknown sorts of fruits, beautiful in appearance and agreeable in taste, either cultivated in the gardens or growing wild in the woods, which were among the daily bounties of the kings and of the nobles. One of the courtiers told me that the King had mentioned my fondness for fruits; and the consequence was that many spontaneous offerings were brought to the palace, and found their way to my table. These are true courtesies, which I could only the more appreciate, as we had been given to understand that we should witness nothing but cold ceremonials, extorted urbanities, and a proud and repulsive policy. We were led to expect that we should find rapacity intrusive, insatiable, and extortionate,—every art employed to obtain much, and to give little in return. Far different was my experience. It seemed as if nothing was expected from me, while upon me and around me every kindness was profusely and prodigally showered. Even the children brought their garlands, which they hung on our arms; coronals of fragrant flowers, fresh roses, were every morning upon my table. In great things as in small, I found a hospitality that was almost oppressive, and of which I retain the most grateful memory.

The Siamese nobles generally occupy elevated benches or thrones, leaning on stuffed triangular cushions, the ends of which are ornamented with gold embroidery. One of these was presented to each of the principal members of the Mission, more or less decorated according to their rank. We were informed that the use of such cushions was prohibited to the people. On presenting it, the giver said, "When you rest your head upon it, sometimes think of me."

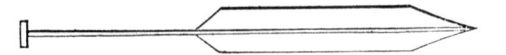

Almost all locomotion is by water. The barges are generally scooped out of a single trunk, and are sometimes as much as one hundred and twenty feet in length, and moved by as many as a hundred rowers or paddlers. Those of the official barges are clothed in scarlet, and have a woollen head-gear somewhat in the shape of a helmet. The strokes of the paddle are given with great regularity and order. The stem and stern of the barges are raised high above the body of the barge, and generally represent the head and tail of some monster. The barge is guided by means of long oars, by one or more steersmen, who from their elevated position on the poop give the word of command to the rowers, who are seated below. There is a roofed cabin, adorned sometimes with curtains of crimson and gold silk, either in the centre or nearer the stern, in which is the place of honour; and the height and ornaments of the cabin designate the rank or the functions of the occupier. On one occasion (the sun blazing most fiercely), the curtains for my protection were forgotten, and the inattention having been noticed by some of my suite, I found that a terrible bastinading had been given to the man who had neglected his duty. In the King's barge there is a high throne erected in the centre. Large outspread umbrellas always accompany the barges of the nobility.

There are certain imposing ceremonies, called *Tham Khuan*, which mark the principal events or eras in the life of a Siamese, such as the shaving his head-tuft, his reception as a bonze, his marriage, the advent of a new sovereign, &c. These commemorations are never neglected, and even in the case of the less privileged classes are made the subject of much display. A sort of altar is erected of planks or bamboos, having seven steps of ascent, which are carpeted with fresh banana-leaves. Each of the steps is ornamented with grotesque figures of angels and animals in clay, paper, or carved out of calabashes. Vessels of metal or porcelain are crowded with meats and fruits. On the upper stages are garlands of flowers, and leaves of tinsel, gold, and silver, in the midst of which is a fresh cocoa-nut. At the foot of the altar are nine chandeliers, whose wax candles are kindled at a signal given by three discharges of a musket. One of the candles is seized by the person in whose honour the ceremonial has been prepared, and he walks three times round the altar; when his friends approach, each seizes one of the wax-lights, which he blows out over the head of "the ordained," so that its smoke may envelop his forehead. Then the fresh cocoa-nut is given him that he may drink its milk, eating with it a hard egg; and a cup containing coins to the value of about four pence is presented to him. At this moment a band of instruments breaks into music, and the ceremony ends. (Pallegoix, ii. 55, 56.)

Marriages are the subject of much negotiation, undertaken not directly by the parents, but by "go-betweens," nominated by those of the proposed bridegroom, who make proposals to the parents of the intended bride. A second repulse puts the extinguisher on the attempted treaty; but if successful, a large boat, gaily adorned with flags and accompanied by music, is laden with garments, plate, fruits, betel, &c. In the centre is a huge cake or cakes, in the form of a pyramid, printed in bright colours. The bridegroom accompanies the procession to the house of his future father-in-law, where the lady's dowry and the day for the celebration of the marriage are fixed. It is incumbent on the bridegroom to erect or to occupy a house near that of his intended, and a month or two must elapse before he can carry away his bride. No religious rites accompany the marriage, though bonzes are invited to the feast, whose duration and expense depend upon the condition of the parties. Music is an invariable accompaniment. Marriages take place early; I have seen five generations gathered round the head of a family. I asked the senior Somdetch how many of his descendants lived in his palace: he said he did not know, but there were a hundred or more. It was indeed a frequent answer to the inquiry in the upper ranks, "What number of children and grandchildren have you?" "Oh, multitudes; we cannot tell how many." I inquired of the first King how many children had been born to him: he said, "Twelve before I entered the priesthood, and eleven since I came to the throne." I have generally observed that a pet child is selected from the group to be the special recipient of the smiles and favours of the head of the race.

Though wives or concubines are kept in any number according to the wealth or will of the husband, the wife who has been the object of the marriage ceremony, called the Khan mak, takes precedence of all the rest, and is really the sole legitimate spouse; and she and her descendants are the only legal heirs to the husband's possessions. Marriages are permitted beyond the first degree of affinity. Divorce is easily obtained on application from the woman, in which case the dowry is restored to the wife. If there be only one child, it belongs to the mother, who takes also the third, fifth, and all those representing odd numbers: the husband has the second, fourth, and so forth. A husband may sell a wife that he has purchased, but not one who has brought him a dowry. If the wife is a party to contracting debts on her husband's behalf, she may be sold for their redemption, but not otherwise. On the whole, the condition of woman is better in Siam than in most Oriental countries.

The education of Siamese women is little advanced.

Many of them are good musicians, but their principal business is to attend to domestic affairs; they are as frequently seen as men in charge of boats on the Meinam; they generally distribute alms to the bonzes, and attend the temples, bringing their offerings of flowers and fruit. In the country they are busied with agricultural pursuits. They have seldom the art of plying the needle, as the Siamese garments almost invariably consist of a single piece of cloth.

There is an extraordinary usage connected with childbirth. The event has no sooner taken place, than the mother is placed near a large fire, where she remains for weeks exposed to the burning heat: death is often caused by this exposure. So universal is the usage, so strong the prejudice in its favour among high and low, that the King himself has vainly attempted to interfere; and his young and beautiful wife, though in a state of extreme peril and suffering, was subjected to this torture, and died while "before the fire,"—a phrase employed by the Siamese to answer the inquiry made as to the absence of the mother. A medical missionary told me he had been lately called in to prescribe for a lady who was "before the fire;" but ere he had reached the house, the patient had died, and both body and funeral pile had been removed. There seems some mysterious idea of pacification, such as in some shape or other prevails in many parts of the world, associated with so cruel a rite. Mothers nurse their children till they are two or three years old, nourishing them at the same time with rice and bananas. (Pallegoix, i. 224.)

Shaving the hair-tuft of children is a great family

festival, to which relations and friends are invited, to whom presents of cakes and fruits are sent. A musket-shot announces the event. Priests recite prayers, and wash the head of the young person, who is adorned with all the ornaments and jewels accessible to the parents. Music is played during the ceremony, which is performed by the nearest relatives; and congratulations are addressed, with gifts of silver, to the newly-shorn. Sometimes the presents amount to large sums of money. Dramatic representations among the rich accompany the festivity, which in such case lasts for several days.

Education begins with the shaving the tuft; and the boys are then sent to the pagodas to be instructed by the bonzes in reading and writing, and in the dogmas of religion. They give personal service in return for the education they receive: that education is worthless enough, but every Siamese is condemned to pass a portion of his life in the temple, which many of them never afterwards quit. Hence the enormous supply of an unproductive, idle, useless race.

When a Thai is at the point of death, the talapoins are sent for, who sprinkle lustral water upon the sufferer, recite passages which speak of the vanity of earthly things from their sacred books, and cry out, repeating the exclamation in the ears of the dying, " Arahang! arahang!" (a mystical word implying the purity or exemption of Buddha from concupiscence). When the dying has heaved his last breath, the whole family utter piercing cries, and address their lamentations to the departed:—" O father benefactor!

why leave us? What have we done to offend you? Why depart alone? It was your own fault. Why did you eat the fruit that caused the dysentery? We foretold it; why did not you listen to us? O misery! O desolation! O inconstancy of human affairs!" And they fling themselves at the feet of the dead, weep, wail, kiss, utter a thousand tender reproaches, till grief has exhausted its lamentable expressions. The body is then washed and enveloped in white cloth; it is placed in a coffin covered with gilded paper, and decorated with tinsel flowers; a daïs is prepared, ornamented with the same materials as the coffin, but with wreaths of flowers and a number of wax-lights. After a day or two, the coffin is removed, not through the door, but through an opening specially made in the wall; the coffin is escorted thrice round the house at full speed, in order that the dead, forgetting the way through which he has passed, may not return to molest the living. The coffin is then taken to a large barge, and placed on a platform, surmounted by the daïs, to the sound of melancholy music. The relations and friends, in small boats, accompany the barge to the temple where the body is to be burnt. Being arrived, the coffin is opened and delivered to the officials charged with the cremation, the corpse having in his mouth a silver tical (2s. 6d. in value) to defray the expenses. The burner first washes the face of the corpse with cocoa-nut milk; and if the deceased have ordered that his body shall be delivered to vultures and crows, the functionary cuts it up and distributes it to the birds of prey which are always assembled in such localities.* The corpse being placed upon the pile, the fire is kindled. * * * * * When the combustion is over, the relations assemble, collect the principal bones, which they place in an urn, and convey them to the family abode. The garb of mourning is white, and is accompanied by shaving of the head. The funerals of the opulent last for two or three days. There are fireworks, sermons from the bonzes, nocturnal theatricals, where all sorts of monsters are introduced. Tents are erected within the precincts of the temples, and games and gambling accompany the rites connected with the dead. (Pallegoix, i. 244—7.)

Slavery is the condition of a large part of the population of Siam—not absolute slavery, perhaps, as formerly existed in the West Indies, or now exists in the United States, but such as implies a dependence far less tolerable than that which belongs to ordinary domestic servitude. Every Siamese is bound to devote one-third of the year to the service of the King. This is but an exaggeration of the *corvée* or statute labour of the middle ages. Besides the Siamese, there are Laos, Cambodian, Burmese,

---

* This mode of disposing of the dead is universal among the Parsees whenever they are able to give effect to the arrangements. At Bombay, they place the corpse in an iron chair at the top of a tower, whence, when the birds of prey have devoured the flesh, the skeleton falls into the abyss below. I have heard Parsees regret, in China, that they lose the privilege of having their remains carried by winged messengers to all the quarters of heaven. What they next appreciate is to be buried with their faces turned towards the rising sun; and I have remarked, inscribed on the Parsee tombs at Macao, the beautiful verses of Ecclesiastes, "Surely the light is sweet, and a pleasant thing it is to behold the sun," &c. I once asked a Parsee why they copied from our sacred books: he said, and very truly, that they had nothing more appropriate in their own.

and other races who have been subjugated in war, and who are absolute vassals to their masters, or to the sovereign. I saw few examples of harshness in the treatment of slaves: they are generally cheerful, amusing themselves with songs and jokes while engaged in their various toils.

But the greatest number of slaves so called appeared to be *debtors*; for the non-payment of a debt gives to a creditor possession of the body of the person indebted, of whose labour he can dispose for the payment of the interest due, or the extinction of the debt itself.

In Siamese society, one is alike struck with the vassalage of the subject many, and the domination of the ruling few.

So absolute is submission, that the severest punishments emanating from the authorities are submitted to without murmuring. A mandarin being imprisoned in order to be punished, a Frenchman offered to intercede for him with his superior. "No!" replied he; "I would see how far his love would reach:" and this was not said ironically, but was the Siamese interpretation of what a European would have rendered by, "I wait to see how far his rigour will extend."* The King said to the French envoy that his subjects have the temper of asses, who tremble so long as one holds the end of their chain, and who disown their master when the band is loosed.

The groundwork of all Siamese institutions and habits is a reverence for authority. This principle

---

* La Loubère, p. 105. *Ib.*, p. 100.

is pushed to forms of the most extravagant excess; on the one side of assumption, and on the other of prostration. It influences language so far as to create vocabularies utterly unlike one another, to be employed in the various grades of society; it is exhibited in the daily usages of life in shapes the most inconvenient and ridiculous. No man of inferior rank dares to raise his head to the level of that of his superior; no person can cross a bridge if an individual of higher grade chances to be passing below; no mean person may walk upon a floor above that occupied by his betters. There was an expression of extreme distress from the Siamese when, on board the *Rattler*, some images of Buddha were found in the cabin, over whose heads common sailors were permitted to tread the deck. Honours almost divine, language quite devotional, humiliations the most degrading, mark the distance between sovereign and subject; and to some extent the same reverence is paid to age which is exhibited towards authority. The paternal relations are associated with forms and phrases of habitual respect; and the honouring father and mother has more than the force of a commandment—it is an hourly observance.

Precedence of *position* is thus laid down:—

"The right hand is more honourable than the left"—(this is wholly contrary to Chinese usages, which invariably recognise the left side as the seat of honour)—"the floor opposite the door more honourable than the sides, the sides more than the wall where the door is, and the wall which is on the right hand of him that sits on the floor, more honourable than that on his left hand: in the tribunals no persons sit on the bench which is fixed to the wall directly opposite the door, except the president who alone has a determinative voice. Councillors who have only a consultative voice are seated on the lower benches along the side walls, and other meaner officers along the wall of the side where the door is."*

In addressing an equal, the Siamese use the word *than*, meaning master, and call themselves *kha*, or servant; to a superior they say *Chau Kha*, my lord. But the terms of humility on the one side, and of assumption on the other, fall and rise with the difference and distance of rank. Crouched in the dust before a dignitary, the language employed by the speaker is—" Your slave—a hair—an animal —*dixan*, the diminutive of *devaxan*, a little beast," —or some equally depreciatory phrase. No man approaches a person of the higher orders without prostrating himself,—raising his hands over his head, and bending the body low. To the highest authorities there must be three separate acts of adoration, and the word "khorab," which means "obedience to order," constantly interlards the conversation. "When the Portuguese interpreter saw the Phraklang, though at the distance of twenty or thirty yards, he bent his body, and crept along like a sportsman approaching the game unobserved. In this inclining posture he continued until within a few yards of the object of his reverence, when he laid himself prostrate on the

---

* La Loubère, p. 56.

MODES OF SALUTATION.

ground, and awaited the pleasure of his superior."* This is the universal method of inferiors entering into the presence of persons of higher rank.

Other forms are—" Lord benefactor, at whose feet I am;" to a prince, " I the dust of your august feet" —" I the sole of your foot;" to the King, " Mighty and august lord! divine mercy! I a dust-grain of your sacred feet;" and of the King, the usual phraseology is, "the divine order"—"the master of life"—"sovereign of the earth"—"guardian of the bonzes." The ordinary phrase in the presence of majesty is *ton xramong*, " placed on my head." The most common regal title, and that found in the sacred books, is *Phra ong*, meaning literally, "the divine personage."

Bruguière says that the word *to reign—sarenivat—* means literally, " to devour the people."†

The ordinary mode of salutation is, " Tgiou di?" " Continue well?"—" Kiudi?" " Eat well?" Strange changes of places and positions occur as men of greater or less rank enter. Everybody knows what is the amount of deference to be paid to a particular functionary or a person of birth, and the coming of a noble of high position deranges and redistributes every individual in a company. The head of a great man must not be approached. I recollect, on one occasion, when I was supposed by the nobles in the distance to have approached too near to the tuft of a prince of the blood, and there seemed, from some motion of my hand, an apprehension that I

---

* Abeel, p. 229.   † *Annales de la Foi*, xxvi. p. 172.

might touch that tuft, a general murmur circulated round the walls. The answer made to the King, when his official commands are issued, is literally—"The slave of the high and mighty has heard the royal word; I have put it on my brain—on the tuft of my head."*

A Catholic missionary thus speaks of the prostrations of the Siamese: "When the Siamese salute one another, they join the hands, raising them before the face or above the head. They sit or lie on the ground, according to the quality of the person they address: if obliged to change their places, they walk with a profound inclination, or drag themselves on their hands and knees, which becomes a painful position when the audience is prolonged. Whatever situation a man takes, he is always anxious to be below his superiors. In addressing an equal, they say t'an, sir, and speak of themselves as k'a, *i. e.*, a servant. If they address a superior, they give him the title of chauk'a, my lord; if he be very elevated, they call him khorab, *i. e.*, worthy to receive my homage: in these cases they call themselves by some humiliating term. To reign is called saverinaja-sombat, to enjoy or dispense riches. It is not said of such and such an officer that he is governor of such city, but that he eats the city, which has often more truth than poetry in it.

"The Siamese often speak in the third person, both when they address another, and when they speak of themselves. When they answer affirmatively (it is

---

* La Loubère, p. 58.

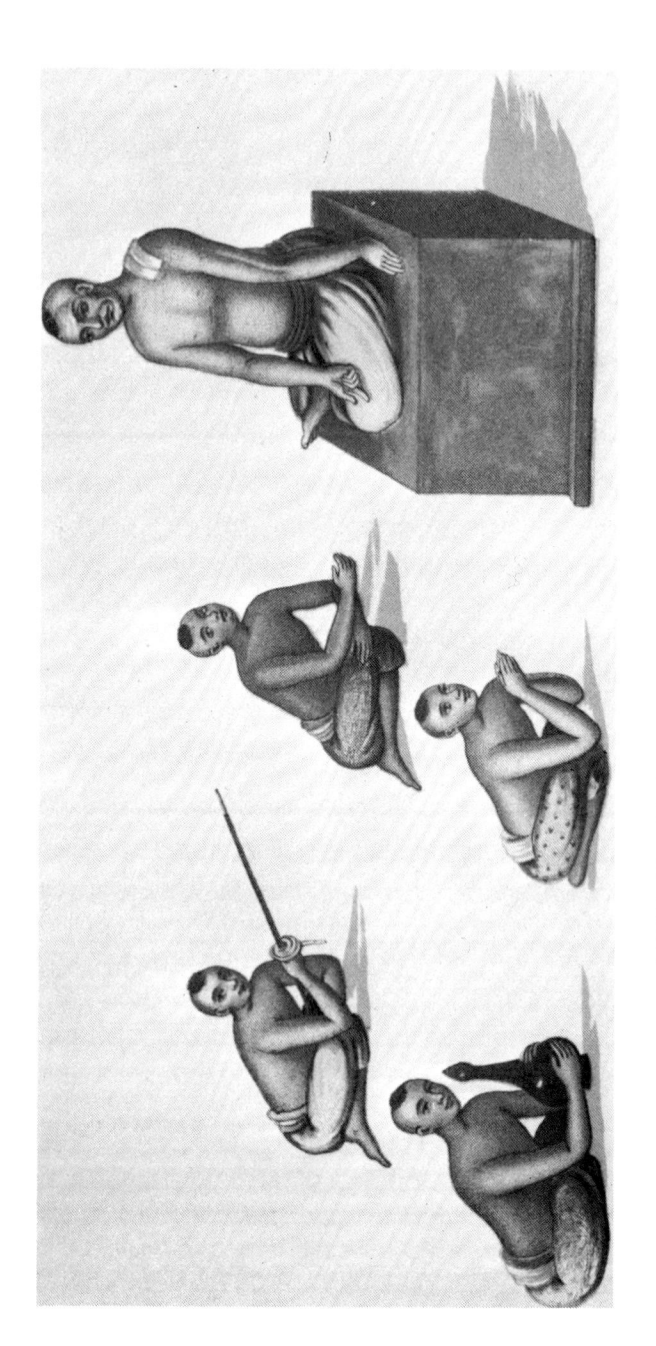

MODE OF APPROACHING SUPERIORS

rare that they say no), they simply repeat the honorary title of the person who interrogates them. Thus: 'Have you done such a thing?' 'My lord' is the reply.* They have personal pronouns, but rarely use them. Kou, which answers to I or me, denotes pride or anger in the person who employs it; to say 'meung,' thou or you, is very offensive; and to employ the word 'man,' him, is little less than shameful. The King, speaking of himself, says 'k'a,' your servant. A man is addressed by his title, but 'nang,' which answers to madam, is the general designation for women; after the age of thirty a female is termed 't'achoi,' or old lady." (Father Bruguière's *Annales de la Foi*, xxv.)

A person of rank is approached by his attendants in a peculiar prostrate position. The number of such prostrate persons is determined by the rank of the individual served. In the case of the kings there are many hundreds: an unnatural protrusion of the left arm is a mark of gentility, all persons of high grade being trained to place their elbows in this, to us, graceless, painful, and constrained position.

The Siamese are a small, well-proportioned race; their skin is of an olive hue; they have black hair, of which they keep a coarse tuft† (which has somewhat the appearance of a brush) on the top of the head, all around being closely shaven. Women adopt

---

* This is also a Malayan custom.

† Little change has taken place for many centuries in the mode of dressing the head among the Siamese: "Os Siameses trazem as cabecas rapadas e sobre as fazes deixão ficar grandes guedelhas." (Couto, vol. iv. p. 9.)

the same practice of cherishing a tuft of hair, which, however, they carefully oil and comb. The preservation of the tuft, and the changes it undergoes under different circumstances, are objects of great interest and attention in Siam.

The head of a child is frequently shorn. At the age of three or four the tuft begins to be cared for, but it is more in front than is usual after the time of puberty. It is prettily knotted and kept together by a golden or silver pin, or, in case of poverty, by a porcupine quill; but it is generally garlanded by a wreath of fragrant flowers. As among the Chinese, long nails are appreciated as a mark of aristocracy; and every art is used for making the teeth black, which is deemed a *sine quâ non* of comeliness. The use of betel and areca helps to accomplish this object.

The ordinary dress of the Siamese is a long piece of cotton printed cloth, passed round the waist between the thighs, the ends of the cloth being stuck in behind. They wear no covering over the head, or upper part of the body; and the legs and feet are quite naked. The higher classes sometimes wear sandals, and have generally a piece of white cloth hanging loosely about the shoulders, which they sometimes use to wrap round their head. Young women employ a sort of silk scarf to screen the bosom; a refinement which, after marriage, is much neglected: indeed, no sense of shame or impropriety appears to be connected with the exposure of the body above the waist. In the sun, a light hat, which looks like an inverted basket, made of palm-leaves, is

MANDARIN IN ORDINARY COSTUME
1.

London, John W. Parker & Son, West Strand, 1857.
M & N. HANHART, LITH.

used by both sexes. On all ceremonial occasions, and in visits from inferiors to superiors, it is usual to wear a silk scarf round the waist. In the presence of the King, the nobles have a garment with sleeves made of *tulle*, of the most delicate texture, and richly ornamented, which they often take from their shoulders and fasten round their waist. The women who ply on the river wear rather a graceful sort of white jacket, fastened in front. In cold weather an outer garment or robe is worn, whose value depends on the rank and opulence of the wearer.

There is a universal passion for jewellery and ornaments of the precious metals, stones, &c. It is said there is scarcely a family so poor as to be without some valuable possessions of this sort. Rings of silver and gold adorn the arms and the legs of children; rich necklaces, earrings, and belts, are sometimes seen in such profusion as quite to embarrass the wearer. Female children, up to the age of twelve or thirteen wear a gold or silver string with a heart in the centre, performing the part often assigned to the fig-leaf in exhibitions of statues. To the necks of children a tablet called a *bai soma* is generally suspended, bearing an inscription as a charm against mischief; and men have a metallic ball attached to a belt, to which they attribute the virtue of rendering them invulnerable. A necklace consisting of seven lumps of gold or silver is worn by girls as a protecting influence.

Though both the head and feet of the Siamese are almost invariably bare, I have seen ornamented slippers used by the nobles, but very rarely. The garments which are on great occasions worn over the shoulders are felt as an encumbrance, and are frequently removed and fastened round the waist, and employed to wipe away the perspiration from the body, even in the midst of the most imposing ceremonies. There is little difference in the costume of the sexes. The demeanour of the women is invariably modest, and the lightness of their garments and nudity of their breasts are considered no more indecorous than an uncovered face or hand among Europeans.

Of the garments worn by the Siamese, the *panung*, called by the Portuguese *panks*, and by French writers *pagne*, is worn round the waist and thighs. Those presented by the King are called *pasompai*. The *panung* is of cotton, linen, silk, embroidered or decorated according to the taste and opulence of the wearer.

The *seva kaau*, or loose muslin shirt, is the ancient garment of the Siamese; it is thrown off in hot weather.

The *pakum*, or upper linen, is thrown over the shoulders and twisted round the arms.

A *chetna*, or handkerchief, is usually carried by a slave, and used to wipe the perspiration off the neck and chest.

The following names and descriptions of the ordinary garments were given me at Bangkok:—

Sumpack. Vesture girded round the waist.

Sacklia. The gold sash.

Succhangua. The robe thrown over the shoulders.

Pa piom. The pagne or principal garment, which

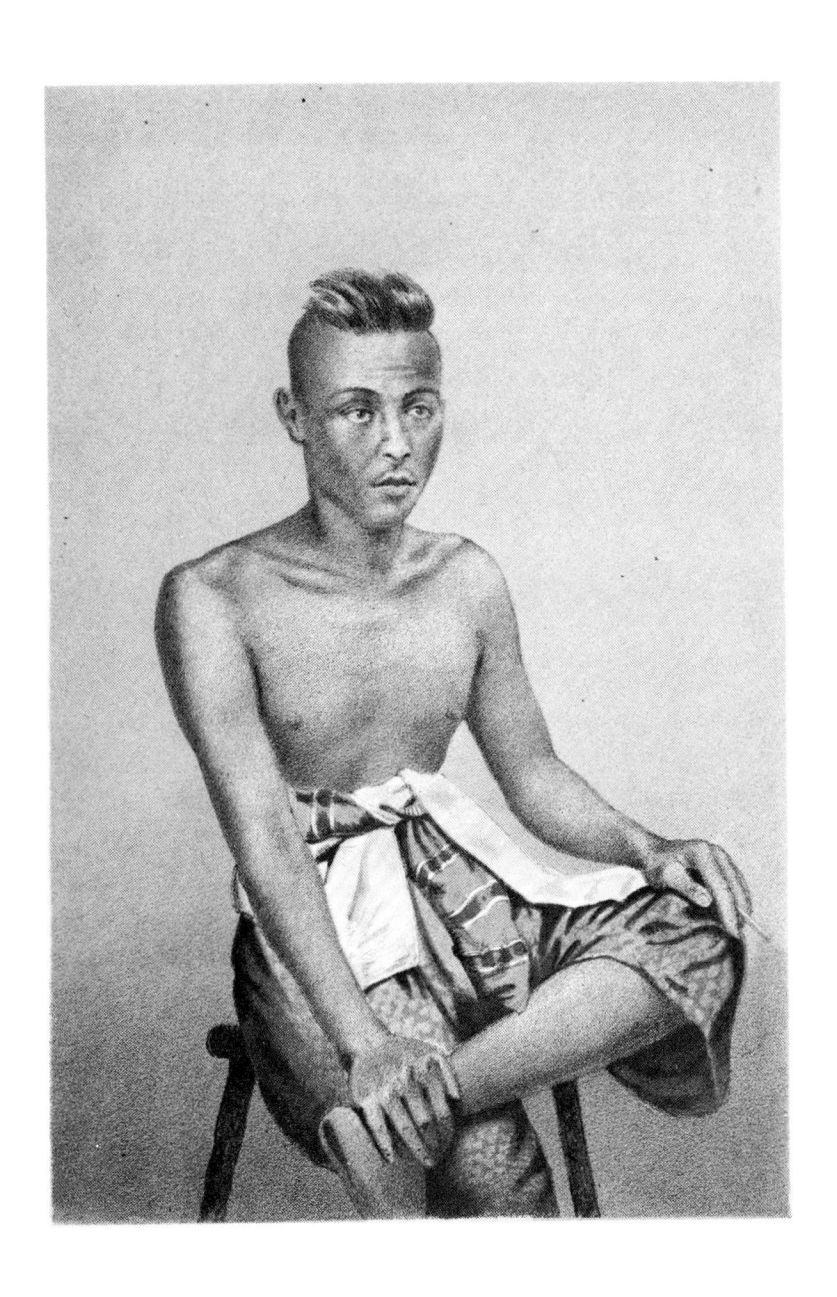

MANDARIN IN ORDINARY COSTUME

2.

London; John W. Parker & Son, West Strand, 1857
M & N. HANHART, LITH.

passes round the body and between the legs, and the ends of which are tucked in behind.

Yang nai. The jacket.

The following remarks upon the Siamese people, written by a Siamese in his native language, and translated by an American missionary (the Rev. W. P. Buell), are not without interest. The footnotes are by the latter.

"In the kingdom of Siam things are thus—viz., The men and women have a form three cubits high (near five feet), it is generally agreed. Some are three cubits and a half. A few are four cubits high; about one man in a hundred.

"Another subject: The complexion of the Siamese is a dark red. Some are light, and they dress after the same fashion. There is no difference. They make their teeth black. They take the shell of a cocoa-nut, burn it and take the dark water which comes out of the shell, and rub it on the teeth. The teeth then become black. When the teeth are well blacked, they take quicklime and spread it on seri leaf to be rolled up—they take of betel-nut quartered, one part, and one seri leaf rolled up—they take tobacco rolled up into a little ball about the size of *the poot-sa fruit* [this resembles our crab apple, but is much smaller], and all being prepared, they eat, taking the tobacco to wipe the teeth, and then depositing it between the lips and the teeth.

"Again: *the men* smoke cigars. These cigars they carry behind their ears. Sometimes they also carry there a scented preparation made with fragrant materials, and a wreath of flowers is worn on the wrist.

"Another subject: They preserve *long* finger-nails. In the cool of the day [evening] they take hog's fat to anoint the nails every day. Another way is to take garlic to rub their nails, and the nails grow long very fast. They take care not to do any labour— they only work at toys. The man who keeps long finger-nails is a man of dissolute mind. His heart rides on primpness. He is the master of harlots, and desires to deck himself that he may stroll about and talk with the women that they may have a heart to love him. Men of this sort are few; amongst a hundred men there will be about forty.

"At the present time, persons fancy pa-nungs.* Chintz pleases *the men*. Pa-nungs of alternate stripes of silk and gold thread—also chintz of a very small blue and white check, with gold thread borders, please *the women*.

"Again: *the men* are pleased with *pa-homs*† of black silk crape [two widths] sewed together, and

---

* "A pa-nung is about three yards of strong India chintz, of star pattern, on deep red, blue, green, and chocolate coloured grounds. The Siamese place the middle of this, when opened, to the small of the back, bringing the two ends round the body before, and the upper edges being twisted together are tucked in between the body and the cloth. The part hanging is folded in large pletes, passed between the legs and tucked in behind as before."

† "A *pa-hom* is a large scarf, about 2½ yards long by 1¾ yards wide, and generally made of silk—two widths sewed together. The middle of the pa-hom opened is placed *under* the left arm, and the two ends passing up before and behind, and crossing *over* the right shoulder, hang down as low as the hips. The labouring *men* have a strip of white cotton cloth about 1½ yards long which they either tie around the waist or head, or throw carelessly over one shoulder; but, perhaps, more generally the middle passes around the throat, and the two ends are thrown loosely over both shoulders, hanging down behind. The lower class of females wear a white cotton shirt or jacket, fitting tight around the body, extending down a very little below the hips, and with long sleeves."

also silk crape of various colours. If they wish them to make merit,* they can. If they wish to go anywhere, they can. If they wish to go to transact business, they can. If they wish to visit their relations, they can according as they fancy a *pa-nung* or a *pa-hom*. There is no particular choice. A *pa-nung* either dark, red, purple, green, light or scarlet, with a silk crape *pa-hom*, answers the same purpose. There is particular choice.

"Again: *the men* cut off their hair. The shape of their hair is like the lotus flower. They cut that hair all around even with the edge of the hair on the forehead. On the back part they shave off the whole. They preserve only what is on the crown.†

"As to the *women*, they cut their hair like the *open* lotus flower. They never shave, but preserve the whole head, trimming the forehead, the eyebrows, and a small circle around the crown.‡ And they bore their ears, and insert ear-rings made with pure gold, set with jewels and precious stones. They also wear finger-rings made with pure gold, and set in the same way. They also wear guards—the strands being made with pure gold. They have

---

* "*i. e.* are dressed clean enough to go and see the priests, and carry them presents, if they choose."

† "It is seldom, too, that a Siamese man is ever seen with a beard. This is always plucked out by the roots, and never suffered to grow even to a moderate length. This gives them an effeminate appearance."

‡ "When the women are not very particular to keep this circle distinct, and when the men, too, are careless about keeping their heads shaved, which is very commonly the case, there is no discoverable difference between the hair of the males and females. Immediately after the birth of a child, the mother often shaves her head perfectly bare; and at the death of a relative."

girdles; they have sashes; they have bracelets; and their *pa-homs* are the same with those of the men mentioned above.

"Another subject: The children (male and female) dress themselves, preserving a bunch of hair—some, about a cubit and a half long—others, only a cubit; and it is twisted up into a knot on the crown of the head, and a gold pin is stuck in, and a wreath encircles the knot. Bracelets encircle the wrists, and anklets encircle the ankles. Strands of large beads also encircle the wrists. A large badge is worn about the neck. A double guard is worn athwart the breast, having a roll of gold sheeting strung on it. The *pa-nung* being put on, they take a girdle and gird the loins.

"All these ornaments which are used in the dress of [royal] children are made with pure gold, set with jewels, precious stones, and jet; different ones being made in different ways.

"Another subject. If one be a prince, he fares well. If one be the child of a prince, he fares well. If one be the nephew of a prince, he fares well. If one be the offspring of the royal family, he fares well. Would such visit any one, he can. Would he walk for pleasure in any direction, he can. Would he go anywhere, he has four men to carry him on their shoulders. He has an umbrella spread over him. He has men to attend him, and various marks of distinction—viz., a royal waiter, a royal goglet, and a royal betel-bag prepared according to the rank of princes.

"Again: public officers and the children of public

officers act according to their several grades, agreeable to established customs.

"Another subject. Gardeners' and farmers' *pa-nungs* and *pa-homs* are different [from princes']. They are vulgarly short, and they wear a jacket [short white shirt, buttoned up before] and a hat suitable to keep off the rays of the sun.*

"We have a season in the first, second, and third months that is considered very cool.† All the inhabitants of the exalted city [Bangkok] put on jackets, because it is very cool. But in the hot season *the men* prepare themselves cloth of light materials, in width about two cubits, in length about two cubits and a half, and they dip this *pa-hom* in water [*i. e.*, it is kept moist about the shoulders].

---

* "The Siamese most generally go bareheaded, except some of the labouring class, who have a hat formed of a species of palm-leaf, stitched together in the form of an inverted milk-pan. Inside of this is constructed a simple ratan frame, fitting the head, and which keeps it on. They never wear shoes or sandals. Go where you will, from the king to the peasant, you will see all classes and sexes barefooted."

† "*The cool season* here commences about the middle or full moon in November, and lasts until the same time in February. During this time there is a clear sky, cool atmosphere, and pretty constant and bracing winds. The thermometer stands usually at 72° F., although the older missionaries have seen it at 59° F.

"*The hot season* commences about the middle or full moon of February, and continues until the same time in June. This season is trying to Europeans; but with prudence, perhaps, not more so than the summer and autumn months in our Southern States in America. The thermometer rises usually to 96° F.

"*The rainy season* commences about the middle or full moon in June, and lasts until the same time in November. During this season the atmosphere is usually very pleasant, except in the middle of the day, when the rays of the sun striking the wet earth with great power, cause a steam to arise which is unpleasant while it lasts. Our showers come only once or twice a day, and but for an hour or two at a time. This season is almost equal to a second cool season, and not to be dreaded, as some at home suppose."

"In this explanation respecting the kingdom of Siam, [it will be seen that] the manner of dressing is, in general, the same throughout the kingdom."

The superstitions of the Siamese are not originally traceable to their religious creed, nor to the primitive teachings of Gaudama (Buddha), who prohibits his disciples from consulting soothsayers, putting trust in auguries, or valuing charms and prognostics. But the infusion of a corrupted Brahminism from India, and of a low Buddhism from China, working upon the credulity of a wretchedly-instructed population, have fed that passion for mystery and belief in invisible agencies by which the ignorant seek to explain inexplicable phenomena, and to frame excuses and find consolations for their individual misfortunes. Independently of the official astrologers of the Court, there are men called *modu* who are paid by the people for their professional advice as to the daily business of life, the result of commercial speculations, the desirableness of a matrimonial engagement, the fit time for shaving the head-tuft, for beginning a journey, how to win at play, how to recover lost or stolen property, &c. Their functions differ little from those of the white wizards and witches who, to this hour, are not without influence in the ruder parts of Great Britain, and whose supernatural knowledge of events is firmly believed in by a considerable portion of the agricultural population at the present hour.*

Confidence in *talismans* may have been of Malayan

---

* In my native county (Devonshire) I could cite recent examples of extraordinary credulity.

or Mahomedan origin; and the belief in alchemy is probably traceable to the same source. Many charms are supposed to render their wearer invulnerable, among which a ball of solid mercury is deemed of undoubted efficacy. Now, the art of freezing quicksilver was probably possessed by the Arabs, and there may be abundant traditional evidence of the existence of the metal in a solid state. To some rare woods mixed with various ingredients, the same virtues are attributed as to hard quicksilver.

But the ordinary amulets are composed of gold and silver beads, strung on a thread which has been blessed by the bonzes, or of small metallic plates on which mysterious characters are engraved. The necklaces of the women have been almost all steeped in holy water. Magicians are called in when invalids are supposed to be in a dangerous state, who make images of clay, which they convey to the woods and bury, promising by their incantations that the disease shall be transferred to the image.*

The strange prejudice in favour of odd numbers, which dates from the highest antiquity, and is spread through the western world, exists in all its force among the Siamese. They will build no staircase having an even number of stairs; no house must have an even number of rooms, doors, or windows: yet the *decimal* system is the universal medium by which all the associations connected with eternity and infinity are impressed on the Siamese mind; and the gradations from tens to hundreds, thousands, mil-

* Pallegoix, ii. 48, 49.

lions, billions, are favorite elements of religious speculations among the bonzes.

Of an ancient ceremony frequently referred to by travellers, which required the immolation of three human beings when any new gate was constructed in a Siamese city, I could find no vestige in Siam. Though many details are given of the proceedings in a letter from Bishop Bruguière, Pallegoix doubts the existence of such a usage. It has probably fallen into desuetude.

The *ghoule* and vampire superstitions have made their way into Siam, modified in their details, but preserving the great outlines of the Oriental type. Infants born before their time are generally delivered to the magicians, as such premature birth is deemed of evil augury. Among the strange fancies is one that a magician can reduce a buffalo to the size of a pea, which being swallowed by the person he is employed to bewitch, the pea re-assumes its former shape, and bursts the interior of the wretch who has swallowed it.

Love-philtres are sold by the magicians, and are believed to be efficacious in winning the affections and exciting the passions of those to whom they are administered.

Demons are believed to be the keepers of hidden treasures, which demons are frequently invoked; and many tales are told of the success of those who have conciliated, and the punishments of those who have exasperated them.

The dread of ghosts and demons is universal among the Siamese. We often saw little rafts of bamboo, with small images of human beings (representing families), and offerings of betel-nut, rice, fruits, and flowers, lighted with small tapers, the whole floating on the river for the purpose of conciliating the spirits of the waters. When epidemics attack the people, similar offerings are placed on four cross roads. One mode of conciliating is by tying a cotton thread round the waist, to show that the doctors are held in remembrance.

As to the fabulous creations which are crowded into the legendary tales and current superstitions of the Siamese, there is no end to the catalogue: mermaids and sirens on the waters, ogres and giants on the land, nymphs in the forests, ghosts and spirits everywhere, dragons and fire-spitting serpents, birds, some of which attack and feed upon living men, some with women's breasts, and others with elephants' trunks. The field of investigation may be left to those who like to contemplate the extravagances of prurient imaginations, and dive into the enormous abyss of human folly and credulity.

The wildest superstitions (many of them importations from India and the Malay countries) are connected with pregnancy and the birth of children, as with death and the dead. An *enceinte* woman is supposed to become the object of special visitation from evil spirits, in order to obtain a future mastery over the fruit of the womb, and many incantations and charms are used for her protection. The corpse of a woman dying in child-bed is believed to be an object of particular concupiscence to magicians, who extract from it the elixir of life. Such corpses are not allowed to be consumed by fire, but are interred; and it is held that by the performance, by hired magicians, of certain ceremonies over the grave, the deceased will burst the tomb, mount upwards with a fearful yell, assume a gigantic form, when being again controlled by magic arts, the body re-descends to the grave, having lost all power of molesting the living.

After death, a man's corpse is washed, coloured with turmeric, and rubbed with quicklime; then wrapped in white cloth. The arms are raised as if in adoration, and a piece of gold or silver placed in the mouth. Quicksilver and honey are poured down the throat; after which, the body is placed upright—a tube from the mouth is passed through the roof of the house to carry off the offensive effluvia above—holes are made in the feet, in which bamboos are placed, to convey the depositions that descend. But these and other observances, more or less onerous and costly, depend upon the position and wealth of those concerned. In the case of opulent persons, money is scattered profusely among the crowds who assemble to witness the funeral ceremonials in their various stages.

The study of alchemy was at one time a favourite pursuit among the Siamese. No doubt, the science was introduced under Moorish or Mahomedan influence. La Loubère mentions (p. 63) a King of Siam who wasted two millions of livres in search of the philosopher's stone. The opinion entertained of the supernatural power of amulets, or talismans, may probably be traced to the same source. But such is the supposed influence of such charms, that if it can be proved that either a plaintiff or defendant has worn one during the proceedings of action at law, he is condemned, *ipso facto*, to lose his suit.

The bonzes are charged with the public education, and schools are attached to most of the religious establishments. Instruction in the creeds and rites of Buddhism constitutes, naturally, a very important part of the system of instruction. A considerable portion of the male population are able to read and write, but there are few means of acquiring any of the higher branches of knowledge. There is, notwithstanding, especially among the nobles, much devotion to the study of the mechanical arts, and even considerable acquaintance with the use of nautical and philosophical instruments.

"The average amount of payment for tuition in common schools at Bangkok is eight dollars per annum, thirty-five shillings, from each boy; and fifteen dollars more cover all his expenses for board, clothes, stationery, &c. Some wealthy Chinese have private teachers, at a cost of eight dollars per month. A school-room may be hired at two dollars and a half per month, or even less." (*Chinese Repository*, vii. p. 309.)

The education of women is much neglected in Siam; there are few among them that can read or write. At the theatrical exhibitions within the palace, however, a woman was the prompter, and turned over, with great alacrity, the MS. pages of the play which was being acted. Many of them are taught music; and the wives and concubines of the nobles are frequently engaged in singing, and giving concerts for the amusement of their lords and their lords' guests. Some of them practise the arts of embroidery—make garlands and other ornaments of flowers for the adornment of the houses, and prepare sweetmeats and delicacies for the table. Among the courtesies of the King, we were in the habit of receiving boxes of cakes, on which was written, "Prepared by the ladies of the palace for royal service."

The medical science, though under the immediate patronage of royalty, cannot be deemed in a very advanced or satisfactory state. I observed, however, that the Siamese had much confidence in their native doctors; and on one occasion, when I offered to the senior Regent of the Kingdom the services of the medical gentleman who accompanied the Mission, the offer was accepted with great unwillingness and distrust, though the treatment of the native physicians had obviously failed, and the patient was suffering extreme pain. The head of the physicians is located within the King's palace, and has a considerable body of "royal doctors" under his orders, who hold the office hereditarily from father to son. The Siamese divide the profession into two departments—those who treat external and those who deal with internal ailments; which is, in fact, the broad distinction between surgery and medicine. The number of the professional doctors is immense, from the lowest quacks to the class that, by long experience, have attained to some real understanding of the action of particular medicaments on the human frame. The arts of *charlatanerie* are as rife in Siam as elsewhere;

but a custom prevails there for the protection of the patient, which might, perhaps, be introduced with advantage into other countries, of which the simple condition is, "No cure, no pay." When a person is ill, the doctor is sent for, and the first inquiry is, "Can you remove my complaint?" After deliberation or examination, the reply is generally in the affirmative. Then the negotiation commences as to the sum to be paid for the cure, and the amount is settled by a written contract, the doctor always demanding two wax candles for an offering to the god of medicine, and six salungs (equal to 3s. 9d.) for the cost of medicines. If the patient's health improve under the doctor's care, the visits continue; if the doctor think the case hopeless, his visits cease, and there is an end of the contract.

There are said to be two medical schools or systems in Siam contending for the mastery—the Indian and the Chinese—and it would be difficult to say which is the most crowded with follies and superstition. Here is a Siamese *recipe*, which seems to combine the nonsense of both. It is a prescription for what was called "morbific fever:"—"One portion of rhinoceros horn, one of elephant's tusk, one of tiger's, and the same of crocodile's teeth; one of bear's tooth; one portion composed of three parts bones of vulture, raven, and goose; one portion of bison and another of stag's horn, one portion of sandal. These ingredients to be mixed together on a stone with pure water; one half of the mixture to be swallowed, the rest to be rubbed into the body; after which the morbific fever will depart."*

There are books on medicine translated into Siamese from the Pali. As regards anatomy, they are, of course, like all ancient works on the subject, exceedingly rude, and full of false notions; but as regards the application of herbs and simples, many of the instructions are valuable, and the nature of various portions of the vegetable kingdom is well understood. There is a general treatment of sick persons which is often successful. They are dieted to a thin rice-soup, with a small infusion of dried fish as a condiment. Shower-baths are used three or four times a day. The attendant nurse takes a large quantity of hot water, in which there is a strong infusion of medicinal herbs, and squirts it with great violence in a shower of vapour over the body of the patient: this operation is frequently repeated. Rubbing all the joints and limbs and surface of the body, in the manner of Oriental shampooing, is an habitual practice. Sometimes the doctor stands himself on the knees of the patient, and rubs the whole frame with the soles of his feet.

The general character of diseases in Siam differs little from that of other Oriental tropical climates. Vaccination has been introduced. The cholera has several times visited Siam. On the whole, the average mortality is less, and the chance of life greater, than in most countries under the same latitude.

The Siamese are a musical people, and possess a

---

* Pallegoix, i. 342.

great variety of both wind and stringed instruments—cymbals, drums, great and small, many of which are singularly shaped; indeed, almost every combination of materials is employed out of which the ingenuity of man has produced sweet sounds.

The *Khong-bong* is an instrument of great power; it is composed of a semicircle of suspended tongues, or flat pieces of sonorous wood or metal; in the centre of which the musician stands and strikes the notes with two wooden hammers. The harmony is perfect, and is heard at a considerable distance.

The *Ranat* is a *Khong-bong* on a smaller scale, in which the tongues are disposed in a straight line before the player. They have a species of guitar or violin, the surface (over which are the strings) being made of the skin of the boa, or some other serpent, stretched on half a cocoa-nut shell. This instrument I have seen in China. One of their flutes is played through the nostrils. The *Takhe* is a species of guitar placed on the ground, with metal chords, which are struck by the artificial nails, or claws, of the ladies, fixed like thimbles on the tops of the fingers. They are several inches long, and are bent outward, ending in a sharp point. They are invariably worn by the women in dramatic representations.

I had, on the occasion of the death of a nobleman in Siam, an opportunity of purchasing the musical instruments used in his family.

The following description was furnished me from Bangkok. The first set, Nos. 1, 2, 3, 4, 5, 6, forms a

"Another matter which appears to have created much discussion and frequent reference, regarded the manner in which the members of the Mission should proceed to the place of audience. It was first proposed that, after proceeding to the usual landing-place in boats, they should thence continue on foot to the audience-hall. This proposal was given up for that of going on horseback; and this last, finally, to that of being carried in palanquins.

"Matters were at length settled, and we were given to understand that we were to proceed to the palace at an early hour on the following day.

"I accompanied Mr. Crawfurd on an early visit to the Barkalan, Suri Wong Montree. On this occasion he was seated on a piece of red carpet, and leaned on a velvet cushion: he rose up as we entered, and pointed to a mattress, covered with chintz, placed near to the door, for us to sit on. His manner appeared to me to be stiff, haughty, assuming, and altogether without dignity to support it. The conversation between him and Mr. Crawfurd lasted nearly half an hour, and turned chiefly on commercial matters. He stated that the country could furnish annually fifty thousand peculs of sugar, and thirty thousand of pepper. He appeared to have greatly exaggerated the annual produce in benzoin, and observed that the forests could supply sapan-wood in any quantity. He desired to know if the Siamese would be permitted to purchase arms in our ports in India.

"When we returned on board, Captain Dangerfield remained behind, after breakfast, for the purpose of

necessary shape for forming the body of the violin, and as much as fifty ticals is sometimes given for one. The nut is covered with goat-skin; the small eye-shaped instrument affixed thereto is for regulating the tone. It is held in a slanting position, resting on the ground, when played.

8. Kajape (Guitar). This is a far more simply constructed instrument than the preceding. It is held by the left hand, and rested on the right knee. The strings are struck by the long nails, which the higher classes here, as well as in China, cultivate universally. In case, however, the musician lacks these fashionable ornaments, a piece of ivory, or wood, is substituted.

9. Klue (Flute), made of bamboo.

10. Thôn; a kind of drum, which, when played, is placed horizontally on the knees, and struck with the right hand. The orifice at the other end is closed or opened by the left hand, according to the note it is desired to produce. This instrument is constructed of earthenware: the skin used is that of the boa.

11. Rumana; a kind of drum, beaten by the hand. The piece of wood and cord attached are for tuning the instrument; the string being inserted between the skin and frame by the stick: ox-skin (not buffalo) is here used.

12. Ching (Cymbals).

These form the singing band.

The songs of the Siamese are not wanting in a certain plaintive expression—they are full of repetitions. The subjects are generally historical, recording the feats of ancient warriors, or amorous—and these are frequently gross and lascivious.

The Siamese have no written music; their several tunes are attained by ear alone, and are a curious but not inharmonious *mélange* of the sounds produced by their various instruments. The profession of music is esteemed worthy; indeed, the highest ambition of the fair sex in Siam is to possess the faculty of performing the graceful evolutions and charming tunes of the Lakhon pu ying, or dancing girls. These girls are trained from their earliest infancy; their limbs are contorted into unnatural positions by painful and barbarous processes, and they are otherwise adapted to their profession. Their perception of concord in the notes is as acute as that of an European musician, and they are equally as long in tuning their instruments.

The soft and tuneful notes of their music form an agreeable contrast to the loud, monotonous, and discordant tones of the music of the Chinese; a fact much to be wondered at, when the civilization of their respective countries is taken into consideration. Perhaps, however, the great apathy of the Siamese, compared with the industry of the Chinese—their consequent fondness for amusement, and their system of polygamy, offer the best explanation of the marvellous difference. The close of each day, in fact, at every nobleman's house, is the signal for the commencement of music and dancing; and the concert is continued without interlude till the next day has been encroached upon by some hours. Add to this the time given to it daily by the numerous women, whose almost sole occupation it is, and it might well be a matter of surprise that the Siamese have not attained greater proficiency in the art.

Among the amusements of the Siamese is the game of chess; but it differs from the Indian or European game, and has no doubt been imported from China, as the chess-board, the pieces, and the moves, in all respects resemble those of the Chinese.

The chess-board of the Siamese, like ours, has sixty-four squares, which are not distinguished into black and white. They place their pieces on the corners of the squares; the board is divided into two portions by a space they call the river. There are nine points on each line, and forty-five on each half of the board. The number of pieces is the same as with us. Each player has a king, two guards, two elephants, two knights, two chariots, two cannons, and five pawns. Each player places nine pieces on the first line of the board, on his own side; the king in the centre, a guard (minister) on each side of him, two elephants next, two knights next, and then the two chariots upon the extremities of the board; the two cannons in front of the two knights, and the pawns on the fourth line.

The king moves only one square at a time, but not diagonally, and can only move in an *enceinte* (or court) of four squares—his own, the queen's, and queen's-pawn's and king's-pawn's—and they never castle.

The two guards remain in the same limits, and can only move diagonally; the elephants move diagonally, but only two squares at a time, and must not pass the river. Their knight moves like ours, but must not pass over pieces; he can pass the river, which is considered as one square. The chariots move like our castles, and cross the river, and the cannons the same. The pawns always move one step; they cross the river, and they may move sideways as well; they take in the same way that they move. The object of the game is, as among us, to give checkmate. The cannons are allowed to pass over any piece. The king must not be opposite the other king without a piece between. The cannon can only take where there is a piece between itself and the piece it takes; but the intervening piece may belong to either player. (La Loubère, vol. ii., p. 122.)

It is deemed a sin for the Siamese bonze or talapoin not to have made himself acquainted with the hidden powers of numbers; and, like other Orientals, the priests employ their leisure hours in solving mathematical problems. Agrippa, in his second work, *De Occulta Philosophia*, chap. 22, gives a great many curious examples of what are called Magic Squares: they represent the art by which a large square being divided into any number of small squares, the figures representing the whole number of squares should be so arranged by arithmetical progression, as that, whether added up perpendicularly, horizontally, or transversely, the sum-total of the figures shall always be the same. The following are examples:—

CURIOUS PROPERTIES OF NUMBERS.

MAGIC SQUARES.

15.

4	9	2
3	5	7
8	1	6

34.

1	15	14	4
12	6	7	9
8	10	11	5
13	3	2	16

65.

17	24	1	8	15
23	5	7	14	16
4	6	13	20	22
10	12	19	21	3
11	18	25	2	9

65.

11	24	7	20	3
4	12	25	8	16
17	5	13	21	9
10	18	1	14	22
23	6	19	2	15

Regular Arrangement from Left to Right.

65.

```
                    1
              6         2
        65                    65
           11      7      3
        16     12      8      4
   65  21     17     13     9      5
        22     18     14    10
           23     19     15
              24        20
                    25
```

15.

```
        1
   15         15
     4     2
15 7     5     3
     8     6
        9
```

34.

8	11	14	1
2	13	12	7
9	6	3	16
15	4	5	10

260.

1	63	62	4	5	59	58	8
56	10	11	53	52	14	15	49
48	18	19	45	44	22	23	41
25	39	38	28	29	35	34	32
33	31	30	36	37	27	26	40
24	42	43	21	20	46	47	17
16	50	51	13	12	54	55	9
57	7	6	60	61	3	2	64

505.

1	99	98	4	96	5	7	93	92	10
90	12	88	87	15	16	84	83	19	11
80	79	23	24	76	75	27	28	72	21
31	69	33	34	66	65	37	38	62	70
60	42	58	57	45	46	44	53	49	51
41	52	48	47	55	56	54	43	59	50
61	39	63	64	35	36	67	68	32	40
30	29	73	74	26	25	77	78	22	71
20	32	18	17	85	86	14	13	89	81
91	2	3	97	6	95	94	8	9	100

Cock-fighting is a favourite sport of the Siamese. Though strictly prohibited, one cannot pass the streets without seeing crowds surrounding the scenes of combat. A courageous game-cock is a great treasure, and the object of special attention. The race is smaller than the English, and more resembles the pheasant in size and shape. There is a small bellicose fish, too, which attacks its fellow with great ferocity—bristling its fins, and exhibiting the utmost excitement: one of these, seeing its reflection in a glass, will violently advance, head foremost, against the shadow. The battles of crickets and the formica-leo are favourite sports of the people, from their childhood up. Lotteries have been introduced by the Chinese, and often lead the Siamese to utter destitution. In fact, the passion for gaming and betting seems unchecked, either by public opinion or the power of the law.

Kite-flying is the amusement of young and old. I do not think the art is so well understood as in China, where not only kites of a great variety of size and shape are seen, but they are made musical. When certain winds prevail, kite-battles are much in vogue; the sport being to entangle the kite of your adversary, and to drag it and the string into your own possession. Much noise and excitement accompany these aërial combats.

Boat-races are not unfrequent, nor are pugilistic combats. Dancing on the tight and slack rope, puppet-shows, sleights of hand, optical illusions, wrestling, and sham fights, are among the ordinary recreations of the people. They share the love of amusement with the Chinese, but have few of the laborious and persevering virtues which characterize the people of China.

Computation of Time.—Two eras, a civil and a religious, are used by the Siamese. The latter is dated from the death of the present ruling Buddha (*Somana Khodom*), five hundred and forty-three years before Christ; so that the present year (1856) is the 2399th of the religious epoch. The civil era dates from the reign of a Siamese monarch whose capital was *Sangkhalok*, A.D. 638; so that A.D. 1856 in the Siamese civil calendar should be 1218.* In the treaty I made with the Siamese, there were several corrections as to the dates in which the first King took a particular interest; and the 18th April, 1855, the day when the treaty was signed in quadruplicate, is there recorded to be the second day of the sixth month of the 1217th year of the civil era of Siam.

The year is composed of twelve lunar months, generally beginning in December, and having alternately twenty-nine and thirty days. Every three years an intercalary month is introduced. The months are called the first, second, third, and so on to the twelfth moon. There are two cycles—the small consisting of twelve years, bearing the names of the year of the Rat, the Ox, the Tiger, the Hare, the Great Dragon, the Little Dragon, the Horse, the Goat, the Monkey, the Cock, the Dog, and the Pig. The great cycle is a fivefold repetition of the small cycle, arranged in decades, the first beginning with the Rat and ending with the Cock. The second decade begins with the Dog; and the decades proceed regularly through the years of the smaller cycle—a new cycle recommencing every sixty years.†

---

* This corresponds with the year 4493 of the Chinese, or the 53rd year of the 75th cycle of 60 years. It is the 1219th year of the Parsee era of Yezdèjird.

† The Chinese cycle, also of 60 years, is composed of combinations of two sets of characters,—the celestial (or stems) consisting of 10, and the terrestrial (or branches) of 12. The branches are used to divide the day into periods of 2 hours each. They bear the same name as the Siamese, except that the Little Dragon is called by the Chinese the Snake.

COMPUTATION OF TIME.

The *Thai* reckon, not by days, but by nights: repose, instead of activity, is the instrument by which time is measured. They generally inquire, "Where did you rest?" instead of "What did you do?" They say, "This is the first night of the moon; how many nights did you take for your journey?" The days of the week must have been adopted from the West: they are *Sun*day, *Moon*day, *Mars*day, *Mercury*day, *Jupiter*day, *Venus*day, and *Saturn*day.* The names of the stars and constellations are taken principally from the Sanscrit. The day is divided into four equal parts of six hours, counting from sunrise. There is a subdivision into watches of three hours, which reckon from sunset; the hour is divided into ten *bat*, and the *bat* into six *noths*, which therefore correspond to the European minute.

According to Kämpfer, the days of the week are—

Sunday . .	Van athet .	Day of the sun.
Monday .	Van chau . .	„ moon.
Tuesday .	Van ngankau	„ labour.
Wednesday	Van poeth .	„ meeting.
Thursday .	Van prahat .	„ hand day.
Friday . .	Van sok . .	„ rest.
Saturday .	Van saun .	„ attraction.†

The Siamese divide the day into twelve hours—

---

* Though the Gothic and Scandinavian nations have, in the cases of Tuesday, Wednesday, Thursday, and Friday, given the names of Scandinavian deities to those days of the week—Tuisco, Woden, Thor, Friga—most of the Northern nations have preserved the Latin names, as in—

French, *Mardi, Mercredi, Jeudi, Vendredi.*
Spanish, *Martes, Miercoles, Jueves, Viernes.*
Italian, *Martedi, Mercoledi, Giovedi, Venerdi.*

While for Saturday they have taken the Sabbatical word.

† Kämpfer, p. 41.

from sunrise to sunset; the night (according to the custom of the ancients) into four watches, the last ending with the broad daylight. The eighth and fifteenth days of the moon are considered holy by the Siamese, and are observed as days for rest and worship: on them the temples are visited, and offerings made to Buddha, and to the priests, who preach to the people in a large open hall. No fishing or hunting is permitted on these days, and neither fresh fish nor meat is sold in the bazaar, under pain of fine and corporal punishment. The new year, *Song Kran*, is celebrated for three days; and the astrologers predict the character of the year by associating it with some animals, upon whose back it is represented to be mounted on its approach. The *Visa Khabuxa*, on the 15th day of the 6th month, is another holiday, when the King sends presents to the bonzes of fruits and flowers, and odoriferous woods for cleansing their teeth. On the *Rëkna*, beginning the 6th day of the 6th moon, the King keeps his palace for three days, and a mock king is invested by the people with temporary sovereignty, who sends out his ministers to catch what they can in the bazaars or open shops, and even confiscates junks that arrive during the exercise of his precarious authority. His mock majesty proceeds to a field in the town, and makes some furrows with a golden plough: leaning against the branch of a tree, he places his right foot on his left knee, and is bound to stand on one leg as evidence of his legitimacy. Hence his popular title is *King Hop*. A variety of vegetables are scattered in his presence, and a cow being brought in, whatever she first eats is pronounced likely to be scarce, and the people are advised accordingly. The whole farce is probably intended to throw scorn upon popular influences, and reconcile the subject to the authority of a *real* King; for the reality of the royal authority of a King of Siam is a fact not to be mistaken, and may well be contrasted with the doings of a transitory impostor. The *Khao-vasa*, 6th of the 8th month, is a sort of Lent, when all the wandering bonzes are required to return to their temples: it generally ushers in the rainy season. *Sat*, the last day of the 10th moon, when presents are made of cakes of the new rice. *Kathin*, the 16th day of the 11th month; after which the King makes, during seven days, his royal visits to the great pagodas, and distributes new vestments to the bonzes. These processions are in magnificent barges; and the King is accompanied by the princes and high officers of the state, each in a separate barge, the whole number of rowers not being less than 8,000 to 10,000. When the royal processions are over, those of the people follow. *Loi Kathong*, on the 15th day of the 12th moon, the festival of the angel of the river, whose forgiveness is then asked for every act by which the waters of the Meinam have been rendered impure. Offerings are made of little rafts of plantain leaves, bearing lighted tapers, and ornamented by flags and flowers. These tributes are launched at night, and carried by the current into the sea. *Phapa*, at the beginning of the 12th month, when nightly processions take place to the pagodas, and alms and offerings are left by boys and girls for the bonzes, while they are supposed to sleep: they are waked by stones and bricks flung against the doors of their cells, when, as if exasperated, they turn out to scold the invaders of their repose, but are soothed by the gifts they bring. The young people all take flight, and return home with shouts, and songs, and laughter. On the *Jinga-tana*, at the close of the 4th month, a cord is made of dog's grass, which is taken to be blessed by the bonzes; and the cord is fastened round the walls of the city. At a signal given by the astrologers, successive bursts of artillery are heard, which are supposed to frighten giants and plague-demons, who are known to attack the city on that particular night. *Trut* is the festival of the close of the year, being the end of the 4th moon, when visiting and playgoing are universal.*

Though our acquaintance with the capital of Siam is now tolerably complete, the interior of the country has been so little explored, that it would be idle to undertake any general description of the provinces. I shall, therefore, content myself with giving some extracts from different sources which are not without interest or instruction.

In reporting one of his excursions into the country, Bishop Pallegoix speaks of a large assemblage of gaily-ornamented barges, filled with multitudes of people in holiday dresses, whom he met above Ayuthia, going on a pilgrimage to the "foot of Buddha." The women and girls wore scarfs of silk, and bracelets of gold and silver, and filled the air with their songs,

---

* Pallegoix, i. p. 250—2.

to which troops of priests and young men responded in noisy music. The place of debarkation is Tha Rua, which is on the road to Phra-bat, where the foot-print of the god is found. More than five hundred barges were there, all illuminated: a drama was performed on the shore; there was a great display of vocal and instrumental music, tea-drinking, playing at cards and dice, and the merry festivities lasted through the whole night.

Early the following day, the cortege departed by the river. It consisted of princes, nobles, rich men, ladies, girls, priests, all handsomely clad. They landed, and many proceeded on foot, while the more distinguished mounted on elephants to move towards the sacred mountain. In such localities the spirit of fanaticism is usually intemperate and persecuting; and the bishop says, the governor received him angrily, and accused him of "intending to debauch his people by making them Christians." But he was softened by presents and explanations, and ultimately gave the bishop a passport, recommending him to "all the authorities and chiefs of villages under his command, as a Christian priest (farang), and as his friend, and ordering that he should be kindly treated, protected, and furnished with all the provisions he might require."

Of his visit to the sacred mountain, so much the resort of Buddhist pilgrims, Pallegoix gives this account:—

"I engaged a guide, mounted an elephant, and took the route of Phra-bat, followed by my people. I was surprised to find a wide and excellent road, paved with bricks, and opened in a straight line across the forests. On both sides of the road, at a league's distance, were halls or stations, with wells dug for the use of the pilgrims. Soon the road became crooked, and we stopped to bathe in a large pond. At four o'clock, we reached the magnificent monastery of Phra-bat, built on the declivity, but nearly at the foot of a tall mountain, formed by fantastic rocks of a bluish colour. The monastery has several walls surrounding it; and having entered the second enclosure, we found the *abbé-prince*, seated on a raised floor, and directing the labours of a body of workmen. His attendants called on us to prostrate ourselves, but we did not obey them. 'Silence!' he said; 'you know not that the *farang* honour their grandees by standing erect.' I approached, and presented him with a bottle of sal-volatile, which he smelt with delight. I requested he would appoint some one to conduct us to see the vestige of Buddha; and he called his principal assistant (the *balat*), and directed him to accompany us. The *balat* took us round a great court surrounded with handsome edifices; showed us two large temples; and we reached a broad marble staircase with balustrades of gilded copper, and made the round of the terrace which is the base of the monument. All the exterior of this splendid edifice is gilt; its pavement is square, but it takes the form of a dome, and is terminated in a pyramid a hundred and twenty feet high. The gates and windows, which are double, are exquisitely wrought. The outer gates are inlaid with handsome devices in mother-of-pearl, and the inner gates are adorned with gilt pictures representing the events in the history of Buddha.

" The interior is yet more brilliant; the pavement is covered with silver mats. At the end, on a throne ornamented with precious stones, is a statue of Buddha in massive silver, of the height of a man; in the middle is a silver grating which surrounds the vestige, whose length is about eighteen inches. It is not distinctly visible, being covered with rings, ear ornaments, bracelets, and gold necklaces, the offerings of devotees when they come to worship. The history of the relic is this:—In the year 1602, notice was sent to the King at Ayuthia, that a discovery had been made at the foot of a mountain, of what appeared to be a footmark of Buddha. The King sent his learned men, and the most intelligent priests, to report if the lineaments of the imprint resembled the description of the foot of Buddha, as given in the sacred Pali writings. The examination having taken place, and the report being in the affirmative, the King caused the monastery of Phra-bat to be built, which has been enlarged and enriched by his successors.

" After visiting the monument, the *balat* escorted us to a deep well cut out of the solid stone: the water is good, and sufficient to provide for crowds of pilgrims. The abbé-prince is the sovereign lord of the mountain and its environs within a circuit of eight leagues; he has from four to five thousand men under his orders, to be employed as he directs in the service of the monastery. On the day of my visit, a magnificent palanquin, such as is used by great princes, was brought to him as a present from the King. He had the civility to entertain us as well as he could. I remarked that the kitchen was under the care of a score of young girls, and they gave the name of pages to the youths who attended us. In no other monastery is this usage to be found.

"His highness caused us to be lodged in a handsome wooden house, and gave me two guards of honour to serve and watch over me, forbidding my going out at night on account of tigers. The following morning I took leave of the good abbé-prince, mounted my elephant, and taking another road, we skirted the foot of the mountain till we reached a spring of spouting waters. We found there a curious plant, whose leaves were altogether like the shape and the colours of butterflies. We took a simple breakfast in the first house we met with; and at four o'clock in the afternoon we reached our boat, and after a comfortable night's rest, we left Tha Rua to return to our church at Ayuthia."

I received from a gentleman, now resident in Siam, the following notes of an excursion to the city of Pechaburi :—

"1855, *July* 9*th*.—We left Bangkok about three in the afternoon, and although we had the tide in our favour, we only accomplished five miles during the first three hours. Our way lay through a creek; and so great was the number of boats, that it strongly reminded me of Cheapside during the busiest part of the day. Although I had been in Bangkok four months, I had not the least conception that there was such a population spread along the creeks. More than four miles from the river, there appeared to be little or no diminution in the number of the inhabitants, and the traffic was as great as at the mouth of the creek.

" Having at last got past the crowd of boats, we advanced rapidly for two hours more, when we stopped at a *wat*, in order to give the men a rest. This *wat*, as its name ' Laos' implies, was built by the inhabitants of the Laos country, and is remarkable (if we can trust to tradition) as being the limit of the Burmese invasion. Here, the Siamese say, a body of Burmans were defeated by the villagers, who had taken refuge in the *wat;* and they point out two large holes in the wall as the places where cannon-balls struck. After leaving this, we proceeded rapidly until about 12 P.M., when we reached the other branch of the Meinam (Menam mahachen), and there we halted for the night.

" 10*th*.—Our journey to-day was most delightful; most of it lay through narrow creeks, their banks covered with atap and bamboo, whilst behind this screen were plantations of chilis, beans, peas, &c. &c. Alligators and otters abounded in the creeks; and we shot several, and one of a peculiar breed of monkey also we killed. The Siamese name of it is *chang*, and it is accounted a great delicacy: they also eat with avidity the otter. We crossed during the day the Hai-chin, a river as broad as the Meinam at Bangkok. Towards evening we entered the Mei-Klong, which we descended till we reached the sea-coast. Here we waited till the breeze should sufficiently abate to enable us to cross the bay.

" 11*th*.—We started about 4 A.M., and reached the opposite side in about three hours. The bay is remarkably picturesque, and is so shallow, that, although we crossed fully four miles from the head of the bay, we never had more than six feet of water, and generally much less. Arrived at the other side, we ascended the river on which Pechaburi is built. At the mouth of the river, myriads of monkeys were to be seen. A very amusing incident occurred here. Mr. Hunter, wishing to get a juvenile specimen, fired at the mother, but, unfortunately, only wounded her, and she had strength enough to carry the young one into the jungle. Five men immediately followed her; but ere they had been out of sight five minutes, we saw them hurrying towards us, shouting, ' *Ling, ling, ling, ling!*' (*ling*, monkey). As I could see nothing, I asked Mr. Hunter if they were after the monkey. ' Oh, no,' he replied; 'the monkeys are after them!' And so they were—thousands upon thousands of them, coming down in a most unpleasant manner; and, as the tide was out, there was a great quantity of soft mud to cross before they could reach the boat: and here the monkeys gained very rapidly upon the men, and when at length the boat was reached, their savage pursuers were not twenty yards behind. The whole scene was ludicrous in the extreme, and I really think, if my life had depended upon it, that I could not have fired a shot. To see the men making the most strenuous exertions to get through the deep mud, breathless with their run and fright combined; and the army of little wretches drawn up in line within twenty yards of us, screaming, and making use of the most diabolical language, if we could only have understood them! Besides, there was a feeling that they had the right side of the question. One of the *refugees*, however, did not appear to take my view of the case: smarting under the disgrace, and the bamboos against which he ran in his retreat, he seized my gun, and fired both barrels on the exulting foe; they immediately retired in great disorder, leaving four dead upon the field. Many were the quarrels that arose from this affair among the men.

" The approach to Pechaburi is very pleasant: the river is absolutely arched over by tamarind trees, whilst the most admirable cultivation prevails all along its course.

" The name Pechaburi is derived from *pet*, a diamond, and *buri*, a town (only used in composition): this, I imagine, is connected with our word *borough*.

" The first object which attracts the attention is the magnificent pagoda, within which is a reclining figure of Buddha, one hundred and forty-five feet in length. Above the pagoda, the priests have, with great perseverance, terraced the face of the rock to a considerable height. About half-way up the mountain, there is an extensive cave, generally known amongst foreigners as the ' Cave of Idols:' it certainly deserves its name, if we are to judge from the number of figures of Buddha which it contains.

" The talapoins assert that it is natural. It may be so in part, but there are portions of it in which the hand of man is visible: it is very small, not more than thirty yards in length, and about seven feet high; but anything like a cavern is so uncommon in this country, that this one is worth notice. We now proceeded to climb the mountain: it is very steep, but of no great height—probably not more than five hundred feet; it is covered with huge blocks of a stone resembling granite: these are exceedingly slippery, and the ascent is thus rendered rather laborious. But when we reached the top, we were well repaid. The country for miles in each direction lay at our feet—one vast plain, unbroken by any elevation: it appeared like an immense garden, so carefully was it cultivated; the young rice and sugar-cane, of the most beautiful green, relieved by the darker shade of the cocoa-nut trees, which are used as boundaries to the fields—those fields traversed by suitable footpaths. Then towards the sea the view was more varied: rice and sugar-cane held undisputed sway for a short distance from the town; then cocoa-nuts became more frequent, until the rice finally disappeared; then the bamboos gradually invaded the cocoa-nut trees; then the atap palm, with its magnificent leaf; and, lastly, came that great invader of Siam, the mangrove. Beyond were the mountains on the Malay peninsula, stretching away in the distance.

" With great reluctance did we descend from the little pagoda, which is built upon the very summit; but evening was coming on, and we had observed in ascending some very suspicious-looking footprints mightily resembling those of a tiger.

" Pechaburi is a thriving town, containing about twenty thousand inhabitants. The houses are, for the most part, neatly built, and no floating houses are visible. Rice and sugar are two-thirds dearer at Bangkok than they are here; and the rice is of a particularly fine description. We called upon the governor during the evening. Next morning we started for home, and arrived, without any accident, on Saturday evening."

CHAPTER V

LEGISLATION.

THE following short notice of the constitution of the judicial establishments and of the laws of Siam was furnished to me from a native source. But, in a country where the authority of the sovereign is absolute, it is obvious that the organization of the tribunals and the protecting power of legislation can afford but very inadequate security, should the supreme royal will at any time supersede the ordinary course of justice. To a great extent, also, the power of interfering with the action of the tribunals is possessed and exercised by the high nobles, according to their rank and influence.

Any party having a complaint to prefer does so before the *San Luang* (*San*, building; *Luang*, king). This court is presided over by "*K'un Li Támarat*" and "*K'un cha san;*"—these officiate alternately for fifteen days. They take down the complaint in writing, and hand it over to the LUK K'UN. This tribunal is composed of four *Luang** and eight assessors. Their business is to examine the complaint that has come down from the *San Luang*. If they consider that it is a fit and proper case for trial,

---

* The nobility are graduated in the following order:—*Somdets; Chau P'aya; P'aya; P'ra; Luang; K'un.*

they pass it over to P'RA RACHANICHAI. He decides to what department it belongs. The courts of the various departments are named K'UN SAN. Of these there are four—viz.,

(1) *Chau P'aya Kralahom's.* This department takes cognizance of cases belonging to the Southern Provinces.

(2) *Chau P'aya Nikorabudin's* court entertains cases belonging to the Northern Provinces.

(3) *Chau P'aya P'ra Klang's* court entertains cases relating to the Foreign department.

(4) *Chau P'aya Yumaret,* criminal cases.

The "*K'un San*" are the courts in which the whole proceedings of a case are carried through, embracing the examining witnesses, receiving bail, &c.

Bribery is said to flourish from the judge down to the lowest clerk,—all have their price. The judges in these courts are the only lawyers in the kingdom, and generally exceedingly clever men.

The case being finished, it is sent back to the "*Luk K'un*" for decision. The decision is then handed to the "*P'ra Krai Si,*" or "*P'ra Krai Lem,*"— officers whose duty it is to deliver the sentence: this sentence they also put in force after it has been approved of by the King.

Appeal.—Appeal is allowed, not against the decision, but against the sentence. This appeal is made to the King.*

---

* During a certain part of one day in the week, the King sits in public for the purpose of receiving complaints. As, of course, he is far above the people, he lets down a small case, into which the paper containing the complaint is put, and his Majesty draws it up with a cord and reads it.

Bail.—Bail is required both from plaintiff and defendant before the case is commenced by the "*K'un San;*" and in case of either party not appearing, the bail is held responsible for him. Bail is not allowed in criminal cases.

Punishments.—Decapitation is awarded for treason, murder, aggravated robberies, piracy, and arson.*

Coining is punished by cutting off the right hand of the actual coiner, and the fingers of the man who passed the bad money. Most of those who suffer this punishment die, in consequence of the ignorance of the doctors.

Debtors are imprisoned, or work in irons for the King, during the pleasure of the creditor.

If, even *by accident*, a house should catch fire, the owner of it is seized, and led through the town, three days on shore and three days on the river. He is obliged to repeat, every few minutes, "My house caught fire; take care, and be warned by me." He is then, if rich, put into prison, and only released by paying a heavy fine. This severity is not unnecessary in Bangkok.

One peculiarity of the judges may be mentioned here. Every nobleman has a certain number of "marks of dignity" (it is impossible to convey the exact idea by any corresponding phraseology). If a nobleman insult another of the same rank, but holding a greater number of "marks of dignity," he is considered as insulting his superior, and punished accordingly. The judges, in order to preserve them

---

* Princes of the blood-royal are put to death either by strangulation, or beating them to death with clubs. No royal blood must fall to the ground.

from insult in their office, have each "ten thousand marks," although they are only *Luang*. This is the number the *Kralahom* holds; so that, if he were insulted by the judge, or *vice versâ*, it would be held that they were equal.

A sort of synopsis of the laws of Siam has been published by Col. James Low;* but he seldom gives the text, and has availed himself of the titles of the chapters to introduce sundry curious details and observations on Siamese customs and manners, the result rather of desultory reading than of local observation and personal knowledge. I have selected a few of the commentator's gatherings, which, though in many particulars unsatisfactory, are not without interest. The laws of a country are among the most prominent and practical evidences of its civilization and advancement; and, on the whole, the Siamese must be deemed superior to the Chinese. "Will you not look into our laws?" was an inquiry made of me by one of the Regents of Siam. I had objected to allowing British subjects to be rendered amenable to laws of whose character I was but little informed. I asked how many volumes I should be required to study? "About seventy," he said. My answer may easily be anticipated. But who shall answer the question—In how many volumes must the laws of England be looked for?

The principal articles of the Siamese code were printed a few years ago at Bangkok, in a quarto volume, which is reported to contain nineteen out of

* *Journal of Eastern Archipelago*, vol. i., p. 429. Singapore, 1847.

the seventy volumes of manuscript laws. But though this portable and useful publication was intended for general use, it is now only obtainable by favour and with considerable difficulty.

The Siamese generally divide their laws into three principal sections:—

1. The *Phra-tam-ra*, which prescribes the titles and duties of public functionaries.

2. *Phra-tam-nun*—codes of the ancient Kings.

3. *Phra-raxa-kam-not*—modern codes, under the various heads of Robbers, Slaves, Conjugal Duties, Debts and Contracts, Disputes and Law-suits, Inheritance, and Generalia. Pallegoix says he has made himself master of the codes, and speaks favourably of them, and of their adaptation to the national character and wants. The groundwork is traceable to the institutions of Menu. There is a provision that all the provincial judges shall have a copy of the laws, and that the King shall read a portion of them every day; which is probably as much practically in force, as the enactment that "all law-suits shall be terminated in three days:" such days are frequently prolonged to years.

Judicatures, or Courts of Law.—There are practically in Siam three principal tribunals for the administration of justice,—those of the King, the princes, and the provincial governors.

A governor holds daily sittings in the portico of his official residence. His auxiliaries are—*Balat*, or lieutenant-governors; the *Jokabat*, who is a sort of public accuser, and check upon the governor; the

Mahat thai, who is the executive officer of the governor; the *Sassade*, or keeper of the popular records, and especially of the census. The *Luang muang* is an officer charged with the local police; the *Luang pheng* is the reader of the law applicable to the case under judgment; the *Khun-khueng* is the inflictor of punishments. This tribunal is called the *Kromakan*, but it invariably refers all important matters to the judgment of the King.

Every high functionary has a court, named a *Chang wang*, exercising a sort of authority; but the supreme tribunal of the King, called the *Sala luk khun*, is the great resort of judicial action. This court is presided over by the *Phaja rong muang*, who has a number of subordinate officers, charged with investigations, and, to some extent, with decisions. They occupy raised seats in separate halls, on the stairs and neighbourhood of which crowds of prostrate suitors are to be seen, while the judges converse, smoke, drink tea, and chew betel.

The action of the judiciary is tolerably prompt and despotic. A deposition having been laid before a judge, messengers are despatched to arrest the accused, around whose neck a white cloth is tied, and he is brought to the *Them*, or provincial prison, and is placed in fetters, unless he can pay for exemption. He must be provided for while in prison by his friends; and when he is conducted to the presence of the judge, the indictment is read, and the witnesses interrogated; their depositions are committed to writing, and the accused is allowed to call any number of witnesses in his defence. A false accuser is condemned to punishment, and to the costs of the suit. Blows of bamboo are used to force criminals to confess—to name their accomplices, who are seized as soon as denounced. Pallegoix says that there is a universal venality among the judges, and that litigated cases end generally in the ruin of both the contending parties,*—a result not confined to Siam.

The capital is divided into districts, each being under the control of a commissary of police; but there is no patrol, nor ambulatory watch. Disorders and tumults are rare, and dealt with in so summary and arbitrary a way, that it seems everybody's interest to keep the peace. When it is disturbed, the police seize upon all persons indiscriminately; and lucky is the man who escapes from prison without having been severely fleeced.

The ordinary *modus procedendi* before a Siamese tribunal is sufficiently simple. The plaint is brought forward in writing, copied, and read to the complainant; it is sealed with prepared clay, and an impression made in the clay by the complainant's nail. A synopsis of the plaint is sent to the defendant, who puts in his answer, which is copied and sealed. When the case is appointed for hearing, an attempt at conciliation is made; if it fail, the depositions on both sides are read. The witnesses may be examined as to their depositions. When the evidence is gone through, the subordinate judges give their opinions in writing; these are referred to the chief

---

* Pallegoix, i. 361.

judge, who pronounces the award: there are appeals from the lower to the higher courts, and, in all cases, to the King. The expense of an ordinary suit is from 12 to 30 ticals (30s. to 75s.): this is paid by the losing party.

Legal reasons for excluding witnesses are so many, that they would appear seriously to interfere with the collection of evidence. Those shut out by moral impediments are:—Drunkards, opium-smokers, gamblers, notorious vagabonds, goldsmiths, braziers, blacksmiths, shoemakers, executioners, beggars, potters, dancing women, women who have been thrice married, adulterers, clerks, orphans, players and tumblers, undutiful children, contemners of religion, slaves, intimate friends and inmates of parties concerned, quacks, strumpets, liars and sorcerers, personal enemies. Some of these exclusions are the result of ancient prejudices and traditions, especially those which refer to particular trades, as in the instance of potters, who are shut out in consequence of a murder committed on a virtuous man by a potter ages ago. A bad reputation attaches to the other excluded trades.

By physical causes:—Virgins and unmarried women, pregnant females, blind and deaf persons, persons above seventy or under seven years of age, persons on their deathbed, hermaphrodites, persons suffering under loathsome and cutaneous diseases. Midwives are excluded, probably because their services may be suddenly required.

By intellectual incapacities:—Persons who cannot read, persons who cannot reckon up to ten, persons ignorant of the law and of the eight cardinal sins (*i.e.*, idiots), persons who cannot distinguish right from wrong, persons excluded by mental incapacity from the priesthood, lunatics.

In contrast to these exclusions, the code directs that special weight shall be given to the evidence of priests and religious persons, to those learned in the law, to individuals of rank and good character, to laymen who have been in the priesthood, &c.

The following is a copy of the Siamese oath, or *Sapath*, which is administered to witnesses in the Siamese courts:—

"I, ——, who have been brought here as an evidence in this matter, do now, in the presence of the divine *P'hra P'hoott hee rop* (meaning Buddha), declare that I am wholly unprejudiced against either party, and uninfluenced in any way by the opinions or advice of others; and that no prospects of pecuniary advantage or of advancement to office have been held out to me: I also declare that I have not received any bribe on this occasion. If what I have now spoken be false, or if in my further averments I should colour or pervert the truth so as to lead the judgment of others astray, may the three holy existences, viz., Buddha, the Bali [personified], and the Hierarchy before whom I now stand, together with the glorious Devattas of the twenty-two firmaments, punish me.

"If I have not seen, yet shall say that I have seen— if I shall say that I know that which I do not know, then may I be thus punished:—Should innumerable descents of the Deity happen for the regeneration and salvation of mankind, may my erring and migrating soul be found beyond the pale of their mercy. Wherever I go, may I be encompassed by dangers and not escape from them, whether arising from murderers, robbers, spirits of the ground, of the forest, of the water, or of the air, or from all the T'hewatda [or divinities who adore Buddha], or from the gods of the four elements, and all other spirits. May blood flow out of every pore of my body, that my crime may be made manifest to the world. May all or any of these evils overtake me three days hence. Or may I never stir from the place on which I now stand; or may the Hatsanee ["lash of the sky"—viz., lightning] cut me in twain, so that I may be exposed to the derision of the people; or if I should be walking abroad, may I be torn in pieces by either of the four preternaturally-endowed lions, or destroyed by poisonous herbs or venomous snakes. If when in the water of the rivers or ocean, may chárákhe [or alligators], hera [the fabulous horned alligator], mang kan [a fabulous animal, which in Siamese astronomy represents Capricorn], maché [or large fishes], devour me; or may the winds or waves overwhelm me: or may the dread of such evils keep me during my life a prisoner at home, estranged from every pleasure; or may I be afflicted by the intolerable oppressions of my superiors; or may cholera morbus cause my death: after which, may I be precipitated into hell, there to go through innumerable stages of torture; amongst which, may I be condemned to carry water over the flaming regions in open wicker-baskets, to assuage the heat felt by Y-haan Wetsoo-wan, when he enters the infernal hall of justice, [he is one of the thirty judges in hell, who relieve each other alternately, and was once a king on earth,] and thereafter may I fall into the lowest pit of hell. Or if these miseries should not ensue, may I after death migrate into the body of a slave, and suffer all the hardships and pains attending the worst state of such a being during a period of years measured by the sands of the four seas: or may I animate the body of an animal or beast during five hundred generations; or be born an hermaphrodite five hundred times; or endure in the body of a deaf, blind, dumb, houseless beggar, every species of loathsome disease during the same number of generations: and then may I be hurried to narok [or hell], and then be crucified by P'hreea Yom [one of the kings of hell]."*

The *codes* contain many lessons to the judges, recommending them to enforce the claims of justice; to be impartial; to resist plausible and sophistical arguments; to follow the example of an illustrious rajah, a king of the Dog nation, who compelled his subjects to stuff their ears with cotton, lest they should be stunned when their country was invaded by the king of the nation of Lions. An unjust judge is to be cut on the forehead with a sword; to be exposed in the pillory; and if he shall falsify any document, to be imprisoned in chains. The King is required to furnish any ignorant judge with copies of the codes, so that he may not plead his unacquaintance with the law as an apology for his errors.

---

* The Siamese text of this oath is in *Jones' Grammatical Notices of the Siamese Language*, p. 68—71. It is extracted from a native volume on the Law of Evidence.

Coroners' Inquests.—When the body of a murdered person is found, the nearest officers of police gather together and inspect it. They seize all the suspected characters in the neighbourhood, who are detained in prison until the judges see fit to order their liberation. The heads of police are punished if within a certain time they are not on the track, or have not succeeded in arresting supposed offenders. The police are authorized to call upon the inhabitants to assist their search.

The capital punishment of nobles is extraordinary in Siam. They are put into a sack, and beaten to death in a public place. Such, a few years ago, was the fate of the son of the most powerful noble in the land, the present Somdetch, who was supposed to have been intriguing with one of the wives of the late King.

Coining is so common in Siam, that it is said more than one-tenth of the whole silver circulation (ticals) is spurious. On conviction, the man who blows the bellows is punished by having his right-hand fingers chopped off; he who forms the coin has his right hand cut off; he who impressed the King's mark will lose his right arm. These punishments were inflicted in a case which occurred just before I visited Siam.

Executions are rare; beheading is the common mode of their infliction. In case of murder or suicide, the houses within a circle of sixty fathoms from the spot where it has been committed are made responsible, and subjected to a heavy fine. Thus, there is a great anxiety to prevent quarrels terminating in bloodshed, and a general confederation to remove and to fling into the river any dead body that may be found, lest the neighbourhood be compromised.

Some offences are visited by very barbarous punishments. The penalty for melting an idol of gold or silver, stolen from a temple, is to be burnt alive. Adulterers are punished by marking with a hot iron on the cheeks, and the forehead is sometimes branded for other crimes. A bonze convicted of adultery is stripped in public of his yellow robes, flagellated till the blood springs, and condemned to cut grass for the royal elephants to the end of his days. This is one of the most infamizing punishments, from which the criminal is never redeemed. The *ta ven* is another punishment to which particular opprobrium attaches. The convict, loaded with chains, and wearing the *cangue*,* is marched through the principal streets of the town, preceded by cymbals and accompanied by police-officers; he is compelled to cry without ceasing, in a loud voice, "My crime is—[so and so]. Be warned by my example." When his voice is weak or silent, he is beaten with swords. He is thus escorted for three successive days through the town on foot, and three times in a boat round the city, subjected to the same conditions.

Murder is punishable with death: but executions, which are ordinarily by beheading or piercing the body with spears, are unfrequent. After death, the bodies are impaled, and left to be devoured by birds of prey.

I had no opportunity of visiting the interior of the prisons of Siam, of which I heard a miserable

---

* A collar of wood, fastened round the neck.

account from all who had obtained access. But the prisoners are mostly turned out by day, and employed in public works of all sorts. At night they are all fastened together by one long chain, and it is said they are so crowded that there is scarcely room for their bodies on the ground where they lie. Groups of criminals are constantly met with in the streets, bearing fetters from the lightest to the heaviest, and escorted by the police, armed with muskets or thick staves of bamboo. A majority of those who bear the least quantity of irons were said to be debtors, who could at any moment be redeemed on the payment of their debts; but no criminal convicted of any serious offence could be released without the interposition of the King. The worst convicts carry a collar of iron round the neck, handcuffs, leg-gyves, and an iron belt round the waist, to all which the cangue is sometimes superadded,—the sufferings caused by which depend upon the weight of the instrument.

Personal Relations, Successions, &c.—The practice of adoption is common in Siam. The first official person whom the King sent to me, on my arrival at Bangkok, was "an adopted son," who was the child of a deceased friend of his Majesty, and who had a considerable influence at Court, and was the depository of all the King's wishes. The terms of adoption are generally announced publicly by the adopter, and many enjoy all the privileges of an heir. A wife, with the husband's consent, or a widow, after his death, may adopt; and as the performance of funeral rites is expected from the heir of the deceased, it is natural that childless persons should provide for their becoming ministration.

Marriages are the subjects of much negotiation; but the contract is a civil, not a religious one, although the bonzes frequently take a part in the ceremonials — as, indeed, they do on most occasions of display. There are none of the difficulties of access between the sexes which frequently exist in Oriental countries; and there is little disposition on the part of the parents to force the marital engagement upon their children, when repugnant to them. Independently of the arrangements as to dowry, spontaneous gifts are made for the domestic comforts of the espoused. The bridegroom removes to the vicinity of the lady's residence, and she conveys his meals to him for three days before the marriage. The form pronounced is one taken from the *Pali* books,—" Be ye married, and live together until ye be separated by death." The rank of an unmarried woman is regulated by that of her father; of a married, by that of her husband. In Siam, women appear to take an active part in the direction of household affairs; but in the presence of their husbands (at least, when strangers are witnesses) they always appear prostrate. The deportment of married women is generally modest and decorous, exhibiting much timidity when foreigners approach, but less than Chinese women of rank ordinarily display.

Wives—Widows.—There are four classes of wives in Siam:—1st. The wife of royal gift, who takes precedence in rank. 2nd. The legal wife, who has been married according to the legal forms. 3rd. The wife of affection. 4th. The slave wife; that is, the handmaid with whom the owner has cohabited, and who, in consequence, becomes emancipated.

I imagine that this classification is rather the result of opinion than of legal *status*. I observed only two grades of wives among the Siamese, the first wife, and the subordinate and subsidiary wives. Marriage is only allowed beyond the seventh degree of blood affinity: a widow may marry her deceased husband's brother, and a widower his deceased wife's sister. The opprobrium of incontinence attaches to a woman on her *fourth* marriage; and her rights of inheritance are limited to the dowry she brought her husband, and to property personally acquired. A third of a man's property goes to his widows; but on the subdivision, a larger proportion to the legal wife. The ordinary period of marriage for men is about twenty; that of women, about fourteen. As regards Sovereigns, they may marry a sister or a daughter to preserve the royal race. The ancient Egyptians were not scrupulous on this head, nor are some other Oriental nations.[*] A wife may be pawned by her husband as security for a debt; but there is a power of protection, for, on public announcement from the wife that the affairs of the husband are becoming embarrassed, she cannot be made a victim of the consequences. Property is disposable by will or gifts, but, in case of intestacy, escheats to the King. In ordinary cases, it is divided into three parts—one of which goes to the

---

[*] Low, p. 347—50.

parents and grand-parents, one to the widow, and one to the children and near relations on the male side: if there be no ancestors or widow, the children and relatives divide the whole.

There is a registrar of the estates of deceased persons, and claims are expected to be put in before the obsequies are terminated. The claim must be personally put forward. Provision for the payment of outstanding debts must be made before the property is distributed. A Siamese leaving his country without the consent of his parents, forfeits his claim to their property; but the law is modified, if he prove his return to provide for their wants before death, and attended the administration of the funeral rites.* Traitors and rebels are excluded from the right of inheritance—slaves, of course. There are many forms as to the making gifts, so as to secure the heirs to property against being deprived of their rights; such as requirements that such gifts shall be made at certain periods before the death of the giver.

Low states that on the death of a minister, the King inherits one-fourth of the property, on the assumption that the public functions can in no instance have been honestly performed; and the remaining three-fourths are distributed in the usual manner. If among the wives there be any who have been bestowed by the King, she receives half a portion more than that which reverts to an ordinary wife. Three years' cohabitation are necessary to the establishment of a widow's claim; a wife emancipated by her husband

---

* Low, p. 345—6.

from slavery does not inherit—her children do. On the demise of a wife bestowed by the King, the King receives one-third of her property, her husband one-third, and the remaining third is partitioned among her relatives.*

All rights in a country whose government is absolutely despotic are, of course, held on sufferance. As regards the soil, a title is, however, created by the fact of a party having cleared it and brought it into cultivation, the produce being subject to the tax payable upon it. Authority must be obtained for clearing the land, and it becomes alienable and heritable. An old law, or recorded usage, gives to the cultivator a claim on the Sovereign of land for sowing, on the condition of paying a fourth of the gross produce; and the same record says that the Sovereign should lend money without interest to industrious and meritorious subjects.†

The great Chinese ceremonial of honouring agriculture by the Emperor's guiding the plough, and furrowing a portion of land, was formerly a Siamese custom; but it is delegated now to the keeper of the granaries. The Siamese hold that the condemnation of man to cultivate and harvest by the sweat of his brow, is the punishment of sins committed in a prior state of existence; and the failure of a crop is still attributable to the prevalence of sin, which leads the Supreme Intelligence to order that the grain, instead of multiplying upon earth, shall ascend spiritualized to heaven.

---

* Low, p. 351—3.
† Bali Meelent Nara Melinda Raja, quoted by Low, p. 337.

Commercial Laws.—The maximum rate of interest in Siam is six per cent. per month; but after three months the rate is reduced to three per cent. per month, which is the average rate: compound interest is not allowed. If money be borrowed on productive property, such as stores, cattle, carts, or articles which may be beneficially used by the parties to whom they are pledged, no interest is charged; but the ordinary mode of borrowing, is to pledge the person and property of the borrower.

The Pali code allows a Sovereign to charge seventy-five per cent. interest for money lent from the Treasury, and half that amount to private lenders; but when the sum of interest due reaches that of the capital lent, the interest ceases, unless on a new agreement. Money is borrowed on deposits placed in the hands of third parties. The deposit cannot be sold without the consent of the depositor, but may be transferred to other parties who will give effect to the original conditions. For effecting sales, bargain-money is usually paid down. The more important contracts are in writing, but the handwriting must be that of a disinterested person. Secret associations, according to Colonel Low,* are bound together by mingling the blood of the conspirators with arrack, salt, and chillies (capsicums); and the swords of the parties are rubbed with the mixture—swords which have been used in battle, and stained with the blood of an enemy, being preferred. All the spirits and deities are invoked to

---

* P. 393.

witness the contract, and to visit the perjurer with all imaginable evils; after which, the mystic compound is tasted by all the associates.

The following information respecting the state of slavery and slaves has been furnished me by a gentleman resident at Bangkok; and, as containing a more correct description of the laws which regulate and the position occupied by a large portion of the population of Siam, I have thought the details not unworthy of the reader's notice:—

"Throughout the whole of this paper I have used the terms 'slaves' and 'slavery' to express the Siamese words '*bau*' and '*b'at*.' I have used them in deference to the opinions of preceding writers, but I consider that some other words would much better express their meaning.

"The various classes of slaves were distinguished by a King of Siam who reigned in the year 1359, Siamese sacred era—that is, about 937 years ago. He divides them into seven classes; but as some of these bear a great resemblance to each other, I have taken the more common division, and make only three distinct classes:—

"1st. Slaves captured in war.
"2nd. Slaves by purchase.*
"3rd. Slaves by birth.

"I. Prisoners of war (now in Siam) may be divided into the following nations:—

---

* Slaves by debt, which at first sight might appear to be a separate class, will, upon closer inspection, be found to belong to this class.

"(1) Malays, amount to 5,000
(2) Cochin Chinese ,, ... 10,000
(3) Peguans ,, ... 10,000
(4) Laos ,, ... 20,000
(5) Burmese ,, ... 1,000*

"These nearly all belong to the Kings: some few are given to the principal nobles; but, even in that case, they are always considered as '*bau chauchawit,*' or 'King's men.'

"The Cochin Chinese mostly belong to the second King, the first King having a great antipathy to that people.

"The Malays and a few Peguans are employed as sailors—average pay eight ticals a month, whilst the serang gets from twenty to thirty ticals.

"The Cochin Chinese, some Malays and Peguans, and the Laos men, are employed as soldiers. Their pay, whilst on service, amounts to four ticals *per mensem*; they also get their rice during that time.

"They must serve three months during the year; the remaining nine they may employ as suits them best. Their children, if sons, become slaves to the King; if daughters, their parents are at liberty to sell them the same as Siamese.

"Of these nations, the Malays and Cochin Chinese hold a high character for honesty—the Burmese quite the reverse; in fact, the Burmese village of Kok-kwai, immediately below Bangkok, is so well known, that when a boat is stolen, the loser goes

---

* "The numbers here are different from what the Bishop gives; but this includes only the *fighting men*."

directly to Kok-kwai, and it is seldom that he fails to recover it for a consideration.

"All these various nations have small villages scattered about the country; for instance, the Malays at Ayuthia, the Peguans at Paklat, &c.

"King's men consider themselves decidedly superior to any other slaves, and presume considerably upon their fancied superiority.

"II. Slaves by purchase.

"These are divided into two classes,—redeemable and irredeemable. The latter class are not numerous; they are chiefly young girls sold by their parents. With these no security is given, and, as a natural consequence, more than four-fifths abscond when they get an opportunity, and the owner has no redress. They thus become rather a losing investment.

"We now come to the principal class of slaves in Siam,*—slaves by purchase, and redeemable. These are either sold by their parents, or sell themselves after having once been free. No one can sell a slave without his own consent.† Prices of slaves vary from eighty to one hundred and twenty ticals for men, and from sixty to one hundred for women. The method of selling and buying is very simple:— every slave has a paper; which paper his master retains, but must give it up whenever the slave pro-

---

* "The Bishop gives a third of the population as about the number of slaves. I suppose by this he includes Chinese, for there are distinctly much more than a third of Siamese who are slaves."

† "I stated this upon the authority of several very learned Siamese; but, upon looking over the laws, I found that it was not absolutely correct."

duces the amount mentioned in it. A copy of a female slave's paper is given in Bishop Pallegoix' book. The difference between that and a man's paper is very slight.

"'Wednesday,* the 7th day of the waning moon of the 11th month of the year 1217 of the little era (Chuulasakkarat). I, Kow, the husband, and Nu, the wife, sell our son Pau to L'uang Lurassakon, for the sum of one hundred ticals; our son being the slave of no one else, nor of the King. For the truth of which I hold myself responsible; and if the said Pau should run away, I hold myself responsible for him.'

"Such is the bill of sale; but as nearly always the father and mother are slaves, some other surety is required, which is given in another paper.

"Anything that the slave may break, or whatever money he may borrow from his master, is added to the original amount; so that we have instances where the papers represent four hundred ticals.†

"Masters are bound to furnish rice and salt fish, but not clothes; and it has always remained a mystery to me how they ever manage to get new sarongs. The only way I can suggest is, that sometimes they manage to pick up a stray fowl or duck; or if they are hired out, sometimes the master will, in an excess of generosity, throw them an old *panlung*.

"III. The position of slaves by birth differs in no

---

* "Nine-tenths of the documents are dated Wednesday, even if the agreements are made on another day."
† "Redeemable slaves are said to be bought '*K'ai fak;*' irredeemable, '*K'ai kat.*'"

respect from that of slaves by purchase; the treatment is the same, and the mode of purchase, with the exception that there is a fixed price for them when they reach manhood, viz., forty-eight ticals.

"The laws with reference to this class of slaves are so accurately defined, that it is not necessary for me to say any more respecting them.

"I will now proceed to make a few remarks upon slavery in Siam, and endeavour to give my reasons why it cannot, with reference to the two last classes, be considered as slavery in the European sense of the word.

"Bishop Pallegoix states that slaves are 'well treated in Siam—as well as servants are in France;' and I, from what I have seen, would be inclined to go even farther, and say, better than servants are treated in England. This is proved by the fact that whenever they are emancipated, they always sell themselves again. Masters cannot ill-treat their slaves, for they have always the remedy of paying the money they represent; and he must be a very worthless character who cannot get somebody to advance the sum. If they are treated harshly, you may make certain that generally it is the man's own fault. The only punishment which can be considered severe is the being put 'into chains;' and this is rarely done until every other means have been tried. If no improvement takes place from this last punishment, the slave is handed over to the King, and takes his place with the convicts—a punishment to which death itself is far preferable. But these are men whose crimes would be as heavily punished in England. It is true, there is no trial required; but no man is so foolish as to lose his slave unless there are weighty reasons for so doing.

"In small families, the slaves are treated like the children of the masters; they are consulted in all matters, and each man feels that as his master is prosperous, so is he. The slaves, on the other hand, are faithful, and when their master is poor, will devote every *fuang* they can beg or steal to his necessities, and, as long as he will keep them, will pass through any amount of hardship. Seldom do you see such attachment between masters and *paid* servants in England.

"Despite of what the Bishop says about the humanity and virtues of the Roman Catholics in Siam, I believe that no slaves are so ill treated as those of Christians; and he should, when mentioning the cruelties practised upon Christian slaves by the Siamese, have made some mention of the opposite case.

"The principal hardship that slaves suffer is an insufficiency of food; and as their food is so simple, they require plenty of it—and they certainly do consume an enormous quantity.

"Men purchased '*K'ai fak*' cannot be considered slaves, as they have the power of redemption in their own hands.

"That the slave is a simple debtor, and gives his services for the interest of the money lent, may be proved from the fact, that the surety, in case of the man dying while in your service, must refund to you the original sum; that if a man is sick, and is attended to in his master's house, the surety is liable for the interest during the time of the man's illness; that men may borrow money upon interest, and live apart from their master's house, and yet in some cases they are liable as his servants. If we consider them, then, as debtors, we shall probably be correct; and especially as the rate of interest in Siam is about thirty per cent., it does not appear astonishing that a man should prefer working to paying such an extortionate rate.

"*Laws of Slavery.*—There are seven classes of slaves—viz.,

"1. Bought with money. 2. By birth. 3. Left by legacy. 4. By gift. 5. Those who become so from gratitude. 6. Voluntary slaves in time of famine. 7. Prisoners of war.

"These seven classes may be claimed, and compelled to work.

"The following six classes cannot be compelled to work:—

"1. Manumitted slaves. 2. Those slaves whom the master has allowed to become talapoins. 3. Those whom their master has given to the talapoins. 4. When the master himself has become a priest. 5. Those who come to live round the man's house. 6. Those who come to live upon his lands.*

---

* "Useless as these two last clauses may appear, yet they are often infringed in a country where might is right."

" Slaves bought with money are subdivided into three classes:—

" (*a.*) Those slaves who are free by payment of the debt. [These must have a security.]

" (*b.*) Those who are bought irredeemably. [These have no security.]

" (*c.*) Those who pay interest and do not work.

" Husbands may sell their wives, parents their children, masters their servants.

" When children are sold under the full value, they must not be beaten till they bleed.

" When slaves *K'ai fak* (*a*) take their master's place in prison, half their money must be remitted; but if they are *K'ai kat* (*b*), no part is to be remitted.*

" If a man sell a slave, and after receiving the money refuse to give up the man, he shall pay twice the price,—three quarters to the buyer, and one quarter to the Government.

" If a buyer disapprove of a slave before three months have elapsed, he may claim back his money. If a master strike a slave so that he die, no claim can be had upon the surety, and the master shall be punished according to law.

" Anything that the slave shall break after the money has been paid, shall be added to the redemption-money paper.

---

* " It is a very common thing, when masters have been arrested for debt, to make their slaves take their place till they can collect sufficient money. I never heard, however, of any slave having had any portion of his redemption-money remitted for it."

"If, in minding cattle, he should be negligent, and they be lost, he shall pay; but if more be given than he can possibly look after, he shall pay half. But if robbers *bind* him, and steal the cattle, he is not liable.

" Any claim against the slave must be made before he is sold to another master.

" If a master insist upon a female slave marrying against her will, half her redemption-money must be remitted.

" If a slave go to war in lieu of his master, or by the King's command, and fight there, all his redemption-money must be remitted: if he do not fight, half must be remitted.

"If a slave be placed to plant rice, &c., he cannot leave until the season be finished.

" If a master sell a slave, and then repurchase him, if the master dies, only half can be demanded from the slave.

" If, when rice is dear, a slave sells himself below the standard price (forty-eight ticals for women, and fifty-six for men), when rice gets cheap, his price shall be raised to the standard.

" If a slave injure himself when at work, compensation shall be allowed according to the amount of injury.

" If a slave die in defence of his master, nothing can be demanded from the security.

" In case of any epidemic, and the relations of the slave who is ill with it attend him, nothing can be demanded.

" If a merchant have a slave who has been in the

habit of collecting accounts and selling goods for his owner, and that slave abscond with money received on his master's account, his master cannot claim; or if he has bought goods on his master's account, the seller cannot claim.

"If a man have several wives, the smaller selling themselves to the higher wives, no interest can be claimed, as they are all considered sisters.

"If a master wishes to get rid of a slave and cannot, he may take him to the judges; and if they cannot sell him within three days, and another person buys him after that time, he must be '*K'ai kat.*'

"The children of slaves who are relatives of the master are free.

"If a slave run away, the money expended in apprehending him must be added to his account.

"Slaves having children, the children must be charged for according to age.

"If the parent's price is below twenty-four ticals each, their children are not considered slaves.

"If a slave quarrel with his master, the judges will not receive his complaint until he has paid his money, unless it is a serious charge.

"If a slave makes money while in service, at his death it goes to his master; but if he had money before, it goes to his relatives.

"If a slave accuse his master of capital crimes falsely, he has his lips cut off; but if the charge is true, he receives his freedom. Children always accompany the mother.

" Two slaves, husband and wife, having their names on the same paper, if one of them run away, the other can be charged.

" I have given, I think, all the important laws, and in general they are literally translated,—for the greatest part of which I have to thank Mr. Hunter."

CHAPTER VI.

NATURAL PRODUCTIONS.

Vegetables.

AS regards the productions of Siam for the consumption of its people, and for the supply of foreign countries, the state of agriculture is generally rude and backward. Few or none of the instruments which represent the application of science to the culture of the land are to be found in Siam,— a country whose rural population is comparatively small—whose soil, spontaneously creative alike from its alluvial character, and from an abundance of water and of sunbeams to give vegetation every possible impetus, rewards the cultivator by large harvests for a small outlay of capital or labour. Immense tracts remain to be recovered from the jungle; and there can be no doubt that, under the influence of peace and commerce, vast districts will be subjected to the beneficent sway of the husbandman. China, that has already poured her millions of men into Siam, is at hand to provide from her teeming and superfluous multitudes the principal element wanting for the full development of the territorial opulence of Siam; while the presiding presence of European settlers will no doubt furnish the appliances which knowledge, wealth, and civilization are able to bring to regions so inviting.

Though there is much land occupied by the Chinese where the state and mode of agricultural cultivation resemble that exhibited in the " middle kingdom," from whence the settlers came, the general condition of the productive land is far less favourable than in China. China, indeed, in all her populous provinces, represents, under the action of an immense repartition of property, and the presence of a superabundant supply of hands, a surface rather resembling a continuity of gardens than of fields or meadows. It is horticulture more than agriculture—at all events, in the adjacency of cities and large towns, which afford cheap and abundant supplies of manure, whose value is thoroughly appreciated by the cultivator.

In many parts of Siam, the land is prepared during the rainy season by turning in herds of buffaloes to trample down the weeds and move the soil, which is afterwards harrowed by a coarse rake, or a bush of thorny shrubs. The seed is then broadcast upon the surface. But wherever the Chinese are established, they introduce their native usages and improvements.

I do not feel myself competent to present a complete catalogue of the natural productions of Siam, and I shall principally notice those which more peculiarly characterize the country, or which excited my special attention. In its great outlines, the animal, mineral, and vegetable world resembles that of other tropical regions, though in every part of the field there are varieties in detail which belong to the domain of the naturalist. They will become in time the objects of particular attention, and no portion of the East is probably so inviting as the Siamese regions, from their extent, their richness, and their novelty. There is, indeed, almost everything to explore; and the inquirer may now " expatiate boldly," with a certainty of having a full recompence for his exertions and investigations.

The production of *rice* is estimated at twenty-five thousand tons. Rice is sold by the coyan of one hundred baskets: a basket is supposed to be sufficient for the food of a man during a month. The ordinary cost of a basket is about $7\frac{1}{2}d$. sterling.* The extent of cultivable rice-land is capable of being doubled or trebled: there is now only one rice-harvest in a year, and there might well be two. There can be little doubt that Siam is able to provide a supply of one hundred thousand tons of rice per annum by improved and extended cultivation.

Moor says,—" The rice of Siam is equally famed with its sugar. Rice is produced in immense quantities all along the banks of the river, in a rich alluvial soil, irrigated by the waters of the Menam. The exportation of this article is prohibited; notwithstanding which, it finds its way to Singapore and other parts in the Straits. At Singapore, I once had an opportunity of seeing the rice of Manilla, Java, Bengal, Cochin China, Siam, and Queda, all exhibited at the same time; and, if I recollect right, that of Siam was pronounced to be superior to all the rest."†

---

* Mr. Low says that the medium price of a measure of rice of $31\frac{1}{4}$ gallons is $3s$. sterling. P. 341.
† *Notices Ind. Arch.*, p. 236.

The removal of the prohibition on the export of rice is one of the great benefits conferred by the late treaty. It is now allowed to leave the country, unless a royal ordinance shall proclaim the existence of a dearth; but as already the prospect of large foreign demands is extending the field of cultivation, free trade in this all-important article will certainly give more security against the visitations of famine than could ever be hoped for from any restriction upon its exportation.

The present amount of *sugar* produced is very large, and it may be increased indefinitely with the demand. " It is produced almost everywhere in the kingdom, under the direction of the Chinese settlers. Its quality, which yields to that of no sugar in the world, is too well known for me to enlarge upon it in this place. The principal part of it is sent to China, and the Americans have lately taken away several shiploads of it."[*]

There are extensive sugar plantations in the province of Nakhon-Xaisi. Pallegoix counted more than thirty manufactories, each employing from two to three hundred workmen, almost all Chinese. Among these the Catholic missionaries have met with much success. On one occasion the governor threatened to burn their church, but the King interfered for its protection.

Sugar is largely manufactured in various other parts of Siam. The principal establishments are the property of the Chinese. The manufacture is carried on

---

[*] Moor's *Ind. Arch.*, p. 236.

in very primitive style: the motive power consists of buffaloes; the cane is crushed between two cylinders of hard wood. Large fires are applied to the enormous vessels in which the juice is subjected to evaporation; and when it has reached the required consistency, it is poured into cones made of clay. Quicklime is employed for the purification of the saccharine matter. A single building generally serves, not only for the manufacture of the sugar, but for the abode of all the labourers employed.

Sugar will probably become the most important of all the exports of Siam. The soil is admirably adapted to its cultivation.

Aquila or *eagle wood* (lignum aloes) is known for its fragrance, especially when burnt. Many medicinal virtues are attributed to it by the Siamese, who employ it to cure a great variety of diseases. Only one species of tree contains the odorous element. The natives go forth into the woods to seek it, provided with saws, hatchets, and scissors, of various forms. When by certain signs they have discovered the tree of which they are in search, they fell it, saw it into fragments, which they examine with great care, and throwing aside the white, they only preserve the dark wood, which is obtained in various shapes, and is sold at about ten shillings per pound. Every Christian family in the districts where it grows is bound to pay to the King a tribute of two pounds weight of eagle-wood. This wood is " an article of great consumption as a perfume among the nations of Eastern Asia, who use it in all their funeral, marriage, and other ceremonies. It is the diseased part of a tree, and, perhaps, is only to be found in one tree in twenty, and in that one only in a very small quantity. The labourers employed in finding it frequently cut up several trees before they find the smallest portion of it. It is principally found in the islands situated in the Gulf of Cambodia."*

Gutta-percha has of late years become an important article of commerce. The remarkable qualities of this extraordinary and valuable gum are generally appreciated in its application to so many purposes of manufacture, art, and science. The tree grows in the maritime districts of Siam; and the gutta-percha which used to be sold at about five dollars a hundredweight, fetches now five or six times that price.

Cardamums are the produce of a tree of about a man's height: at the end of the branches grow groups of flowers, which produce the three-lobed fruit with whose aromatic and piquant taste we are familiar.

Gamboge is extracted by an incision in the tree, whence the gum flows into a hollow bamboo, which when filled is withdrawn and broken, and the gum being thoroughly hardened, is taken out.

The *bamboo* performs among the Siamese a great portion of the multitudinous services which the still more ingenious and inventive inhabitants of China have extracted from it. It is employed for building, for baskets, mats, and vessels of every sort. In some shape or other, it is used for food,† for clothing,

---

* Moor's *Notices Ind. Arch.*, p. 236.
† The ancients were not unacquainted with its use. See Ælian, lib. iv. cap. 34.

for shelter, for navigation, for comfort, for ornament. It is the plant alike of the utilitarian and the poet,—one perpetually turning to account its infinite variety of uses, the other celebrating its multifarious beauties: it is the raw material of the shipwright and the builder, the tool-maker and the carver; out of it are constructed instruments of music and weapons of war. The hardness of the wood, the facility with which it is split into the minutest threads, the straightness and regularity of its fibres, its smoothness of surface, the rapidity of its growth, all add to its value. It lends itself from the most exquisite and minute carving to the coarsest usages of the crate and the hurdle, collecting, conveying, or distributing every species of fluid. It supplies fire by friction, and is the great water-conductor, being an almost ready-formed conduit. In some species, the knots or separations in the stalk are distant six or seven feet; in others they are adjacent. For boxes, for nets, for cordage, for thread, for numerous implements and instruments, it is the ever-present material. Perhaps, amidst the many gifts of Providence to a tropical region, the bamboo is the most benignant, appropriate, and accessible. The author, the sculptor, the architect, and the painter have all laid it under contribution in the field of imagination and the development of art; and if the camel is characteristic of the desert, the bamboo may be considered typical of the Indo-Chinese nations. Its leaves, its stems, its branches, its roots, all contribute to multitudinous objects, a detailed description of which would fill thousands of pages.

Next to the *bamboo*, the *rattan* has place for the services it renders to the community. Its formidable prickles furnish an excellent fence; it interlaces its long stalks with the forest-trees, and these are often the most valuable from their length and strength.

The drug called dragon's blood is the produce of one of the varieties of the rattan. Its tenacity, its polish, its flexibility, the ease with which its fibres are separated into any size, render it invaluable for twine and cordage, for sofas and chairs, for trellis-work, for sieves, panniers, baskets, mats, for every species of ligatures; and last, but certainly not least, for the castigation of malefactors and slaves.*

The tree called *rak* by the Siamese is a species of banana, and furnishes the beautiful varnish so much valued in the lacquer-ware of China. Incisions are made in the bark, from whence exudes a thick, viscid, dirty-white gum, which is passed through a cloth, and put into jars of water, in which it is preserved from drying by contact with the air. This varnish is so caustic, that not only does it burn and ulcerate the skin, but its vapours produce inflammation of the eyes, and pustules on the face. When exposed to the air, it becomes first brown, and then intensely black. It is used for book-covers, baskets, furniture, and especially for gilt idols. It is neither affected by sun nor rain. Pallegoix expresses surprise that it has not been employed in Europe as a protection for gilded works, which so soon perish when exposed to the fluctuations of the seasons.

* Pallegoix, i. 143.

The fan-palm grows to an immense height in Siam. It produces fruit after fifteen years, and lives to an incredible age. Amidst the fan-shaped leaves which crown the top of the tree, branches of fruit, which is used for food, are produced in the shape of almonds. During the flowering season, an incision is made at the foot of the blossoms, to which a hollow bamboo is suspended, and a sweet liquid exudes. It becomes intoxicating in twenty-four hours; but if immediately evaporated, it gives an uncrystallizable sugar, which is sold in earthen pots. The fan-palm produces the leaves which are employed for writing.

The cocoa-nut palm is very abundant. The white pulp of the fruit is rasped, kneaded in hot water, and the juice being expressed through a piece of cloth, is much used for making cakes. When boiled, this juice is converted into an oleaginous substance, which becomes speedily rancid.

The sago-palm is also a native of Siam, but is principally found on the Malayan side. Boiled with sugar and the milk of the cocoa-nut, it is much esteemed.

The *curcuma*, or Indian saffron, is a bulbous, fleshy root, of a deep golden colour, and an aromatic smell. It is reduced to a fine powder, and employed to colour the skins of women and children. In the morning, Siamese mothers may be seen industriously engaged in *yellowing* their offspring from head to heel. So universal is the custom, that in caressing the children of the Kings or the nobles, you may be certain to carry away yellow stains upon your dress. A small quantity mingled with quicklime makes a paste of a bright pink colour, of which the consumption is so large for spreading on the betel leaves which are used to wrap round the areca nut, that I have seen whole boat-loads moving about for sale amidst the floating bazaars on the Meinam. Curcuma is known to be the colouring matter in the curries, mulligatawnies, and chutnees of India.

A plant called *guncha*, which possesses many of the intoxicating properties of opium, is grown abundantly and consumed largely in Siam. It is smoked, and its effects, at first exhilarating and sometimes even infuriating, are followed, after three or four hours, by deep sleep, ultimately producing a train of diseases similar to those which the inordinate use of opium creates. The consumption of this latter drug in Siam is large, but principally among the Chinese population. The importation is said to amount annually to about twelve hundred chests, but I saw no reason to suppose that it is much used by the Siamese people; indeed, the cost of the luxury must, to a great extent, be prohibitory.

The following is the account given by La Loubère of the fruits of Siam. Since he wrote, Europeans have become familiarized with many of the fruits he describes, such as the pine-apple, the tamarind, the cocoa-nut, and even the banana. In addition to the fruits described by La Loubère, we found many which have no doubt been introduced since his time, such as the mangosteen from the Straits, the lichee from China; and no doubt we should have discovered many others, had our stay been prolonged.

" The Indian figs, which the Siamese call elephants'

trunks (*clouey-ngouan chang*), have not the taste of our figs, and are, in my opinion, not so good. The Siamese melons likewise are not real melons, but the fruit of a tree known in the American Islands by the name of papaya. The fig is of the size and shape of a sausage. The green skin, which becomes dark, separates easily from the flesh; and it has none of those little pips which are like specks of gravel in our figs. Its taste is strong, and is at the same time sour and sweet.

"The banana the Siamese call *clouey-ngau-chang*, or elephant's tooth; it is longer and greener than the fig. These fruits hang in bunches from the top of the trees. The bananas exposed to heat become like dried apples.

"The guava, (in Siamese, *loue kiae*) is about the size of an apple. The skin is greyish green, and beneath it the fruit is about the consistence of a lemon, but not so white. It at first tastes like strawberries, but it is much stronger. This flesh is of the thickness of a crown-piece, and contains a liquid full of little pips.

"The jac (in Siamese, *ca-noun*) is of the shape of a large melon. They have a grey skin, and contain a great number of pips or kernels, which are about the size of a pigeon's egg. These, when roasted, are like our chestnuts. The fruit is yellow and succulent, of a sweet taste and a powerful smell.

"They preserve a fruit like plums; it has the taste of a medlar, and has sometimes two and three stones, larger than those of the medlar. They call it *moussidà*.

" The heart-of-beef is so called from its size and shape; the skin is thin, and within it there is a material like white cream, very pleasant. They call it *mancout.*

" The *durian* (in Siamese, *tourrien*) has a most disagreeable odour. It is of the size of a melon, covered with prickles. It contains several shells, within which is the fruit; and fewer of these shells the better is the fruit, but there are rarely fewer than three.

" The *mango* (in Siamese, *ma moüan*) has the taste of the peach and apricot, but stronger. They are sometimes as big as a child's hand; they are flat and oval, in the shape of an almond. The skin is like that of a nectarine, with a yellowish colour; and the fruit itself is like a pulp, and covers a large stone.

" The Siamese have acid fruits with which they quench their thirst; they are in the shape of plums.

" The tamarind is also sour, and has a covering like the almond, and many of them again are inside a husk. The syrup is very agreeable, but receives the taste of the pimpernel by long keeping.

" I speak nothing about sugar or pepper, as I have not seen them. The pepper hangs down in little berries like currants.

" The anana (in Siamese, *separat*) tastes like our nectarine. They say it is unhealthy, as its juice eats into iron. Its shape is that of a large fir-apple. The plant which produces it is only three feet high. Sometimes there spring from the large one, one or two smaller fruits. Each plant bears but one fruit.

" The coco (in Siamese, *ma pr'au*) is a nut, but very large. In the wood of the coco is a very agreeable liquor, which, as the fruit ripens, congeals, and forms a very agreeable beverage." *

The *durian* is deemed by the Siamese the king of fruits. Its smell is offensive to European sense, and I have heard it compared to the stink of carrion and onions mingled. But the exquisite flavour of the fruit renders even its fragrance attractive to its *habitués*, and it is the only fruit which has ever a considerable money-value in the Siamese market. It is the produce of a fine tree, whose branches stretch out almost horizontally. The durian is of the size of a melon, covered with sharp pyramidical points, more prominent than those of the pine-apple. The external skin opens spontaneously when it is ripe, and the interior consists of four lobes, of a creamy consistence and a whitish colour, in which are nuts more or less in number. The Siamese, who are passionate gamblers, make the quantity of nuts to be found in a durian the constant subject of their betting.† João de Barros places the passion for the

---

* La Loubère, vol. ii., p. 84.

† The following curious notice of the "duriaoen" is given in Linschotten's *Travels*:—

"In Malacca there is a fruit so pleasant, both for taste and smell, that it excelleth all other fruites, both of India and Malacca, although there are many both excellent and very good. This fruit is called in Malayo (which is the province wherein it groweth) *duriaoen*, and the blossomes *buaa*, and the tree *batan*. It is a very great tree, of solide and firme wood, with a grey barke, having many branches, and excessive great store of fruit: the blossome is white and somewhat yellow; the leaves halfe a handfull long, and two or three fingers broad, rounde, and somewhat hollowe; outwardly darke greene, and inwardly light greene, and some-what after a red colour. It beareth a fruit of the bignes of a *mellon*, covered with a harde husk, with many small and thicke sharpe prickles; outwardly greene, and with strikes downe along the sides like the *mellon*. They have within them foure holes, or partitions, according to the length thereof, in each of the which holes are yet three or foure cases; in each

durian as almost on a level with the attractions of the " mogas Malacas,"—the dark Malayan maidens.

Mangosteens are produced contemporaneously with durians, and are generally eaten after them. The Siamese consider the durian a heating fruit, and that it is desirable to temper its action by the delicious and refreshing mangosteen. This beautiful fruit grows on a leafy tree, which rises to the height of fourteen to fifteen feet. The fruit, of the size of a small orange, is contained in a smooth shell, of a deep mahogany colour; the number of its internal lobes being marked by a sort of star at the top, which look as if they had been artificially carved upon the shell. The inside of the shell is of a bright red, and surrounds a fruit of snowy whiteness, divided into

case, or shell, a fruite as white as milke, and as great as a hennes egge, but better of taste and sauour, like the white meat which the Spaniards make of ryce, capons flesh, and rose-water, called *mangiar blanco*, yet not so soft or slymie; for the other that are yellow, and not white within, are either spoyled or rotten, by evil aire or moysture: they are accounted the best which have but three nuttes in each hole, next them those that have foure, but those of five are not good, and such as have any cracks or cliftes in them.

"This fruit is hot and moist; and such as will eat them must first treade upon them softly with his foote, and breake the prickes that are about them. Such as neuer eate of it before, when they smell it at the first, thinke it senteth like a rotten onyon; but having tasted it, they esteeme it above all other fruites, both for taste and sauour. Here you must note a wonderful contrarietie that is between this fruit *duriaoen* and the hearbe *bettele;* which in truth is so great, that if there were a whole shippe, shoppe, or house full of *duriaoens*, wherein there lay certaine leaves of *bettele*, all the *duriaoens* would presently rotte and bee spoyled. And likewise by eating over many of those *duriaoens*, they heat the maw, and make it swell; and one leafe of *bettele*, to the contrairie, being laide colde upon the hart, will presently cease the inflammation, rising or swelling of the maw. And so if, after you have eaten *duriaoens*, you chance to eat a leafe or two of *bettele*, you can receive no hurt by the *duriaoens*, although you have eaten neuer so many. Hereupon, and because they are of so pleasant a taste, the common saying is, that men can neuer be satisfied with them."

segments, some of the larger of which have seeds in the centre. The mangosteen has the reputation of possessing the flavour of the strawberry and the fragrance of the raspberry. It may be eaten in large quantities with safety, and is, perhaps, on the whole, the most popular of tropical fruits. The shell is used as an astringent in cases of dysentery, and as a mordant for fixing a black colour in dyeing.

The *jack* is to the durian what coarse earthenware is to porcelain. There are two species of the jack-tree in Siam, the fruit of both of which is used for food. The first has long deeply-serrated leaves, and bears a huge oval fruit, sometimes as large as a man's head. Under a thick skin there is a mealy and fibrous pulp, which is succulent, but somewhat laxative when fully ripe. The fruit is gathered before it reaches its complete maturity, when its flesh is white and firm. It is roasted, or boiled in water, scraped, and eaten without any condiment. It is a healthy and agreeable food, something resembling wheaten bread in taste: it is often cut into slices and cooked in sauce of palm-sugar with cocoa-nut milk.

The second species of *jack* is a fine oval-leaved tree, whose trunk, of a bright yellow, is used for dyeing the garments of the priests. Its enormous fruits sometimes weigh from ten to forty pounds, and are attached either to the trunk, or the larger branches capable of supporting them. The fruit is cut into thick slices, and large nuts are taken out, enveloped with a yellow, thick, and odorous pulp, which is then eaten: the nuts being roasted or grilled like chesnuts, are liked by children. A single fruit will suffice for the meal of fifteen to twenty persons, and a single tree will produce a hundred of such fruits in a year.

The *mangos* of Siam are excellent: there is a species called the durian mango which is superlatively so. Some of the mango-trees grow to the height of from thirty to forty feet. The fruit resembles in shape a flattened egg. It has rather a thick skin, which is easily removed, and has beneath it a golden, fragrant, and delicious pulp, of the consistency of a peach or pear. It is a wholesome fruit; when half ripe, it makes an excellent and appetite-exciting pickle.

The *tamarind* grows to an enormous size, and lives for centuries. Under its shade the Siamese are accustomed to assemble for most of their social games. Its young leaves are used for seasoning ragouts; its pods contribute to almost every Siamese dish. When the seeds are removed, the pulp may be preserved for a whole year: it is much valued for medicine.

The *guava*, the *papay*, the *plantain*—the orange, of which there are twenty varieties—lemons, citrons, *pomelos*, pomegranates, jujubes, pine-apples—are in abundance.

The plantain, or banana, deserves special mention, as the Siamese say there are no less than fifty sorts, in size from a little finger up to an elephant's tusk, sweetish, sugary, acid, succulent, mealy, fragrant—in many varieties of odours and flavours. It is the first fruit given to children at the breast. Mahomedans say the plantain was sent by Allah to the Prophet, when he lost his teeth in his old age. It grows at every period of the year, and is eaten by everybody, whatever his rank or station. The green plantain leaves are employed for a thousand domestic uses; they make coverings and wrappers, whether loose or sewed into many shapes, and give to everything a character of spring-like freshness.

The *makok* produces a sharp and acid fruit; after eating which, if water is drunk, a sweet taste is left in the mouth and palate, which remains for a whole day. Under the tree called the Indian poplar, Somanakhodom is said to have indulged his divers contemplations, and by religious exercises to have reached that sanctity which made him a Buddha. Hence the tree has the same holy character in Siam which the Hindus give to the *ficus religiosa*, a tree also found in Siam. The wild vine produces grapes, of which a bunch sometimes weighs as much as from ten to fifteen pounds. Pallegoix says that a tolerably good wine is made of this fruit, but I had no opportunity of tasting it in Siam.

Other fruits excited our attention: the rose-coloured *jambo*, fragrant as a rose, and esteemed for its medicinal qualities; the *maprang*, a species of plum, yellow or gold, with a fibrous nut instead of a stone; the *hamut sida*, reddish brown, with a sweet pulp around a smooth nut; the *takhob*, a hairy plum, having a green pulp filled with small seeds, which are eaten with it. There are several varieties of the *lichee*, probably introduced from China: one of the species is so attractive to the bats, that it is necessary to protect every bunch in a net-work of bamboo to prevent its being devoured by them.

The *rambutan* is well known in the Straits settlements. The *sathon* is of the size of a peach, its flesh acid but pleasant; its thick and fleshy skin is made into preserves. The *makhuit*, round as a ball, with a hard, white, ligneous shell, contains a sort of apple-marmalade mixed with small seeds. The shell of the *matum* is still harder, and can only be broken with a hammer; within is a yellow viscous jelly, with a balsamic perfume.

The most common vegetables are maize, cucumbers, gourds, radishes, cabbages, mustard, lettuces, melons and water-melons, tomatoes, celery, mint, parsley, chervil, cummin, coriander, garlic, onions, leeks, peas, beans, and a great variety peculiar to the tropics and to Siam itself. The sweet potato and the yam abound; the latter grows to the weight of twenty to thirty pounds. Many nutritious roots are cultivated, and others grow wild. The *kloi* is remarkable for its snowy whiteness, but it is poisonous until cut in slices, steeped in water, and exposed to the sun.

A root which Pallegoix calls the ground pistachio produces a quantity of almond-shaped nuts, which are employed for making cakes, and from which an oil is expressed for domestic use. The oil of the small *sesamé* is employed for the same purposes.

The *nïeng-lak*, a large tree, bears a minute fruit, of which a pinch being put into a glass of water, suddenly swells, impregnates the water, and gives it a refreshing and agreeable taste.

The seeds of the lotus, the aquatic chesnut, a water-lily whose stalks when cut grow so rapidly as to be visible to the naked eye, and a fleshy cress that floats upon the ponds, are among the most appreciated vegetable food.

There is an enormous demand, and of course a vast production, of fragrant flowers in Siam. They are used in the religious services of the temples, for the adorning the persons of women and children, for domestic ornaments, for presents to guests; they are largely employed in all processions and ceremonials, and their cultivation is an object of primary attention to the peasantry.

The *lotus*, among all the Buddhist nations, is the sacred and the favoured flower. In Siam there are seven varieties. The smallest has a white flower scarcely larger than a daisy, and is found in rivers, principally at the time of inundations. Its stems are esculent, and are eaten both raw and cooked. The red lotus serves only to ornament ponds. There are lotus-flowers (nymphæa), blue, green, light, and dark yellow; but they are rare. The great lotus is a magnificent rose-coloured flower, whose golden stamina breathe a delicious fragrance. It is the ornament of all festivities, and is sent habitually as an offering to the King, the priests, and to Buddha himself. When the flower is impregnated, it produces from seven to eight nuts, which are surrounded with green pulp. These nuts, boiled or grilled, are considered a great delicacy. The seeds of the nymphæa are placed in balls of soft earth, which are flung into ponds; and soon small leaves develop themselves on the surface of the water, and continue to increase in size to the extent of a foot in diameter.

The *mali* is a fragrant flower, growing on a shrub

of about a yard high. There are gardens around Bangkok wholly devoted to its cultivation. It is of the size of a small pink, of the purest white, and is always gathered before it is fully opened, to preserve its rich odours. With it water is perfumed, and medicine made palatable; the wreaths and topknots worn by children are braided from this flower, and it is used for necklaces and bracelets, and often presented to guests in garlands which are hung upon the arm or carried in the hand. I have received these flowers in purses of silk, or of silver, from the Kings and the nobles of Siam. They are presented in a variety of shapes, concealed under gauze, or sheltered beneath cases made of the banana leaf; sometimes they are suspended in festoons from the mosquito curtains of your bed, or placed on your table in vessels of silver.

A yellow flower, called the *champa*, is one of the most fragrant; it is almost always worn behind the ears of children, and it gives variety to the garlands which are so commonly distributed. A single *champa* will fill a room with its odour.

The *kadanga* is a flower from whose calyx four yellow petals hang, diffusing a sweet perfume, and rendering an essential oil. The *phut*, which somewhat resembles a white rose, is also a favourite and fragrant garden-flower.*

Animals.

Elephants are abundant in the forests of Siam, and grow sometimes to the height of twelve or

---

* Pallegoix, i. 147—8.

thirteen feet. The habits of the elephant are gregarious; but though he does not willingly attack a man, he is avoided as dangerous; and a troop of elephants will, when going down to a river to drink, submerge a boat and its passengers. The destruction even of the wild elephant is prohibited by Royal orders, yet many are surreptitiously destroyed for the sake of their tusks. At a certain time of the year, tame female elephants are let loose in the forests. They are recalled by the sound of a horn, and return accompanied by wild males, whom they compel, by blows of the proboscis, to enter the walled prisons which have been prepared for their capture. The process of taming commences by keeping them for several days without food; then a cord is passed round their feet, and they are attached to a strong column. The delicacies of which they are most fond are then supplied them, such as sugar-canes, plantains, and fresh herbs; and at the end of a few days the animal is domesticated and resigned to his fate.

Without the aid of the elephant, it would scarcely be possible to traverse the woods and jungles of Siam. He makes his way as he goes, crushing with his trunk all that resists his progress; over deep morasses or sloughs he drags himself on his knees and belly. When he has to cross a stream, he ascertains the depth by his proboscis, advances slowly, and when he is out of his depth he swims, breathing through his trunk, which is visible when the whole of his body is submersed. He descends into ravines impassable by man, and by the aid of his trunk ascends steep mountains. His ordinary pace is about four to five miles an hour, and he will journey day and night if properly fed. When weary, he strikes the ground with his trunk, making a sound resembling a horn, which announces to his driver that he desires repose. In Siam the howdah is a great roofed basket, in which the traveller, with the aid of his cushions, comfortably ensconces himself. The motion is disagreeable at first, but ceases to be so after a little practice.

Elephants in Siam are much used in warlike expeditions, both as carriers and combatants. All the nobles are mounted on them, and as many as a thousand are sometimes collected. They are marched against palisades and entrenchments. In the late war with Cochin China, the Siamese general surprised the enemy with some hundreds of elephants, to whose tails burning torches were attached. They broke into the camp, and destroyed more than a thousand Cochin Chinese, the remainder of the army escaping by flight.*

Of elephants in Siam, M. de Bruguières gives some curious anecdotes. He says that there was one in Bangkok which was habitually sent by his keeper to collect a supply of food, which he never failed to do, and that it was divided regularly between his master and himself on his return home; and that there was another elephant, which stood at the door of the King's palace, before whom a large vessel filled with rice was placed, which he helped out with a spoon to every talapoin (bonze) who passed.†

* Pallegoix, i. 150—4. † *Annales de la Prop.*, xxv., p. 74.

His account of the Siamese mode of capturing wild elephants is this:—In the month of March, a number of female elephants are turned out into the woods: they are recalled by the sound of horns, and are always accompanied by a number of males, who follow them into a park, surrounded by high palisades; having entered which, the doors are shut upon them. Men are placed upon a terrace, protected by large trunks of trees, from whence they throw round the legs of the elephant they propose to capture a rope, by which he is bound. Every species of torture is used: he is lifted by a machine in the air—fire is placed under his belly—he is compelled to fast—he is goaded with sharp irons, till reduced to absolute submission. The tame elephants co-operate with their masters, and, when thoroughly subdued, the victim is marched away with the rest.

Some curious stories are told by La Loubère of the sagacity of elephants, as reported by the Siamese. In one case, an elephant upon whose head his keeper had cracked a cocoa-nut, kept the fragments of the nut-shell for several days between his fore legs; and having found an opportunity of trampling on and killing the keeper, the elephant deposited the fragments upon the dead body.

The Siamese certainly treat the elephants as reasonable beings; and La Loubère says that when the three were despatched which the King of Siam presented to Louis XIV., they whispered these words in their ears:—" Go; depart cheerfully. You will, indeed, be slaves,—but slaves to the greatest monarch in the world, whose sway is as gentle as it is glorious." No doubt, this sort of invention was suited to the taste of the *Grand Monarque*, and the temper of the times.

I heard many instances of sagacity which might furnish interesting anecdotes for the zoologist. The elephants are, undoubtedly, proud of their gorgeous trappings, and of the attentions they receive. I was assured that the removal of the gold and silver rings from their tusks was resented by the elephants as an indignity, and that they exhibited great satisfaction at their restoration. The transfer of an elephant from a better to a worse stabling is said to be accompanied with marks of displeasure.*

The Emperor Galba is reported to have trained elephants to dance upon ropes.

Tigers abound, especially in the Laos country. They sometimes prowl about the tents, and carry off oxen and buffaloes; but their common prey is the wild deer and pigs of the forests. The Laos people capture the tiger by making an enclosure of heavy piles, in which they place a live dog. They surround the inner by an outer enclosure, leaving a suspended door open. The tiger, attracted by the cries of the dog, enters the outer enclosure, and, in prowling round, touches the spring which holds the door, and it closes upon him, when the inhabitants come and destroy him. The skin of the spotted tiger is much valued for its beauty.

Tiger-cats are common. Kümpfer, on arriving at the Dutch factory called Amsterdam, whose ruins are yet to be seen at about two leagues from the mouth of the

---

* La Loubère, p. 41—8.

Meinam, visited the governor, a Swede by birth, and Core by name. He was " under some grief, having lost a tame Suri cat, which he found again to-day, but in the belly of a snake he had killed, and which, as he complained, had robbed him before of many of his hens, having always been lurking in corners under the houses. We had an accident with another sort of thief, who at night had got under the house where seven of us fellow-travellers lay together. He had laid hold of the corner of a waistcoat hanging through a crevice of the floor, which was made of split *bamboons*, and was pulling it through with such a force, that one of us awaked, who, suspecting a thief, seized it, and called to his sleeping companions for help. While they were thus pulling and hauling who should have it, Core, who from former experience immediately suspected a tyger, fired a gun and frightened him away."

The *rhinoceros* is sought principally for his horns and skin, which latter is supposed to possess great medicinal virtue for strengthening the sick. Though so thick and tough, Pallegoix says that, being grilled and scraped, and boiled with spices until reduced to gelatine, it becomes a very agreeable food.

Horses are rarely seen, except within the Kings' palaces; and they are only small ponies, mostly brought from a distance. When our Mission was publicly received by the second King, several carriages with horses were sent for the reception of myself and suite, and the first King offered me a pair as a present for my use in Hongkong.

Tame *buffaloes* and *oxen* are not allowed to be killed,

but the prohibition does not extend to the wild races of the woods. We found it difficult to obtain *beef* for our sailors. Many of the Brahminical prejudices are associated with Buddhism. In China I have seen vehement proclamations against the killing of oxen and buffaloes. I remember one issued to this effect: — " Kill pigs—they are dirty and useless, except to eat; kill sheep—they cannot plough or help you in your agricultural labours: but how can you dare kill buffaloes and oxen, that work with you in the fields? and is not the Bull one of the celestial signs? Have you thought of this? Tremble and refrain."

Bears, wild pigs, porcupines (which, the Siamese insist, fling their quills against both men and dogs), elks, deer, roebucks, gazelles, goats, and other animals, tenant the jungles and the forests of Siam. There is a large consumption of dried venison, and great multitudes of deer are killed during the inundations. Civet cats, monkeys (the ourang-outang is found on the Malayan side), squirrels, flying squirrels, otters, whose skins are an article of some importance in trade, hares (a popular animal, and a frequent actor in the tales and fables of the Siamese, who attribute to " puss" an unusual amount of sagacity), rats, musk-rats, and mice, may be mentioned among the quadrupeds most common in Siam.

Dogs and cats are seen in large numbers in the streets and houses of the Siamese. The dogs are fetid and filthy, quite of the Pariah race; their presence, in the temples especially, is an annoyance and an offence. Of the cats, many are of colours and shapes unlike the common European races. They have long tails, and short tails, and curled tails, and no tails at all. The best ratcatchers are of a dun colour, with black and white spots, of which we brought more than one specimen away; and they became favourites for their virtuous dispositions and useful qualities.

Bats abound. The larger species do much mischief in the gardens, as they live principally on fruit. They are black in colour, are nearly as big as a cat, and invade the mango and lichee trees by hundreds and thousands. Their principal domicile is amidst the thick foliage in the courts of the pagodas and temples, and among the tufts of the bamboo. Multitudes are caught in the net with which the fruit-trees are protected against their ravages. They are skinned and eaten by the Siamese; but Pallegoix says they have a *urinous* taste, which the employment of red pepper is not sufficient to subdue. At night they hang over the city of Bangkok like a dense black cloud, which appears to be leagues in length.*

Some of the birds attracted our admiration:—The *karien*, a noble stork as tall as a man, having black, grey, and white plumage, with a neck and crest of brilliant red: they cannot, when running, be overtaken by the swiftest greyhound, and form most picturesque objects when fishing on the borders of the marshes and lakes; the snowy pelicans, busied by day in the pursuit of their prey, and seeking, in triangular groups, solitary trees in the forest for rest at night. The wonderful beauty of the plumage of

---

* Pallegoix, i. 172.

the halcyons (kingfishers), some of which gave us the first announcement of our adjacency, was among the earliest objects of delight.

The white ibis is everywhere found. The male peacock, of enormous size, and with plumage of singular lustre, may be seen on the top of a tall tree, gathering the females around him by his inharmonious cries.

The Argus-pheasant is common, and its feathers are an article of commerce. There is a species called by the natives "heaven's hen." Toucans, parrots, parroquets, are seen in the forests, in which pigeons and turtles sometimes crowd the branches of the trees.

Of the falcon races there is a great variety in Siam. The common vulture is a useful conservator of the public health, and scavenger for the removal of public nuisances. He devours the carrion and putrid animal substances, which would otherwise be intolerably offensive. The adjutant is a valuable auxiliary in the same good work, but he does not wait for his prey till death has made it noisome.

The singing-birds are many. There is a species of thrush which imitates all the sounds he hears,—the barking of a dog, the mewing of a cat, the crowing of a cock, and the human voice, so as to be an almost perfect imitation. A little black-and-white bird, which, from the colour of its plumage, Pallegoix calls the dominican, sings very sweetly at daybreak, and in the spring season. A variety of humming-birds are found in the gardens, the feathers of one of which, of a purple colour with white spots, are exported to foreign countries.*

The number and audacity of the crows in Bangkok, and other populous places in Siam, are amazing. Pallegoix says, " They devastate the gardens, and eat all the ripe fruit; carry away chickens, and all eatables exposed to the sun: they enter houses by door or window; will steal cakes and plantains from the hands of children; will raise up the covering of pots and pans, and carry off their contents, not only for present use, but to be stored for future supply. They conceal their robberies in the roofs of the houses, or in hollow trees, and often assemble to make war upon jays, pigeons, and less courageous birds. Of the food that is given to dogs, cats, poultry, the crows invariably steal the largest portion. No doubt, they destroy many nuisances, in the shape of insects and animals more annoying than themselves. If you fling a stone among them, their number only increases, and they salute you with a tenfold clamour; if you kill one, a thousand come to inquire what you are doing, and, instead of getting rid of the plague of their presence, you augment it a hundred-fold."†

The reptiles of Siam are multitudinous. Crocodiles are found in the rivers, from their mouths to their shallows. They deposit about twenty eggs in the sand, each about double the size of goose-eggs. The eggs are esteemed rather a dainty; but they are only carried away when the thief has a horse at hand on which he can take immediate flight from the

---

* Pallegoix, i. 171.   † *Ibid.*, i. 165—6.

irate mother, who, according to Pallegoix, invariably rushes forth to protect her progeny. Of the young crocodiles, multitudes are destroyed by the larger fish, and by their own race.

At Bangkok there are professional crocodile-charmers. If a person is reported to have been seized by a crocodile, the King orders the animal to be captured. The charmer, accompanied by many boats, and a number of attendants with spears and ropes, visits the spot where the presence of the crocodile has been denounced, and, after certain ceremonies, writes to invite the presence of the crocodile. The crocodile-charmer, on his appearance, springs on his back, and gouges his eyes with his fingers; while the attendants spring into the water, some fastening ropes round his throat, others round his legs, till the exhausted monster is dragged to the shore and deposited in the presence of the authorities. Father Pallegoix affirms that the Annamite Christians of his communion are eminently adroit in these dangerous adventures, and that he has himself seen as many as fifty crocodiles in a single village so taken, and bound to the uprights of the houses. But his account of the Cambodian mode of capture is still more remarkable. He says that the Cambodian river-boats carry hooks, which, by being kept in motion, catch hold of the crocodiles; that during the struggle, a knot is thrown over the animal's tail; that the extremity of the tail is cut off, and a sharp bamboo passed through the vertebræ of the spine into the brain, when the animal expires.*

---

* Pallegoix, i. 175.

There are many species of lizards; the largest is the *takuet*. His name has passed into a Siamese proverb, as the representative of a crafty, double-dealing knave; as the takuet has two tongues, or rather one tongue divided into two. The noisy *tookay* never fails to make his presence known. He is excused for his clamours, on account of the services he renders in destroying vermin. The inhabitants call him the clock, and say he announces the hours.

Cameleons, flying lizards, serpents from the most gigantic to the smallest species, are noticeable among the reptiles. The larger are eaten by the Siamese; and, if Pallegoix is to be believed, the *boa* now and then eats a child in return.* The boa is reverenced by the Chinese, and is frequently found on board the junks, where he is considered as a tutelary guardian, and daily sacrifices are offered to him.

Serpent adoration is one of the most widely-spread of human superstitions. Serpent-charmers practise their arts in Siam. They exhibit vipers which are trained to dance, to fight with one another, and to exhibit all sorts of extraordinary tricks, and acts of submission to their masters. They have been rendered harmless by the extraction of their poison: and I heard of no instance of a serpent-charmer being injured in educating his sometimes exasperated subjects.

Pallegoix has an account of a "fiery serpent," said to redden and burn the plant over which he passes. But he doubts the tales he had heard. He speaks with more personal knowledge of a serpent

---

* Pallegoix, i. 178.

that is attracted by fire, and follows any light or torch in the darkness, and is only escaped from by abandoning the light which has excited his attention. There is a snake called by the Siamese "sunbeams," from its very brilliant colours; it is inert and easily avoided, but its bite is said to be mortal.

An immense frog sings the bass in the great chorus of grasshoppers, crickets, cicadæ, and other musicians, which, especially during rain, fill the whole atmosphere with their varied music.

Sea, river, and land turtles are used for food by the Siamese. The sea-turtle sometimes weighs 150 pounds; and they are so abundant, that ships are laden with their eggs, which are principally consumed by the nobles. One species of the river-tortoise is taken by the line and hook, a plantain being used for bait, while for another species the bait is a fish. There is a variety which is a regalia of the crown, and is regularly watched by guards, who surprise it when it lands at night to deposit its eggs in the sand. The eggs are sent to the palace; the animal is allowed to escape, after being branded with a hot iron, as the property of the King. The field-tortoise is often hunted by dogs: both the flesh and the eggs of the animal are a favourite Siamese dish.

Whales, dolphins, porpoises, flying-fish, sharks, sword-fish, bonitos, dorys, and a vast number of other fishes, are found in the Bay of Siam. Rays, soles, salmon, &c., abound in the mouths of the rivers. The fishing and salting of prawns and shrimps is a considerable trade: crabs, crawfish, and lobsters are also prepared for food. The *bicho de* *mar* forms a very important article of export to China. Pallegoix speaks of a large fish, called the *mëng-phù*, weighing from thirty to forty pounds, of a bright greenish-blue colour, which will spring out of the water to attack and bite bathers. He says there is also a *tetraodon*, called by the Siamese *the moon*, without teeth, but with jaws sharp as scissors: it can inflate itself so as to become round as a ball; it attacks the toes, the calf, and the thighs of bathers, and, as it carries away a portion of the flesh, a wound is left which it is difficult to heal.[*]

Land and sea crabs are the common food of the people. A favourite condiment is the *kapi*, which is made of shrimps pressed into a paste, and salted after the first stage of putrefaction has commenced.

If in the more salient portion of the field of animal existence I feel unable to do more than point out a few of the most prominent objects, I dare not attempt to penetrate into that multifarious population of the insect world, which to describe requires knowledge which I do not possess, and space of which I cannot dispose. The centipede and the scorpion are too troublesome not to be specially mentioned. The exquisite pain caused by the bite of the centipede may be alleviated by the application of quicklime. There is a luminous centipede which gives a bright light even when crushed; it is a small variety, and is said sometimes to enter the orifice of the human ear, and to cause extreme suffering. The scorpion is very intrusive: it will conceal itself

---

[*] Pallegoix, i. 193.

in the folds of your garments, enter your pockets, hide itself in the leaves of your books; no known application will save from great annoyance the person whom it bites. A large species is called the elephant-scorpion: when it attacks the huge beast, he roars with intolerable agony; it is seldom known to bite a human being, and from its size is easily avoided. The cockroach is a universal, all-devouring, ever-present pest: the mosquito, from the pain it inflicts, is still more annoying. Ants of all colours, sizes, and shapes invade everything, and attack everybody: some of them sting sharply. The white ants are as insinuating, as destructive, as in any part of the tropics.

How can I pass the fire-flies in silence? They glance like shooting stars, but brighter and lovelier, through the air, as soon as the sun is set. Their light is intense, and beautiful in. colour as it is glittering in splendour—now shining, anon extinguished. They have their favourite trees, round which they sport in countless multitudes, and produce a magnificent and living illumination: their light blazes and is extinguished by a common sympathy. At one moment every leaf and branch appears decorated with diamond-like fire; and soon there is darkness, to be again succeeded by flashes from innumerable lamps which whirl about in rapid agitation. If stars be the poetry of heaven, earth has nothing more poetic than the tropical fire-fly.

" The glow-worms (cicindelæ) settle on some trees like a fiery cloud, with this surprising circumstance, that a whole swarm of these insects, having taken possession of one tree and spread themselves over its branches, sometimes hide their light all at once, and a moment after make it appear again, with the utmost regularity and exactness, as if they were in a perpetual systole and diastole."*

The white ants commit great ravages in Siam, and are as much a pest to dwellings as are the mosquitoes to their inhabitants.

Minerals.

Metals.—*Gold* is found in many parts of Siam. The most productive locality is that of *Bang Taphan*, in the province of *Xumphon*, at the foot of the high mountains called the *Three Hundred Peaks*. Grain-gold and nuggets are collected. The soil containing the gold is crushed and washed in wooden bowls, and, by agitation, the metal is separated from the mass. The gold-mine is guarded by orders from the King, and worked only under special authority. Private individuals are allowed to collect gold, on condition of their paying for the privilege a certain amount per day; but the climate is most unhealthy, and the yellow fever carries off in less than a month the greatest part of the adventurers.

Silver is only found in combination with copper, antimony, lead, and arsenic.

Copper is produced in large quantities. Pallegoix says there are mountains of copper ore which give thirty per cent. of metal, but that the copper has

---

* Kämpfer, p. 45.

hitherto been mainly used for the manufacture of idols.

Tin is an important article of production and export. It is principally worked in the provinces of *Xalang*, *Xaija*, *Xumphon*, *Rapri*, and *Pak Phrëk*. The Chinese are the most active tin-miners, and work in associated bands.

Lead is brought abundantly from mines in the mountainous districts of *Pak Phrëk* and *Suphan*. The ore is argentiferous.

Antimony and *zinc* are found in the mountains of *Rapri*; but the metals not being used by the Siamese, the ores are not worked.

Iron mines at *Tha Sung* are wrought by the Chinese, the principal openers of the various sources of productive industry in Siam and other countries to which they migrate. The ore is very rich, and spread over an extensive plain. It is collected by the Siamese, and sold to the Chinese, to whom it is conveyed in Siamese boats plying on a canal which divides the plain. Above six hundred Chinese are engaged at the furnaces, occupied night and day: the iron being converted into thick plates, is sold in Bangkok.

Precious Stones.—Pallegoix says that a great quantity of precious stones are collected in the neighbourhood of the *Sabab* mountain, and that they are found still more abundantly on the frontiers of the *Xong* tribes, where they are gathered by the peasantry, who sell the whole at prices varying from sixteen to sixty francs per pound. Among the stones so collected, the Governor of Chantabun showed him rock crystals, cats'-eyes as large as a nut, topazes, hyacinths, garnets, sapphires of deep blue, and rubies of various colours. The Bishop says that, in wandering through the Chantabun mountains, they collected in an hour two handfuls of precious stones. There are certain localities in which the King forbids their collection, except for his own account.

CHAPTER VII.

MANUFACTURES.

THE manufacture of the precious metals by the Siamese into a variety of vessels,—particularly vases, urns, tea and coffee pots and urns, boxes, and other articles, in which gold is embossed on silver in a style somewhat resembling that for which the Russians are celebrated,—has obtained for the Bangkok goldsmiths an Oriental celebrity. Their number must be great, as the King informed me he had employed no less than six hundred for several months in making the tomb of his brother, the late King. The gold vessels of Siam are almost all of an orange colour, which, I was informed, was produced by exposing them, in a certain state of manufacture, to the action of sulphur. Mother-of-pearl is much used for inlaying woods. The glass manufactures are numerous, particularly for the production of variegated vitreous substances, mingled with metallic oxides, with which the temples are covered, and which glitter gaily in the bright sun. Gold-beaters are also abundant; and there is an enormous demand for their work, particularly for gilding statues of Buddha, for ornamenting temples, pictures, and other decorations. Copper and iron founders are also ingenious workmen; and Pallegoix says that by a supply of metal from a multitude of crucibles not containing more than 100 pounds each, a colossal statue of fifty feet in height has been produced in the capital.*

Some of the most costly of the garments worn by the people of high rank were, as we learnt, manufactured in their houses; and they prided themselves on their being able to produce textures more valuable than any they imported from foreign countries. The laws forbid the use of certain garments to any but persons of elevated condition. As to the ordinary dresses of the people, they are almost wholly made from cotton stuffs of foreign origin.

Earthenware of coarse quality, tiles, and the common productions of the potter's wheel, are provided by native manufacturers: so are vessels of brass and iron, and the domestic utensils for daily use.

I have received the following native account of the mode of manufacturing a peculiar species of cloth, the use of which is confined to the nobility, who boast that it has never been successfully imitated out of Siam:—

"This description of cloth, called Pha Poom, is used by gentlemen of distinction and rank in Siam and Cambodia, as sarongs or dresses, and is also worn by the nobles and followers of his Majesty and his ambassadors. This description of cloth has been manufactured to perfection in Siam and Cambodia from ancient times.

"In the manufacturing of this cloth, white silk yarn is used, and dyed in the following manner:—

---

* Pallegoix, i. 354.

"The silk yarn is taken in the quantity of about a handful; and the parts that it is desired should remain undyed are tied round with the leaves called ka pho, and then put into the dyeing matter, the parts exposed only taking the dye.

"The leaves are then removed, and tied round the parts that have been dyed, and other parts that it is desired should remain white or undyed, and is again put into the dyeing matter of a different colour, the parts exposed only taking the dye. This process of removing and tying of the leaves is repeated; the silk yarn is all dyed of the requisite colours, and then it is woven into cloth, having flowers on both sides nearly alike. This description of cloth is only manufactured in Siam and Cambodia, but when it was first invented is unknown."

The arts of drawing and painting are mostly formed on Chinese models, but in a ruder shape. Most of the sculptured images are imported from China, and have all the monstrous forms which are popular among the Chinese. But the Siamese paint, decorate, and gild their temples far more ostentatiously than the Chinese. They have a class of men who study caligraphy, and are proud of exhibiting specimens of their art. The books of the Siamese open in one continuous sheet, folded fan-like; the usual length of the page from eight to twelve inches, the breadth three or four: the paper is black, and the characters are written generally with gamboge, though sometimes with white paint. All hasty records are made with chalk, which is easily removed when the record is not intended to be permanent.

Indian (*i. e.* China) ink is also used for writing on light-coloured paper. The leaves of a sort of palm-tree (koi) are employed as tablets, which are written on by a *stile*, but principally for the re-production of the sacred books. These are fastened loosely together by strings, so that they can be easily turned over. They are preserved under richly-painted and gilded coverings, and are highly appreciated. Pallegoix says that there are a number of ladies in the palace specially occupied in writing these books.*

An American missionary says:—" On our way to Ayuthia (from Bangkok) we stopped a little to examine a paper-manufactory. The paper is made here from the bark of a tree or plant called khri. It is reduced to a pulp by manual beating, soaked in water, and then run into a mould, which consists of a rectangular box, about fourteen by twenty inches, with a piece of coarse cloth stretched over the bottom for a strainer; and then, instead of pressing, it is exposed to dry in the sun before it is removed from the mould. When dried, it is ready for use, but cannot be written upon with ink, as it spreads; and the texture is coarse, resembling wrapping-paper. The Siamese use a kind of soft stone, or steatite pencil, for writing."†

---

* Pallegoix, i. 348.   † *Missionary Herald*, Berlin, 1840, p. 73—4.

CHAPTER VIII.

COMMERCE.

TIME was when Bangkok occupied the third place among the commercial cities to the east of the Cape of Good Hope—(first, Calcutta; second, Canton)—and as many as sixty British vessels were engaged in trade with the River Meinam; but such has been the baneful influence of bad legislation—such the destructive progress of monopoly—that when I visited Siam, all that remained to represent foreign trade was one English (half-caste) merchant, one Armenian, and a few Anglo-Indians from Bombay and Surat. The existing commerce, carried on in square-rigged vessels, was wholly possessed by the King and the nobles, while the mass of the junk coasting-trade had passed into the hands of the Chinese; but even this latter branch of commerce had been so interrupted by the pirates on the coasts of China and in the Gulf of Siam, that the junks employed had been reduced to one-tenth of the number formerly engaged.

Yet, looking at the wonderful aptitudes of Siam, it is obvious that nothing but mismanagement and misrule could have prevented the rapid growth and extension, instead of the decline and decay, of the commerce of so feracious a region. Four great rivers, navigable at a considerable distance from their mouths, open cheap and easy communications with vast regions of cultivable lands; multitudes of canals lend their auxiliary aid; the general spirit of the people is favourable to maritime pursuits, and the trader occupies a respectable position in public opinion. In fact, from the monarch to the meanest of his subjects, everybody is disposed to barter and to turn to profit the exchange of commodities.

The greater activity of the multitudinous Chinese, and their roving and adventurous spirit, have made them the principal channels of trading operations in all parts of the country: there are no districts too remote to be explored by them, no object of traffic too small to escape their notice,—they are awake to everything which is to leave lucre in their hands; they are masters of the art of exploring and of *exploiting*, (we want an English word, though *exhausting* would be hardly too strong,) and their presence often reminds me of the vultures which I have seen gathering from all quarters of the heavens to feed upon a camel that has fallen down in the deserts, or the tens of thousands of black ants which collect around and devour or carry away the body of a cockroach which has had the misfortune to be trodden upon.

Let it not, however, be supposed that I look with any feelings but those of complacency upon the exodus of the Chinese from their native land, and their outpourings on all adjacent regions. I believe there is no class of settlers who, under proper control, are so likely to be useful—that the very quality, the passion for acquiring wealth, which leads them to dare all danger and difficulty, is a most valuable recom mendation. Their own habits of subordination,—their inborn and inbred respect for authority—their gregarious spirit, which drives them into associations of every sort, private and public, praiseworthy and pernicious,—only require a thorough knowledge of their character to be turned to the best account. Already they constitute nearly half the population of Siam. Every year there is a considerable influx, principally from the Island of Hainan, and from the provinces of Kwang tung and Fookien; the two latter districts affording, indeed, the chief supply of emigrants not only to Siam, but to Cochin China, the Straits, California, Australia, Western America, and generally to the countries in which Chinamen are located.

As most of the Chinese junks come down by the north-east and return by the south-west monsoon, their trading affairs are very sluggishly conducted; and long credits, irregularities, and delays have, no doubt, added to the profits, but have increased the risks of commerce, especially to the foreign trader desirous of realizing his import cargo and obtaining produce in return. It was an ancient joke of one of the Catholic bishops, that every foreigner who came to Siam should be accompanied by three cargoes—one of presents for the King and the ministers, another of the commodities which he desired to sell, and a third loaded with patience to enable him to wait for their sale.* The establishment of capitalists, with warehouses for stowing goods, ready to purchase the

---

* Pallegoix, i. 326.

produce of the country, or to exchange the goods they import for such produce, will in future years regulate or supersede the existing state of things.

Van Schouten (1636) reports on the commerce of Siam,—" The principal traffic of the country is in stuffs which come from the Coromandel coast and from Surat, Chinese manufactures, jewels, gold, benzoin, gum-lac, wax, sapan-wood, eagle-wood, tin, lead, and deer-skins—more than one hundred thousand deer being annually caught, the skins of which are sold in Japan at a great profit. They also deal largely in rice, of which all the Oriental nations consume great quantities. The King is the greatest merchant in the whole kingdom, annually sending to the Coromandel coast and to China, where he is held in high honour. Each year he obtains large sums by trafficking in the kingdom of Pegu, at Jongoma and Langhojangh.

" The coinage of the country is of very pure silver. The tical is worth 30 sols, the mace $7\frac{1}{2}$ sols, and the foang 3 sols 9 deniers. They usually reckon by catties of silver; each catty being worth 20 taels, or 144 livres; for the tael is worth somewhat more than 7 francs. All commerce is conducted by this money, no other being current in the country: but from Manilla and the islands of Borneo and Legneo is brought a shell, of which eight or nine hundred are worth a franc; and this is used in purchasing the necessaries of life, which are exceedingly cheap." (P. 34.)

In La Loubère's time all foreign trade was monopolized by the King. He says that no individual was allowed to sell imported articles; and that the King was not contented with selling by wholesale, but had shops in the bazaars where his commodities were dealt out in retail. He not only monopolized the sale of imports, but compelled his subjects to buy the wares he imported; and parents were ordered to clothe their children before the accustomed age for wearing garments. Tin, ivory, areca, and some other articles could only be sold to the King, and by him were supplied to foreigners; but the export was free of many important articles of produce,—rice, sugar, fish, salt, gums, birds' nests, oils, spices, &c.

The ancient commerce of Siam was, when La Loubère wrote, in a state of decadence, in consequence of the King's monopolies; and he reports that only two or three Dutch barks traded with the country. Ferdinand Mendez Pinto, the famous exaggerator, states that, in his time, more than a thousand foreign ships were engaged in the Siamese trade. "Commerce," the French ambassador well remarks, "requires a certain liberty;" and when the prices at which imports were to be bought and exports to be sold were arbitrarily fixed by the King, there was little encouragement for the commercial adventurer. (P. 113.)

In the former days of Siamese commerce, teak, cassia, oil of turpentine, sandal-wood, resins, ginger, pepper, tobacco, coffee, cotton, sugar, benzoin (gum benjamin), eagle-wood, cardamums, gutta percha, cardego, and a variety of oils, were the principal vegetable commodities for exportation.

The *dyewoods* of Siam were objects of considerable

trade, consisting of shumac, rosewood, *kĕlē*, (for yellow,) jackwood, sapan or campeche wood, *jo*, and laclake, for red dyes; ebony fruit (name not mentioned) for black, and a fruit called *carthame* for rose colour.

Metals, ivory, skins and horns of animals, contributed largely to the export cargo. Mr. Crawfurd furnished Mr. M'Culloch (*Dictionary*, article Bangkok) with the following list of exports from Siam:—

"Black pepper, sugar, tin, cardamums, eaglewood, sapan-wood, red mangrove bark, rosewood for furniture and cabinet work, cotton, ivory, stick-lac, rice, areca-nuts, salt fish; the hides and skins of oxen, buffaloes, elephants, rhinoceros, deer, tigers, leopards, otters, civet cats, and pangolins; of snakes and rays, with the belly-shell of a species of landtortoise; the horns of the buffalo, ox, deer, and rhinoceros; the bones of the ox, buffalo, elephant, rhinoceros, and tiger; dried deers' sinews; the feathers of the pelican, of several species of storks, of the peacock and kingfisher, &c.; and, finally, esculent swallows' nests." He omits one of the most important articles of produce and export—teak-wood for ship and other building.

Gutzlaff gives the following accurate account of the Chinese junk trade with Siam:—

"The junks, every year, in February, March, and the beginning of April, arrive from Hainan, Canton, Sookah (or Soo a chen, in Chaou-chow-foo), Amoy, Ningpo, Seang-hae (or Shang-hae heen, in Kiangnan), and other places. Their principal imports consist of various articles for the consumption of the Chinese, and a considerable amount of bullion. They select their export cargo according to the different places of destination, and leave Siam in the last of May, in June, and July. These vessels are about eighty in number. Those which go up to the Yellow Sea take mostly sugar, sapan-wood, and betel-nut. They are called *pak-tow sun* (or *pih-tow chuen*)—white-headed vessels,—are usually built in Siam, and of about two hundred and sixty or three hundred tons, and are manned by Chaou-chow men from the eastern district of Canton province. The major part of these junks are owned either by Chinese settlers at Bangkok, or by the Siamese nobles. The former put on board, as supercargo, some relative of their own, generally a young man who has married one of their daughters; the latter take surety of the relatives of the person whom they appoint supercargo. If anything happens to the junk, the individuals who secured her are held responsible, and are often, very unjustly, thrown into prison. Though the trade to the Indian Archipelago is not so important, yet about thirty or forty vessels are annually despatched thither from Siam.

" Chinese vessels have generally a captain, who might more properly be styled supercargo. Whether the owner or not, he has charge of the whole cargo, buys and sells as circumstances require, but has no command whatever over the sailing of the ship. This is the business of the *hochang*, or pilot. During the whole voyage, to observe the shores and promontories are the principal objects which occupy his attention day and night. He sits steadily on the side of the ship, and sleeps when standing, just as it suits his convenience. Though he has nominally the command over the sailors, yet they obey him only when they find it agreeable to their own wishes; and they scold and brave him just as if he belonged to their own company. Next to the pilot (or mate) is the to-kung (helmsman), who manages the sailing of the ship: there are a few men under his immediate command. There are, besides, two clerks—one to keep the accounts, and the other to superintend the cargo that is put on board: also, a comprador, to purchase provisions; and a heäng-kung (or priest) who attends to the idols, and burns every morning a certain quantity of incense, and of gold and silver paper. The sailors are divided into two classes: a few, called tow-muh (or headmen), have charge of the anchor, sails, &c.; and the rest, called ho-ke (or comrades), perform the menial work, such as pulling ropes and heaving the anchor. A cook and some barbers make up the remainder of the crew.

"All these personages, except the second class of sailors, have cabins,—long, narrow holes, in which one may stretch himself, but cannot stand erect. If any person wishes to go as a passenger, he must apply to the tow-muh in order to hire one of their cabins, which they let on such conditions as they please. In fact, the sailors exercise full control over the vessel, and oppose every measure which they think may prove injurious to their own interest; so that even the captain and pilot are frequently obliged, when wearied out with their insolent behaviour, to crave their kind assistance, and to request them to show a better temper.

" The several individuals of the crew form one whole, whose principal object in going to sea is trade, the working of the junk being only a secondary object. Every one is a shareholder, having the liberty of putting a certain quantity of goods on board, with which he trades wheresoever the vessel may touch, caring very little about how soon she may arrive at the port of destination.

" The common sailors receive from the captain nothing but dry rice, and have to provide for themselves their other fare, which is usually very slender. These sailors are not usually men who have been trained up to their occupation, but wretches who are obliged to flee from their homes; and they frequently engage for a voyage before they have ever been on board a junk. All of them, however stupid, are commanders; and if anything of importance is to be done, they will bawl out their commands to each other till all is utter confusion. There is no subordination, no cleanliness, no mutual regard or interest.

" The navigation of junks is performed without the aid of charts, or any other helps except the compass: it is mere coasting, and the whole art of the pilot consists in directing the course according to the promontories in sight. In time of danger, the men immediately lose all courage; and their indecision frequently proves the destruction of their vessel. Although they consider our mode of sailing as somewhat better than their own, still they cannot but allow the palm of superiority to the ancient craft of the 'Celestial Empire.' When any alteration for improvements is proposed, they will readily answer, 'If we adopt this measure, we shall justly fall under the suspicion of barbarism.'

"The most disgusting thing on board a junk is idolatry, the rites of which are performed with the greatest punctuality. The goddess of the sea is Matseo po—called also Teën-how, or 'queen of heaven.' She is said to have been a virgin who lived some centuries ago in Fuh Kien, near the district of Foo Chow. On account of having, with great fortitude and by a kind of miracle, saved her brother, who was on the point of drowning, she was deified, and loaded with titles not dissimilar to those bestowed on the Virgin Mary. Every vessel is furnished with an image of this goddess, before which a lamp is kept burning. Some satellites, in hideous shape, stand round the portly queen, who is always represented in a sitting posture. Cups of tea are placed before her, and some tinsel adorns her shrine.

"When a vessel is about to proceed on a voyage, she is taken in procession to a temple, where many offerings are displayed before her. The priest recites some prayers, the mate makes several prostrations, and the captain usually honours her by appearing in a full dress before her image. Then an entertainment is given, and the food presented to the idol is greedily devoured. Afterwards, the good mother, who does not partake of the gross earthly substance, is carried in front of a stage, to behold the minstrels, and to admire the dexterity of the actors: thence she is brought back, with music, to the junk, where the merry peals of the gong receive the venerable old inmate, and the jolly sailors anxiously strive to seize whatever may happen to remain of her banquet.

"The care of the goddess is entrusted to the priest, who never dares to appear before her with his face unwashed. Every morning he puts sticks of burning incense into the censer, and repeats his ceremonies in every part of the ship, not excepting even the cook's room.

"When the junk reaches any promontory, or when contrary winds prevail, the priest makes an offering to the spirits of the mountains, or of the air. On such occasions (and only on such), pigs and fowls are killed. When the offering is duly arranged, the priest adds to it some spirits and fruits, burns gilt paper, makes several prostrations, and then cries out to the sailors, 'Follow the spirits,' who suddenly rise and devour most of the sacrifice. When sailing out of a river, offerings of paper are constantly thrown out near the rudder.

"But to no part of the junk are so many offerings made as to the compass. Some red cloth, which is also tied to the rudder and cable, is put over it, incense sticks in great quantities are kindled, and gilt paper, made into the shape of a junk, is burnt before it. Near the compass, some tobacco, a pipe, and a burning lamp are placed, the joint property of all; and hither they all crowd to enjoy themselves. When there is a calm, the sailors generally contribute a certain quantity of gilt paper, which, pasted into the form of a junk, is set adrift. If no wind follows, the goddess is thought to be out of humour, and recourse is had to the demons of the air. When all endeavours prove unsuccessful, the offerings cease, and the sailors wait with indifference."

For the last twenty years, the number of junks employed in the Siamese trade has been gradually diminishing, and they have been to some extent replaced by vessels built on European models. In 1832, only three or four square-rigged vessels were in the habit of visiting the Meinam,—mostly Arabian vessels bearing the British flag. Under the impulse given by the present Prime Minister, a considerable number of trading-vessels have been built for Siamese account on excellent models, and ship-building is likely to become a very extensive and prosperous undertaking in Siam.

It was in the year 1835 that the present Phra Kalahom began the building of ships on the European model; and he has pursued the meritorious work with great perseverance and success. These vessels belong to the two Kings and principal nobility. In a few years, square-rigged vessels will, no doubt, supersede junks altogether for foreign voyages.

The Parsees have been called the Jews of India. Their commercial spirit has led them into the remotest regions. I found some of them in Siam, carrying on a trade with Surat and Bombay. They are mentioned by Joâo de Barros as established in Siam in the beginning of the sixteenth century,* and are said to have influenced the King of Malacca to throw off his subjection to the Siamese.

---

* *Decadas*, vol. iv., p. 15.

Pallegoix gives the following list of articles exported, their prices and quantities. He does not mention his authorities for the estimate; but I doubt, on the whole, if the quantities be stated in excess: the statement at best is, however, only approximative.

ARTICLES.	PRICE.	QUANTITIES SHIPPED.
Clean rice	20 ticals the coyan*	1,500,000 coyan.
Teak-wood		130,000 trees.
Sapan-wood	1 tical p. picul	500,000 piculs.
Cocoa-nut oil	10 ,, ,,	700,000 ,,
Sugar	7 ,, (averg.) p. picul	250,000 ,,
Palm sugar	1 fuang the jar	180,000 jars.
Salt	6 ticals the measure	12,000 measures.
Pepper	10 ,, p. picul	70,000 piculs.
Cardamums	200 ,, ,,	700 ,,
Bastard cardamums		6,000 ,,
Laclake	16 ticals p. picul	11,000 ,,
Tin	24 ,, ,,	5,000 ,,
Iron		20,000 ,,
Ivory		500 ,,
Gamboge	80 ticals p. picul	600 ,,
Rhinoceros horns		70 ,,
Small deer horns		30,000 pairs.
Stag horns		200 piculs.
Buffalo horns		300 ,,
Deer sinews		250 ,,
Rhinoceros hides		300 ,,
Tigers' bones		70 ,,
Buffalo and ox hides	1 tical p. hide	120,000 hides.
Gum benjamin	100 ,, picul	200 piculs.
Edible birds' nests		20 ,,
Dried fish	Various prices	100,000 ,,
Dried prawns		20,000 ,,
Balatchang, or *kapi*		20,000 measures.
Wood-oil	5 to 6 ticals p. picul	25,000 piculs.
Rosin		16,000 ,,
Rosewood		250,000 ,,
Damars, or torches	1 fuang p. packet	300,000 packets.
Rattans	1 ,, ,,	260,000 ,,
Bark for dyeing		300,000 ,,
Sea-slugs		5,000 piculs.

* The coyan is 100 baskets.

ARTICLES.	PRICE.	QUANTITIES SHIPPED.
Gold-dust		
Raw cotton	. . . .	200,000 bales.
Indigo paste	. . . .	60,000 jars.
Kēlē (yellow wood)		
Lead	8 ticals p. picul . .	6,000 piculs.
Aquila-wood	4 ,, catty	
Tobacco	1 tical p. 1000 bundles	
Precious stones . . .	20 to 60 ticals p. catty	
Ebony		
Fish-oil	2 to 3 ticals p. picul	
Capsicums		
Tortoiseshell		
Feathers		
Onions	1 tical p. picul	
Ginger		
Iron stoves, &c.		
Sardines (salted) . . .	. . . .	90,000 piculs.
Coffee	16 ticals p. picul . .	12,000 ,,

The prices of Siamese produce given to me at Bangkok in April, 1855, were—

Sugar, white	7¼ to	7½	ticals per picul.
,, 2nd quality . . .	6¾ to	7 ,,	,,
,, 3rd quality . . .	6½	,,	,,
,, red	3	,,	,,
Pepper, black	8 to	9 ,,	,,
Lac, old	11	,,	,,
,, new	8	,,	,,
Gamboge	30 to	35 ,,	,,
Gum benzoin	40 to	60 ,,	,,
Cardamums	230 to	400 ,,	,,
Tin	30 to	35 ,,	,,
Tallow	8 to	12 ,,	,,
Cotton	12 to	13 ,,	,,
,, uncleaned		4 ,,	,,
Cocoa-nut oil		9 ,,	,,

Rice	30 ticals per coyan of 100 baskets.
Hides	4 ticals per picul.
Horns	6 ,, ,,
Sapan-wood	½ to 1 tical ,,
Hemp	10 ticals ,,

Opium has become one of the most important articles of importation; its consumption is said to be about 1200 chests, which represent a value of nearly 150,000*l.* sterling. The vice of opium-smoking is mostly confined to the Chinese, and among them it seems as ineradicable as the consumption of spirituous liquors among many of the European nations. The former laws against the importation and use of opium were as helpless as they were severe. I give in the Appendix the last decree, which was issued in 1839 by the late King. Ten thousand copies were printed at the American Missionary press. The decree originated in a contest between Chinamen (engaged in smuggling opium) and Siamese, which led to the loss of many lives. For some time an active search was carried on, and severe punishments were inflicted on the traders in and smokers of opium. The King allowed a certain quantity to those who would suffer from a sudden cessation of the habit. But the influence of the Chinese, the wants of the Treasury, the impotency of prohibitions and punishments to arrest the evil, have led to the legalization of the drug, and the establishment of an opium farm, for which a large sum is annually paid by an opulent Chinese contractor.

The custom-house service is carried on with considerable activity. We found several revenue-boats at the entrance of the Meinam, in the Gulf of Siam, whose business it was to report the arrival of ships. All along the banks of the river are small custom-house stations; and they are said to practise many exactions, and to connive at many irregularities. This would be only according to Oriental custom, and the small pay received by the officers, no doubt encourages their venality. They interfere little with the barques of the nobles, and, no doubt, make amends for their abstention from acting against the influential and strong by their heavier oppressions upon the weak and the unprotected. In this respect Siam offers no exception to the rest of the Eastern world. Under former treaties, foreign vessels were not called upon to pay duty on imports or exports; but the enormous charge for tonnage-dues, whatever might be the value of the cargo, had nearly destroyed the foreign trade.

The tonnage-dues collected from Chinese and Siamese vessels are very various. Sailing-boats able to proceed to sea pay from 8 to 40 ticals (1*l.* to 5*l.*); small junks, from 40 to 60 ticals (5*l.* to 7*l.* 10*s.*); large junks, from 80 to 200 ticals (10*l.* to 25*l.*) The English and American Treaty established, in lieu of all other charges, a tonnage-duty of 1700 ticals (215*l.*) per fathom of 78 English inches. This amount, though reduced by royal decree to 1000 ticals (125*l.*), was too heavy to be borne. This mode of taxing cargo is so obviously unjust, as by it the most and the least valuable commodities are subjected to the same

THE COINAGE.

imposts, that it seems strange such a scheme could have been concurred in by British and American negotiators. However, by the new treaty, tonnage-dues are *wholly* abolished, and moderate duties on exports and imports substituted.

The money that circulates in Siam consists principally of silver *ticals* or *bats* of the value of 2*s*. 6*d*. sterling, with smaller coins, constituting its subdivisions. The coin is an irregular ball, but has two impressions, made by blows, bearing the King's mark. There is a double tical—a half tical, called *song-salung*—a quarter tical, the *salung*—and the half *salung*, or *fuang*, which represents 1200 cowries. These shells are generally employed for the small purchases of the people, about 100 of them representing a farthing. They are collected on the Siamese coast. Pallegoix says, that for a *fuang* (less than 4*d*.) fifty or sixty varieties of vegetables may be purchased in the public markets. Four ticals make the Siamese ounce —20 ounces the catty, or Siamese pound of silver. The larger amounts are reckoned in pounds of silver, of which the sterling value is about 10*l*. Gold coins, resembling the silver in form and size, are issued, but in small quantities. Copper coins are issued by individuals in the provinces; and stamped glass, or enamel bearing inscriptions, is also used as a circulating medium. The Government issues promissory notes of various amounts, even to one-eighth of a tical. They do not seem extensively current, and, I believe, have not experienced any depreciation.

The French authorities quote the Siamese weights as:—

Avoirdupois Weight.

			cwt.	qr.	lb.	oz.	dr.	sc.	gr.
Hùn	=	45 centigrammes =							7·6170
Fuang	=	2¼ grammes =						3	8·0949
Salung	=	4½ ,, =					2	1	6·1898
Bat	=	18 ,, =				10	0	4·7597
Xang	=	1440 ,, =			3	2	12	2	0·7811
Cati	=	720 ,, =		1	9	6	1	0·39055
Kab	=	72 kilogrammes =	1	1	18	11	14	2	4·460

Measures.

Va = 2 mètres = 78·742 inches.
Cubit = 50 centimètres = 19·6855 ,,
Empan = 25 centimètres = 9·84275 ,,
Kabiet = ¼ of an inch.
Sen = 20 va.
100 sen = 4000 mètres = 2 miles, 3 furlongs, 35·2 poles.
400 sen = 1 jôt, or 1 Siamese league.
Kanan = about ½ litre.
Thang = 20 kanan, or small bushel.
Sat = 25 kanan, or large bushel.
Kien = 80 sat, or waggon-load.*

---

* Mr. Jones, in his *Siamese Grammar*, gives the Siamese weights and measures as follows:—

4 pic = 1 fuang.
2 fuang = 1 salung.
4 salung = 1 tical, or *bat*.
4 tical = 1 tambung.
20 tambung = 1 chang.
50 chang = 1 hab or picul.
100 hab = 1 para.

Long Measure.

12 niu = 1 kab = 19½ inches.
2 kab = 1 sok.
4 sok = 1 wa.
20 wa = 1 sen.
400 sen = 1 yōt.

Dry Measure.

25 kanan = 1 săt.
80 săt = 1 koyan = 20 piculs.

---

20 kanan (cocoa-nut shell) = 1 tang.
100 tang = 1 koyan.

But the real measures are so inaccurately established, that great misunderstandings and quarrels result among buyers and sellers from the want of a legal standard.

The ancient weights and measures of the Siamese, as given by La Loubère, are as follows.

Siamese long measure is composed as follows:—
Peet met can pleüde (that is, 8 grains of whole rice before the husk is removed) = 1 inch (Siamese, *niou*).

12 *niou* = 1 *keub* or palm, measured from the thumb's point to the middle finger.

2 *keub* = 1 *sok* = 1 cubit, from the finger-point to the elbow.

2 *sok* = 1 *ken* (the length from the points of the fingers to the middle of the chest).

2 *ken* = 1 *voüà* = 1 fathom and an inch.

20 *voüà* = 1 *sen*.

100 *sen* = 1 *róë neng* (róë = 100, neng = 1) = nearly 4000 mètres.

4 *róë neng* = 1 jod.

The moneys and weights of the Siamese are here arranged together, as most of the names equally apply to both.

4 ticals = 1 tael, 20 taels = 1 catty, 50 catties = 1 pic. The tical is of the weight of half an ounce, and is also a silver coin = 4 *mayons* = 8 *fuangs* = 32 *payes*. The *paye*, however, is not in use; but there is a coin = 2 *payes*, or *song-paye*.

The *paye* = 20 clams = 24 grains of rice: so that, according to this calculation, the tical = 768 grains of rice.

Many of these words are not Siamese: the *pic*, for example, in the Levant, is the name of a measure, about a yard long; in Siam it is 25lb. of 16 oz. *Catty* is Chinese, and in Siamese is called *schang*; but the Siamese catty is only equal to half the Chinese. *Tael* is also Chinese, = in Siamese language "tamling."

The *tical*, or *baat*, and the *mayon*, or *selung*, are words of doubtful origin. *Fuang, paye,* and *clam* are native words.

The *tical*, although it weighs as much as half-a-crown, is equal to 37½ sous of France. (La Loubère, vol. ii., p. 59.)

The Siamese moneys are quoted by Mr. M'Culloch in his *Dictionary*, on Mr. Crawfurd's authority, thus:—

200	bia or cowries	=	1 phai nung.
2	phai nung	=	1 sing phai.
2	sing phai	=	1 fuang.
2	fuang	=	1 salung.
4	salung	=	1 bat or tical.
80	ticals	=	1 cattie.
100	catties	=	1 picul.

But the picul of commerce contains only fifty catties,—the commercial cattie being double the weight of the Chinese, which is 1⅓ lb.

The long measures, as given by Mr. M'Culloch (from Mr. Crawfurd), are—

12	finger-breadths	=	1 span.
2	spans	=	1 cubit.
4	cubits	=	1 fathom.
20	fathoms	=	1 sen.
100	sen	=	1 yuta.

He says, the fathom is about 6 feet 6 inches.

La Loubère says, the Siamese scarcely use any other instrument of calculation than the pen; but the Chinese employ a sort of *jetton* (the abacus), the invention of which Father Martini, in his *History of China*, carries back to a period of from 2600 to 2700 years before Jesus Christ. However this may be,

Pignorius, in his work *De Servis*, informs us that the ancient Roman slaves were familiar with the use of this instrument, which they employed in their calculations.*

---

* La Loubère, i. 230—1. 1691.

CHAPTER IX.

REVENUES.

THE ancient sources of Siamese revenue, according to La Loubère, were a land-tax, somewhat capriciously levied; an impost on boats, at the rate of a tical (2s. 6d.) per fathom in length; a licence on the manufacture and sale of arrack; taxes on fruit-trees; produce of Crown lands; tribute from dependent countries; fines and confiscations; the personal services of all the subjects of Siam, estimated (in 1690) at 2 ticals (5s.) per month; commercial monopolies. The ready money paid to the King annually was 600,000 crowns.*

Independently of the taxes paid in money or produce, all the subjects of Siam were formerly bound to give their personal services for six months of the year, to be employed in public works, or any species of labour for the King's profit. This time of servitude is now reduced to four months, but it is deemed the most productive source of the royal revenues.

The Treaty between Great Britain and Siam which it was my privilege to negotiate must lead to a complete revolution in the financial system of the country, as it destroys many of the present and most fruitful sources of revenue. That it will be more productive

---

* La Loubère, p. 95.

hereafter to the State, while it confers very great benefits on the people, may safely be anticipated. The extension of privileges, of farms and monopolies, was really undermining all the foundations of the national prosperity, as was visible in the diminution of supplies, and the consequent decline of trade. A nobler emancipation than that brought about by the Treaty of Bangkok has seldom honoured the annals of a nation's history; and if the state of things described by Pallegoix in 1854* be compared and contrasted with that which the Treaty has secured for 1856, the results cannot but be welcomed by every commercial, civilized, and Christian man.

The present sources of revenue are six:—
1. Tributes from princes dependent upon the King of Siam.
2. Land, garden, and plantation taxes.
3. Farms and monopolies.
4. Custom-house duties.
5. Tonnage and harbour charges.
6. Fines and confiscations.

The forms of tribute are very various: the token of subjection is mostly represented by trees or flowers of gold and silver, and gold-dust, which are presented (principally by the Malayan States) every three years.

Most of the other dependent States pay tribute in the produce of the country, which the King either sells in Bangkok, or exports on his own account to

---

* Pallegoix, i. 302—312.

foreign markets, principally to China. Both Kings possess a number of square-rigged vessels, which trade with the islands of the Indian Archipelago, and with Canton, Amoy, Shanghae, and even as far north as the Gulf of Pecheli.

The land-tax is a tical per acre, and is collected at the rice-harvest; it is often exacted in produce, much to the loss of the cultivator. The lands are *cadastred* at the beginning of every new reign. Every fruit-tree is registered: a durian pays annually 1 tical (2s. 6d.); mango, mangosteen, and jack trees, a salung (7½d.); a tuft of bamboos, a fuang (3¾d.). There are special taxes on sugar-plantations—on pepper, tobacco, and all the principal articles of production; and they had so grown in amount, and their collection had become so vexatious, as to lead to the abandonment of many agricultural enterprises. The new treaty provides that produce shall only pay *one* tax; which will relieve the producer from the annoyances that have lately so sorely and severely pressed upon his industry.

But the system of monopoly, gradually invading almost every article in use, and under which the dealing and right of purchase was confined to the person who purchased from the King the exclusive right to farm the article, was one of the most intolerable grievances ever inflicted on a people. Tradition says—but I know not the authority—that it was by the advice of an Englishman that a former King of Siam was induced to introduce the system of monopoly, as the simplest form of collecting the greatest revenues. I may say, at all events, with some pride, that it was an Englishman who overthrew the system, and was enabled to persuade the King and the great nobles that monopolies were pernicious to the country, and not profitable to the treasury; and that though there might be a present sacrifice on their abandonment, free interchange would be found, in the long-run, a wiser and better policy than that of restraints and impediments. "But what are we to do during the transition from one state of things to another? How can we make the present sacrifices which you expect from us?" were questions frequently put to me in Siam. To which I could only answer: That free commerce was buoyant and elastic, and soon made for itself new channels; that the period of transition would neither be so long, nor the sacrifice so great, as the Siamese anticipated; that a change of the existing system was called for, alike by the evidence of its own mischievousness at home, and by the fair and friendly expostulations of other nations, who felt that they also were injured by what was so injurious to Siam; that one monopoly had followed in the footsteps of another monopoly, till production was checked, trade diminished and menaced with extinction; that a change would be alike acceptable to the people of Siam and the world at large; that nations were more and more brought into contact with one another, by easier and cheaper communications, by the general diffusion of knowledge and civilization, by new wants, by the augmentation of wealth, by greater commercial enterprise, and by the great tide of tendency which could not be resisted, and which it was not safe to attempt to resist; that all fertile countries had their superfluities, which other nations were desirous of obtaining in exchange for superfluities of their own; that varieties of climate, and soil, and condition, gave to all the means of interchange; that commerce bound remote nations together, and gave them common interests; that commerce is the natural parent and ally of peace; that in the progress of events, questions are always settled by the interference of the warrior with violence and outrage, or by the negotiator in a spirit of amity and good-will; and that commerce was, of all negotiators, the most effectual. No doubt, thoughts like these had been working in the minds of many of the influential Siamese; but it was my business to suggest and to enforce them, and, on more than one occasion, it was no small satisfaction to me to hear from men of the highest station, " What you say is true: the shopkeepers complain they cannot sell, the peasants say they cannot produce; we have only a few, instead of, as in former times, many ships in our river; and matters grow worse, instead of better." On one occasion, the most influential noble in the kingdom said to me, " We must work together; we must put an end to these monopolies; and the blessing of the people will be on your head."

The system of monopoly began by farming spirituous liquors; then tobacco, gaming, oils, torches, leaves for covering roofs, combustibles, timber, condiments, markets, fisheries, mining, hunting—one after another every species of industry was subjected to the ravages of an invader more and more rapacious as he destroyed the very element on which he fed. Chinese settlers have beaten the Siamese out of the market in the competition for farms. It was said that one Chinese mandarin had obtained possession of ninety different monopolies. And the Chinese, having obtained the farm of a particular article, are merciless in their prosecutions and punishment of all who invade their privilege. In such cases, they have been in the habit of "protecting their rights," as it is called, by their invasions of the domiciles, seizure of the goods and persons of delinquents, who can obtain no redress for any such visitations, inasmuch as the Chinese farmer has invariably behind him the noble through whose influence he obtained the monopoly, and to whom, of course, he paid the market-value. There is no class of men who exercise power in a more arbitrary spirit than the Chinese—to their exactions there are no bounds; and as they are unchecked by those influences which at home place some control upon rapacity, all their bad qualities are exhibited where they are for the most part "birds of passage," and certainly, at the same time, "birds of prey;" for though multitudes of Chinese become permanent settlers in Siam, there is, perhaps, no example of an utter abandonment of the intention of returning to the "flowery" fatherland, of worshipping in the ancestral hall, of performing the religious rites demanded by the *manes* of their progenitors, and of revisiting the graves of those whom to reverence is the part of a Chinaman's nature, formed by education and habits absolutely despotic, and pervading all classes of society.

Pallegoix gives the following table of the revenues

of Siam. They are obviously only approximate estimates.*

	Ticals.		Ticals.
Rice-grounds	2,000,000	Brought forward	10,097,100
Gardens	5,545,000	Rattans	12,000
Plantations	500,000	Bark for tanning	10,000
Teak-wood	80,000	Timber-spars	9,000
Sapan-wood	200,000	Bamboos	90,000
Cocoa-nut oil	500,000	Palm-leaves for roofing	15,000
Sugar	250,000	Firewood	15,000
Palm-sugar	10,000	Opium farm	400,000
Rice exported	100,000	Arrack	500,000
Salt	50,000	Gambling-houses farm	500,000
Pepper	400,000	Fisheries do.	70,000
Cardamums	10,000	Markets do.	100,000
False cardamums	20,000	Floating bazaars	150,000
Laclake	12,000	Tobacco monopoly	200,000
Tin	60,000	Aquila-wood	45,000
Iron	60,000	Turtle-eggs	6,000
Ivory	45,000	Custom-house revenues	300,000
Gutta-percha	24,000	Exemption from corvées	12,000,000
Rhinoceros horns	2,000	Chinese capitation-tax	2,000,000
Stag horns	4,000	Tonnage-dues on shipping	80,000
Buffalo horns	500	Gold-mines of Bang Taphan	10,000
Hides	2,600	Prostitutes	50,000
Gum benjamin	1,000	Fines and receipts from tribunals	15,000
Birds' nests	100,000	Revenues of Northern Provinces	50,000
Dried fish	30,000	Do. Southern Provinces	40,000
Dried prawns or shrimps	6,000	Lotteries	200,000
Balachang, or *kapi*	10,000		
Wood-oil	8,000		
Rosin	7,000		
Rosewood	40,000		
Torches, or *damar*	20,000		
Ticals	10,097,100	£3,370,512 10s.—Ticals	26,964,100

* I find in Moor's *Notices of the Indian Archipelago* (1837) an estimate of Siamese revenues, which, except in a few instances, is wholly discordant from that furnished by Pallegoix; but Moor's information must have been singularly imperfect, as I observe he gives no credit for some of the most productive sources of income—such as compositions for personal labour, capitation-tax paid by Chinese, &c. He estimates the tax on rice and paddy to be only 862,350 ticals, instead of 2,000,000; pepper, 23,200, instead of 400,000. But Moor's tables are so obviously full of errors, that I notice them merely to prevent their being received as authority.

I do not find a return of the amounts received by the Treasury for fines and confiscations. In almost all cases, a portion of the fine is ordered to be appropriated to the King. Confiscations often take place on a large scale, but the receipts from this source must always be capricious and uncertain.

Sundry local functionaries are charged with the collection in their district of the public taxes, and pay them to the *phra xajot*, the chief of the King's pages, through whom they are transferred to the Treasury, which provides, under the King's orders, for the expenses of the State. There are about eight thousand bonzes in the royal pagodas who are provided for by the King's revenue, which is also charged with military and marine expenses, and all public works throughout the kingdom.

CHAPTER X.

LANGUAGE AND LITERATURE.

I FIND in several authors an opinion that the Siamese language is a connecting link between the Chinese, the Sanskrit, the Pali, and their derivatives, and even with the Polynesian dialects. I see no ground for such a theory. The introduction of a small number of words from India and the Indian Archipelago is easily explained; but the broad general deductions which are drawn from a few resemblances are quite unwarrantable, and the results of very imperfect knowledge. The character and construction of the language are peculiar: tradition refers its origin to the Laos country, the idiom of which it resembles in many particulars; but the Siamese has a distinct type of its own.

Mr. Jones published, at Bangkok,* some short notices of the Siamese grammar. He represents the roots of the language to be few, all monosyllabic, and generally confined to visible objects. The pitch of the voice gives various meanings to the same word. He thinks that the polysyllabic words in the language are all of foreign origin. Nouns are not susceptible of declension, nor verbs of conjugation. Auxiliary

---

* *Brief Grammatical Notices of the Siamese Language, with an Appendix.* By J. Taylor Jones. Bangkok: Printed at the Mission Press. 1842.

particles stand in the stead of cases, moods, and tenses, as in Chinese. Mr. Jones estimates the number of persons speaking Siamese at from three to four millions. If his work be somewhat crude and imperfect, the writer must be allowed to have presented himself with very modest claims to attention.

The best grammar of the Siamese language with which I am acquainted is that of Bishop Pallegoix: it is in Latin, and was printed in Bangkok in 1850.* In the same year, a Siamese dictionary, in Latin characters, was printed for the use of the Catholic Mission.† A far more important contribution than either to our knowledge of the Siamese is, no doubt, the great Dictionary which has been lately published in Paris, under the care of the Bishop, and at the expense of the Imperial Government.

The Siamese alphabet consists of twenty vowels, half-vowels, or diphthongs, and forty-four consonants. The forty-four consonants are divided into seven gutturals, six palatals, six linguals, six dentals, eight labials, and eleven half-letters, sibilants, and aspirates.

With few exceptions, the Siamese is a monosyllabic language; and those exceptions are almost wholly found in foreign words. In proportion to the eleva-

---

* *Grammatica Linguae Thai.* Auctore D. J. Pallegoix, Episcopo Mallensi, Vicario Apostolico Siamensi. Ex Typographiâ Collegii Assumptionis B. M. V. in civitate regiâ Krŭng Thĕph Măhá năkon sí Ajŭthă ja, vulgo Bangkok. A.D. 1850. 4to.

† *Dictionarium Latinum Thai, ad usum Missionis Siamensis.* Ex Typ. Coll. Assump. B. M. V. Bangkok, A.D. 1850.

tion of style is the number of words of Sanscrit and Pali origin, but accommodated to Siamese pronunciation. The highest idiom is that of the sacred books; the second is the language of the higher orders; the lowest, that of the people. It is a language of tones or cadences, which give a different meaning to words whose alphabetic forms would be the same. Hence the language lends itself to jokes and equivoques of all sorts; and many a word *idem sonans* to an unpractised ear, presents distinctions marked and obvious to a Siamese.*

The tones are exhibited by the addition to the written characters of letters and of accents. Of course, the variety of tones reduces the number of separate written words as directed to a European eye; but the language is crowded with synonyms, which are used as a protection against the many meanings which belong to the same or nearly the same sound. There are, for example, no less than twelve Siamese words for *head*. Many compound words have a descriptive or poetical character. River is "mother of waters;" milk, "breast-water;" the horizon, "heaven's support;" the will, "heart-water;" fruit, "child of the tree;" cook, "father of the kitchen;" rudder, "tiger's tail;" compass, "raven's beak;" plough, "pig's head." These terms resemble the Arabic in many particulars.

---

* In the following, the various meanings of the word *kháo* are embarrassing enough: "kháo bok khao và klài krung kao mi kháo pen rùb kháo mi khào kháo mén khao klún mài khào." The translation is, "It is reported that near the ancient capital there is a horn-shaped mountain with white rice, smelling so disagreeably that it cannot be eaten." (Pallegoix, i. 377.)

Auxiliaries are employed to give to nouns and verbs the various significations which result from declensions and conjugations. Most words may be used as subjectives or adjectives, verbs or adverbs, by changing their position, or adding another word to modify the sense. Auxiliary words express the past, the present, and the future; and a single particle transfers an active into a passive verb.

The language is written from left to right. The sacred literature of the Siamese, though translated into the vernacular, but not written in the common character, is mostly in the Pali language. The principal collection is the *Trai Pidok*, or "Three Vehicles," by which we are understood to pass through the great sea of the world. It is divided into three parts: the *Phra vinai*, rules or regulations; the *Phra sut*, sermons and histories; and the *Phra baramat*, philosophy. The whole is composed of four hundred and two separate works, making three thousand six hundred and eighty-three volumes. Of profane literature, Pallegoix says the Siamese have about two thousand volumes.

The slight modification of sounds and words apparently the same, and which give a completely different signification, makes the pronunciation of the Siamese language difficult to strangers, and leads to many mistakes as to the meaning. For example, in the sentence, "Khai khai kai khai na khai? ha nie khai pha-khai khai," the import is, "Is nobody selling eggs in the city? the seller is ill;" but the various *khai*, by shortening and lengthening and intonating them according to their meaning, leave no doubt of the meaning in the mind of a Siamese hearer.* There are no less than six tones in the language,—the abrupt, the short, the long, the high, the low, and the middle. They have been compared to musical notes: the abrupt, to a demi-semi quaver; the short, to a semi-quaver; the long, to a double note; the high, an ascent from sol to si; the low, a descent from sol to re, touching slightly the intermediate notes. But the printing types employed by the Siamese are not accompanied with accents in the European style. The French missionaries contend that, notwithstanding all these difficulties, a person by six months' application may understand common conversation and make himself understood: but Mr. Jones says that, from a want of attention to the inflections of the language, he has known "good proficients" expose themselves to ridicule and be unintelligible for years.

La Loubère avers that it is quite impossible to convey in French characters any accurate idea of Siamese pronunciation; that of ten words written in any French alphabetic form and read by a Frenchman, not one would be understood by a Siamese. Mr. Jones abandons all attempts to represent the combinations of Siamese characters by the English alphabet.†

There is much that is poetically paraphrastic in

---

* So in Chinese—*Chi chi chi chi* lu: "I know the way that leads to the place." Hioh *chi chi* poh wei jü *chi chi chi* yaow, *chi, chi, chi* yaow wei yü *chi chi* shih: "To know the requirements of virtue is more important than to know what virtue is; but the knowledge of these requirements is less important than the practice of them."

† *Grammatical Notices*, p. 18.

the Siamese language. The word for content is "good heart." Lips are designated by words meaning "the light or beauty of the mouth;" a flower, "the world's glory;" a crocodile, "son of the water." An augmentative is made by the use of the word *mother;* a diminutive, by that of *son.* La Loubère says, he could not discover *any* word in Siamese resembling European, except Po (father) and Me (mother): but these two sounds, or something approaching them, being the first lispings of infancy, he might have found indicating the parental relations in almost every language of the world.

The modes of address are as various as the various ranks of society, and any failure in the proper forms of conversational respect to a superior is immediately resented. A child of low condition is called "you rat!" simply; to a child of the middle ranks a more respectful prefix is added, equal to "Master Rat" or "Miss Mouse." Children of the nobles are called "father" and "mother" by their subordinates. A title equivalent to mister and mistress is in use among equals; but it is deemed courtesy to add some term of family endearment, as mother, father. A woman younger than the person addressing her is called "my young sister;" if older, "my elder sister:" to a magistrate is used the term "benefactor," "fatherly benefactor;" to a prince, "Mighty sovereign, the dust of your feet, the sole of your foot, waits your orders." The phrase "I ask for your orders" occurs at every stage of conversation with dignitaries. The name of the King must not be uttered by a subject: he is always referred to by a periphrasis, such as "the master of life," "the lord of the land," "the supreme head." A short specimen, among many, furnished to Bishop Pallegoix* by a learned bonze, exhibits, in a verbal discourse between the King and one of his pages, the literal phraseology employed:—

"The order of the most merciful King having descended upon the hairs and the head of Saraphet Phakdi, his Majesty said, 'Mr. Saraphet! get a ship ready; take merchandize from the royal warehouses, and fill the ship.'

"*Page.* My august lord! I receive your orders on my hair and my head.

"And the page worshipped, and crawling away, he examined the ship, which he manned and loaded with merchandize, and returned to the court, and worshipped, saying—'I supplicate by the power of the dust of your feet which cover my head, the slave of the Sovereign has loaded the ship.'

"*King.* With what?

"*Page.* My august lord! I receive your orders; I have loaded three hundred piculs of cardamums.

"*King.* No more?

"*Page.* My august lord! I receive your orders.

"*King.* What besides?

"*Page.* August lord! the hair of your head has also shipped thirty thousand piculs of pepper.

"*King.* Any sapan-wood?

"*Page.* My august lord! there is sapan-wood.

"*King.* When is she to sail?

---

* See, for many other examples, his *Grammatica Lingua Thai*, and *Description*, i. 381—398.

"*Page.* My august lord! I receive your orders; she will be ready on the 13th day of the moon.

"*King.* Regulate and inspect properly.

"*Page.* My august lord! I receive your orders."

Another example will explain the mode of intercourse between the priests and the laity:—

"There was a bonze in office who was laying down the floor of his house. Two planks were wanting. He was embarrassed, and said, 'Where can we find two planks?' Then one of the attendants said, 'I have seen plenty of planks; I receive your orders.' 'Where, sir, did you see them?'—*Servant.* 'I receive your orders; it was in the house of the mandarin *Si*. I receive your orders; if you ask them as alms, I think he will present them; I receive your orders.' Then the bonze went to the house of *Si*, who observing him, said, 'Master benefactor, I invite you; I receive your orders.' And the bonze sat down. And the mandarin said, 'The master benefactor is come; what does he want?' 'Persevere in my benediction, great mandarin! my person comes to ask two planks as alms.' 'Master benefactor! why do you ask two planks?' 'Persevere in my benediction; my person will have them conveyed to finish the floor of my chamber.' 'But, master benefactor! are two planks enough?' 'Persevere in my benediction; a portion of the floor is made.' 'Master benefactor! and you have made a portion of the floor? I, a hair, thought you had not yet begun it.' 'Rest in my benediction; I have made a part.' Then the mandarin called, '*Ma!* go and choose good planks, and present them to the benefactor.' And the bonze blessed the mandarin, and went with the slave *Ma* to choose the planks in the store of the sawyers; and having chosen them, he returned to his pagoda."

The following interlineal translation of the Lord's Prayer will serve to show the collocation of words:—

Father our who art in heaven, name God must glorify
Pon raon yon savang, Shen Phra hai phra kot
all places people all offer God praise. Kingdom God
tonk heng kon tang tai tonai Phra pon. Muang Phra
ask find with us must finish conformable heart God
io hai dai ke raon hai leon ning chai Phra
kingdom earth equally heaven. Nourishment we (our)
muang pon-din semo savang. Ahan raon
all day ask must find with us day this; ask pardon
toak van co hai dai ke raon van ni; co prot
offences we (our) equally we pardon persons do offences
bap raon semo raon prot pon tam bap
us. Not must fall into cause sin. Must deliver out
ke raon. Ya hai raon tok nai kouan bap. Hai poun krai
misery all. Amen.
onerai tang poang.

The cardinal numbers precede the substantive: as, *Sain dënan*, three months. When the cardinal numbers follow the substantive, they become ordinal: *dënan sain*, the *third* month.

The earliest specimen that exists in the Siamese character is an inscription of about the date of A.D. 1284. It was found on a stone pillar in the city of Sukhoday, the then capital of Siam. The King informs me that the date, according to the astronomical era, is 1206. He says that this is about the time in which letters were introduced into Siam from Cambodia, and that the form of alphabet superseded that (the Sanscrit) which the Brahmins had brought from India.

It is known that King Phra Khrom Ram Khom huang, a distinguished monarch of Northern Siam, introduced the Siamese alphabet sixty-six years before the building of Ayuthia,—namely, in 1284 of the Christian era.

I may remark here, that a literary spirit was not an uncommon merit among the ancient Siamese Kings. Naret, in the sixteenth century, is said to have caused complete copies to be made of no less than eighty-four thousand distinct treatises, comprising the sacred books. La Loubère says that the Sovereign who ruled while he was at Ayuthia caused Quintus Curtius to be rendered into Siamese, and had made himself well acquainted with the history and policy of European nations. And far higher praise than this may be given to the present Kings of Siam.

The first literary work in Siamese of which we have any knowledge is a book on war and military tactics, written in the year 860 of the Siamese era (A. D. 1498), under the orders of King Rama, who also directed that public business should be conducted by means of written documents, and not left to the uncertain interpretation of verbal commands.

Siamese types for printing were first prepared by the Protestant missionaries in 1835.

Literature.

It is not unusual for the Siamese to invite a priest to their houses, in order that he may repeat some tale of history or fiction to the household, or to a crowd invited or permitted to become listeners. A translation of one of these romances, made by an American missionary lady,* is given in the Appendix.

I have collected a few specimens of the prose and the poetry of the Siamese, which will serve to exhibit the general character of the literature of the country. Latin translations of most of these will be found in Pallegoix's *Grammar*.

EXAMPLES OF ODES.

Ex Phra păramăt.

Jani: Human tortures are not one hundred thousandth part equal to the tortures of hell. He who is condemned by the king of hell will be exceedingly tormented.

His sin has brought to pass that he is confined in a dungeon, bound to a beam with chains, on account of his sin in unmercifully binding others with fetters. They stretch him on a heated iron plate, they stab him, his blood gushes forth, he dies, and is born again seven times in a day.

Being greedy of rewards, he feared not to lie; his tongue shall be plucked out, because he judged unjustly.

When he was a judge, he threatened in order to extort money; having received which, he held false evidence to be good. Assuredly, after his death he shall not escape punishment; he did not pronounce judgment in accordance with the truth, therefore will he be subject to hell for a long period.

---

* See *Chinese Repository*, vol. iii., p. 505.

He was blind to crime, he despised the institutions of his ancestors; therefore dogs as large as elephants, vultures, and ravens shall devour his flesh.

The preceding ode has a reference to the appropriate punishments which are said by the Buddhists to be inflicted in hell on those who have committed particular sins. Representations of tortures in the most horrible shapes are often found on the walls of the Buddhist temples. A glutton is sometimes represented reduced to a skeleton, while devils surround him tormenting him with the presence of all sorts of luxuries and delicacies, which they snatch away and place beyond his reach.

A drunkard is chained on his back to the sands, under a burning sun, with water at hand which he cannot approach.

An adulterer is visited by devils, some of whom tear away the peccant parts with red-hot pincers; and other devils compel him to devour them as they are torn away.

A liar or slanderer has one devil lacerating the upper and another the under jaw, while a third pulls out his tongue by the roots.

A person who has refused to clothe the naked is first deprived of his garments by one set of demons, and then another set flays him of his skin.

There are paintings of almost every form of anguish or agony, almost every mode by which pain can be inflicted or life destroyed, but always with a frightful prolongation of suffering in all conceivable shapes. Starvation, impaling, crucifixion, exposure to the elements, and the many processes of lingering death, have occupied the busy and brutal fancies of priests and painters.

Ex Săvătdĕrăksá.

Lest thou shouldst forget thyself and commit sin, give thy attention to the Happy State in the way which thy ancestors have instructed thee.

When thou hast arisen at dawn of day, thou shalt restrain thy anger, turn thy face towards the east, and from thence to the west; thou shalt consecrate water according to the sacred rites, especially with the prayer of Phra p. trăi Sărăna thrice repeated; then shalt thou wash thy face, and repeat some good sayings, and thus thou wilt become glorious and happy. For in the morning glory rests in the countenance, at noon in the body : the body must, therefore, be washed, and the breast sprinkled with sweet scents; and thus thou wilt escape disease and be spotless.

When night has set in, glory rests in the right and left feet : thou shouldst, therefore, wash and cleanse them; but care must be taken lest a woman place her hands on thy feet. When thou hast taken food, turn thy face towards the east; thou shalt be glorious and long-lived.

The preceding ode has reference to Buddhist usages and opinions. The *Happy State* is that concentrated abstraction from worldly cares and concerns which results from devout contemplation, and is enjoyed in its supreme perfection by Buddha himself. The control of the passions is among the most frequently-taught lessons of the Buddhist priest;— ablutions, purifications, meditation, and the repetition of moral sentences, are observances habitually insisted on. The presence of women in connexion with religious services, and especially in communication with the priesthood, is deemed of a desecrating and degrading character.

Xăn lăn lóng.

At that time the heavens were overcast with clouds; the moon, stars, and sun were obscured by the impending rain. The rain was pouring down, eclipsing the solar rays; the air was resounding with the tumult.

Two kings joined battle with innumerable forces from the right and from the left, shouting, and charging each other.

Then King Indra despatched a celestial charioteer, by name Matŭli;

That he might lead forward his chariot and celestial horses, to offer them to the most powerful of the royal combatants.

Indra, king of the heavenly host, sent me to offer this chariot to thee, the greatest king.

POETICO-HISTORICAL FRAGMENT.
Păthŭmăxăn.

There was formerly a most puissant sovereign, the elder brother of other sovereigns; he was named Phrŏmăthăt. He was a most prudent king, well acquainted with science, and expert with the bow and balista; the kings his brothers were in great fear of his power; the fame of his name was spread over all countries.

Xanthăbaĭn.

Two birds approach'd the mournful king:
"O birds! sweet birds! condolence bring!
Fly to my lady! quickly fly,
And tell her here I weep and sigh.
Then hasten back, and tell me where
She dwells, and I will hasten there."
The little birds flew gaily o'er,
And sang as they had sung before—

But never to the king return'd,
And still he groan'd, and sigh'd, and mourn'd.

Phra Părămăt.—A Mother's Merits.

A mother's merits, who can say
   How inappreciable they?
A mother's merits, earth can bring
Nought 'gainst them in the scale to weigh.
The fire-fly's light 's a lovely thing;
But these are bright as noon-tide ray.
Wide is the air, vast heaven's arched ball;
Yet they are narrow, they are small,
With mother's merits when compared:
The sea—the stream—the waterfall—
Mount Meru* to its summit bared,
   Are trifling, and unworthy all.
Yes! mother's merits, high and true,
They can eclipse, outweigh, outvie
The earth, with towering Mount Meru,
   And the huge ocean and the sky.

Ex Sŭphărĕt.

Hateful, repulsive to the eye,
The ugly vulture floats on high;
Yet, harmless, crimeless in his ways,
Upon the dead alone he preys;
And all his acts, in every place,
Are useful to the human race.

The snowy ibis, beautiful
And white as softest cotton-wool,
Preys on the living, and its joys
Spring from the life that it destroys.
So wicked men look sleek and fair,
Even when most mischievous they are.

---

* The Holy Mountain of the Buddhists.

The force of this composition can hardly be estimated by a European; but to a Buddhist, whose primary and paramount duty is to reverence life in all its forms, the contrast presented by the poet is very striking.

Siamese Proverbs.

When you go into a wood, do not forget your wood-knife.

Place not your boat across the stream (in the way of the current).

An elephant, though he has four legs, may slip; and a doctor is not always right.

Go up by land, you meet a tiger; go down by water, you meet a crocodile—(Difficulties on all sides).

Nobility is seen in the race; good manners, in the individual.

If a dog bite you, do not bite him again.

He who lives under the sky should not fear the rain.

Nourish no worms that eat timber: *i. e.* Be cautious in the selection of your friends.

The Siamese can hardly be said to have a national drama; but theatrical representations seem never wanting in the capital. They are mostly conducted by the Chinese, who bring with them all the habits of their native country, and seldom adopt the usages of the country to which they emigrate. Most of these representations are fragments of traditional history, in which the actors (all men or boys) are clad in the ancient costume of China. The theatre is generally an elevated stage, and the crowds fill the space in front below. The play is noisy, often libidinous, and lasts sometimes for days and nights. There is a mingling of buffoonery, tumbling, quarrelling, and fighting. The vices of the mandarins are the frequent subject of the comedy. The expenses of the representation are paid by the community: the theatre is open to everybody; reserved seats are sometimes erected for " the quality," but on these occasions I have observed little exhibition of the wonted respect for rank. The Siamese dramatic representations are almost always fragments of history or fable, with music and dumb-show. Now and then, a shriek, or a word, or a song is heard; but the general character is pantomimical, or of dumb-show.

CHAPTER XI.

RELIGION.

Doctrines of Buddhism.

I SUSPECT that modern Buddhism in all its forms represents the gross corruptions and adulterations of a simpler and truer philosophy emanating from remote ages, and that these corruptions and adulterations are mostly traceable to the craft of priests and the tyranny of princes, practising upon the ignorance, credulity, and prostration of the masses of the people. The present King of Siam, who must be deemed one of the very highest authorities as to the *real* character of Buddhism, contends that there is nothing in Buddhism properly understood which is repugnant to the facts established by astronomical and geological science. Such an opinion is, however, clearly incompatible with the teachings of modern Buddhist bonzes as to the cosmogony of the universe.

There are some broad analogies between the Buddhism of China, Ceylon, Burmah, and Siam; but when we look into the various ramifications, refinements, and glosses which the various Buddhist teachers have introduced into different countries, the analogies and resemblances are lost in the huge mass of invention and fable which an imaginative temperament, ministered to by habits of seclusion and contemplation, has gathered round the original doctrine.

The great outline is everywhere the same. The primary cause, by whatever name it may be called, is a sort of omnipotent and almighty *Repose*, whose original work was the Universe, launched into being at a period so remote as not to be distinguishable from a past eternity; and the machinery once constructed, rolls on, in virtue of its own elementary principles, as it has rolled on for infinite ages and will continue to roll, performing its functions, never deviating from the original law of its existence, and causing neither care nor concern to that pantheistic and spiritual essence called *Phra-thain*, whose complacency is not to be disturbed by the movement of the spheres, still less by the trifling events which agitate successive generations as they appear and disappear from the stage of being in an infinite variety of forms. Yet, from time to time, and in the course of millions upon millions of years, an emanation from the great Spirituality appears upon earth, the world being always in a state of pregnancy with these emanations. As regards mortal man, he is doomed to pass through countless changes of being, accompanied by a higher order of existence for virtuous deeds, or punished by a lower order of existence for faults and vices; but his ultimate supreme felicity is to be absorption or annihilation, the loss of the individual sensation, and absolute forgetfulness of all that can interfere with eternal, dreamless rest and peace.

It will be seen that, in its prominent features,

Buddhism bears a strong resemblance to Brahminism, and, in fact, to much of that Western philosophy which denies or doubts the *active* immortality of the soul, and which deems life to be as the lightning, or the electric spark, or any other transitory vitality, shining for a moment, and then lost for ever.*

The Buddhism of the Siamese is to be found in a collection of sixty volumes, prepared, by order of a King of Ayuthia, in the year 2145 of the Sacred era of Siam (A.D. 1654). Its title is *Trai-phum* (The Three Places), and it was composed, by a synod of learned bonzes, from the sacred books. It would be profitless to wander over the waste which these collections display,—utterly vain the endeavour to drag forth historical truth from the masses of fiction, valuable knowledge from clouds of ignorance, or to separate a sound morality from the entanglements of so many childish and useless observances which are deemed merits, and so many unimportant acts which

---

* This utter-absorption Buddhist beatification is in Chinese represented by characters meaning "heaven without thought," or "annihilation of thought is heaven."

> Abstraction from all thought, all care, all love,
>   All hatred, and all sympathy—can this,
>   This soul-annihilation, be heaven's bliss?
> This, virtue's highest recompence above,
> After life's turbulent troubles?—*this* divine,
>   This worthy of the Godhead? Higher far,
>   Even as infinities to nothings, are
> The very feeblest dreamings which enshrine
>   Our GOD, our Father; for though faint and dim
>   Our visual organs, yet we see in *Him*,
> All-active as creation, neither rest
>   Nor weariness,—but from the source of Might
>   He pours out ceaseless tides of love and light,
> Blessing with busiest energies, and blest.

partake of the character of sin, and to which reference will be made hereafter in speaking of the duties of the bonzes or talapoins.

But there are few questions connected with the earlier history and present condition of man more interesting than that of the Buddhistic belief and practice: for Buddhism is the most extensively professed religion of the world; it is the faith of two-fifths of the whole human race; and if Brahminism be considered one of its branches or modifications, one-half of mankind may be classed as recognising the great outlines of the Buddhist dogmas. It would thus number as its votaries more than all the Christian, all the Mahomedan, all the other sects of the world united. Such a religion is well worthy of being studied.

Its main feature, as above mentioned, is the recognition of the existence of a succession of manifestations of Deity in various shapes and at different periods of the world; that essential Deity can scarcely be said to be personalized, but is rather a calm and cold abstraction into which the human races are ultimately absorbed by the annihilation of all individuality. The mortal life of every human being is, as has been said, but one of a succession of stages through which he is passing,—a stage of reward or punishment, the consequence of the deeds of former forms of existence. The individual may be degraded hereafter if his conduct be unworthy and deserving future discipline, or elevated if he shall so discharge his duties as to entitle him to recompence. The great object of all religious observances is to become entitled to be lost in that vast infinity of vague beatitude where all separate and personal sensation shall terminate. The name of atheism can scarcely be properly appended to such a creed,—it may be doubtful even if we can properly call it idolatrous; for I cannot discover that any Buddhist deems the images he worships are the real God whose auspices he seeks, or are anything more than a visible representation of one of those incarnations of the Deity by which His will has been revealed for the instruction and guidance of mankind.

There is a class of household or tutelary divinities to whom most of the Siamese pay their adorations, erecting altars and offering incense to them in their houses and gardens. With these a sort of friendly and colloquial intimacy is preserved, under a somewhat vague notion of the value of their intercessions with superior agencies.

That ignorant devotees would confound the representations of the Godhead with the Godhead himself, is but the natural result of a low civilization, and of a craving after some visible and tangible evidence, something satisfactory to the senses, in the relations between the created and the Great Cause of creation. Christianity, of all the forms of religious belief, is undoubtedly that which best lends itself to the great law of progress and the development of mind, and in this perhaps will be found the best evidence of its substantial truth; for, after all, this will be the ultimate test, and the sole security for the final triumph of religious teachings.

The truths of philosophy must make their way,— their irresistible, all-conquering way. Nothing can permanently oppose the power of evidence which becomes mathematical from its cogency, or invincible from the demonstrations it brings to men's sense and men's experience. Hence the doctrines which are built upon fallacious theories of the universe, upon false histories and vain traditions, must ultimately be swept away; and that religion can alone become universal which progresses with the progress of knowledge, and whose conquests are conquests over every species of error and darkness. If this were more constantly kept in mind by those who "go forth" to enlighten and instruct "the heathen," their success would be more assured.

Vague and wandering thoughts, finding utterance in language which gives a wide range to the imaginative faculties, are by no means incompatible with religious speculations, as they characterize some of the most successful flights of poetry. The sublimest passages of Milton are probably those in which, by some vague but felicitous expression, he calls up a whole train of associations presenting new and striking images, by which his idea is aptly conveyed to and appreciated by the reader. So—

"No light, but rather darkness visible."

Again—

"What seemed his head,
The likeness of a kingly crown had on."

"He fell—and to this hour
Had still been falling."

The Buddhists, whose contemplations lead their

thoughts into calculations of infinite ages, as connected with the incarnations of the Divinity, have sought to convey notions of eternity by images in which the fancy is made the handmaid to speculations the most adventurous. For example, they teach that, in order to estimate the ages needful for all the transmigrations which are preliminary to the creation of a Buddha, you are to fancy a granite rock of enormous extent, which is to be visited once in a hundred thousand years by a celestial spirit clad in light muslin robes, which should just touch the rock in flitting by; and that until by the touch of the garment, which must remove an infinitesimal and invisible fragment of the stone, the whole stone should be reduced in successive visitations to the size of a grain of sand, the period of transmigrations of a Buddha would not be completed. Again, the priests say, so many must have been those transmigrations, that there is no spot on earth or ocean which you can touch with the point of a needle where Buddha has not been buried in some form or other during the incalculable period of his transitions from one to another mode of existence. So, the descent into one of the lesser hells of Buddhism is said to occupy three thousand years, and the same period is required to mount again from its abyss,—this being the penalty of a minor offence; the greater crimes demand a proportionate era for their purgation or punishment.

In every emanation or revelation of the Godhead, active and energetic virtue would seem extinct. The divine attributes of Gaudama—as, indeed, of all the

Buddhas that preceded him—are altogether of a passive or contemplative, but never of an enterprizing character. Omniscience is the groundwork of the God-like nature, which dwells in an atmosphere of eternal complacency and repose; no greater sympathy with good than with evil,—no displeasure against sin, no manifestation of approval of virtue. If, on the one hand, there is nothing carnal, so, on the other, there is nothing spiritual in their notions of the Godhead. It may be a question whether, independent of the incarnation of Deity in successive Buddhas, there is not in the minds of Buddhist worshippers—as there is certainly in the teachings of the bonzes—a vague sense of a higher element of order and authority—the great Creator of the created, the God of gods.

As regards the ultimate disposal of man after he has passed through his various transmigrations, and reaches a state of *Nirvani* (Pali) or *Nishvan*, there seems no small variety of opinion as to what is to be understood by that state of anticipated blessedness, which some call annihilation or extinction, others repose, others complacency, and some infinite felicity, be that felicity what it may. But it is given to none to penetrate into the darkness beyond the grave: "it doth not yet appear what we shall be;" "eye hath not seen nor ear heard" the pleasures in store for the virtuous: and if we, to whom so much has been revealed, but from whom so much more has been concealed, are but wanderers in mists and clouds when we follow the dead into the regions unexplored, we ought not to wonder that others less enlightened, less instructed, should be more at a loss than ourselves.

As regards the belief in the immortality of the soul, from all that I can gather from books and conversation, the idea of final beatitude in the mind of a Buddhist is represented by an ultimate and absolute abstraction from all the cares and concerns of mundane existence; and while the Christian hopes are associated with the noblest associations of active and progressive felicity,— eternal peace, tranquillity, inaction, and, as some contend, insensibility, are the leading associations of the votary of Buddha. But how far this repose is to be accompanied by a perception of its existence, appears to admit of doubt. Neither annihilation, nor extinction, nor absorption, appears to me accurately to represent that vague dreaming which hangs over the Buddhist futurity. It is an ignorance of all that we shall be, except to know and to believe that everlasting rest is the final destiny of the tried, the purified, the sanctified, who have gone through all the trials, temptations, and changes, the discipline of which was necessary to the great consummation. The belief in ultimate absorption into the essence of the Deity would seem to necessitate more of controversy as to the attributes of that Deity, of whom Buddha himself is but an emanation and a revelation; but at the threshold of this revelation inquiry seems strangely arrested: all beyond—all referring to the Causer of causes, to the Lighter of lights, to the Sender of the sent, to the Inspirer of the inspired,— all is left in doubt and darkness, as on the other side of a gulph which mortality is not permitted to cross.

The Buddhist teacher seems to avoid the question as to the eternal existence of matter, by losing himself in calculations which represent infinite and uncountable epochs of time, during which the world has been undergoing perpetual changes which have altered, and may alter, its essential character without bringing about its final destruction. The animals now existent are different from those which in remote ages were the occupiers of the earth; and future generations will produce creations unlike the present inhabitants. Heaven and the heavenly bodies are subject to the same law of mutability—life and death are but the portals of change to a higher or a lower position than that previously occupied, as reward or punishment. The human race may disappear to be replaced by an entirely different order of beings; but the process of mutation is infinitely slow.

To be entirely disconnected from the world is represented to be the most exalted stage of mortal virtue: so, one of the highest acts of merit, and which more than any advances the devotee towards final absorption (Nivana), is the sale of all his property, and his own person, and the dedication of the proceeds to acts of charity. Several instances of such self-sacrifice are recorded in the Pali writings.

In the teachings of ancient sages who have become the honoured among nations, there will be found much more of resemblance and affinity than would be anticipated from the exercise of independent thought emanating from the minds of men placed in situations extremely remote from and unlike one another. The Book of Job contains much of Platonic wisdom, and the words of Confucius and Gaudama might well have fallen from many a Western philosopher. "Attach not yourself," says Gaudama, "to the pleasures of this world; they will fly from you in spite of yourself. Nothing in the universe is really your own. You cannot preserve it unchanged, for even its form is perpetually varying." "Be not the slave of love or hatred, but learn insensibility to the vicissitudes of life; be indifferent to praise and blame, to rewards and persecutions. Endure hunger and thirst, privations, diseases, and even death, with the tranquillity of an imperturbable spirit."

The real and invincible objection to Buddhism is its selfishness, its disregard of others, its deficiency in all the promptings of sympathy and benevolence. Its highest virtue is exhibited in fruitless contemplation; its noblest reward is to be found in eternal repose. A bonze seems to care nothing about the condition of those who surround him; he makes no effort for their elevation or improvement. He scarcely reproves their sins, or encourages their virtues; he is self-satisfied with his own superior holiness, and would not move his finger to remove any mass of human misery. And yet his influence is boundless, and his person, while invested with the yellow garments, an object of extreme reverence. Three hundred *Phra* receive daily their alms from the hands of the King; and this almsgiving is, in the minds of the Siamese, a merit of a high order, entitling them to expect recompence in the next stage of their existence, be that what it may. It is not unusual for a noble, as a work of pre-eminent excellence, to emancipate a slave that he may become a bonze. In the fifth month, at the full moon, the Phra wash the feet of their superiors, and the people wash the feet of the Phra. Compared with the privileges and exemptions which the bonzes enjoy, their privations are few: "they toil not, neither do they spin;" they make no contributions to statute-labour; they pay no taxes, render no services to the Sovereign or the State. Once in every year, they are required to pass the nights of three weeks in the forests, in frail huts built of bamboo and palm leaves, when they are supposed to be engaged in lonely contemplation. The people believe not only that they are safe from attack, but that wild beasts come and lick their hands and feet while they are occupied in their meditations. Among the *Phra*, some may be seen who appear wholly absorbed in thought: however near you approach, you can obtain no attention, or only a repelling frown; they have their eyes fixed on the ground, an expression of perpetual gloom in their visage, and their lips cease not to repeat prayers in the Pali tongue. But in others, the force of nature breaks down all restraints and acerbities, and they will be found busy, talkative, curious, and even courteous. In fact, whatever mask he wears, in whatever garments clad, to whatever laws subjected, by whatever engagements bound, the original type is seldom wholly effaced, and the *man* is found hidden beneath the vestments of the *Phra*.

There are some curious reasonings with reference to the religion of the Siamese written by the Abbé de Fleury in the *Lettres Edifiantes*,* which are worth referring to and preserving.

"What shows that the Siamese have no clear notions of the Divinity, is their acknowledgment that those they call gods have a beginning and an end; that the Sommanakodom (Gaudama) was born at a certain time, that he died, and was annihilated, or at least reduced to a condition in which he takes no part in anything, and no longer acts upon men or upon the rest of the world. Before the birth of Sommanakodom, or rather before he became a god, there was no God. If there were another, had he begun to exist? Thus may they be forced to acknowledge an Eternal Being. As the religion of Siam came from the Indies, it would seem that it is founded on the same principle and the same fables: there are certainly many points of resemblance between them.

"The Brahmins invest their sovereign deity, whether Vishnu or Esomara, with a body and a human countenance; they also give him a wife and children, and represent him as subject to anger and all the passions; much as the Greeks spoke of Jupiter, who was their sovereign god, though he could not resist destiny, and frequently quarrelled with the other gods. The general terms, therefore, in which they speak of an almighty, supreme Deity

---

* Vol. xxv., p. 98—99. Ed. Toulouse, 8vo, 1811.

are of little import. The reasoning of the Siamese would lead us to the conclusion that the power of their god would lead to self-annihilation."

Again:*—

" With regard to the Siamese, it is necessary to distinguish the variety of causes, in order to destroy their mistake as regards the cause of merit. Men, they say, are punished or rewarded according to their merits; as though merit were an efficient or acting cause, not referring to a God to punish or reward them. They should be shown the difference between the means and the end to which it moves. A workman, for instance, builds a house in the hope of gain; will you say that interest built the house? Will you speak of it as an existing being who can move wood or stone? A criminal is punished for his crime; did the crime take the sword to decapitate him? Do you not see that his crime was the motive which induced the judge to condemn, and the headsman to execute him, as gain was the motive which incited the mason to build? Endeavour to make them understand the subject, without troubling yourself to teach them the names of efficient, final, or material cause. If you can once establish the idea of an infinite and acting mind—in a word, of a Divine Creator—it will not be difficult to establish the necessity of our faith. The whole universe has but one Master: we must not, then, say your God, or ours; the Master must be served, not according to the will of His servants, but in His own way. He

---

* P. 101—103.

is the lawgiver; but, they say, He is great enough to be served differently by different nations; since He permits their diversity, it is not displeasing to Him. He allows, likewise, of diversity of colours and form, of manners and language. All this is but conjecture; and according to this principle of toleration, it might be imagined that God approves of crimes; for He might, doubtless, absolutely have prevented them. We must, then, recur to other proofs of His will; for the question is whether He has revealed it to man, and to know His word. I imagine that all idolaters have books they esteem sacred, and believe to be the word of God, whether approximating to true religion or not. They blindly receive all that is written therein, believing it wrong to doubt of their divine origin, or anything they teach: in a word, they oppose their pretended faith to every argument. This point deserves examination."

Nothing can more exhibit the reverence which is attached to the image of Buddha than the severe laws which are to be found in the *Code* with regard to Buddha's likenesses.

By section 47, a thief who steals an image of Buddha, of whatever it may be made, is, with his friends and accomplices, first to receive sixty lashes; he is to be slain to pay for his wickedness, and they are to have their hands and feet cut off and to be fined 700,000 cowries.

By section 48, if by washing, smelting, or otherwise, the thief remove the gildings or ornaments of Buddha, he is to be put in a furnace and treated in like sort. If he strip off the gold, he shall be taken to a public square, and a red-hot iron rubbed over his skin till it is stripped as he stripped the image. If he scrape off the gold or ornaments of a Buddhist image, pagoda, temple, or sacred fig-tree, on conviction his fingers shall be cut off; or, at least, he shall receive sixty lashes, or be fined double the value of repairing the damage. But a repetition of the offence is to be punished by decapitation and the cutting open the heart. If the guardians of the images abet the criminal, they are to be put to death.

By section 50, the stealing in order to sell articles dedicated to Buddha, such as ornaments, sacred books, garments, &c., in addition to the ordinary penalties for theft, is to be punished with exposure on the pillory, with sixty lashes, the cutting off the fingers, and a fine of four times the value of the stolen articles.

By section 51, neglect to denounce offenders is made liable to eight degrees of punishment, according to the degrees of guilt. 1st, to death; 2nd, to have their mouths cut off; 3rd, to confiscation of goods, and condemnation to cut grass for the elephants; 4th, to flogging, from twenty-five to fifty stripes; 5th, disability to hold office; 6th, a fourfold fine; 7th, a twofold fine; 8th, a onefold fine.

By section 52, the destruction of a priest's dwelling, bridge, or consecrated shed, is to be punished by the obligation to repair the damage, and to receive from thirty to sixty lashes.

To dig into or undermine a Buddhist image,

temple, or pagoda may be punished with death, loss of fingers, or sixty lashes.*

On board the *Rattler* were some images of Buddha which had been brought from Burmah. Being placed where officers and men, walking upon the deck, were, in the opinion of the Siamese, subjecting the images of the god to indignity, I was applied to by one of the highest nobles in the land to speak to the owners, and to request them to sell the images. This interference was earnestly pressed upon me, as it would enable the nobleman to do a deed of merit, and to release " the god" from degradation and slavery; and a large sum would have been willingly paid. I said, I could not ask the officers of the vessel to dispose of their property, which they valued as mementos of their adventures in Burmah. I gave great pain by refusing to comply with the wish so urgently expressed, but I was apprehensive my compliance might involve other questions of delicacy and difficulty in my relations with the Siamese.

The Buddhist heavens, with all their attractions, occupy far less prominence in the temples to influence men's hopes than do the Buddhist hells to act upon their fears. In truth, it is far less easy to give a vivid portraiture of felicity—which to a great extent may be concealed from the outer view—than of sufferings whose agonies may be depicted in a thousand visible shapes. Some of the ideas of heaven and its inhabitants are poetical enough. There are angels whose finger-tops are so radiant as to illu-

---

* *Chinese Rep.*, xix. p. 551.

minate worlds: some of them are the controlling genii of the sun, the moon, and the stars. One has a mouth three hundred leagues wide, and a body in proportion; and he seeks to snap at the sun and the moon, that he may devour their beautiful palaces for his repasts; but they always escape him by their never-tiring speed. The rain-angel lifts his hand when showers are to fall, and accompanies his mandate with song. The lady-angel Mekhala dwells among the clouds, carrying a crystal mirror, which she moves when the lightnings break out. A giant frequently attacks her with an arrow or a stone; these fall to earth, and are what mortals call thunderbolts. In one of the heavens are fragrant flowers which spring into the hands of those who invite them. There is a body of angels who sit in judgment on man: they mourn over his errors, follies, and crimes, and send the records written on dogskins to the king of hell; but they are more delighted to listen to the history of men's virtues and merits, which they engrave on tablets of gold and deposit in the archives of heaven.

Of the present reigning Buddha (Gaudama), who was born five or six centuries before the Christian era, the sacred books say, that if a man had a thousand heads, and each head a hundred mouths, and each mouth a hundred tongues, and they were all employed from the eternity in which the universe had its beginning to the eternity when it shall have its end, all would be insufficient to describe the various excellences of Buddha. In all the elaborations of the Buddhist bonzes, the decimal system enables them to launch into regions of infinity. Thus, they say, that of ten millions of millions of worlds the destruction is gradually going on at the rate of one in an *asongkhai;* a period which requires one hundred and sixty-eight cyphers to record, with the figure of unity (1) placed at their head. Throughout all these worlds, and through all these *asongkhai*, the majesty and holiness of Buddha penetrate; yet our earth is always his birthplace, and here he plants his foot. Gaudama is to reign about twenty-five centuries longer. He is the fourth Buddha of our age; the fifth is to appear under the name of *Phra Metrai*, and is destined to rule for eighty thousand years. He is to introduce the golden age. Wars, diseases, poverty, and crime are to cease; the earth is to produce fruits without cultivation, and there will be no longer any excesses of cold or heat. This new Buddha will plant at every angle of every town the *Kamaphruk* tree, which will produce whatever is an object of desire,—gold, silver, rich garments, luscious foods and drinks. Eighty-four thousand vast cities will suddenly spring into existence. Ferocious animals will all become tame; and if a seed be dropped, it will produce more fruit than can be estimated.

The eight Buddhist hells have given full play to the most horrible fancies. In the first, where the victim is condemned to be cut to pieces, there is a wind which restores the separate parts to their vitality; and the operation is performed again and again, till another life begins in the regions of monsters. In this hell one day has the length of nine hundred thousand earthly years.—The second hell has a floor of molten iron, in which the sufferers are subject to horrible torments. They die in agonies, but are renewed, again to pass through the same agonies; and a day passed is equal to thirty-six millions of mortal years.—In the third hell, mortals all take the bodies of animals, but preserve the human head, or *vice versâ*. Devils drive them from mountain to mountain, which fall upon and crush them, but leave them to be resuscitated and to be crushed anew, and then to be transferred to other hells. — The fourth hell is the hell of screams: the floors are covered with lotus flowers and iron spikes, upon which the damned are flung, and where, uttering horrible wailing, they are condemned to pass four thousand years, every day of which is equal to seventy-six millions of mortal years.—The fifth hell resembles the fourth, except that there are devils who, when the damned seek to escape from the flower-leaves and red-hot spikes on which they are impaled, prevent them by heavy blows on their body from an iron hammer.—In the sixth hell, the damned are roasted on spits before blazing fires. When roasted, enormous dogs with iron teeth come in and devour them; but they are re-born, again to be roasted and eaten for a period of sixteen thousand years.— The seventh hell is that of cruel kings. It is more tormenting than the sixth hell; for it seems to offer a chance of escape, having a steep and rugged mountain, up which the damned climb, and having reached the summit, a fierce wind blows them down, to be impaled below upon spikes of hot iron. Here the sufferings last an *antarakab*—a period of uncountable years.—The eighth hell is that of unquenchable fire. It is so crowded, that the damned cannot move. It is the deepest and the widest of the hells, and its torments will continue till the cloud shall be seen which announces the destruction of the world.

These eight hells present horrors enough to satisfy any passion for awful warnings; but as there are a number of subordinate hells, the bonzes indulge their fancies by describing and the artists by depicting an infinite variety of other sufferings. Each major hell has sixteen minor or subordinate hells, thirty leagues in length and breadth and height. In one of these the damned are tormented with excessive thirst. Through it a salt river flows, which when the wretches reach and fling themselves into the waters, multitudes of devils fish them out with burning hooks, tear out their entrails, and, as they cry for water, pour melted iron down their throats.

The more enlightened party among the Siamese Buddhists owes its strength to the influence of the present King while he was associated with the priesthood. One of the earliest grounds of difference was a determination to restore the purity of the text of the Pali books, and the accuracy of the Pali pronunciation. Many of the more childish observances of the modern ritual were also pronounced to be without authority; but the more important reform was the repudiation of a vast mass of commentaries and fabulous inventions, which the new party declared to be interpolations and corruptions of pure Buddhism. An American missionary having asked one of the principal bonzes at Bangkok to explain the differences between the two parties, the priest gave the following illustration:—" 'Here are two piles of books. The first contains the instructions of Buddh; the second contains the writings of eminent teachers of the religion of Buddh who lived in ancient times. The first pile our party receive as authority in religion; the second we examine and compare with the first. So far as it agrees with the first, we receive it; so far as it disagrees, we reject it.' I then inquired whether they actually found much in the second pile to reject. 'Yes,' he said, 'much, very much;' and then mentioned one set of books, consisting of more than five hundred volumes, the whole of which they rejected."*

The form of *Brahminism* is found in Siam, and under the direct patronage of the King.

The official astrologers, called *Hon*, are natives of India; and they have a pagoda, built at the Royal charge, dedicated to the worship of Bramah, Vishnu, and Siva. In this temple are seen all the monstrous idols of Hindoo worship. These soothsayers are habitually consulted on State affairs. I observed in most of the dramatic representations of the Siamese that a body of Brahmins, clad in white, were introduced, and performed sacerdotal ceremonies; and I learned that when my negotiations for a treaty were about to be commenced, the astrologers were called upon to fix "an auspicious day" for entering upon them. They are required to prognosticate the changes

---

* Report of Mr. Carswell. *Missionary Herald for* 1849, p. 199.

of the weather, the results of public policy, the chances of peace and war. If their prophecies are verified, they are loaded with rewards: their failure brings castigation from the bamboo, degradation, and loss of office.

Father Bigandet bears the following testimony to the favourable influences of Buddhism on the condition of women:—" In Burmah and Siam the doctrines of Buddhism have produced a striking, and to the lover of true civilization a most interesting result—viz., the almost complete equality of the condition of women with that of men. In these countries, women are not so universally confined in the interior of their houses, without the remotest chance of ever appearing in public. They are seen circulating freely in the streets; they preside at the *comptoir*, and hold an almost exclusive possession of the bazaars. Their social position is more elevated, in every respect, than that of the persons of their sex in the regions where Buddhism is not the predominating creed. They may be said to be men's companions, and not their slaves. They are active, industrious, and, by their labours and exertions, contribute their full share towards the maintenance of the family. The marital rights are fully acknowledged by a respectful behaviour towards their lords. In spite of all that has been said by superficial observers, I feel convinced that manners are less corrupted in those countries where women enjoy liberty, than in those where they are buried alive by a despotic custom in the grave of an opprobrious slavery. Buddhism disapproves of polygamy, but it tolerates divorce. In these respects the habits of the people are of a damnable laxity."*

The Siamese name of the present Buddha is *Phra Kodom*, or *Somana Kodom* (Gaudama). The sacred books profess to give his history, as narrated by himself, for five hundred and fifty generations, during which a great variety of transmigrations took place, from angelic elevations down to the serpent; once an incarnate white elephant, and several times man. It was when he appeared in the form of a sovereign that he was raised to the beatitude; his father being Prince Siri Suthot, and his mother the Princess Maha Maja. He was born in the midst of prognostications, signs, and wonders—for a hundred thousand worlds shook with ecstasy, and five hundred beautiful children had their birth on the same day, to be devoted to his special service. Many are the legends which record his words of wisdom while yet in his cradle, and the miracles which were wrought for his preservation and comfort. The god Indra busied himself in surrounding him with honours. At sixteen he married, and had a son; but the king of the angels (Indra) weaned him from all sensual pleasures, and conveyed him to the shadow of the sacred Banyan, in the solitudes of Himalaya, where Indra shaved his head and invested him with the yellow garments of the priesthood. He remained in seclusion, engaged in prayers and meditations—passed through unnumbered temptations of every sort, his soul and body growing

---

* "Notes to Legend of the Burmese Buddha," chap. ii. *Journal of Indian Archipelago*, vol. ix. 158.

purer and lighter, till the whole blaze of holiness and omniscience enveloped him, and he became a Buddha. On one occasion, King Phajaman, who had failed to seduce him by all the invitations of lasciviousness and ambition, advanced with a huge army of one hundred thousand giants, whose missiles, ere they reached the saint, were invested with flowers which turned themselves into a rampart for his protection. But the goddess of the earth became wroth with Gaudama's enemies, and raising herself up, she twisted her long locks, and rained from them such torrents that the giants could only escape by ignominious flight. To this hour the spilling of water upon the earth is held by the bonzes to be a work of merit, and they assert that Buddha's outpourings in the various stages of his transmigrations formed a vast ocean. A magnificent throne raised itself out of the earth to receive him, of which he took possession, with crossed legs, to receive the adorations of the multitude. Phra Indra, with a deputation of angels, implored him to open his lips and to instruct the people; and thenceforward he began his journeyings, accompanied by his five hundred favourite disciples, among whom were many princes; and they visited the great cities of India, making Benares their principal abode.

On one occasion, being desirous of giving to his mother in heaven the benefit of his instructions, Indra caused a golden ladder to be made for his accommodation; and millions upon millions of angels descended to listen to his teachings; and they were so effective, that immense multitudes passed into the beatitude of *Niphan*, or absorption, reaching thus the supreme felicity. When Buddha descended from heaven, angels accompanied him, and, as they flew, scattered flowers of celestial fragrance and beauty, every one of which spread its perfumes over a distance of ten leagues.

The sacred books state that the Brahmins exhibited, from the first, symptoms of ill-will and jealousy. This is probably a story of later invention, to justify the ill-will which, in process of time, grew up between the Brahminical and Buddhist priests. On one occasion, it is averred that the Brahmins hid under a mountain of flowers, which the votaries of Buddha had brought to the spot where he preached, the dead body of a beautiful woman they had caused to be murdered; and when a cadaverous stench was perceived, the Brahmins announced that Buddha had violated and destroyed a virgin, whose corpse he had concealed beneath the heap of flowers. Failing in this attempt to overturn the reputation of the saint, they hired a fair young woman to profess the greatest zeal for the doctrines of Buddha, and then publicly to announce that she had been defiled by intercourse with him and was then pregnant; but Indra, alive to the wicked plot, sent a rat which concealed itself in the garments of the woman, and while she was denouncing the impurity of Gaudama, the rat gnawed the belt which supported the bundle, exhibiting the factitious *grossesse* of the woman. It fell to the ground, and a universal burst of indignation broke from the assembled multitudes.

Many such tales are associated with Buddha's early

history. His eloquence is said to have been so irresistible, that he terminated destructive wars by simply appealing to the sovereigns engaged in them; he subdued the fiercest robbers by the magic of his presence; he revealed the most extraordinary secrets of nature, which he had learned in the progress of his metempsychosis.

It is strange to find an Esopian fable in the midst of these records and traditions. On one occasion, when Gaudama was justifying himself to his disciples in reference to a prince (Thevathat) who had been seeking to undermine his influence, he said—" Once, when I was a stork, he was a lion. In his haste to eat, a bone stuck in his throat. He implored my assistance, and, with my long beak, I took the bone from his throat. When I asked him for the reward he had promised me for the service, he answered, 'it was quite enough that he had allowed me to withdraw my head safe from his gullet.'" Thevathat was afterwards convinced, and asked pardon for his faults; but the earth opened beneath his feet, and he fell into the great hell of *Avichi*, where his body, eight thousand fathoms high, is now impaled on three great iron spits amidst horrible flames, and he cannot lie down nor move: he is condemned to these torments for one hundred thousand cycles (kab). When reformed and purified, he will return to earth to become a Buddha.

Gaudama, when in his eightieth year, was poisoned by Phajaman, the same prince whose army of giants had been scattered by the goddess of earth. He died on Wednesday, the fifteenth day of the sixth moon of the year of the Small Dragon. His funeral exceeded in magnificence anything that had ever been exhibited in the world. After the burning of his body, the relics were distributed in golden urns among the greatest sovereigns of India. Indra, the king of the angels, possessed himself of his hair and one of his teeth, which he carried to the *Davadung* (one of the celestial abodes), and erected over it a pyramid, where angels worship his name.

There is reason to believe that Gaudama is not altogether a fictitious person. He was probably some intelligent sovereign who lived about the sixth century before Christ; whose deeds and words were admired during his life, exaggerated after his death, associated with a succession of fables and inventions, till the passion for hero-worship laid the foundation upon which the future deification of a great and good man was constructed: and the doctrines of Buddhism have become the profession of a far larger number of human beings than belong to any other faith. Perhaps nothing has contributed to this more than the wide diffusion of the languages in which the sacred books of the Buddhists are written,—namely, the Sanscrit, the Pali, and the Chinese.

Among the qualities attributed to Gaudama was supernatural strength, which enabled him to subdue monsters and giants. He possessed the power of making himself as large or as small as he pleased. At will, he could transport himself to any part of the world. He could annihilate himself, and transfer his identity to any other being. After his death and arrival at the beatitude of eternal repose, the Siamese pretend that he interested himself in their behalf, and now listens complacently to the prayers addressed to him by their bonzes.

There is no end to the fables and traditions respecting Gaudama which are found in the sacred books. Some of the ancient Catholic writers report that his mother's name was Maha Maria—the great Mary—and that there were bonzes who represented him as a brother of Jesus Christ.* But there is, I repeat, sufficient evidence of the existence of Gaudama,—that he was a sagacious and a benevolent prince—probably the son of a monarch of some consideration—a sage and a hero deified by the admiration of after-days.

" Men first made heroes—then those heroes gods," in the same way that priests begin by making their heroes saints, and to these saints are afterwards ascribed attributes of divinity. Such creations are not confined to any one portion of the globe: they are the tribute which ignorance and vanity pay to credulity and pride.

La Loubère gives, from the Pali books, a translation of a curious Life of Thevathat, the brother of Gaudama according to the Siamese traditions, but represented in the Pali text as only his relation and contemporary. This "Life" is full of marvellous and miraculous events connected with Gaudama's history.†

Of the most famous of the images of Buddha, I received the following account from the King. The

---

* La Loubère, p. 136.   † *Ib.*, p. 145—147.

accompanying engraving is a most correct representation of the idol in the garments in which he is clad at different seasons of the year, as described in the narrative:—

(Copy.)

"Those persons having understanding, both those who are followers of the Buddhist religion and those who are friendly to his Majesty the King of Siam, are invited to listen to the following account of the image of the Budh Gotam,* made of a solid beautiful green stone, or jasper. It is supposed to have been made by the ancient followers of the Budhist religion, but by whom it is not certainly known by the people of the present day, for its narrative account is lost in antiquity. The image was made to represent the Budh Gotam, but at what time it was made it cannot be ascertained; yet it is ascertained that it must have been made many years ago, probably within the first 2000 years after the death of the Budh Gotam, corresponding to the year 1457 of the Christian era, for it has been worshipped for a long period.

"We cannot give an account which is certainly worthy of belief, because many of the Cambodians, the Northern Siamese, and the Laos Shiang and Laos Kao, have a tradition, which is handed down to the present day, that this jasper image has been in each of their respective countries at such a time; but the evidence of these persons cannot be trusted, as they

---

* Kodom.

IMAGES OF BUDHA

London; John W. Parker & Son, West Strand, 1857.

exceed the bounds of truth, and they do not agree with each other. These traditions are probably mere conjectures, and are not worthy of credit. We shall, therefore, omit these statements, and give the account which is most current in Siam, from the time it was certainly known, and cannot be gainsaid.

"1979 years after the death of the Budh Gotam, corresponding to the year 1436 of the Christian era, a small pagoda, which was within a large one, in the city of Chiangrai in the kingdom of Zemmi, was struck by lightning and destroyed, when this jasper image was discovered; but it was supposed to be made of common marble, and not of jasper. It was then placed in a temple. After being there two or three months, the gilding wore off, when it was discovered by all that the image was made of jasper. It was then removed to the city of Lampang, one of the then capitals of the kingdom of Zemmi, where it remained 32 years. In the 2011 of the Siamese Budhist era, or the year 1468 of the Christian era, it was removed to the new city of Zemmi, the new capital of the kingdom, where it remained 84 years. In the 2095 Budhist year, or 1552 of the Christian era, the kingdom of Zemmi became weak, and the kingdom of Lao Kao became powerful, and obtained this jasper image, and removed it to the city of Lau, then the capital of the kingdom of Lao Kao, where it remained 12 years. It was then removed to the town of Kiang Chan, the new capital, where it remained 215 years. In the year 2322 of the Budhist era, or 1779 of the Christian era, the present capital of Siam was established, and the first king of the present dynasty, who then reigned under the title of Phra Bad Somdetch Phra Budh Yot Fa Chulatoky, and occupied the present royal palace, subdued the whole Laos people, who consented to yield to his authority. He removed the jasper image to the capital of Siam, and placed it in the town built on the west bank of the river, in a place called Dhanapung, where it remained 3 years. Immediately after the jasper image was brought down here, he commenced to build the present capital of Siam on the eastern bank of the river opposite the old town, and after 3 years it was completed.

" In the 2325 Budhist year, or 1782 of the Christian era, in the 6th month, corresponding to the month of May, this jasper image was removed to the new capital, and placed upon a golden throne 34 feet $2\frac{3}{4}$ inches high, and gorgeously arrayed with ornaments of gold and precious stones, which are changed 3 times each year, according to the manner represented in the drawings. His Majesty Phra Bad Somdetch Phra Budh Yot Fa Chulatoky, the first king of the present dynasty, reigned 27 years; and then his Majesty Phra Bad Somdetch Phra Budh Lord Luh Nob Kalay reigned 16 years, and was succeeded by his Majesty Somdetch Phra Nang Klau Chau Yu Hua, who reigned 26 years. The united reigns of these 3 kings were 69 years. The jasper image during these three reigns remained in the same place, until the reign of his present Majesty, Somdetch Phra Paramendr Maha Mongkut, who is the grandson of his Majesty Phra Bad Somdetch Phra

Budh Yot Fa Chulatoky, the son of his Majesty Phra Bad Somdetch Phra Bud Lord Luh Nob Kalay, and the younger brother of his late Majesty, Phra Bad Somdetch Phra Nang Klau Chau Yu Hua, and who ascended the throne in the 2394 year of the Budhist era, or 1851 of the Christian era, in the 6th month, corresponding to the 15th May. His Majesty reverences and worships this jasper image the same as if the Budh Gotam was yet alive, and, desiring that the people of friendly nations who are not in the habit of visiting [Siam] his capital should see this jasper image, has had three representations of it painted upon one piece of cloth, representing the 3 different kinds of ornaments which decorate him in the three different seasons of the year. His Majesty has had many of these representations painted, and has also caused to be written an account of the jasper image in the Bali, Siamese, and English languages.

"Dated at Bangkok, Siam, 7th August, 1854.

" This from
" S. P. P. M. MONGKUT,
"The King of Siam and
Sovereign of Laos, &c."

European writers have generally given the Buddhist bonzes, or priests, the name of *talapoins*,—probably from their usually carrying a fan, called *talapat*, meaning palm-leaf. But their Siamese title is *Phra;* by which is meant what is great, distinguished, sacred. They generally live in convents attached to the temples. In several places the number in a convent is small, but in the capital they are congregated by hundreds. In Bangkok there are more than ten thousand bonzes. The whole number in Siam exceeds a hundred thousand.

Their garments are all of yellow, and consist of a *langouti* (a sort of toga), a belt, a cloak, and a scarf. The yellow colour which is used for the costume of the bonzes, is said to have been adopted from its resemblance to that of gold, the most precious of metals, as a mode of showing reverence to Buddha. Their head and eyebrows are shaven, and they carry suspended from their shoulders an iron pot placed in a sort of satchel. They hold a fan over their eyes, which is intended to prevent their attention being distracted by distant objects.

Every Siamese becomes, at some period of his life, a candidate for the priesthood. Clothed in white, and accompanied by his relations and friends—with a numerous band, and offerings for the pagoda—the novice makes his way to the hall of reception, where ten or a dozen *Phra* are in attendance for the ordination. The principal bonze sits on a carpet, accompanied by an equal number on his right and left. The novice is introduced by one of the bonzes with the words—" I present this person, who desires to be ordained a *Phra:*" upon which the candidate comes forward, crawling on his knees, and after three salutations, and joining his hands over his forehead, says —" Venerable president, I own you as my *upaxa*" (the ordainer); and he withdraws twelve cubits back. Then the introducing bonze subjects him to the following interrogations:—

Bonze. Candidate! to the questions I ask, you must answer in all truth. Are you free from leprosy?

Cand. Sir, I am free.

Bonze. Have you ever been mad?

Cand. No, sir.

Bonze. Have magicians exercised over you an evil influence?

Cand. No, sir.

Bonze. Are you of the masculine sex?

Cand. Yes, sir.

Bonze. Are you free from debts?

Cand. Yes, sir.

Bonze. Are you a slave or fugitive?

Cand. No, sir.

Bonze. Have your parents given their consent?

Cand. Yes, sir.

Bonze. Are you above twenty years old?

Cand. Yes, sir.

Bonze. Have you provided yourself with the yellow *langouti*, the belt, the mantle, the scarf, and the pot?

Cand. Yes, sir.

Bonze. Then come forward.

He again advances on his knees, and, with joined hands, says three times—" O father benefactor, I pray to be admitted to the dignity of *Phra*. Take pity upon me: raise me from the lowliness of one of the laity; give me the perfect condition of a *Phra*."

Then the officiating bonze says—" Brethren, if

there be any objection to the admission of the candidate, now is the time for speaking;" and after a pause, he adds—" No objection having been made, the candidate must be admitted."

A book is produced, and while the name and date are recorded, the new *Phra* clothes himself in the yellow garments. A fan is placed in his hand, an iron pot under his arm, and he is thus addressed by the officiating priest:—" Now that you are received, I must instruct you as to the duties to be done, and the sins to be avoided. Daily you must collect your alms; you must always wear your yellow dress; you must dwell in the pagodas, and not in the houses of the laity; you must abstain from carnal pleasures—from lying, thieving, and the destruction of life."

The novice must remain three months at least in the monastery; after which he may resume the secular dress; but if he wish to return, he must be re-ordained. Many remain a year or two in the monasteries, and then marry; but this is an infraction of the ancient institutions of Buddhism, which allowed no abandonment of the monastic vows. But at the point of death the yellow vestments must be laid aside, as it is a sin to connect them with putrefaction or offensiveness.

In the hierarchy of the *Phra*, the *Sangkharat* (meaning the King of the Cenobites) is appointed by the King, and his authority is supreme over all the pagodas and bonzes of the kingdom. He reports on religious matters to the King, and presides over the assemblies of the priests when they are convened for any special object. Next in rank are the *Somdetch Chau* and *Raxakhama*—princes of the bonzes, who are the abbots of the royal monasteries: these are also appointed by the King. Each abbot has a vicar and a secretary. Then come the whole body of *Phra*, beneath whom are a body of youths not having attained the age of twenty, but who wear the yellow garments, and perform menial services in the convents. These have three obligations imposed on them, independent of the five primary obligations:— not to eat after noon till the next sunrise; not to inhale the fragrance of flowers; not to sit on mats, or elevations above twelve inches from the ground.

La Loubère gives in his second volume the maxims of the priestly orders, translated from the Siamese. They are curious, as developments of the principles of the Buddhist religion. In many points they will be found to resemble the outlines of monastic life. All energetic action, all virtuous exertion, would be paralysed under such influences. In seeking to be harmless, a man becomes absolutely useless; and in attention to absurd observances, in abstention from natural and sinless enjoyments, in the exaggeration of minor virtues—such as humanity to animals, respect for life, for personal decorums, and the subordinate or secondary moralities,—all elevation of character is lost, and a talapoin becomes little better than a cumberer of the soil. The maxims are:—

Kill no human being.
Steal not.
Avoid the sins of the flesh.
Boast not of your own sanctity.

Do not break up the ground.
Destroy no tree.
Kill no animal.
Drink no intoxicating beverage.
Eat no rice after mid-day.
Regard not song, dance, or music.
Use no perfumes about your persons.
Neither sit nor sleep in a place higher than that occupied by your superior.
Keep neither gold nor silver.
Speak of nothing but religious matters.
Do nothing but what is religious.
Give no flowers to women.
Take no water from a spot where worms are engendered.
It is a sin not to provide water to wash after nature's necessities.
Do not court secular persons for the sake of alms.
Borrow nothing from secular persons.
Lend nothing on interest, not even a cowrie.
Keep neither lance, nor sword, nor warlike weapon.
Eat not to excess.
Sleep not much.
Sing no gay songs.
Play upon no instrument; avoid sports and games.
Judge not your neighbour: say not, this is a good, and that is a bad man.
Swing not your arms in walking.
Mount no tree.
Bake no bricks, and burn no wood.
Wink not in speaking, and look not round in contempt.

MAXIMS OF THE PRIESTLY ORDERS.

Work not for money.

Give no strong medicine to pregnant women.

Seek not pleasure by looking upon women.

Make no incisions which bring blood.

Buy not—sell not.

When you eat, make no noise like dogs—chibi, chibi, chiabi, chiabi.

Sleep in no exposed place.

Administer no poisonous medicine.

It is a sin to walk in the streets in a non-contemplative mood.

It is a sin not to shave the head, the eyebrows, and to neglect the nails.

It is a sin to stretch out the feet when sitting.

Keep not the leavings of your meals.

Have not many garments.

It is a sin for a priest to love and caress young priests as if they were women.

It is a sin to appear as austere as a priest of the woods—to seem more strict than other priests—to meditate for the sake of being seen—to act differently in public from in private.

To receive alms and to give them to another is a sin.

To speak to a woman in a secret place is a sin.

It is a sin to meddle with royal affairs, except where religion is concerned.

It is a sin to cultivate the ground—to breed ducks, fowls, cows, buffaloes, elephants, horses, pigs, or dogs, as secular people do.

It is a sin to preach in any but the Pali tongue.

It is a sin to think one way and speak another.

To sit on the same mat with a woman is a sin.

To cook rice is a sin.

To eat anything which has not been offered with joined hands is a sin.

To dream of a woman, and to be awaked by the dream, is a sin.

It is a sin to covet another man's goods.

To make water on fire, on the earth, or in water, is a sin.

To speak injuriously of the earth, the wind, of fire, or water, or anything else, is a sin.

It is a sin to mount an elephant or a palanquin.

It is a sin to be clothed in costly garments.

It is a sin to rub the body against any substance.

It is a sin to ornament the ears with flowers.

To wear shoes which hide the toes is a sin.

To plant flowers or trees is sinful.

It is sinful to receive anything from the hand of a woman.

It is a sin not to love everybody alike.

It is a sin to eat anything having life, such as seeds which may germinate.

To cut down or tear away anything which has life is a sin.

It is sinful to make an idol.

It is sinful for the priest not to fill up a ditch which he has dug.

It is a sin to fold the end of the garment, unless there is work to be done.

To eat out of gold or silver vessels is a sin.

It is a sin to sleep after meals, instead of performing religious rites.

Having eaten what is given in alms, to say that it was good or not good is a sin.

To exhibit self-glorification, by saying, I am a mandarin's son, or My mother is rich, is sin.

It is a sin to wear red, black, green, or white garments.

It is a sin, in laughing, to raise the voice.

It is a sin, in preaching, to alter the Pali text in order to gratify the hearers.

To employ charms, in order to become invulnerable, is a sin.

To boast of being more learned than another is a sin.

To desire gold or silver, saying, When I leave the convent I will marry and live expensively, is a sin.

It is a sin to mourn for dead relations.

To go out at evening in order to see any one but mother, or sisters, or brothers, and to amuse oneself by talking on the way, is a sin.

To give garments, or gold, or silver, to any but father and mother, brothers or sisters, is sin.

To leave the convent in order to recover garments, gold, or silver, supposed to be stolen, is sin.

To sit on a carpet of wrought gold or silver which has not been given, but ordered to be made, is a sin.

To sit down without stretching the garment appropriated to sit upon, is a sin.

To walk in the street without having buttoned the proper button, and to enter a boat without unbuttoning the same button, are sins.

To cough or sneeze, in order to win the notice of a group of girls seated, is a sin.

It is a sin not to have the under garment hemmed; and it is sinful to wear over the shoulders a garment in one piece only.

Not to put on the garments at break of day is sinful.

To walk in the streets as if some one were following is a sin.

After washing the feet, to make a noise with them on wood or stone, and then enter the house of a secular, is to commit a sin.

To be cognizant of the influence of numbers* is sinful.

It is a sin to make a noise with the feet, or to walk heavily on ascending a staircase.

It is a sin to raise the garment in making water.

It is a sin to pass judgment on other men, or to say, this is well, this evil done.

To look fiercely at other people is a sin.

To mock or to rail at another is sinful.

To sleep on an elevated place is a sin.

To clean the teeth with certain long pieces of wood, or while speaking to others, is a sin.

To eat and to talk at the same time is a sin.

To eat so that the rice drops while eating is a sin.

If, after eating and washing the mouth, the teeth are picked, and the lips whistled through in the presence of seculars, it is sinful.

---

* Many Orientals are full of superstitions as to the hidden virtues of particular numbers. Father Martini (*Histoire de la Chine*, p. 16) speaks of the fondness of the Chinese for the number 9, which is the most fortunate, while 10 is the most abhorred. The Emperor has 9999 boats; some of the provinces have 999 reservoirs: 9 is the most respectful number of prostrations.

MAXIMS OF THE PRIESTLY ORDERS.

To gird the garments below the navel is a sin.

To take the garments of the dead before they are percolated is sin.

To menace a person with arrest (*i. e.*, bonds), with the cangue, with blows, or any other punishment—with complaints against him to the King, or any high personage, in order to excite alarm,—is sinful.

To be moving anywhere without thinking of keeping the commandment (*i. e.*, the Buddhist law) is sin.

It is sin to wash the body in a current of water above the spot any older priest is washing in.

It is sinful to forge iron.

It is sinful, in thinking of religious matters, to dwell upon that which is not clearly understood, without consulting another priest who might give an explanation.

Not to be acquainted with the three seasons of the year, and the conferences which belong to each, is sinful.

A priest who knows that another priest owes money, and who enters the temple with the money-owing priest, commits a sin.

A priest in enmity with another priest, and who nevertheless accompanies him to religious conference, sins.

It is a sin to cause alarm to any one.

If a priest arrest any one, knowing he has no money, he sins, if the amount be less than a tical; and if it be more than a tical, the priest must be driven from his religious profession.

A priest who gives medicine to a man not sick commits a sin.

A priest who whistles for his amusement sins.

It is a sin to shout as thieves do.

The habit of envy is sinful.

To light a fire, or to cover a fire, is a sin.

To eat fruit out of season is sinful.

It is a sin to eat of the flesh of man, elephant, horse, serpent, tiger, crocodile, dog, or cat.

To ask alms every day in the same place is a sin.

To make a bandage or cup of gold to receive alms therein is a sin.

A priest sleeping in the same bed with his disciples, or any other persons, commits a sin.

A priest who puts his hand into the cooking-pot sins.

A priest who crushes, fans, and cleans rice, or draws water to cook it, sins.

To serve sin is a sin.

A priest sins who, in eating, slobbers his mouth like a little child.

A priest asking alms, and taking more than he needs for a day's use, sins.

He commits a sin by yielding to nature's necessities in an open place.

If he take wood, or anything, to make fire in a place where an animal is accustomed to rest, he sins.

If he cough in order to be noticed when he asks alms, he sins.

He sins, if, walking in the streets, he covers his head with his robe, or wears a hat, as seculars sometimes do.

He sins, if he removes his robes in order that his body may be seen.

If a priest go to sing or to recite near a dead person, he sins if he do not reflect upon death, and that everybody must die, and on the instability of mortal things, and the fragility of the life of man.

A priest sins if he eat without crossing his legs.

If he sleeps in a place where others have slept together, he sins.

A priest sins if, when speaking with seculars, he stretches out his legs.

A bonze may not wash himself in the twilight or the dark, lest he should unadvisedly kill some insect or other living thing.

Notwithstanding all the precepts which are supposed to be protective of personal purity, the paintings seen in the Buddhist temples are often of a licentious and libidinous character.

The persons and property of the priesthood are removed from the general action of the law. There is a sort of ecclesiastical court, presided over by a bonze of high rank, in which the sacred code, written in the Pali language, constitutes the rule of judgment, in precisely the same way as the text of the Koran becomes the paramount law in the superior courts of the Mussulmans. Within certain limits, a priest may both inherit and bequeath property; but its possession does not emancipate him from those privations to which he is condemned by his religious vows. In case of intestacy, the property falls to the convent of which the bonze was an inmate.

A priest is not allowed to take an oath. His affirmative answer to a question is received when he raises his fan; his negative is conveyed by letting the fan drop.

As the priesthood, as an institution, is more dovetailed into the social system than in any part of the world, no jealousy seems created by its laziness, no resistance is exhibited to its claims. It is supported by the spontaneous offerings of the whole people, in whose minds *merit* and its recompences are constantly associated with reverence for the functions of the servitors of Buddha, the depositaries of his will and the expounders of his teachings. Among the priests will be found some subtle polemics, who are by no means unwilling to enter the fields of controversy. The Mohamedans aver that a few of the priesthood have recognised the authority of the Prophet, but the cases must be very rare.

The police to which the *Phra* are subjected is superintended by one of the princes, who has a number of commissaries, who are authorized to bring them up for judgment. On the proof of their delinquencies, they are unfrocked, flogged with the rattan, or condemned to prison, or other penalties, according to the gravity of their offences.

During the rainy season,—*i. e.*, for three months of the year,—the *Phra* are compelled to remain in their convents. During the other nine, many of them lead a wandering, vagabond life; and some of them trade, and practise alchemy or medicine, in spite of the prohibition of such employments.

Their daily life is thus described:— At cock-crowing, they ring their bells and beat their drums, to announce their coming to those from whom they are to collect. They summon their attendants to get ready their boats. They bathe, visit the temple, and recite prayers in Pali. They then take their rounds, and gather from the multitudinous almsgivers— mostly prostrate women—the contributions of rice, fish, fruits, vegetables, and cakes. When their pot is filled, they return to their houses, select what pleases them of the food they bring, and give the remainder to their attendants. They then smoke, drink tea, converse, or enjoy their promenade. A few of them have literary tastes, but such cases are quite exceptional. At eleven to half-past eleven o'clock they take their second repast, as they are not permitted to *eat* anything after mid-day till the next sunrise; but drinking tea, cocoa-nut milk, &c., is not prohibited. When asked to private houses to celebrate domestic festivities, great honour is done them, and they are welcomed with a variety of gifts,— money, pieces of silk and cotton, tea, fruits, and preserves. On such occasions they perform a religious service in Pali, which lasts an hour, and is principally composed of sentences in praise of the excellences of Buddha.

A volume called the *Patimok* contains the regulations which the bonzes are bound to obey. This is an abbreviation of a larger work in several volumes, entitled *Phra Vinai*.[*]

In China, the Buddhist priests often subject them-

---

[*] Pallegoix, ii. 23—32.

selves to voluntary torture; burning off the joints of their fingers in the fire, inflicting terrible wounds on the body, and even condemning themselves to voluntary and painful death. But suicide and self-mutilations are rare in Siam. An example of self-immolation occurred in 1821; but the poor wretch who had announced his intention to sacrifice himself jumped out of the burning pile, and ran into the river. (Bruguière, *Annales*, xxvi. 162.)

There is a body of female devotees called *Nang-xi*, who are dedicated to the service of the pagodas. They are a sort of nuns, wearing white dresses, and are allowed to collect alms for themselves, and for the temples to which they belong. They have their prayers to recite, and their services to perform.

As to hospitals for animals, reptiles, vermin, which are said by some travellers to be under the special care of the bonzes, I know of none such in Siam; though, no doubt, the temples are the recipients of a multitude of living creatures—peacocks, geese, ducks, fowls, pigs, fish, apes, beetles, crocodiles—whose lives are safe and sacred, unless under strong temptation. Dogs and cats are found in multitudes within the walls of the temple inclosures, where they

"Live unmolested lives, and die of age."

Of course, they become a nuisance; but Bangkok is scarcely worse than Damascus or Constantinople.

CHAPTER XII.

CHRISTIAN MISSIONS TO SIAM.

I.—*Christian Missions and Missionaries.*

THE diversity of the religious instructions of the Catholic and Protestant missionaries is an immense difficulty in the way of both. I am sorry to say, they frequently exhibit towards each other a spirit which is not that of Christian concord. The Catholic denounces the Protestant as a schismatic and a heretic, and the Protestant tells his hearers that the Catholic is but a teacher of a corrupt and indefensible faith. The whole field is too much occupied with jealousies and misunderstandings; and I have heard it alleged by natives against their foreign visitors—" They quarrel with one another; they do not understand one another; they teach different religions: how should we understand their differences? When they can agree about what we are to receive, we shall be more disposed to listen seriously." Now, I am much disposed to think that if the various sections of missionaries would only regard one another as coadjutors—fellow-labourers—promoters of a common object, though pursuing it by dissimilar modes of action,—that each should allow to the rest even the merit of good intention and honest effort,—all would be benefited by the concession, and the great work would be thereby much promoted.

It must be acknowledged—and, indeed, the fact is not denied by the missionaries themselves—that, as far as the Siamese are concerned, the labours alike of Catholics and Protestants for their conversion have been almost or altogether fruitless. The early hopes announced with great rejoicing and abundant confidence* have been sadly disappointed. The number of professing Catholic Christians is far less than in the remotest days of missionary exertions; and the augmented numbers, unwearied zeal, and undoubted merits of those who represent the American Missions have produced no visible effect. Yet there is no persecution, scarcely any impediment to religious teaching, and thousands of Bibles and hundreds of thousands of religious books have been circulated in the language of the people. Moreover, much influence is really possessed by the missionaries: they have rendered eminent services in the medical and chirurgical field; they have lent great assistance to the spirit of philosophical inquiry; many of them have been councillors and favourites of kings and nobles, admitted to intimate intercourse, and treated with a deference which could not but elevate them in the eyes of a prostrate, reverential, and despotically-governed people. But Buddhism, by habit and education, is become almost a part of Siamese nature;

---

* The early correspondence of the United States' Missionaries is remarkable for its encouraging tone—" This land is soon to be all Immanuel's." (*Missionaries' Herald*, 1839, p. 202.) It is doubtful whether there are ten professing Protestant Christians among the Siamese at the present moment.

and that nature will not bend to foreign influences. The Siamese, whether or not they have religious convictions, have *habits*, which the teaching of strangers will not easily change. Many of them enter not unwillingly upon discussions connected with religion, propound doubts, and exhibit a wonderful freedom from uncharitableness and censoriousness. I have taken from the reports of the missionaries a few examples of their mode of conducting a controversy. " Will God pardon a great sinner—a murderer, and reward him like a virtuous man? If so, he is not just." " What you say is very good, but we wish to see how you persevere." " If God be the father of all, why did He not reveal His will to Eastern as well as Western nations?" " If miracles were worked to convert your forefathers, why do you not work miracles to convert us?" " You say we are all lost if we do not listen to you: this is dangerous teaching—will it not offend the King?" " You say that God will be angry with those who do not believe you: ought God to be angry on this account?—is He a good God if He is angry?" " You say God is very mighty and very benevolent, and that He makes His sun shine equally upon the just and the unjust: how, then, can He punish sinners everlastingly in hell?" " How are we to know that your books are true? You tell us so, and we tell you our books are true; and why do you not believe us, if you expect us to believe you?" On one occasion, one of the Buddhist priests said to the missionaries—" Do you think you will beat down our great mountains with your small tools?"

Controversies have already broken out in Siam, but they have not taken the character of exasperation which has been exhibited in China, as to the proper terms to designate the Divine Being. I am quite of opinion that it is impossible to associate with words employed by heathen nations any correct idea of the spiritual Deity of the Jewish, Mahomedan, and Christian creeds. In the Siamese language, Buddha is called "Phra poo-te chau;" "poo-te" being the nearest approach to Buddha in sound; and the word "Phra" means Lord; and "chau," any object entitled to respect and reverence.

The Missionaries called God *Phra Chau;* but with these terms Buddhism and *corporeal* entity are distinctly connected, and the only meaning conveyed is that of *Buddha* without his name. The wisest course is, at once, to adopt the Scripture word "Jehovah" or "Jah:" as Mahomet insisted on the employment of the word *Allah* alone as the spiritual God of the Koran, and repudiated every name which he found employed by idolaters in any shape, so I think it would be far better that we should not seek to accommodate the attributes of the God we worship to the low standard which the vocabularies of idolatry offer to our choice.

In most cases, words have been selected merely because they seemed the best, and often on a very imperfect acquaintance with the language, without duly considering the pernicious consequences of introducing false notions with missionary teaching. The impression has often been left that Christianity merely brings a new God into the already-crowded Pantheon.

La Loubère gives some valuable advice to Catholic missionaries as to the best mode of proceeding towards the conversion of the heathen, grounded on the fact that small success had attended missionary labours in Siam. He says, that if the teachers of Christian truth have not the gift of miracles, they must be cautious as to the manner in which "the mysteries of Christianity" are pressed upon the attention of their hearers; that the removal of one set of idols, to be replaced by another having similar attributes but with Christian names, will be a task of some difficulty; and that the only safe course is to commence the work by insisting on the existence and spiritual character and perfect attributes of God, leaving the development of "peculiar doctrines" to be brought about in due time. He dwells upon the prudence of St. Francis Xavier, who, when the Japanese represented to him that it was impossible they should believe that their dead parents should fall into the "horrible misfortune" of eternal damnation, for want of having embraced Christianity, of which they had never heard, "sought to prevent and nullify that thought" by reference to the beneficence and omnipotence of the Divine Being. He points out the consequences which the rash zeal of propagandists had produced by their denying all authority to the writings and all respect for the characters of the ancient sages who are venerated in heathen lands. He says, that by pointing out to them their errors in scientific matters, by the communication of positive knowledge, by the evidence of superior civilization—by teachings in the mathematical, astronomical, and anatomical field,—influence may be acquired; but especially he points out that a virtuous example is more likely to be effective than a dogmatical creed, and concludes by observing, that if the beauty of Christianity have not convinced the Orientals, it is principally by reason of the bad opinion which the avarice, treachery, invasions, and tyranny of the Portuguese and some Christians in the Indies have implanted and riveted in them.*

It is only when the missionary gets into the field of his labours that he is really able to appreciate the magnitude of the task he has undertaken, and the difficulties that surround him on every side. He is sent into a vast forest, and is expected to re-mould and re-form the huge trees he finds there. The habitual modes of thought, the common education of a nation, cement every man to his neighbour, till the whole becomes like a gigantic pyramid; and a few strangers are "sent" to cause the huge pile to disappear. It is a labour beyond their strength. Fancy that men had a mission to persuade a Chinaman to abandon his beloved and cherished tail, or a Siamese to sacrifice the tuft of hair he honours: the attempt would certainly fail, yet the task would be less difficult than that of revolutionizing his very nature.

It is really sad to read the records of unrewarded zeal, of untiring devotion, of disappointed hopes, of feeble consolations, which the honest records of missionaries present. I take Dr. Judson as an example,

---
* La Loubère, p. 141—143.

a man distinguished by every quality that honours a missionary—no toils too great, no perils too alarming, no sufferings too intense, to arrest him on his heavenly way; yet what tales of dejection, what failures, what confessions, and how unsatisfactory as a final triumph the conversion of a few barbarous Kareens!

La Loubère points out that one of the main causes of the failure of missionary efforts is the disregard of the real excellences of the religions professed by those whom we seek to convert. We should, as far as possible, turn their prejudices and opinions to account, and group our influence upon their education. We want to make a *tabula rasa*, and we fail. We cannot root out the traditions, overturn the habits and the recollections of ages; we cannot dogmatize and condemn with any credit to ourselves, or thus exercise a beneficial influence upon others. He says of the Siamese, they, with other Orientals, believe that different religions belong to different nations; they do not molest us in our opinions, why should we trouble them? They do not deem faith a virtue, and say there can be no one faith in the world, any more than one opinion in matters not religious. Their priests do not tell their hearers they will suffer eternally, if they do not receive their dogmas; for, in fact, nobody denies the dogmas, nor do they deny the dogmas of the missionaries, but say they see no reason for changing the faith and rites of their fathers. Show them that their books contain inconsistencies and absurdities: their learned men own it, and ask whether there are none in the ancient books of other nations. They say their best men taught them their religion, and own that the best men of foreign nations have also taught those nations. But they will not hear of sinless creatures—they have had no experience of such. In many of the rites of Christianity, they perceive analogies with their own,—prayers, incense, hymns, saints and saints' days, sacrifices, expiations, good angels and evil spirits.

Why should we, who have not the gift of miracles, scandalize them by suddenly opening, asks La Loubère, all the mysteries of Christianity? Teach them first a knowledge of God, but do not begin by requiring an assent to the doctrine of the Incarnation. The mysteries of the redemption, of imputed righteousness, of the atonement, will be invincible stumbling-blocks if presented in the shape usually employed by missionaries. The doctrine of the Eucharist is unintelligible and offensive if pressed upon a heathen. The doctrine of eternal torments he will not receive; and the teaching that all his unbelieving ancestors, family, and friends can be destined to damnation, he most absolutely repudiates.

The Scriptures, La Loubère says, cannot be safely given to them without proper preparation and comment. How could the language of our Saviour with respect to His mother and His brethren be received among nations trained to reverence a mother as the very groundwork of all morality? "Let the dead bury their dead"—what more abhorrent than such counsel among peoples whose funeral rites form the most sacred of duties and obligations? St. Francis Xavier, when the Japanese expressed their horror at his telling them that their parents would be damned for not believing in a religion of which they had never heard, had, as just mentioned, the wisdom to alter the whole tone of his preaching, and his success was the result of the discretion with which he developed Gospel truths.

La Loubère quotes a curious example in illustration of his views. Father Jerome Xavier, a Portuguese Jesuit, wrote a book called *The Mirror of Truth*. He was answered by a Mahomedan of Ispahan, named Lin el Abeden, in a volume called *The Mirror Repolished*. The Propaganda thought it necessary to have the Islamism refuted, and directed Fr. Philip Guadagnot to do so. He published a work full of abuse of the Prophet; and the Mission, foreseeing that the cause would be damaged by the publication, requested Father Guadagnot to re-write his book—which he turned into so strong an encomium on Mahomet, that the Propaganda sent him a severe reprimand.

Why should not the sages of the heathen be praised when praise is becoming? Why should their merits be concealed? Is there nothing divine in the attributes ascribed to Brahma or Buddha? Is the Sommana-Kodom of the Siamese devoid of high qualities? Are the teachings of the bonzes wholly worthless? Is the doctrine of the metempsychosis so utterly absurd as to be worthy only of scorn? Is there nothing praiseworthy in the horror of blood, in the ideas of the sacredness of life, which are the creed of the talapoins? Is the reverence of ancestors worthy of no deference or regard? Is the declaration of

Confucius, that the foundation of all religion is reverence and obedience, of no value? Are the avowals of that great philosopher, that we ought not to be too curious in our inquiries as to the relations existing between the living and the dead—his unwillingness to give instructions in matters of which he was utterly ignorant—to be forgotten when we address the third of the human family, to whom the authority of his name has a sacredness almost divine?

La Loubère quotes the example of the celebrated Jesuit Nobilibus, who converted forty thousand persons in Madura, having adopted all the rigid observances of a Brahmin's life,—barefooted, bareheaded, almost naked, in privations and in sufferings almost incredible.

But if it be unwise and unbecoming to press our own opinions in an offensive way upon those we seek to convert, how much less excusable is it that we should speak to them of their own faith in opprobrious and insulting language!*

---

* Pallegoix mentions as an evidence of the imprudence sometimes displayed by earnest controversialists, that one of his catechists declared publicly at Muang Phrom, during a hot polemical dispute, that Buddha was in hell; upon which the Buddhist priests armed themselves with bricks, and were proceeding to stone the Christian advocate. He got a good scolding from his superior for his zeal, and the tumult was appeased.

As regards the general spirit in which religious discussions are conducted, I have seldom met with so much tolerance as among the Siamese. They seem never unwilling to listen to arguments recommending religions different from their own. Pallegoix says that one of the Laos princes, whom he met on his way to Bangkok, on the Meinam, invited him to wait his return, saying, "I will conduct you to my country; I will give you a pagoda; you shall preach the religion of the Farangs" (Christians). And even in the remoter parts of the country, the same spirit of charity prevails.

In 1834, Bishop Pallegoix was arrested in the neighbourhood of Nophaburi, in consequence, no doubt, of his teachings among the Laos people. He was kept two days in prison, and conducted by four soldiers to Muang

It cannot be denied that in Siam, as in all non-Christian countries with which commerce has brought us into friendly intercourse, a great shock has been given to idolatry in all its grosser and more offensive forms. This may have been less the effect of Christian teaching than of that knowledge—the knowledge of a demonstrative character—which philosophical instruments and books bring with them. It may be that the mysteries and miracles connected with Christian teaching are as unacceptable and unintelligible to the objects of missionary zeal, as are those of the religion we seek to supplant to our habits of thought and feeling: but where experiments and positive facts come to undermine the Brahminical or Buddhistic cosmogony, how can the force of their evidence be resisted by any reasoning and reasonable intellect? The King of Siam, as I have before remarked, attributes the false philosophy found in Buddhist books, their erroneous teachings as to the creation and condition of the universe, to corruptions which have polluted the pure dreams which emanated from Gaudama. So the Vedanter of Bengal repudiates the authority of the Shasters, and of the various commentaries which, as he contends, have made the books of the Veds of no account, by interpolating unauthorized traditions and ungrounded deductions from the sacred text.

Phrom, with beat of drum. He arrived there exhausted with hunger and fatigue. Under the accusation of the Governor of Nophaburi, he was brought before the Governor of Muang Phrom, who said, " What was the use of arresting this inoffensive priest? Nay! go and look at his boat; and if there be no opium nor other prohibited article in it, let him depart in peace!" And he was freed, as a matter of course.

II.—*Catholic Missions.*

There can be no doubt that a burning lust for conquest and the extension of political influence, mingled with religious zeal for the propagation of Catholic Christianity, led to and sustained the heroic labours of the early Portuguese adventurers in the East. They were alike encouraged by the ambition of their own sovereigns and the mighty authority of the Roman pontiff. Camoens states their purposes with great truth and sincerity:—

The law of Christ they bring,
New customs to establish and new King.*

They were to plant the cross, to overthrow dynasties, to possess themselves of pagan territories, and to introduce the Christian *régime*. The policy was manifest enough in the proceedings of the valorous Lusitanians; but it broke out in a less mistakeable form in the reign of Louis XIV., under the guidance of that extraordinary adventurer Phaulcon, of whom more anon.

The honour of being the first teacher of Christianity in Siam is claimed by St. Francis Xavier, who undoubtedly preached both in Malacca and Singapore, at that time dependent upon the Siamese King; but the first formal Catholic Mission established in Siam was headed by De la Mothe Lambert, a Frenchman, Bishop of Berythus (Beyrout), who, with a small body of followers, travelled from Rome overland, through Syria, Persia, India, and the Straits of Malacca, and, after three years, reached Ayuthia, on the

---

* Vem semear de Christo a lei,
E dar novo costume e novo Rei.—*Os Lusiadas.*

22nd August, 1662. Great discussions and difficulties were raised by the Portuguese residents in Siam, but they were ultimately reconciled.

Pope Sixtus V., in a Bull dated 1588, in the following words, had deprived the Spaniards of jurisdiction in ecclesiastical matters over the kingdoms of Siam and Cochin China, and the city of Malacca, and conferred it upon the Portuguese:—" But so that the provincial minister of the province thus newly constituted shall altogether abstain from the foundation or institution of new establishments or convents in Malacca, and in the kingdoms of Siam or Cochin China, or in their provinces or dominions, also in their territories and settlements to which the just-mentioned Franciscus, minister general, whose commission and authority are and shall remain intact, has appointed, by his letters patent, certain other brethren of the Minores de Observantia of the Custodia of St. Thomas, established in the East Indies, to found other Custodiæ in the latter kingdoms, or their provinces and dominions aforesaid. Neither let him presume to exercise jurisdiction in the establishments or convents of the city of Malacca or the above-mentioned places newly formed and instituted, or superiority over the brethren and persons resident therein; nor let him intrude any other authority towards or in them."

The small success which attended the early efforts of the Catholic missionaries among the Siamese, led them to minister more particularly to the Chinese and Cochin Chinese settlers, among whom they made many converts. They were also cordially welcomed by a small body of Japanese Christians who had fled to Siam in order to escape the fierce persecution which raged in their native land.

The accounts the missionaries give of their early controversies with the Siamese are curious and instructive. They say, the Siamese do not deny the sublime truths of Christianity, nor the moral purity of its doctrines; but insist that their religion is equally attractive, equally holy, equally suited for man's salvation, and that their sacred books have all the authority which Christians claim for the Bible. The Siamese Revolution of 1688 proved a great drawback to missionary hopes and prospects, as it implanted in the Siamese mind the conviction that the religious conversion of the inhabitants was only a stepping-stone to the political subjugation of the country by a Christian sovereign.

The present obstacles to the conversion of the Siamese are represented by the Catholic missionaries to be—1st, the universality of polygamy; 2ndly, the education of youth in the pagodas; 3rdly, the fear of the political invasions of foreigners, especially of the British; and 4thly, the absence of consular protection. The truth is, that where any religious institutions, be they what they may, form a part of the education, habits, and social organization of a whole people, the work of conversion will be one of extreme difficulty: it has been easier to change the dress, the food, the laws of a nation, than to turn backwards the whole current of their daily thoughts, and to root up opinions which have grown with their growth and strengthened with their strength.

I found no indisposition among the Siamese to discuss religious questions; and the general result of the discussions was—" Your religion is excellent for you, and ours is excellent for us. All countries do not produce the same fruits and flowers, and we find various religions suited to various nations." The present King is so tolerant, that he gave three thousand slaves (prisoners of war) to be taught religion by the Catholic missionaries, saying, " You may make Christians of these people."

Pallegoix reports several conversations with the first King, which do honour to his liberal spirit. " Persecution is hateful," he said; " every man ought to be free to profess the religion he prefers:" and he added—" If you convert a certain number of people anywhere, let me know you have done so; and I will give them a Christian governor, and they shall not be annoyed by Siamese authorities." I have a letter from the King, in which he says that in the inquiries into the abstruse subject of the Godhead, " we cannot tell who is right, and who is wrong; but I will pray my God to give you his blessing, and you must pray to your God to bless me; and so, blessings may descend upon both."

I know not what is to impede religious teachings in Siam, but, at the same time, I fear there is little ground to expect a change in the national faith. Neither Catholics nor Protestants speak hopefully on this subject. Their converts are principally looked for among foreigners, especially the Chinese and the Cochin Chinese. The religious teachings of the Catholics do not necessarily interfere with the domestic and civil institutions of these settlers, except in the overthrow of polygamy; and there are cases in which I have heard Buddhists avow that a man is likely to be happier with one wife than with many: but in the case of the Siamese more is asked of the convert than he is willing or likely to surrender.

The account given by Bishop Pallegoix of the Catholic missions to Siam partakes of the general character of such records. He does not hesitate to declare that miraculous interventions assisted the progress of the early Catholic missionaries. He asserts that on one occasion, when the King of Siam called upon the missionaries to give evidence of their divine calling by moving his paralytic brother, saying that on such evidence he would become a convert, the bishop did, by force of prayers and actions of grace, and wrestlings and agonies, obtain the cure of the palsied man; but after the miracle was wrought, the King informed the bishop that " sudden changes might excite troubles." He, however, gave them liberty to build a church and enclose a burying-ground. And the Bishop goes on to assert that a bonze was truly converted and baptized, to the great joy of the Church. One rich person was restored to perfect health, while in the very agonies of death, by pronouncing " *Et Verbum caro factum est.*" A good deal of curiosity was manifested by the highest authorities to be informed as to the doctrines taught by the missionaries, who certainly have always exhibited a zeal, a patience, a devotion the most perfect and persevering. Their converts seem to have been compelled to make many concessions; for example, that a mandarin, whose death took place in all the odour of sanctity, should be buried with pagan, instead of Christian rites.*

A great struggle took place in the middle of the seventeenth century (1668) between Christian and Mahomedan missionaries; and the Catholics were deeply disgusted when the King, whose conversion they deemed secure, received with magnificent honours the ambassadors from Achen and Golconda, who were sent to persuade him to follow the example of many of the adjacent sovereigns, and to adopt Islamism as the true faith. " There was reason to fear that this embassy, by introducing the detestable religion which flatters the desires and the passions, would have utterly ruined all: but the mercy of God rendered it without effect." Christian catechisms, books explaining the mysteries of the Trinity and Incarnation, were printed in the Siamese language and circulated; and a grammar and dictionary, both of Siamese and Pali, were published.

In the field of philology the world owes much to Catholic missionaries; and many have been their works of piety and charity, especially in administering to the sick, and in aiding the cause of education. They have frequently, as in Siam, obtained great influence, but have been little alive to the far mightier opposing influences and interests. Hence, in their ardour to advance, they have lost the ground on which they seemed to stand. " Ripeness is all," as Shakspeare wisely says; and in the snatching at the unripe fruit, the harvest may be wholly lost. For the vast

* Pallegoix, ii. 135.

machinery which was put in motion by the Pope and Louis XIV., under the instigation of the Jesuits, in order to convert the King and the people of Siam; multitudes of missionaries, bodies of soldiers, ambassadors to and fro; a grand scheme, political and religious, which filled the eager and expectant vision of the Catholic world, as one of the most glorious projects of the Holy Father and the *Grand Monarque*; —for this the Siamese were wholly unprepared, and the entire scaffolding fell to the ground with a great crash, burying its most active artificers in the ruins. We ought to feel no surprise at the credulity of that age—we who have witnessed an example in our own even more instructive and remarkable. The sort of electric passion with which the near advent of the evangelization of China was announced through the Protestant world, on the authority of a few enthusiastic, ill-informed persons, will remain as a singular record of the readiness with which we welcome whatever is flattering to our hopes and dreams, especially when religious feelings are concerned. That a single convert to *Christianity* is to be found in the great movement which was expected to christianize a third of the human race, nobody who has any knowledge of the matter would be now bold enough to assert. But there is no imposture which can last a day without some elements of truth and reason; and if we determine to dwell only on these, and to ignore and forget the rubbish and the falsehood which form the essential ingredients of the whole, it is easy enough to make Joe Smith a prophet, and Johanna Southcote the hopeful mother of Shiloh.

Whether from a high estimate of the power of Louis XIV., and a desire to conciliate his favour, or from any other motive, the bishop and missionaries did, after nearly four months' discussion, obtain, on the 18th October, 1673, a most honourable reception for the communications of the Pope (Clement IX.) and the French King, and the letters of both are interesting enough to be recorded here. Of that of the Pope, this is a translation from the Latin:—

Most serene king!—Health and light from grace divine. We have learned with pleasure that your kingdom, always full of riches and glory, was never so flourishing as under the reign of your Majesty. What touches our heart most sensibly is the clemency, justice, and other royal virtues, which impel you, not only to treat with your general equity, but to favour with special goodness, the evangelical preachers who practise and teach to your subjects the laws of true religion and solid piety. Fame has published throughout Europe the greatness of your power and your forces, the elevation of your genius, the wisdom of your government, and a thousand other striking qualities of your august person.

But no one has proclaimed your praises more loudly than the Bishop of Heliopolis. It is from his lips we have heard that your Majesty has given to our venerable brother, the Bishop of Berythus, land and materials for building a house and a church, and that your liberality has added to this good deed other signal favours which our missionaries, who have laboured so long in your States, had never before obtained. My Lord of Heliopolis, full of gratitude, and burning with a holy zeal for the salvation of souls, asks us [leave] to return to your kingdom; and we willingly grant him this permission: and we conjure you to protect and to shelter these two venerable bishops from the hatred of the wicked and the insults of their enemies, by your authority, by your justice and your clemency.

This prelate will offer you some presents from us. They are not of great value, but I pray you to receive them as evidence of the perfect good-will and the great esteem which I have conceived for you. He will tell you that we pray the Almighty God night and day, and at this very moment, in all the effusion of our heart, to obtain from His kindness and mercy, that He shed over you the light of truth, and by this means, when you have long reigned on earth, He may call you to reign eternally in heaven.

Given in Rome, the 24th August, 1669.

Letter of Louis XIV. to the King of Siam.

Most high, most excellent, most potent prince, our very dear and good friend,—Having learnt the friendly reception which you have given to those of our subjects who, moved by an ardent zeal for our holy religion, have resolved to carry the light of faith and of the Gospel through the extent of your territory, we have the pleasure of profiting by the return of the Bishop of Heliopolis to testify our gratitude to you, and to show you, at the same time, that we feel obliged by the present you have made him and the Bishop of Berythus, not only of a field for their abode, but of materials to construct their church and their house: and as they may have frequent occasion to refer to your justice in the execution of an object so pious and so salutary, we have thought that it might be agreeable to you that we should ask for them, and for all other of our subjects, every sort of kind treatment, assuring you that the favours you shall grant to them will be very dear to us, and that we shall joyfully embrace the opportunities of showing our gratitude, praying God, most high, most excellent, most potent prince, our very dear and good friend, that He may be pleased to augment your greatness to a happy end.

(Signed)   Louis.

(Countersigned)   Colbert.

Everything for some time bore a promising appearance. In 1680, the King of Siam sent ambassadors to France, by way of the Cape of Good Hope; but they were never heard of after they left Paknam. In 1682, the Bishop of Heliopolis arrived with a letter and presents from Louis XIV.: to his influence the Catholics attribute the elevation of Constantine Phaulcon to the post of prime minister. M. de Chaumont arrived in Siam on the 22nd September, 1685. His reception was in all respects most honourable. The special purpose of his mission was to convert the King, the Court, and the people to the Romish faith. Two Siamese families, consisting of twelve persons, were baptized. The King is reported to have shown a disposition to profess the Christian doctrines. The missionaries report that he had a crucifix in his chamber, and talked about Christianity with the bishop and his prime minister; but he asked for time; he said he must think more about the matter, but meanwhile the prime minister might present a written statement of the privileges the King of France wished him to grant to the missionaries. They were—

1. Permission for the missionaries to preach, and for the Siamese to profess, the Catholic faith.
2. That the missionaries might instruct their pupils without molestation.
3. That converted Siamese might be freed on Sundays and feast-days from the obligation to work for their masters.
4. That any Christian who by age and infirmity

should be unable to serve his master might obtain exemption.

5. That a mandarin should be summoned to decide all questions where Christians were concerned.

The King made these concessions, and ordered them to be published throughout the kingdom. It is said that the neighbourhood of the Dutch, who had just conquered the Malacca peninsula, decided the King to meet the advances of the French monarch, whose alliance, he thought, might assist him against the forces of Holland. He offered the town and territory of Singor to the French, and desired that troops might be sent to his assistance. A French regiment arrived in 1687, and insisted on having the two fortresses of Bangkok surrendered to them. The King was compelled to give way; and they remained there for three months, when four companies were transferred to Mergui; but the public mind was disquieted, and on the punishment of two Malayan nobles, the Malays rose, were attacked by the French troops, under Phaulcon's orders, and though for a short time tranquillity was restored, the flame of discontent soon broke out in several parts of the kingdom, and the insurgents increased daily in strength and daring.

The King had long been intending to give his daughter in marriage to a young noble, named Monphit, and to place the crown on their heads; but the scheme was unacceptable to the leading nobles. The King fell ill, and one of the principal mandarins, of royal descent, Phra-phet-raxa (the Lord of the Elephants), was nominated by a secret council to conduct public affairs. From that hour the King and his prime minister were doomed. Phaulcon would have fled, but knew not whither to go: he was imprisoned and put to death.* The French troops and the Siamese were at open war. The detachment at Mergui, after valiantly defending themselves, embarked in an English and a Siamese vessel, and reached Pondicherry in safety. Those at Bangkok finally capitulated, and were escorted to Pondicherry, the bishop and the missionaries having become hostages for the safety of the Siamese who conducted them. The missionaries were subjected to many indignities, and a heavy cangue and chains were placed upon the bishop. In the progress of the persecutions to which they were exposed many of the missionaries perished. The details of their sufferings exhibit noble instances of heroism and patience. They complain bitterly of the absence of sympathy on the part of their Portuguese brethren. The want of cordiality between the two great sections of the Catholic Church east of the Cape, the one receiving its influence through the Archbishop of Goa, the other through French ecclesiastics, is a sore which still rankles.

In 1689, five French ships arrived in Siam. The bishop was released, and wrote to the commander in the following words:—" We shall all perish miserably if you do not settle matters, and you will be the sole cause of our condition. Submit to anything, and I doubt not that the King of Siam and his

---

* See Appendix for a translation of Father Orleans' *Histoire de M. Constance*.

ministers will do what is becoming in order to preserve the amity of the French King." It had little effect; French influence grew more feeble in Siam, while that of the Dutch was strengthened.

Some advances were made by the new King of Siam towards reconciliation in 1703. The missionary cause supported itself feebly. In 1730, the missionaries were prohibited from writing, in Siamese or Pali, any books on the Christian religion; from preaching its doctrines to Siamese, Peguans, or Laos; from deceiving or encouraging them in any way to become Christians, and from attacking the established religion. The missionaries were required to place these prohibitions, carved in stone, in their churches. They refused, but consented to erect them outside. The King, at this time, died of a cancer. The missionaries declared his death to be the judgment of God. This exasperated his successor, though he seems to have wished to avoid further misunderstandings with the missionaries.

Persecutions were renewed in the Tenasserim provinces. In 1761, the missionaries say that "Christianity visibly declined, on account of the misfortunes of the times." Internal troubles, invasions from and wars with the Burmese, persecutions and annoyances more or less entirely directed against the missionaries and their converts, occupy the pages of the missionary annals in Siam. In the *Lettres Édifiantes*, one, dated Canton, September 1st, 1767, has the following passage respecting Siam:—" I learn from the missionaries that the kingdom of Siam has been destroyed by the Brahmins [Burmans]; that it has become a vast wilderness; that almost all the Christians have perished miserably; and that the church and college of the missionaries had been razed." In 1772, many were imprisoned. Refusing to join in the public processions as idolatrous, the Christian soldiers were stopped by the King; many indignities were offered to the cross and other symbols of the Christian faith. Flagellations and incarcerations were inflicted upon the missionaries; and in the year 1776, when the King left Bangkok to make war upon the Burmese, he left the bishop and missionaries imprisoned and in chains.

There is in the *Lettres Edifiantes** an interesting episode, throwing so much light upon the state of the Catholic Missions in Siam in the year 1775-6, that I have thought a translation would be acceptable:—

"It is a very old custom in the Kingdom of Siam, and may be considered a fundamental law of the country, to take an oath of fidelity to the King. This custom is not in any way contrary to our holy religion, but among the heathen it is taken in the following manner:—On the appointed day, all the mandarins and officials have orders from the King to repair to a pagoda, filled with idols, where are assembled the talapoins, priests of their false gods. The latter take pure water, over which they make prayers and perform sacrilegious ceremonies, afterwards plunging into it the sabre and arms of the King. This done, the mandarins call upon the idol and

---

* Letter of M. Condé, missionary to Siam. Vol. xxv., p. 390—401.

their other gods to witness, while they drink a little of the water, which, through the prayers of the talapoins, has the power of destroying all who become traitors to their sovereign.

"Among the Christians are several mandarins who, like the rest, receive the King's order to repair to this pagoda, and take the oath of fidelity in the heathen fashion. Fear of the King, who is terrible when his will is opposed, had induced them to join the rest; but although not actually drinking of the water, they pretended to do so. Their names were written down, and the ceremony was complete; but our religion admits of no dissimulation, and we constantly repeated to them that the pretence alone made them guilty in the sight of God. In September, 1775, our Christian mandarins resolved to do as we recommended, and sacrifice life rather than fail in Christian duty. On the appointed day, which this year was the 21st September, they absented themselves from the water of sacrifice; and on the 22nd, they were accused at the tribunal as having refused to take the oath of fidelity. They persisted in saying that they would not do so after the heathen manner, as it would be contrary to our religion, and that they had taken it as Christians do, which was indeed the case. The affair was reported to the King, with malicious exaggerations, while he was celebrating a religious festival, which was to last three days. He gave orders to have the affair examined into, and if the Christian mandarins were traitors, they should be put to death. They were therefore immediately all three thrown into prison, with chains on their feet and necks, a cangue (an instrument of torture) on the throat, their feet and hands thrust into stocks. We did not fail, as their pastors, to visit, console, and encourage them in their prison, where we were allowed to enter, and had the consolation of seeing them firm, contented, and prepared for death.

"On the 25th September, the day on which the affair was brought before the King, the chief of the tribunal sent for the bishop, my fellow-pastor, and myself. We expected to share in the sufferings of our Christian brethren, but repaired immediately to the hall of audience, where the King was awaiting us. We were conducted before him as criminals, and not as we were accustomed to be received on other occasions. The King was very wrathful; and immediately our mandarins were brought forward, with chains on their feet and necks, an honour which we had not yet received. The King put several questions to us, but his irritation prevented him from understanding our replies. We assured him that we did not hinder Christians from tendering him the oath of fidelity; that they had indeed taken it in our presence, but that our holy religion forbade its followers to participate in pagan superstitions; that Christians did not worship the idol, in whom they had no faith; that as they did not fear the false gods, they would not swear by them. We would have spoken at greater length, but the King would not listen. He gave orders to have us seized, stripped, bound, and beaten with rods. The order being given, we were dragged away, and stripped of our cassocks and shirts. I cannot express the feelings of that moment. We both received the benediction of the bishop; and hardly had the venerable prelate bestowed it, when he was thrown upon his back, to be dragged from the presence of the King. I saw no more. Each was bound to a pillar, on the bank of the river, in presence of the people and of the whole Court. Thank God! I felt no terror, and, while being bound, saw only the crucifix which I held. We were seated on the ground; a cangue ten or twelve feet long on our necks, the two ends of which were fastened to a wooden pillar; our feet tied by a cord, by which we were bound to the pillar at the foot of which we sat: another cord, tied round the body, bound us closely to a pillar behind us; our hands being tied to the cangue, which was on our necks, so that we could not stir. The other three Christians were in the same condition, as the King directed that each should receive fifty blows, which were immediately inflicted. We heard their cries, but no blows were given to ourselves, though the reason for this forbearance was not known. Every one was surprised, and some said that the ground under the King shook: this, however, was never ascertained. They unbound us all, we not having been thought worthy to suffer with our beloved Christian brethren, whose blood was shed before our eyes. We envied their happiness: we knew not what had been the King's orders. We consoled these dear confessors while their wounds were dressed, for we were taken with them into the hall: a moment later we saw fetters and chains brought for ourselves. I acknowledge, candidly, that I beheld them with delight; kissed them, and rejoiced in the privilege of wearing chains in a kingdom in which I had expected to find only ease and quiet. A thousand times did I bless God for leading me to Siam contrary to my wishes and inclinations, so to honour me six months after my arrival.

"After having loaded us with irons, we were taken to the dwelling of the Barcalan, close to the river; (the Barcalan is the mandarin charged with the foreign affairs; everything relating to foreigners being taken before his tribunal;) there the cangue was put on our necks, and our hands and feet were placed in the stocks. In this state we passed the night of the 25th and 26th, accompanied by guards. They questioned us all night, yet without listening to us. The next morning the King went out to give audience, and the affair was brought before him, especially in maintaining that it was not lawful for Christians to take such an oath, or to participate in pagan ceremonies. On our side, we were prepared to submit to the will of God, not knowing what was to become of us.

"About seven o'clock in the morning, we were dragged to the palace, and immediately after, the King ordered us to be brought before him. He put the same questions to us that he had done the evening before, and we gave the same answers. He grew angry, and declared we should be put to death: he gave orders that we should be seized; we were stripped and bound, as on the preceding evening, and each received on his bare shoulders one hundred blows. They were counted aloud, the King remaining present. At the very first stroke, I felt the blood flow, and expected every moment to breathe my last. My crucifix, which I had retained, was my support. We all three kept silence, uttering no cries or lamentations, the Lord giving us strength, that all might be convinced of our innocence. The strongest persons of the country generally faint, but I kept my strength. The King was surprised; the tormentors striking with all their might, lest the King should accuse them of sparing us. At length the scene was over, and we retired wounded and bleeding. God grant that it may be for His glory that the palace of the King has thus been watered with our blood!

"We were taken to prison, where were many Christians, who showed us every kindness. Four or five days after, we were conducted to the palace, where those are imprisoned who have taken part against the King. We were resigned to the will of God, but we felt our unworthiness, and martyrdom—how great a favour! such a crown is worthy of an apostle, rather than of a sinner like me.

"We were left in chains nearly a year, till the 2nd September, 1776. Every day we were assured that the King was about to pardon us, but still he delayed. It was in the cause of God that we suffered: the Lord had decreed that we should be released in such a manner as to prove our innocence and His providence. Many mandarins interested themselves for us, and the King had often promised to set us at liberty; but the moment did not arrive.

"Some time after our imprisonment, the Birmans

came with a powerful army, sacked two or three of the provinces of Siam, and besieged one of the strongest towns in the kingdom. The King sent troops, who were unable to resist them. He set out himself, with a troop of Christian soldiers; but his presence, which had once been so powerful to animate the soldiery, had no effect. When it was known how he had treated us, the greatest mandarins declared that the kingdom was lost. The pagan Siamese murmured at our being kept in prison for nothing, and attributed the ill-success of the war to this injustice. The town was taken and sacked; the King himself appeared to lose courage. Up to that time he had always been victorious; he was heard to complain of his misfortune, declaring that he had injured no one, but that he did good to the different nations who were in Siam, without, however, mentioning the Christians. One day, indeed, he told the Christian soldiers not to distress themselves on account of their bishop and their clergy, as he would set us at liberty on his return. During this time we were treated with some consideration; but our irons were not removed, neither was the chain which bound us each to a pillar. We could sit or stand, but were unable to walk. For the rest, we were all together, and no one molested us, but all testified their esteem, seeing how joyfully we suffered. Often have I looked back with regret to that happy time. Two things alone were painful to us: we had not the consolation of celebrating the holy communion, and our flocks were left without a pastor.

"On his return from the army, the King appeared

sad and confused: it was feared that the enemy would come to the capital, and, in that case, Siam itself was lost; but Providence did not permit this. Our protectors and the mandarins who were favourable to us, sought a convenient opportunity to mention us to the King, but none presented itself. While they waited, the King himself spoke, but it was difficult to answer him suitably. Of us, it was expected simply that we should ask the King's forgiveness, and acknowledge our fault; but we persisted in saying that we were not guilty of any, and that we could not be wanting in our religious duties. No one dared, therefore, to present us to the King, who was, indeed, himself unwilling to enter into a discussion with us. He would certainly have gained nothing; for, by God's assistance, we should have been firm.

"At length, on the 14th of August, the eve of the Assumption, the King, who caused all the other prisoners to be brought before him, to pardon or to punish them, directed the high mandarins to examine us, and send us back to our people. They came to set us free, and every one testified pleasure. Nevertheless, we were taken in our shirts, with irons on our feet and a chain round our necks, into the hall, beyond the palace, before the mandarins. They told us that the King pardoned us, but that we must give in writing an acknowledgment of our fault, and a promise that we would not again commit it. We had always dreaded this demand; which we refused, saying plainly, that if the King dismissed us, we must still teach our religion, as we had done before our imprisonment; that we were but the ministers of the true God, and could not change our religion, like the pagans. 'If you are not guilty,' said the mandarin, 'why were you scourged and kept in prison for a year?' 'For nothing,' we replied. 'Why did you not say so?' rejoined he. 'No one would listen to us, and the King was angry.' 'What do you want of me?' he said. We answered, 'We may be again imprisoned, banished, or put to death; but we shall not change.'

"It was already late, and nothing was determined on. The mandarin directed his guards to take us back to prison, but not to that in the precincts of the palace. We entered our new prison, not knowing how things would turn out. We were, however, more comfortable, and we prepared to celebrate the festival of the Holy Virgin. The next day, our fetters were removed; but, as the King had not yet given orders respecting us, we were kept in confinement, and had not the consolation of celebrating mass; but we regarded our deliverance on that day as a signal favour of the Holy Virgin. Every one assured us that on the next day (16th August) we should be permitted to return to our church, and so we expected; but, on the contrary, the morning of the 16th saw us again fettered and taken back to the prison of the palace. Nevertheless, we were told that we should soon be restored to freedom; that the King was angry at the grand mandarins being still absent with the troops: four or five mandarins had taken upon themselves to procure our release. We must have patience; the Lord's will was to prove us, and to make our innocence evident to all the judges of the land.

"On the 30th August, all the mandarins, high and low, were assembled. They had many affairs to examine into; but from that very day the highest mandarin, who loves the Christians and esteems their religion, decided that we must be set at liberty as soon as possible. Every one agreed; but as yet they dared not declare their opinion, lest the King should accuse them of partiality.

"On the 1st September, the King himself began to inquire into the affair: he was told that it was being examined into. The next day they notified to his Majesty that all thought we ought to be released. The King gave orders that it should be done, and immediately retired, without speaking of any other affair. When the news was brought to us, we thanked God, and immediately repaired to the church, there to offer a more solemn thanksgiving. They no longer demanded from us any promise, but all the Christians were obliged to answer for our remaining in the kingdom; so that, after having expected banishment, we found ourselves more firmly fixed than before.

"Three months after our release, the King sent for us to an audience. The bishop was ill and could not go, but my fellow-pastor and myself attended. The King showed us every mark of attention and friendship, placing himself below us, offering us tea (which he does not do to the very highest mandarins), and repeatedly inviting us to drink it. He appeared as if he wished to atone this day for all he had caused us to suffer during the past year.

"Since that time, he has frequently given us audience, and received us graciously; but our holy religion differing from his, we are often forced to contradict him. He persists in declaring that he can fly; and being annoyed at our saying it was impossible, he did not send for us for more than a year. No longer being admitted at Court, we have gone much among the people. All nations repair to Siam; Cochin Chinese, Laosians (people bordering on Siam), Chinese, &c. The harvest is, indeed, great; but we want apostolic labourers, full of zeal, who fear neither torments nor death. We are ever on the point of suffering both; we do what we can for our safety, but the Lord has pity on our weakness. This year, we have had the consolation of admitting several adults to baptism. Had we had more labourers, we might have procured the same favour for many adult Laosians who have died in the country. Nearly eighty received baptism before death, and I have seen many who joyfully received the Word of the Lord in the midst of their trial and misery. Among the Laosians, I found many who heard with docility, and desired to be instructed in our holy religion; but the devil soon disturbed this happy beginning. All these beloved catechumens are now dispersed, and I seldom meet them, my other occupations not allowing me to come and go at will. The Lord's will be done!—all this will redound to His glory, and these poor dispersed people will, I trust, make known the name of the true God in whom they believe.

"My fellow-pastor labours among the Cochin Chinese, who are very numerous. The Siamese show us respect, and little by little render justice to the sanctity of our faith. Their talapoins are rather losing credit;—to what will this lead? God knows. We have much need of the prayers of the faithful. The number of dying children baptized this year amounts to more than nine hundred;—so many gained for heaven.

"This, Monsieur, is the detail you asked for. I follow your orders literally; but I beseech you to ask of God my sanctification, renunciation of self, and the spirit of self-mortification. I often blush to teach others what I myself practise so imperfectly, and to find in myself so much coldness while exhorting others to fervour. I feel assured, Monsieur, of the assistance of your prayers, and entreat that you will sometimes be pleased to offer a mass for me."

In the year 1780, after another refusal on the part of the Christians to join in some superstitious ceremonies, all the Catholic missionaries were, by a royal decree, banished from the Kingdom of Siam. A few returned in 1782, on the death of Phaja tak, and quietly resumed their labours; but Siam was for many years abandoned, and received no missionary from France. The settlement of the English in Penang afforded an asylum to Christians of all the neighbouring territories; and in 1830, a great impulse was given to Catholic missionary exertions by the nomination of Monsieur Pallegoix, Bishop of Mallos, as Apostolic of Siam; since which period, the exertions of the Catholics have been unremitting in activity, and missions have also been established in Cambodia and Laos. A century ago, the missionaries estimated the number of Catholic Christians in the capital at 5000. A vicar apostolic resided there. The Birmans dispersed both shepherds and flocks. There is a touching report, made by Bishop Pallegoix, of the destruction and desolation which he found to have visited the former seat of Catholicism when he reached Ayuthia, in 1831.* There were the tombs of no less than eleven vicars apostolic among the ruins,—now the abode of owls and bats, and reptiles.

The present state of the Catholic population in Siam is reported to be—

In Bangkok	4050
Ayuthia and Salaburi	200
Petriu and Bangplasoi	300
Nakhonxaisi and Bang Xang	300
Chantaburi	1100
Jongsilang	500
Dispersed and in slavery	600
	7050 in all.

The *personnel* of the Mission consists of the bishop, a pro-vicar, eight European missionaries, four native priests, thirty students, four convents occupied by twenty-five nuns (*religieuses*), five schoolmasters for boys, fifteen catechists (mostly Chinese). It can hardly be said that the Catholic converts have always exhibited a becoming prudence. I give, in the Bishop's words, an account of what took place in 1834:—

" The Annamite converts (Cochin Chinese) had obtained, in the neighbourhood of a royal pagoda,

* *Annales de la Propagande*, xxxv. 590.

a considerable portion of land. Little by little, our Christians began to commit havoc in the spot in which the pagoda is,—to laugh at the bonzes, and to play them all sorts of tricks, so that the Phra could bear it no longer. They quitted the pagoda, one after another, and the pagoda being abandoned, became the prey of our Christians. Every night, they demolished the halls, the cells of the bonzes, the tower, the walls, and the pyramids. However, some pious Siamese who had witnessed the devastation went and complained to the chief of the bonzes, who asked justice from the King. Know you what the King replied? 'Ah bah! how can you expect that the Siamese gods will remain in peace while in bondage among the Farangs (Christians)? Believe me, it is better to remove the idols from the pagoda, and abandon it.'

"The next day, as I passed, accompanied by the chief of the Annamite Station, I saw the priests standing upon the outside roof of the pagoda, lowering the idols by cords tied round their necks; others below were stretching out their hands to receive their miserable, petty gods. They placed them in large baskets to remove them elsewhere. 'What, my friends,' said I, 'are you doing?' One of them replied: 'What are we doing? Do you suppose we are going to leave our gods to your Christians, who will melt them and make them into musket-balls?' He spoke thus, alluding to the fact that most of our Christians are hunters and soldiers. This affair made our Annamites laugh heartily; while I blessed the Lord to see, in the midst of a great pagan city, the idols of a royal pagoda, with a rope round their neck, forced shamefully to seek a refuge elsewhere. When the temple was emptied, it may be supposed the Christians did not delay the work of demolition; and, at this moment, not one stone remains upon another of those beautiful edifices, which formerly shone with gildings and incrustations of coloured glass."*

The Catholic missionaries in Siam wear the common cassock, and live with great simplicity,—without bread or wine (except on very special occasions). They have had small success among the Siamese; but they speak confidently of making progress, under the tolerant spirit of the present King. Of the Protestant missionaries they speak slightingly:— "Twenty-seven years ago, American Protestant ministers established themselves in Bangkok: some dispense medicines; others preach, or keep little schools, which do not prosper. Their great object is to print and distribute versions of the Bible, in Siamese and Chinese. They have four presses in activity; they incur enormous expenses; their Bibles circulate throughout the country; and yet many persons have assured me that in twenty-seven years they have not baptized twenty-seven Chinamen, and those they have baptized are people in their service. The Siamese cannot persuade themselves that one can be a priest and a married man. Thus, they never call them Phra (or priest), but Khru (master), or Mó (doctor). Besides, the six families of ministers are

---

* Pallegoix, ii. 299—301.

divided into three sects, which is not likely to inspire confidence."*

The native Christian priests are provided for by their congregations. The Catholic Mission receives from the Propaganda an allocation of 20,000 francs a year, which, they say, is diminished one-fourth by the state of the exchange. The expenditure is thus accounted for in pounds sterling:—

Viaticum of the Vicar Apostolic . . .	£52 per annum.
„ of 9 missionaries, 26*l.* each .	234 „
Subsidy to indigenous priests	40 „
„ to the nuns	40 „
Expenses of the College Seminary . .	160 „
15 catechists, 8*l.* each	120 „
Printing	40 „
Expenses of the Mission's barges . .	32 „
Chaplets, crosses, images, medals, &c. .	28 „
Total expense of Mission	£746 „

The missionaries state that the Chinese are the best of their converts. "They are the most active and industrious; they succeed in all the departments of trade. They work in the sugar manufactories; cultivate extensive plantations of tobacco, pepper, and sugar: some are excellent gardeners, and by their liquid manures obtain great supplies of vegetables. Many grow wealthy and return to their native country." But among the Christians there are few opulent or prosperous people. There is little to distinguish them from the masses, either in appearance or

* Pallegoix, ii. 319—20.

conduct. They have great enjoyment in the ceremonies of their religion,—its music, incense, altars, images, pictures, masses, processions; an attraction not only to them, but to the natives generally, who are fond of shows and all ostentatious display. But great opprobrium attaches to the abandonment of Buddhism among the native Siamese, who concern themselves little with the religious creed or practices of any foreign settlers.

Many of the Christian communities live apart from the Siamese, in campongs, or camps. They give their three months of service yearly to the King, or pay the regular commutation, and are not molested in other matters or at other times. Disputes among them are usually settled by the missionaries, with an appeal to the bishop. The Siamese authorities seem to consider it an advantage to have the trouble taken off their hands, of arranging questions in which generally they have no concern, and feel no sort of interest. The general sentiment of the Siamese is one of a proud contempt for any but his own people—he looks down on all foreigners (Europeans excepted).

III.—*Protestant Missions.*

Dr. Gutzlaff was the first Protestant missionary who called public attention to Siam. He spent nearly three years in the country. His journal is published in the first volume of the *Chinese Repository* (1832). It is characterized by that extraordinary and sanguine credulity, which no amount of disappointment, no experience of facts, no opportunities of knowledge, seemed in the slightest degree to influence or control. He saw everywhere, and in everything, hope and promise. His theory was (and he was in the habit of saying this to his friends), that even the lies told and the frauds practised upon him might, after all, be the means, under the guidance of Providence, of promoting the very objects he had at heart, and whose triumphs he saw in what others deemed melancholy evidence of difficulty and defeat. He reports of the then Sovereign, that " he acknowledged there was some truth in Christianity." Of the Chau fa noi (the present Second King) he says, " he is a decided friend of Christianity;" of Krom-ma-Khun, that " he greatly approved of Christian principles." He describes priests as " anxious to be fully instructed in the doctrines of the Gospel," and generally represents Siam as one of the fields promising great harvests to evangelical labourers. A succession of labourers have appeared—excellent and persevering men; but it may be doubted if they have made a single convert among the Siamese.

In 1831, Dr. Gutzlaff wrote: " The attention of all the different races of people who inhabit Siam has been universally roused (by the Protestant mission); and they predict the approach of the happy time when even Siam shall stretch forth its hands to the Saviour of the world." The report of the Protestant Mission at this period states that the missionaries had equal access to palace and to cottage,—crowds of visitors, high and low, priests and people, men and women, old and young, natives and foreigners—impelled, no doubt, by a natural curiosity to see the persons of strangers, and to hear what they had to say. But, in 1833, Mr. Abeel, one of the ablest of Protestant missionaries in the East, writes that he cannot respond to these "glowing expectations," nor encourage unjustifiable hopes. He cautions his readers from laying improper stress upon "professions," and says most truly of the then reigning King, that he was one of "the strictest devotees of Buddhism." The King gave evidence of his regard for "the truth of Christianity," by informing the missionaries that they must not distribute the books of which they had brought a large supply; that "if it was their object to change religions, they were welcome to attempt it in other countries, but not in his." In this respect the present King is a remarkable contrast to his predecessor, and has, I understand, in no respect interfered with the distribution of books or the teachings of the Protestants, but has expressed an opinion that it is as likely the Buddhists should convert the Christians, as the Christians the Buddhists.*

It may be doubted if the profuse and indiscriminate distribution of Bibles and books is a judicious proceeding, or likely to be accepted as evidence of the *value* attached by the giver to the gift. One of the missionaries acknowledges that sheets of white paper would be yet more carefully sought. Hundreds of thousands of printed tracts and treatises have been scattered broadcast over China and Siam. Has the result responded to the expectation? Has the seed grown up into the harvest of promise?

* *Chinese Repository*, p. 466—468.

Great reverence is attached to *books*, as books, among the Buddhists. It may well be questioned whether it is wise and prudent to fling them to all the winds, as our missionaries fling "their seed," in the hope that some will fall into good ground and bring forth "a hundred-fold." No such seeds have hitherto fallen—no such good ground has yet welcomed those seeds. I doubt not the ultimate prevalence of truth—of Christian as of all other truth; but it is impossible to close one's eyes to the sad—the very sad, but most undoubted fact, that, spite of sacrifices the most heroic, zeal the most devoted, liberality the most unbounded, little, almost nothing, has been done. I ask not the discontinuance of missionary labours, but the calm consideration of the causes of failure—of the incredibly small returns for immensely great exertions.

What follows is a faithful report of a conversation between one of the most distinguished nobles in Siam and a Christian Protestant missionary:—

Nobleman. After all, my religion is a better religion than yours.

Missionary. Convince me of that, and your Excellency shall be *my* teacher.

N. This is my religion: To be so little tied to the world that I can leave it without regret; to keep my heart sound; to live doing no injustice to any, but deeds of compassion to all.

M. This is excellent; this accords with my teaching; but will your Excellency tell me what those must do who have already committed sin?

N. Why should they sin?

M. Who has not sinned? We should own we have sinned; and we Christians have One who has removed our sins from us, and taken them upon himself: but you—

N. Where have I sinned? I do not acknowledge sin.

M. But it is not enough that men should be honest and kind to one another. They owe allegiance to God, their great Sovereign. To disobey Him, to forget Him, to avoid His presence, to be indifferent to His favour—*this* is sin.

N. And so you think God is censorious and jealous of his creatures, and wants their services and their praises? No! let us treat all men justly. God is absorbed, gone into annihilation. We need not be troubled or think about Him.

M. No! He lives above. He is *our* Master. It is not enough that servants should be honest towards their fellows, kind to their wives and children: they owe to *their* Master service and gratitude, and will be punished if they do not render them.

N. Who is to punish? You call sin what is no sin.

M. But does not your Excellency flog your servants when they disobey? Do you pardon them solely because they have not wronged their fellow-servants?

N. (*much excited.*) What service does God want of us? He is not envious and covetous, as you fancy him to be.

M. Suppose I told your Excellency's servants that nothing was required of them but to live honestly and pleasantly together; to care nothing about you—

neither to seek to please, nor obey, nor serve you, nor be thankful for your Excellency's kindness: will you allow this?

N. Now, I will tell you of your heavy sins.

M. Show it me, and I will confess.

N. Why don't you take a wife?—why don't you provide successors to teach your religion when you are gone? Christ had thirty disciples, had he not? and his disciples had wives and children; and they multiplied, and have overrun the world: but your religion and your name would perish together if others followed your example.

M. Others will take care of this.

N. No! each man has a duty for himself.

M. Your Excellency is right,—I am beaten here; but your Buddhist priests enjoin celibacy.

N. Battle it, then, with the Buddhist priests, and not with me.

On another occasion, this nobleman said—"Now, how long have you American missionaries been here?"

M. Nineteen years.

N. Have you made a single convert?

M. Not among the Siamese; and we acknowledge our disappointment, but are not discouraged. If a merchant sent out his agents and they failed, he would recal them; but those who sent us would think their sacrifices well repaid if a single soul were saved; for a soul is not extinguished by death, but lives for ever: and we know that Siam will become a Christian country.

N. But the Siamese are not savages of the woods, having no religion and therefore ready to receive one. We have our religion, in which we have been brought up from our childhood: it will not easily be rooted out. Has it been in any single instance? The work would be difficult.

I received from an intelligent and well-informed gentleman the following account of the

Protestant Missions in Siam.

" 1st. *Baptist Mission*, representing the American Baptist Missionary Union, was commenced in 1833 by the Rev. J. Lalor Jones, who continued his useful labours till his death in September, 1851. He completed the translation of the New Testament Scriptures in the Siamese, and prepared several useful works in the same language. This Mission has both a Siamese and Chinese department. Now connected with the Siamese department are—Rev. S. J. Smith and wife; Mr. J. H. Chandler (printer) and wife; and Miss H. H. Morse (teacher), absent. In the Chinese department are—Rev. W. Ashmore and family; Rev. Robert Telford and family.

" This Mission has met with considerable success in their labours, especially among the Chinese, some sixty of this class having professed their faith in Christ since the commencement of the Mission. Ten other natives have at different times joined their communion. Thirty-three native members are now connected with this Mission. The Mission lost its printing establishment, dwellings, and most of its property, by fire, in January, 1851. This loss has been but partially repaired.

"2nd. *Mission of the American Missionary Association.*—Present missionaries connected with the Mission: Rev. D. B. Bradley, M.D., and family; Rev. L. B. Lane, M.D., and family (absent).

"This Mission was established in 1850; but its senior missionary, Dr. Bradley, had been previously labouring in this field in connexion with a Mission of the American Board of Commissioners, which was withdrawn from this field, the Chinese department of it being transferred to China. Dr. Bradley then took service under the American Missionary Association. Both these last-named societies are supported by Congregationalists, corresponding to the Independents of England. This Mission has a printing establishment, which, however, is now rented and worked by the Presbyterian Mission. Dr. Bradley first arrived in the country in 1835, and has since resided here, with the exception of an absence of three years. He has laboured very successfully in his medical profession, and prepared many useful books in Siamese, including a very full Old Testament History, which, in the absence of the translation of that portion of the Bible, is very valuable. Other valuable works were written by the several members of the Mission of the American Board of Commissioners, during their labours here, some of which are still in print.

"3rd. *Mission of the Board of Foreign Missions of the Presbyterian Church in the United States.*—Missionaries: Rev. S. Mattoon and family; S. R. House, M.D.; Rev. M. M. Carleton and Mrs. Carleton, at Singapore, on the way to join the Mission.

"The Mission was first established in 1840; but the first missionary, the Rev. Wm. P. Buell, was soon obliged to return to the United States on account of sickness, and the Mission was suspended till the arrival of the present labourers in 1847.

"There are two native converts to Christianity connected with this Mission, and a boarding-school of thirty scholars, in which the Siamese, Chinese, and English languages are taught.

"A revised translation of the Four Gospels and the Acts of the Apostles has been made by this Mission; and they have at present under their superintendence a printing and binding establishment.

"For the most part, the missionaries have been permitted to pursue their work without serious interference on the part of the Government, or open opposition on the part of the people; but those arriving in the country toward the close of the late reign found it impossible to obtain suitable locations for dwellings, it apparently being the policy of the Government to confine the foreign residents within the limits already occupied by them. Immediately after the visit of Sir James Brooke, also, our teachers and some of our servants were arrested and put into confinement, under pretence of examining our teachers as to what they had taught us. The examination had made no progress when his late Majesty was attacked with his last sickness, and our teachers were released, after having paid some thirty or forty ticals each, and given security for their appearance for examination when called for. No call was ever made upon them; and upon the accession of his Majesty the present King, our teachers returned to their work.

"The present King, before his accession to the throne, had personally been upon friendly and intimate terms with the missionaries, and had gained through them most of his knowledge of the English language and Western sciences. Upon the accession of his Majesty, he publicly assured us, in common with other foreigners, of his protection, and that we should be permitted to pursue our several callings without hindrance.

"We readily obtained suitable sites for building, and were permitted to go with freedom in every direction, and without passes; and in no respect had we any cause of complaint in regard to the treatment we received personally, and heard of no complaint on the part of the King or the Government against ourselves, till about the 1st October last, when a Singapore paper arrived, containing a letter, purporting to have been written at Bangkok, reflecting upon the King personally, and not in very respectful terms. A few days after the arrival of the letter, the missionaries were requested to convene at the house of Phya Sri Suriwong, where the letter was put into our hands, and we questioned as to the author, and told that we must clear ourselves from any suspicion of having had anything to do with the letter; and of that we thought the letter itself was sufficient proof, and we in a kind manner protested against being held responsible for anonymous communications concerning Siam. This was not satisfactory, and we were made to understand that we were expected to deny the truth of the statements made in the letter. This, for many reasons, we could not do; and one which was decisive with us was, that it would expose us to be called upon to reply to and deny any and everything published about Siam which did not please his Majesty. We were informed that the King was particularly displeased with the assertions in the letter, that things were in a worse state than during the preceding reign, and that his Majesty had lost the good-will of all European residents. We, therefore, made a brief statement, to the effect that personally we had received every kindness from the King, and that in many respects circumstances had been improved beyond what they were in the previous reign, and that his Majesty had our most hearty good-will.

"This paper, we soon heard, was not satisfactory, and that one of our number was more particularly suspected, and his name was left out of the list of those invited to the Palace upon the birthday of the King, which occurred about that time. At these meetings it had been customary for us to prepare a brief congratulatory address to the King: upon this occasion we were requested to present one as missionaries, independently of the European residents, and to have reference to existing circumstances. From high quarters we were reminded of the benefits we had derived from the King's favour, intimating that we had not a proper appreciation of his Majesty's favours. We were most desirous to assure his Majesty of our friendly feelings, and to show that we appreciated and were truly grateful for all the kindness he had shown us. At the same time, we determined to avoid referring to newspaper articles, or to express any opinion on the politics of the country. These influences gave direction to the address which, without our knowledge or aid, got into the newspapers, and has been the subject of comment.

"For more than a month nothing occurred to interrupt our quiet, and no restrictions were placed upon our movements.

"The King had repeatedly given his consent to the missionaries renting places of residence where and of whom they chose. Mr. Chandler, of the Baptist Mission, who has lately returned from the United States of America, wishing to rent, a woman who had been long connected with this Mission purchased a lot for the purpose of renting it to him. Application was made to the proper authorities, and their consent obtained, when Mr. Chandler commenced collecting materials to build. But, after the lapse of a month or two, quite unexpectedly to us all, the party purchasing the lot, and the party through whom it was purchased, and another woman who was only suspected, and who really had nothing to do with the land, were arrested on the charge of selling land to foreigners. They were put in chains, and at night in the stocks; and although upon examination nothing wrong was found in their proceedings, they were not released till after paying a sum of money; and Mr. Chandler found it necessary to abandon the renting the place, and to remove the materials from the ground.

"Soon after these occurrences, we heard of the proclamation prohibiting our going beyond the custom-house stations in the direction of the sea, and, as we then supposed, in any direction. We applied for a sight of the proclamation, but it was refused; and, ignorant of its real character, and hearing a variety of reports from natives, our situation was more uncomfortable than it would have been had we known the exact truth. We have since ascertained the real character of the proclamation, and find that it prohibits our going to the sea, but leaves us at liberty to go in any other direction. The reason alleged is, that one of our number has had some altercation with some of the King's servants, and the restriction was placed upon others on account of their connexion with the offending party.

"About the same time, our native teachers were arrested, under pretence of questioning them as to their knowledge concerning the letters in the Singapore papers. After a few days, they were dismissed, and told that they could again return to their labours, charged, however, not to bring us any false reports concerning the internal affairs of the country. For the honour of being questioned on subjects of which they knew nothing, they paid more than three months' wages. Although having permission to return to their work, they are very slow to do so, being fearful of further difficulties. The altercation with the King's servants, mentioned in the proclamation, refers, as we learn, to circumstances which occurred in June last, when Mr. Chandler and Mr. Telford, and their families, arrived from Singapore. Mr. Smith, with the verbal consent of the proper officers, went out to the Bar to receive them: after which, as the vessel was detained some time at Paknam, he again went down to get some of their personal clothing, but was not permitted to take anything that could not be opened; and as he had left most of the keys behind him, he obtained very little. Then, if ever, the altercation took place. Mr. Smith says he had no contention with those in charge of the ship, but took what he was permitted to do, and left the remainder. However that may be, it is certain that we heard of no complaints till months afterwards, when the Singapore letters had appeared, and it was understood that he was under displeasure.

"In justice to some of the principal nobles, and our neighbour Prince Krom Hluang Wongsa, and also his Majesty the Second King, I must say that they have ever expressed regret at the course taken by the King on this subject, saying that he did not consult with them in reference to it."

It was my good fortune to render, during my visit to Bangkok, some slight service to the American missionaries. From some misunderstanding, the King, as above reported, had prohibited them from visiting the coast for the sake of their health, which had been their usual practice during the hot season. I took an opportunity of pleading for them with his Majesty, who kindly withdrew the obnoxious proclamation, and I insert the following correspondence with a natural sentiment of gratification.

Bangkok, April 23rd, 1855.
To His Excellency Sir John Bowring.

DEAR SIR,—We, the undersigned American missionaries, cannot forbear to express to your Excellency our lively gratitude for the great favour which your Excellency, wholly unsolicited, has very recently done us, and the cause we have espoused, in requesting his Majesty the King of Siam to remove the late restrictions to our travelling in this country; nor for the good we trust you have done the Siamese nation, England, and the world, by negotiating the new Treaty of friendship and commerce between his Majesty the King of Siam and her Majesty, Sovereign of Great Britain and Ireland, which your Excellency has just completed. It is wonderful with what promptness and peacefulness your Excellency has performed this great work. Surely, the King of kings and Lord of lords has been with your Excellency, His servant, to impart the spirit of wisdom and power; and to Him we are glad to think your Excellency, with ourselves, is disposed to ascribe all the praise.

May your Excellency's precious life be preserved yet many years to bless the great nation of which you have the honour to be a distinguished servant, and the world, of which you are in an extraordinary and praiseworthy sense a citizen.

Your humble and obedient servants,

(Signed) J. H. CHANDLER.   D. B. BRADLEY.
         SAMUEL J. SMITH.   S. MATTOON.
         ROBERT TELFORD.   W. ASHMORE.

H. B. M. S. *Rattler*, Gulf of Siam,
24th April, 1855.

MY DEAR SIRS,—I have to acknowledge your kind address. The slight service I had an opportunity of rendering you was a very inadequate return for the many demands upon your time and labours which my visit to Bangkok has entailed upon you, and for whose cheerful dedication we all owe you many thanks.

With that visit is associated all that is hopeful for the future and grateful for the past. I trust that a better and happier era will smile on the beautiful and productive country in which your tents are raised. That your labours bring with them the peace of an approving conscience is the first initiatory recompence: I pray that higher and nobler ones may be yours.

I am, with great respect and regard,
>My dear Sirs,
>>Your very faithful friend and servant,
>>>(Signed)   JOHN BOWRING.

CHAPTER XIII.

BANGKOK.

General Description of City.

THE principal interest of the Kingdom of Siam is confined to the City of Bangkok. Widely extended as are the provinces and dependencies of Siam, its capital, perhaps more than any capital in the world, unites a greater variety of objects peculiar to itself, and presents a more remarkable contrast to the general character of the surrounding country. This is mainly attributable to the nature of the government—a monarchy, absolute and ostentatious, around which society, in all its forms, is in a state of prostration. The humiliation of one order or rank of men to another, from step to step, is the object which first excites the marvel of the traveller. To me who have been accustomed to witness the subjection of the multitude before high office and dignity in China, the scenes in Bangkok were almost incredible. Every grade is in a state of humble submission to the grade above it, till, culminated in the person and presence of the Sovereign, all the concentrated reverence takes the character of universal adoration, and announces, less a mortal raised above his fellow-mortals, than a god in the presence of trembling, abject men.

The approach to Bangkok is equally novel and beautiful. The Meinam is skirted on the two sides with forest-trees, many of which are of a green so bright as to defy the powers of art to copy. Some are hung with magnificent and fragrant flowers; upon others are suspended a variety of tropical fruits. Gay birds, in multitudes, are seen on the branches in repose, or winging their active way from one place to another. The very sandbanks are full of life; and a sort of amphibious fish are flitting from the water, to be lost among the roots of the jungle-wood. On the stream all varieties of vessels are moving up and down, some charged with leaves of the atap palm, which at once adorn and cause them to be wafted by the wind along the water. A few huts of bamboo, with leaved roofs, are seen; and in the neighbouring creeks, the small boats of the inhabitants are moored. Here and there is a floating house, with Chinese inscriptions on scarlet or other gay-coloured paper; and at greater distances from one another are temples adjacent to the river, whose priestly occupants, always clad in yellow garments, their heads shaven bare, and holding a palm-leaf fan between their faces and the sun, sit in listless and unconcerned vacancy, or affected meditation, upon the rafts or railings which skirt the shore.

But the houses thicken as you proceed; the boats increase in number; the noise of human voices becomes louder; and, one after another, pyramidical temples, domes, and palaces are seen towering above the gardens and forests. Over the perpetual verdure, so emerald-bright, roofs of many-coloured adornings sparkle in the sun. Sometimes white walls are visible, through whose embrasures artillery is peeping; multitudes of junks grotesquely and gaily painted, whose gaudy flags are floating in the breezes; each junk with the two great eyes which are never wanting in the prow; ("No have eyes, how can see?" say the Chinese;) square-rigged vessels, most of which carry the scarlet flag with the white elephant in the centre; while, on both sides of the river, a line of floating bazaars, crowded with men, women, and children, and houses built on piles along the banks, present all the objects of consumption and commerce. Meanwhile, multitudes of ambulatory boats are engaged in traffic with the various groups around. If it be morning, vast numbers of priests will be seen in their skiffs on the Meinam, with their iron pot and scrip, levying their contributions of food from the well-known devotees, who never fail to provide a supply for the multitudinous mendicants (if mendicants they can be called), whose code alike prohibits them from supplicating for alms, and from returning thanks when those alms are given.

Seldom is music wanting to add to the interest of the scene. The opulent Siamese have invariably bands of musicians in their service;—the gongs of the Chinese, the sweet pipes of the Laos, the stringed and wind instruments of the native population, seem never still.

The city of Bangkok extends along the banks of the Meinam a distance of several miles. The greater proportion of the population is on the left side of the river. The number has been variously estimated from 50,000 to half a million, so imperfect are Oriental statistics. My impression, without any accurate means of knowledge, is that the population somewhat exceeds 300,000. Pallegoix says that it may be estimated at above 400,000, composed of—

Chinese (paying taxes)	200,000
Siamese	120,000
Annamites (Cochin Chinese)	12,000
Cambodians	10,000
Peguans	15,000
Laos	25,000
Burmese	3,000
Malays	15,000
Christians of various nations	4,000

In discussing this matter with the Catholic missionaries, they generally concurred in maintaining the accuracy of the Bishop's estimate, and stated that they had made a comparison of the ground occupied by the Catholic Christians, who came immediately under their cognizance, with the whole extent of the city, and had satisfied themselves that 400,000 was about the total number of the inhabitants of Bangkok.

I copy from Moor's *Notices of the Indian Archipelago* the following estimates. They serve to show how imperfect our information is on the subject of the population of Siam:—

Population of Bangkok in 1828.*

Chinese (paying tax)†	310,000
Descendants of Chinese	50,000
Cochin Chinese	1,000
Cambojans	2,500
Siamese	8,000
Peguans	5,000
Carried forward	376,500

* "This table of the population cannot be relied on as giving anything more than a very faint and imperfect view of the inhabitants. The Chinese who pay this triennial tax are those who have emigrated to Siam, or their children, who retain the Chinese habits and speak the Chinese language. Those children who speak only Siamese (and their number is very great) are marked upon the wrist like the Siamese. The Chinese descendants make at least half as many as the pure Chinese. The wives of the Chinese are Siamese, Peguans, Malays, Cambojans, and Burmese; and all speak the Siamese language. The children pay no tax till seventeen or eighteen years of age; nor do the women ever pay any capitation tax. If any considerable portion of Chinese are married (and it would seem that a great proportion of them are) the population of the other classes is much greater than is stated. The Cochin Chinese are said to be 1000; but more than 2000 arrived at Bangkok in 1834. The priests are estimated at 20,000 by Mr. Hunter. Though this estimate is probably beyond the truth, they may safely be reckoned at 15,000; deducting 1000 for other races, 14,000 would remain as Siamese priests,—and yet the number of priests will not equal the number of male Siamese who are not in the priesthood: allowing it, however, to be equal, the male Siamese would be 28,000. Females and children would swell the number to 60,000 or 70,000 at the least. The Peguans, who are estimated at 5000, reside at Bangkok in but small numbers. Their principal settlements are Paek-làte, fifteen miles below Bangkok, and Samkok and the neighbouring villages, fifteen or twenty miles above. Their whole number in Siam is about 40,000. The Burmans and Tavoyers together amount to 1000 or 1200, the Malays to 8000 or 10,000, the *Portuguese descendants* to 500 or 600, and the *Christians* about a dozen. You see I deny the name Christian to some who are very fond of claiming it. I do it on the same principle that I could not call a 'pickpocket' a 'gentleman.' "—Moor's *Notes*, as above.

† A poll-tax amounting to about three dollars is levied upon every Chinaman on first entering the country, and re-collected triennially. This secures to them the privilege of exercising any craft or following any trade they please, and exempts them from the half-yearly servitude required by the King from every other Oriental stranger resident in Siam.—Tomlin's *Journal*.

Brought forward	376,500
Laos (lately come)	7,000
Ditto (old residents)	9,000
Burmans (or Bramas)	2,000
Tavoyers	3,000
Malays	3,000
Christians	800
	401,300

I find in a report from Dr. Bradley some valuable vital statistics, showing among 3650 patients who applied for relief at his Missionary Hospital at Bangkok, in a space of fourteen months (1835-6), the proportions of various races, the state of education, and the ages of the applicants:—

NATIONS.

Siamese		2132
Chinese:—		
Foo Kien	150	
Chaou chow	713	
Kiaying chow	5	
Canton	15	
Hainan	51	
		934
Mussulmans		186
Laos		169
Peguans		105
Cochin Chinese		61
Cambodians		47
Christians:—		
Indo-Portuguese	5	
British	7	
Americans	2	
		14
Burmese		5
Total		3653

Males	2884
Females	766
	3650
Unmarried	2408
Married	1242
	3650
Priests	172
Readers	1308
Illiterate	2342
	3822

AGES.

Under 10 years	177
10 to 20	534
20 to 30	774
30 to 40	859
40 to 50	498
50 to 60	415
60 to 70	268
70 to 80	98
80 to 90	25
90 to 100	3
100	1
	3652

There are a few obvious errors, but Dr. Bradley states the tables to be approximatively true.

The American medical missionaries state, in a report made in 1846, that, including cases of vaccination, they had dealt with between twelve and thirteen thousand patients in Bangkok; and that the daily applications at the dispensary were from fifty to sixty; and that they succeed in about two-thirds of all the cases that apply for remedial aid. Of 1308 persons, the numbers were—

Siamese	601
Chinese	539
Laos	65
Malays	42
Cambodians	18
Surat	13
Indo-Portuguese	10
Bengalese	7
English	5
Peguan	5
Parsees	1
Unknown	2
Males	1017
Females	273
Not noted	18
Single	628
Married	427
Not noted	253
Could read	414
Could not read	503
Not known	391

Tables of Temperature and Rain at Bangkok.

The following Tables, prepared by the Rev. J. Caswell, an American missionary in Siam, give synoptical views of the mean temperature at Bangkok for each month of the eight years ending with 1847; of the extremes of temperature for the same period; of the greatest and least, with the average daily range of the mercury, for the years 1845-6-7; also of the number of rainy days from 1840-44, inclusive; with the amount of rain in inches which fell each month in 1845-6-7.

TEMPERATURE.

Synoptical View of the Mean Temperature at Bangkok each Month and Year for the Years 1840-47, inclusive.

	1840.	1841.	1842.	1843.	1844.	1845.	1846.	1847.	Average Monthly Mean.
January .	77·16	88·77	79·32	77·53	74·59	74·07	77·18	74·72	76·67
February.	80·80	80·84	83·13	79·50	79·32	81·81	78·34	78·51	79·03
March. .	83·58	85·73	83·73	83·71	85·79	82·36	83·35	82·02	83·78
April . .	83·60	87·25	84·50	85·03	85·32	79·97	85·52	82·72	84·24
May . .	84·08	84·67	83·41	84·75	84·58	82·04	83·88	81·82	83·67
June . .	82·27	84·40	83·12	84·44	82·50	81·33	82·19	81·93	82·78
July . .	82·66	84·39	81·92	82·51	81·28	79·89	81·41	82·20	81·99
August .	82·36	84·84	82·16	82·75	80·07	79·85	81·11	80·75	81·73
September	82·83	83·48	82·02	82·01	80·15	79·73	80·37	80·20	81·35
October .	81·77	84·55	80·57	81·27	79·70	78·88	80·73	78·89	80·79
November	81·15	82·58	78·92	80·83	77·52	76·84	77·16	79·02	80·50
December	76·34	80·40	77·11	75·45	76·98	76·86	75·46	76·95	75·89
Mean temp. of the year.	81·55	83·49	81·66	81·65	80·65	79·47	80·56	79·98	81·14

Extremes of Temperature for the Eight Years.

	1840.	1841.	1842.	1843.	1844.	1845.	1846.	1847.	
	Min.Max.	Min.Max.	Min.Max.	Min.Max.	Min.Max.	Min.Max.	Min.Max.	Min.Max.	
January .	61 89	65 90	66 88	64 89	62 90	54 88	62 88	60 89	
February	71 91	70 90	74 90	70 90	62 92	73 90	63 89	56 90	
March . .	73 94	76 94	77 91	73 93	73 97	72 92	74 93	70 94	
April . .	75 95	75 97	77 93	77 94	73 97	72 93	77 93	70 95	
May . .	75 93	78 94	78 93	76 96	73 97	75 94	76 94	75 94	
June . .	76 91	78 93	77 91	77 95	75 90	74 91	76 91	74 90	
July . .	76 91	80 91	77 90	77 90	75 90	73 90	75 90	75 89	
August .	76 91	79 93	76 90	77 91	74 88	73 91	76 89	72 90	
September	75 93	78 89	75 92	75 92	74 88	74 90	75 88	74 88	
October .	74 91	77 93	71 90	71 90	74 89	70 89	75 90	72 87	
November	68 89	75 90	70 90	70 90	64 86	68 86	65 86	72 88	
December	65 87	70 90	61 88	61 88	63 88	64 88	66 84	67 85	
									Min.Max.
	61 95	65 97	61 93	60 96	62 97	54 94	62 94	56 95	54 97*

* Extremes of temperature for eight years.

	Average Daily Range of Mercury.			Greatest Daily Range.			Least Daily Range.		
	1845.	1846.	1847.	1845.	1846.	1847.	1845.	1846.	1847.
January..	16·03	14·38	14·74	24°	22°	20	10°	1°	11°
February	12·64	12·64	15·25	16	20	21	3	5	8
March. .	10·90	11·61	13·48	15	16	20	3	5	1
April . .	10·60	10·50	13·66	15	14	18	4	7	8
May . .	9·84	10·36	10·13	16	14	15	4	3	4
June . .	8·13	9·13	10·10	15	12	14	4	5	6
July . .	10·42	8·03	8·93	15	15	12	3	2	5
August .	9·58	8·06	8·64	16	12	12	4	4	4
September	9·00	8·03	8·53	13	12	18	1	4	5
October .	8·94	7·80	7·64	16	12	11	2	2	5
November	10·03	7·23	8·33	13	12	13	6	3	1
December	12·55	10·80	10·10	16	15	14	7	6	6

	Synopsis of Rainy Days.					Amount of Rain in inches each Month.		
	1840.	1841.	1842.	1843.	1844.	1845.	1846.	1847.
January . . .	1	1	1	0	2	0·	·30	0·
February . .	3	1	2	9	2	0·	1·70	0·
March . . .	2	1	11	3	4	4·72	·50	0·
April . . .	9	5	10	5	8	9·32	·30	8·30
May	18	19	20	10	18	9·84	2·55	8·54
June	21	15	23	12	21	8·13	10·94	5·10
July	16	14	12	18	20	5·03	6·20	6·12
August . . .	19	17	11	15	25	9·58	7·26	11·30
September . .	14	12	18	21	21	18·66	13·84	12·00
October . . .	9	17	14	9	16	8·94	5·94	7·35
November . .	8	11	4	2	12	2·20	3·03	5·46
December . .	6	5	1	6	3	·10	0·	0·
						76·52	52·60	64·17

The winds blow with great regularity in Bangkok. From April to November the south-west monsoon prevails, when the monsoon changes to the north-east. But hurricanes and typhoons are almost unknown in Siam. The rainy season commences with the breaking-up of the north-east monsoon; but rains are not abundant until July, August, and September. The dry season begins in November, and the fall of rain is rare until the middle of April. Though the thermometer scarcely ever falls below 59°, the inhabitants appear to suffer much from the cold season. The highest range of the thermometer observed has been 97° in the shade: the mean annual average is 82·57°; the mean annual range, 13·40°. The general character of the climate is favourable, for a tropical country. Dr. Bradley says, of one thousand four hundred and fifty medical cases which came under his treatment, there were only eighteen of fever, and those cases generally of a mild, intermittent character. Hepatitis, so common in Burmah and British India, is rare, and phthisis almost unknown. People often reach extreme old age, and it is not an unusual thing to meet with persons above a century old.*

Bangkok, like many Oriental cities, has its poetical or metaphorical names,—such as *Krung thepa maha nakhon si ajutthaja maha dilok raxathani*, &c.; the great, royal, angelic city, the beautiful, the un-captured,—*Juthia*, the capital *par excellence*,—which was the name of the ancient seat of the Court.

The town is about twenty miles from the sea; but as there is a considerable bend on the river, the distance by water exceeds thirty miles. There is,

---
* *Chinese Repository*, vi. 127.

however, a shorter cut through a straight and narrow branch, which has an outlet at Paklat, by which the distance is diminished many miles; and this shorter course is ordinarily taken by boats of light draught, or at the time of high water. The limits of the city are marked by a semicircle of the Meinam on the western side, and by a canal on the eastern, whose two extremities joining the river make the city almost circular. There is an inner island, formed by another canal, also joining the Meinam. There are two other canals, viz., one from north to south, and another from east to west, crossing the city at right lines, besides auxiliary canals on both sides the river. The highways of Bangkok are not streets or roads, but the river and the canals. Boats are the universal means of conveyance and communication. Except about the palaces of the Kings, horses or carriages are rarely seen, and the sedan of the Chinese appears unknown in Siam: but a boat is a necessary part of every person's household; to its dexterous management every child is trained—women and men are equally accustomed to the use of the oar, the paddle, and the rudder. From the most miserable skiff which seems scarcely large enough to hold a dog, up to the magnificently-adorned barges which are honoured with the presence of royalty—from the shabbiest canoe, hewn out of the small trunk of a tree from the jungle, up to the roofed and curtained, the carved and gilded barks of the nobles—every rank and condition has its boats plying in endless activity, night and day, on the surface of the Meinam waters.

FLOATING HOUSE ON THE MEINAM.

London John W. Parker & Son, West Strand 1857.

A great proportion of the houses float on large rafters, and are sometimes seen moving up and down the river, conveying all the belongings of a family to some newly-selected locality. It is a curious sight to witness these locomotive abodes, sometimes consisting of many apartments, loosened from the cables which have attached them to a particular spot, and going forth on their travels to fresh destinations. On the borders of the river there are scarcely any but floating houses, which can at any time be detached and removed bodily, and without any inconvenience, at the will of the owner.

There are a few houses in Bangkok built of stone and brick; but those of the middle classes are of wood, while the habitations of the poor are constructed of light bamboos, and roofed with leaves of the atap palm. Fires are frequent; and, from the combustible character of the erections, hundreds of habitations are often destroyed. But in a few days the mischief is generally repaired, for on such occasions friends and neighbours lend a willing hand.

A house generally consists of two divisions; one occupied by the males, the other by the females. The piles on which they are built are sunk three or four feet into the ground; and the floor is raised six or eight feet from its surface, and is reached by a rude ladder, which, if the front of the house be towards the river, is made accessible at low tide. Of the floating houses, some are of boards, others of bamboo, or either wicker-work or palm-leaves. These houses have generally a verandah in front, and a small wing at each end. When used for shops or warehouses, the whole frontage is removed, and the contents exposed for inspection to the boats which pass by on the river.

The existence of the people of Bangkok may be called amphibious. The children pass much of their time in the water, paddling and diving, and swimming, as if it were their native element. Boats often run against one another, and those within them are submerged in the water; but it seldom happens that any life is lost, or mischief done to the persons whose boats are run down. I have again and again seen boats bottom upward, whose owners have floated them to the shore, or otherwise repaired the damage done as speedily as possible. The constant occurrence of petty disasters seems to reconcile everybody to their consequences.

The gilded barges are among the gayest objects which float upon the Meinam waters. They are some of them one hundred and twenty feet long, scooped out of the trunk of a single tree. The prow, rising high aloft, represents the head of a serpent, a dragon, a fish, a deity, a monster, or any fantastic object. The poop, which is also elevated high above the water, is like the tail of a bird or fish, but generally ends in a wavy point.

The concussions of boats, and the knocking of their rowers and crews into the water, are of constant occurrence, and seldom produce any expression of irritation. I have seen cargoes swamped and destroyed, and the calamity has been submitted to without any vituperation of its cause. Generally speaking, the boats are paddled about with consummate dexterity, the practice being acquired from the earliest trainings of childhood.

The walls around Bangkok are said to describe a circumference of nearly six miles. They are fifteen feet high, and twelve broad.

The tides rise from six to seven feet at Bangkok. In October, November, and December, they overflow almost all the ground on which the city is built. In April, May, and June, many of the canals are dry during several hours of the day, when communication is interrupted. These canals, which are multitudinous, are the principal means of intercourse. Much inconvenience is experienced by the inhabitants from the want of highways or paths, for, with the exception of some principal streets within the walls, and a smaller number without, the land passages are scarcely passable, and frequently will not allow two persons to walk abreast.

The streets of Bangkok are crowded with persons in chains—men and women in larger or smaller groups, attended by an officer of police bearing a large staff or stick, as the emblem of authority. The weight of the chains is apportioned to the magnitude of the offence for which the bearer is suffering. I understood a large portion of these prisoners to be debtors. If a person cannot pay what he owes, his body is delivered over to his creditors, at whose absolute disposal his services are placed. There is no redemption but by the act of the creditor, or the payment of the debt: friends and relatives often interfere for its discharge. The legal rate of interest being thirty per cent., it may well be conceived how rapidly ruin will overtake an unfortunate debtor. An individual or family may be released from servitude by any party who is willing to discharge the original debt, and accept the services of the debtor. The value of a slave is about 100 ticals (12*l.* 10*s.* sterling). If the slave can find security, his personal liberty is less restrained. Pallegoix gives the following contract for the sale of a slave:—" Wednesday, the 6th month, the 26th day of the moon of the era 1211, the 1st year of the Cock, I, *Mi*, the husband, and I, *Kot*, the wife, bring our daughter *Ma* to be sold to *Lüang Si* for 80 ticals, or to be taken into his service in lieu of interest. If our daughter *Ma* should take flight, let me be seized and be required to restore her. I, *Mi*, have placed my signature in witness."[*]

The noises of different animals frequently interrupt one's rest. There is a bird which the Siamese call "iron-beater," whose cry is like a rapid succession of blows upon the anvil. There are the lugubrious cries of crows and ravens; there are many-voiced owls; there is the guko lizard, crawling about your chamber and over your bed, loudly crying *too kai, too kai*, a dozen times in succession; not to speak of the buzz of flies and the trumpeting of mosquitoes. Everything is full of active, noisy vitality.

---

[*] Vol. i. 234, 5. See also *ante*, p. 192.

Palace.

The palace of the First King is enclosed within high white walls, the circumference embracing nearly the extent of a mile. It contains a variety of beautiful edifices, temples, public offices, military stations, buildings for favourite animals—and, above all, the white elephant—accommodation for some thousands of soldiers, cavalry, artillery, war elephants, and last, but not least, for an innumerable assemblage of ladies. The pavements are either of granite or marble. In the middle of the principal court rises a magnificent oblong hall, called the *mahaprasat*, which is covered with varnished or glazed tiles, ornamented with rude sculpture, and surmounted by a tall gilt spire. This is the great hall of audience, where foreign ministers are received. The interior is adorned with columns, against which I observed a picture of the Pope, presented by the Catholic missionaries,—an engraving of the Queen of England, and one of the President of the United States. There was also a portrait of the Emperor of China, and of some other notable personages. Pallegoix says that in this hall the body of the deceased King is placed for nearly a year in a golden urn, previous to his cremation: and here, too, the talapoins preach in the presence of the Queen and the concubines of the palace, who are concealed behind curtains during the ceremonies.

The throne of the King is a seat elevated ten or twelve feet from the floor, like the box of a theatre, to which he has access without passing through the hall. A curtain is before the throne, which is drawn when the King makes his appearance. The Royal Family and the nobles are arranged in groups according to their ranks;—all are prostrated on their faces when the King's presence is announced by the sound of music. At the foot of the throne are the princes of royal blood, in two groups, to the left and the right of the Sovereign. Next come the high officers of state,—the somdets, ministers, and functionaries holding the most exalted posts,—and other nobles and officers, whose rank is always indicated by their adjacency or remoteness from the throne. In my reception by the King, I occupied a cushion in the centre, and in an exact line with the Prakalahom, or prime minister,—the minister for foreign affairs being one grade below. Etiquette requires that communications shall be made by an interpreter (and an attendant scribe recording all that passes) to the minister for foreign affairs, who conveys the words of the ambassador to the King; and the King's answer is returned through the same channel. The hall would, probably, contain two or three hundred dignitaries.

At the time of my reception, the governors of all the provinces adjacent to the capital were invited to attend. All wore their robes of ceremony, more or less splendid according to their rank. A passage was left in the centre of the hall, through which I walked, attended by my suite, and the captains and officers of Her Majesty's ships *Grecian* and *Rattler;* and we took our seats in the most advanced position ever accorded to a foreign ambassador, or to the highest functionary not of the royal race.

It is mentioned in the account of M. de Chaumont's Mission, that not having made previous arrangements as to the manner in which Louis XIV.'s letter, of which he was the bearer, should be delivered to the King, the French ambassador moved forward from his seat, and raised the letter over his head, while the King stretched down his hand, and good-humouredly took the letter from M. de Chaumont,—no doubt to the great scandal of the nobles, who would only attribute this violation of all decorum to the ignorance of the barbarians coming from countries too remote to have enabled them to become acquainted with the proper forms of Oriental etiquette.

In the case of M de Chaumont, the presents from the King of France to the King of Siam were ostentatiously exhibited, and made a prominent subject in the ambassador's address. Knowing that such offerings are associated in the Oriental mind with the idea of tribute, I made no reference to a present from the Queen of England, consisting of a diamond watch, writing-case, &c., which lay on the floor for presentation to the King; and I explained to his Majesty, privately, my reasons for avoiding the accustomed usage, which his Majesty very graciously appreciated, —as, indeed, in all my relations with him, when I had occasion to convey to him the motives of my conduct, he was invariably willing to accept those explanations, and to assure me that he should attribute my proceedings not to any want of respect for himself, but to my sense of the duties I owed to my sovereign and my country.

Not far from the grand hall is an elevated platform,

mounted by several marble steps, on which is a throne, where the King gives daily audience in the presence of more than a hundred nobles prostrated around. If anything is to be conveyed to the King, it is pushed forwards by nobles, who advance on all-fours, but whose great care seems to be to elevate nothing above the heads of the surrounding attendants. Any letter from or for the King is conveyed in a golden vase. Enormous statues in granite, imported from China, are generally found at the entrances to the different departments of the palace. These statues often represent monstrous giants, dragons, birds with human heads, and all the devices of a creative but rude and superstitious invention. I have sometimes remarked huge figures in granite, representing European costumes, both military and civil; though the prevailing taste is that of ancient Chinese art, with all the grotesque and cumbrous adornings of by-gone centuries.

There is a house in the palace which has the inscription *Royal Pleasure*, in English, and characters in Sanscrit with the same meaning. This house is fitted up, for the most part, in European style, and is filled with various instruments, philosophical and mathematical; a great variety of Parisian clocks and pendules, thermometers, barometers, telescopes, microscopes, statues,—among which I remarked those of Queen Victoria and Prince Albert, nearly of the size of life, in their Court costumes; pictures of celebrated individuals, a considerable collection of books, copying-machines, handsome writing-desks;—in a word, all the instruments and appliances which might be found in the study or library of an opulent philosopher in Europe. There is a balcony from which the King looks round the palace, and whence he often writes his despatches, and pursues his studies while dramatic representations are exhibited, or musicians and dancers, composed of the ladies of the palace, display their art in the court below.

The apartments of the females of the Royal Family are still further in the interior of the palace. In these more secluded places, no less than three thousand females are reputed to have their abode, among whom six hundred are called the wives or concubines of the King; the remaining two thousand four hundred being either ladies charged with official functions within the palace, or slaves and attendants upon the persons of the King's harem. It is said, there are beautiful gardens attached to the ladies' apartments; and there is a vast collection of treasures in gold, silver, precious stones, rich ornaments, and costly garments, distributed in various parts of the interior. There is, indeed, on every side evidence of great wealth; but it is difficult to form an estimate of the actual value of the royal treasure, the amount of which is, probably, exaggerated by the general inaccuracy of Oriental description. I heard, for example, that every king at his succession deposited in the royal treasury a statue of Buddha of solid gold, and of the size of life; and that there exist a great number of these golden statues collected within the palace. Even the dresses of the ladies must represent a large value,—to say nothing of the quantity of jewels all of them wear as necklaces, ear-rings, finger-rings, belts, anklets, bracelets, and other ornaments.

Within the palace there is a court of justice, and an office for the despatch of local business; a theatre, to which the people are often invited, and in which we saw a dramatic representation in the presence of the King. This is independent of the more private plays exhibited in the less accessible parts of the palace. There is a large royal library, in addition to the King's private collection. There is an arsenal of artillery, and a manufactory of fire-arms and other weapons for the King's use; a large extent of stabling for elephants and horses; while for the white elephant there is a separate establishment, with a variety of attendants to feed him with the most delicate food, to prevent him from being molested with flies and mosquitoes, to attend him with parade and music when he goes forth, and to prepare his ornamented bed when he reposes at night.

One of the temples within the palace is of great beauty. It is crowded with a great variety of costly and curious objects. The floor is of mats of silver; it contains statues from Europe, porcelain vases from China; many a strange *lusus naturæ*, such as elephants' tusks of extraordinary shape and size; ancient garments worn by former kings; specimens of elaborately-carved ivory and wood; gold and silver ornaments, with jewellery in endless variety; many statues of Buddha, one of which is said to be of massive gold. But the great glory of the temple is a cross-legged figure of Buddha, raised high in the midst of multitudinous decorations which surround it. It is about

MONUMENT OF THE LATE KING OF SIAM

London; John W. Parker & Son, West Strand. 1857

a foot and a half in height, and said to be carved out of a solid emerald: the probability is that the stone is a malachite or green porphyry. Of this idol, the pride of the palace, and the special object of Royal veneration, I received the account written by the King himself to accompany the picture representing the Buddha as he is clothed at various seasons of the year, which has already been quoted in these pages.* The different garments of gold, with their rich jewelled adornings, were shown to us when we visited the temple, accompanied by many of the nobles. It is in this temple that the oath of fidelity is taken on the accession of a new king. It is accompanied by the ceremony of drinking fresh water which has received the benediction of the highest order of the priests.

As an example of the costliness of the decorations in some of the temples, the following is a description of the "Monument of Golden Work" erected to the memory of the late King by the present monarch, who furnished me with the particulars in his own handwriting:—

"In the 2394th year of the Buddhist era, corresponding to the year 1851 of Christian era, Phra Bat Somdetch Phra Paramendr Maha Mongkut Phra Chom Klau Chau yu Hua ascended the throne of Siam. In the first year of his reign, his Majesty assembled six hundred goldsmiths, inhabitants of Bangkok, and ordered and hired them to make a funeral urn, high, by Siamese measure, 6 cubits, 2 inches less, equal to 9 feet $10\frac{7}{8}$ inches English, and

---

* See *ante*, pp. 316—9.

to overlay it with gold, of the sixth degree of fineness, to the amount of $30\frac{59}{320}$ catties, in which he deposit the remains of his elder brother, Phra Bat Somdit Phra Nang Klau Chau yu Hua; and also ordered them to make the elevated seat, or throne, upon which the urn should stand, 3 vas and 17 inches Siamese high, equal to 21 feet $2\frac{1}{2}$ inches English, and to ornament it with various figures and ornamental flowers of gold, of the seventh degree of fineness, to the amount of $363\frac{31}{3200}$ catties, making the whole amount of gold in the urn and throne $393\frac{1721}{3200}$ catties.

"It was also inwrought with glasses of various colours. The six hundred goldsmiths completed the work in nine months, in the second year of his present Majesty's reign.

"The throne was made with nine stories:—

"The first story was 3 feet high, or 43 Siamese inches; and 15 feet $5\frac{1}{4}$ inches broad, or 224 Siamese inches.

"The second story was 3 feet $\frac{3}{4}$ inch high, or 44 Siamese inches; and 13 feet 6 inches broad, or 194 Siamese inches.

"The third story was 1 foot 3 inches high, or 18 Siamese inches; and 12 feet $6\frac{1}{4}$ inches broad, or 180 Siamese inches.

"The fourth story was 2 feet $\frac{1}{16}$ inch high, or 29 Siamese inches; and 10 feet $2\frac{3}{4}$ inches broad, or 147 Siamese inches.

"The fifth story was 1 foot $3\frac{3}{4}$ inches high, or 19 Siamese inches; and 9 feet $5\frac{3}{8}$ inches broad, or 136 Siamese inches.

"The sixth story was 3 feet 2⅜ inches high, or 46 Siamese inches; and 7 feet 7¾ inches broad, or 108 Siamese inches.

"The seventh story was 1 foot 4⅝ inches high, or 20 Siamese inches; and 6 feet 8¼ inches broad, or 96 Siamese inches.

"The eighth story was 3 feet 5¼ inches high, or 49 Siamese inches; and 4 feet 9⅝ inches broad, or 69 Siamese inches.

"The ninth story was 1 foot 5⅜ inches high, or 21 Siamese inches; and 3 feet 5¼ inches broad, or 49 Siamese inches.

"Making the whole height, from the base of the throne to the top of the urn, 4 vas 2 sok 5 inches Siamese, or 31 feet 1⅜ inches English."

Temples.

The passion for building costly and expensive *wats*, or temples, is of great antiquity, and those described by the ancient chroniclers do not appear to have differed much either in form of architecture, or character of ornament, from those of the present day. João de Barros describes, in the city of Socotay, which he represents to be the most ancient of the cities of Siam, a metal Buddha of the length of 240 feet. The beauty, splendour, and numbers of the temples of Bangkok—their enormous size, their rich ornaments, their peculiar architecture, the extent and variety of buildings enclosed within their walls—embarrass the powers of description. Dr. House has favoured me with a ground-plan of the Phra Chu Pon temple, which gives the general outline with marvellous accuracy. I measured the length of the reposing Buddha, which is built of brick and covered with a thick leaf of gold, and found it to be, from the top of the head to the sole of the foot, 165 feet: the length of the pedestal on which he rests is 82 paces; the sole of the foot of the image, exactly 6 paces.

Various other Buddhas occupy different temples within the vast enclosure. There are said to be nine hundred gilt Buddhas in the corridors, of the size of life—each, with the throne on which he sits, and the pedestal on which that throne is raised, being nearly nine feet high. I did not count the number of the statues, but, from the length of the corridors, have no reason to suppose there is any exaggeration in the enumeration.

The following description of the temples, pagodas, or *wat*, is given by an American missionary:—

"In the city and suburbs are about a hundred. Upon these the Siamese concentrate all their wealth, and taste, and hearts. As might, therefore, be expected, the temples surpass in richness and beauty all other buildings, the King's palace not excepted. The best locations are chosen for them. The amount of ground occupied by a single *wat*, and its appurtenances, is from three to five acres. A *wat* consists generally of one, two, or more large and lofty buildings of brick. Massive pillars support the centre and roof of their spacious verandahs. The whole is neatly covered with a white cement, which gives the brick somewhat the appearance of marble. The doors are very large and numerous. The windows are closed with double shutters, made of thick planks. Both these and the doors are finished in the richest style. Some are ornamented with many varieties of coloured glass, cut into small pieces so as to represent various images. Some are finished with a profusion of gilding, others are thickly set with pearls. Were it not for an immense gilded Buddha, seated on a throne at its further extremity, a visitor might almost fancy himself in a Christian church.

"These large buildings are surrounded by small pagodas, many of whose spires are gilded. Their bases are set with parti-coloured glass and earthenwares of the most showy character.

"Some of the older *wats* are become so thick and dark with trees, which are frequented by crows and other birds, that they seem somewhat like a superb castle in the wilderness. Multitudes of bats in the twilight give an activity to the gloom which reigns around."*

Another missionary says—"The Royal treasures have been most lavishly expended on the repairs and beautifying of a *wat*, the materials of which have been costly, and from two thousand to five thousand men almost constantly employed for fifteen years. But at the consecration extraordinary sums were lavished: many thousand pieces of silk and crape were given to the priests; fireworks, of unspared expense, were prepared; all manner of ornaments manufactured from cloth and paper, gilt and painted, were furnished; men collected from all the provinces, and every nobleman, with all his retinue of almost countless servants,

---

* *Chinese Repository,* vi. 57—58.

were kept in attendance for *seven days;* and it was rumoured that the King designed to empty his treasury in largesses on the occasion. That was unquestionably not done, but it is certain that an immense amount of gold and silver coins were disbursed among the people. It was generally inserted in oranges, limes, and other fruits, and then tossed, not unfrequently by the King's own hand, about into the crowds of myriads; and it is reported that several lost their lives, being crushed to death in the scramble for the King's gifts."*

Pallegoix' general description† of the Royal pagodas or temples of Bangkok is vividly and correctly drawn. They are of a magnificence, he says, of which in Europe we have no idea. There are among them some which have cost 200 quintals' weight of silver, a value of more than 4,000,000 of francs. There are eleven within the walls of the city, and about twenty extra-mural. In the pagoda of *Xetuphon* is a gilded statue of a sleeping Buddha, 50 metres = 166 feet in length. In that of *Bovoranivet*, no less than 450 ounces of gold-leaf were employed in the gilding only. From four to five hundred priests, with a thousand boys to attend them, are provided for in a single temple. The pagoda is, in fact, only the prominent ornament of a vast expanse filled with beautiful edifices, among which will be found a score of Chinese belvideres; a succession of halls, accessible from the water-side; a vast building for preaching; two magnificent temples—one to hold the image of

---

* *Baptist Missionary Magazine,* 1849, p. 26.
† Pallegoix, i. 64—66.

Buddha, another devoted to the worship of the priests, who occupy from two to three hundred prettily-built houses, some in brick, others in wood. They have ponds with decorated rock-work, in some of which are crocodiles, in others gold and silver fish. They have extensive gardens filled with flowers and fruits; many pyramids of delicate forms, gilded or covered with vitrifications or porcelain, raise their ornamental spires to the height of two or three hundred feet. Tall masts, with golden swans at their tops, from which are hung gay flags in the shape of crocodiles or other fantastic forms, are seen amidst the erections. At the entrances are enormous statues of giants, warriors, sages; lions and monsters brought from China; whilst the pagodas are made accessible for boats by canals and water-courses. They have piles for burning the dead, bridges for the convenience of passengers, libraries for the sacred books. The walls of the temples are gaudily painted, representing the facts of history, the traditions of fable, the costumes of foreign countries, and not unfrequently gross and licentious stories. A detached description of any one of the larger pagodas would occupy a large volume, and leave much to be said. Generally, a colossal figure of Buddha is the prominent object, looking like an inert mass, and surrounded by a multitude of costly ornaments.

Every temple is under the special charge of a superior, or abbot, to whom the internal direction is confided. He is called the *Chaou Wat*, or " lord of the temple."

The teachings of the people are conducted in the Siamese language, but the responses are generally in the *Pali* words *Sa tou sa;* meaning " So it is." When the preacher exhibits any remarkable eloquence, it is usual to recompense him with liberal gifts.

In the temple we saw images of wood-spirits, the belief in whose existence is general among the Siamese. What mermaids are to fishes, these strange genii are to birds: the head is that of a bird; the breasts are human; the body, legs, and tail are birdlike; the wings are those of dragons. They are said by the Siamese to inhabit the densest part of the forests, to be immortal, seldom to have been seen by human eye, and taking no part in human affairs.

A sketch of the pyramidical temple at Bangkok, in which the Mission had its first occupation, on the right bank of the Meinam river, is given by Pallegoix. The height of the principal tower is 300 feet: but any representation would be wholly inadequate to convey a distinct idea of the gay, glittering, gaudy, and gorgeous edifice, and its surrounding towers, turrets, and buildings. It is the most prominent object on the left bank of the river, as you ascend; and rising, as it does, over a great mass of the richest tropical vegetation, the effect is most striking and beautiful.

The First King of Siam.

The Emperor of China claims the rights of sovereignty over the throne and territory of Siam, whose monarch is noted in the official books of the Chinese as a *wang*, or dependent king.

In the collected statutes of the Ta Tsing dynasty

there is the following passage:—" The Siam tribute comes by the Bogue of Kwantung (the Canton river). The time is once in three years. The ambassadors may be two, three, or four; but the men who go up to Peking cannot exceed twenty-six."

No other form of vassalage exists than the payment of the triennial tribute,—the pecuniary value of which (and something more) is returned in advantages conceded to the vessels which bring the *kuing she*, or tribute officers, to China. These pay no duty on imports or exports; so that, far from being onerous, the dependence is represented to be profitable to the Siamese. The pride of China is flattered by the triennial display; and an ancient usage is preserved, with its *prestige* and traditional value, without sacrifice of any Siamese interest.

Considering the enormous multitudes of Chinamen who are settled in the Siamese dominions, it may be a matter of prudence and policy that the King of Siam should seek the ratification of his title to the crown by the recognition of the Chinese Emperor; and the preservation of a religious link between a great Buddhist sovereign and the professors of the most widely extended of the religious sects in China may not be without some value; but the yoke, at all events, sits easy on the shoulders of the King of Siam. One of the Royal official seals is in the Chinese character.

The officers sent to Peking as tribute-bearers have not of late years been persons of high rank or position, and they have met with little consideration at the Chinese Court. The announcement in the *Gazette* is generally to the effect—" The tribute-bearers of Sien Lo Kwo (Siam kingdom) have been graciously permitted to ascend to the capital, saw the Dragon's face (the Emperor's), and received imperial favours, and were allowed to return to their own country." They are generally but shabbily accommodated in their progress to and fro; and in the houses appointed for their abode, the Chinese inscription is generally seen, —" Office of Tribute-bearers from Siam." The fact is, that the whole matter of Siamese dependency has dwindled away into the shadow of a form. It is stated that the language used by the King of Siam in his correspondence with the Emperor, is accommodated by a new version to the pride and pretensions of the Chinese Court.

The authority exercised by the King of Siam, as has been before stated, is altogether absolute. Around his person everything, however exalted elsewhere, is in a state of the most entire and reverential prostration. No one dares stand in the Royal presence or look upon the King's countenance. When he leaves his palace, all his subjects bow themselves to the ground; and the reverence paid him is more like that which mortals accord to a divinity, than the deference which is elsewhere associated with the most uncontrolled autocratical power. The King is master, not only of the persons, but really of the property of his subjects;*—he disposes of their labour, and directs

---

* The late King placed in one of the halls, near the palace, a great drum, in order that his subjects might have access to him, and for some time a page went to receive the representations of any subject who struck the drum; but whether the King got weary of the multitude of petitioners, or the pages found the work too troublesome, or from some other cause,

their movements at will. If any recompence attaches to their services, it is an act of grace and free will. His name is not to be pronounced, or his person referred to, except under certain designations, among which the most usual are—*Chao phen din*, Master of the world; *Chao xivit*, Sovereign of life; *Phra maha Krasat*, August great Emperor; *Phra bat somdetch*, Excellent divine feet; *Phra borom intara*, August perfect sublime; *Tepha ja phong*, Descendant of angels; *Maha raxathirat*, the great Emperor; *Borom thammamika*, Perfect justice; *Phra chom klào ju hua*, August and commanding summit.*

Though the crown is deemed hereditary, it does not always descend to the eldest son of the King. A king is supposed to be invested with the right of nominating his successor; but he must carry with him the opinion of the influential nobles. The late King desired that his own son should succeed him; but the great family of the two regents were opposed to the appointment, and he was superseded, even without any further agitation of his claims, by the present King, the legitimate heir to his father.

The ceremonials connected with the advent of a new sovereign are described by Pallegoix with such completeness, that I transfer his account to these pages:—

"On the death of the King, the declared successor

---

the drumming soon ceased, the pages were relieved, and the King was no longer troubled with the noise. In China drums and gongs are seen in the neighbourhood of the offices of the great mandarins: their original object was to obtain a hearing for those who had unredressed grievances to complain of; but the drum-skins have decayed, and the gong-hammer is not at hand; and the repose of the magistrate is not disturbed by the suitor.

* Pallegoix, i. 260.

is escorted with great pomp to the palace. He then washes the corpse of the deceased sovereign, and all the princes and nobles take the oath of fidelity. The oath contains most terrible imprecations against traitors, and is read in the name of all by the prime minister; after which, all present drink from a large vessel of gold, water over which the bonzes have pronounced imprecatory denunciations, and into which the King's scimitar has been dipped.

" On the day of the coronation, all the houses of the capital are illuminated by lanterns; and at the door of each an altar is raised, which is adorned with rich silks, flowers, wax lights, mirrors, and perfume-bearing boxes, while everybody is busy with sports and amusements. The chief of the astrologers writes the name of the new King on a sheet of gold, which is washed with perfumes, rolled up, and placed in a golden tube, which is again enclosed in a gold-enamelled silver box. Nine mandarins, each holding a chandelier with three wax lights, promenade nine times round the box, keeping their chandeliers in a state of vibration; after which, the priests or astrologers sound their conch shells, and beat gongs and drums. At this moment the King enters the hall, gives new yellow robes to about a hundred of the bonzes, and places a lighted wax candle in the hands of the principal priest. An idol, called the Idol of Victory, is brought in, before which the King performs an act of homage; he then girds himself with a *langouti* of white silk, embroidered with gold, and ascends to a throne, where two princes scatter over him lustral water; and the Brahmins present shells with lustral water, with which he washes himself, and changes his *langouti* for one of yellow silk with gold embroidery. Conchs are sounded, with other musical instruments, during the whole of these proceedings;—after which, the King walks into another hall, where he ascends an octagonal throne, surmounted by a seven-storied, pagoda-like umbrella. Eight Brahmins are seated at a distance, around the King, whose face is turned towards the east. The first Brahmin, who is opposite the King, pronounces a benediction in the Pali language, pours into the King's hand some lustral water, of which his Majesty drinks a few drops, and washes his face with what remains. He then turns to the south, performing the same ceremonies, which are repeated at the eight points of the compass. The King then proceeds to a third (quadrilateral) throne, where he seats himself on a golden lion, turns to the north, while an old Brahmin sings a benedictory hymn, and, prostrating himself, delivers the kingdom to the King's keeping. A page comes forward and presents to the King the seven-storied umbrella,—the *savetraxat* or primary symbol of royalty; another presents the golden tube which contains the King's name; others bring the crown, the royal collar decorated with diamonds, the royal staff, which the King places on his right side, and the royal scimitar, which he places on the left.

" Eight species of warlike weapons are then presented,—the javelin, the lance, the bow, the sword, the poignard, the sabre, the sword-stick, and the musket. His Majesty then, in a loud voice, gives permission to his subjects to use the trees, and plants, and waters and stones in his kingdom. Then one of the great mandarins responds—'Your servants receive the excellent orders of our lord, whose voice is majestic as a lion's roar.' The King then scatters flowers of gold and silver among the people, and pours out water on the ground for the benediction of all that the earth produces of animal and vegetable life. During all this, a tremendous noise of gongs, drums, and conch-shells is kept up by the priests, of whom the principal dignitaries are assembled in another hall, to which the King proceeds, and having selected a chief or bishop among them, distributes alms, and receives their blessings.

" He then goes to the great hall of audience, where a costly carpet is spread, adorned with diamonds and precious stones. Loud prayers are uttered, the sound of which is sometimes quite lost in the noise of the musical instruments. One of the chief nobles then advances crawling, and thus addresses the King:— 'Your Majesty's servant is directed, on behalf of all the dignified nobles here present, to offer our united homage, bending our heads at the sacred feet of your glorious Majesty, *Somdetch phra chrom klao*, our refuge, who are mounted on the diamond-adorned throne, invested with the sovereign power;—seated under the *savetraxat* (seven-storied umbrella),—the terror of your enemies, whose august name is written on the plate of gold. We ask leave to deposit at the sacred feet of your Majesty everything we possess, and all the treasures of the kingdom.' The King answers—'All the dignified nobles shall have the privilege of appearing in my presence, as they desire, to offer their services according to their several functions. So let each, without fear, come and present his service.' Then the *Phaja Phra Klang* (the minister for foreign affairs) prostrates himself, and presents to the King the royal barges, ships o war, arsenals, soldiers, and military appurtenances. The *Phaja Suphavadi* offers the elephants, horses, and the capitals of provinces of the first, second, third, and fourth order, with all their inhabitants. The master of the palace presents the palace and all its contents. The minister of justice presents the city of Bangkok. The minister of agriculture offers the produce of the fields and the gardens. The treasurer gives the twelve departments of the royal exchequer. Being thus richly endowed, the Monarch withdraws to the interior of the palace, where two ladies wash his feet.

" The princesses then present the articles required in the palace, and among the tributes a golden nosegay weighing a pound. They invite him to eat sweetmeats which they have prepared;* after which he mounts his palanquin, and throwing in his way handfuls of money to the right and the left, is conducted to the temple of the Emerald Buddha, where he performs his adorations in the midst of lighted wax tapers and perfumed joss-sticks. The golden urns containing the ashes of his ancestors are then brought; —he offers them incense, lights, and flowers, and having called on the priests for an address on death,

---

* I imagine the ladies of the palace habitually prepare cakes and sweetmeats for the King. Among his presents to me, his Majesty sent boxes of sweet cakes, on which he had written, "Prepared by the ladies of the palace for royal use."

enters his palace, and the formalities of the coronation are considered to be closed."

The ordinary receptions of the King take place almost daily. At ten o'clock the high officers assemble in a large hall in the outer precincts of the palace, where they discuss the topics which are to be suggested for the consideration of the King. Each mandarin is accompanied by a scribe, who records any important proceedings. At eleven o'clock, from a hundred to a hundred and fifty high officers enter the audience hall, where each occupies the place assigned to his rank. Whisperings and low conversations take place until the arrival of the pages, who, bearing the royal ensigns, precede the King. At his Majesty's entrance the whole of the assembly raise their hands, bend their heads to the ground, and remain prostrate on their knees and elbows to the end of the audience.

The King is seated on an elevation under a canopy, with decorated cushions for his support; but he often changes his position. He chews the areca and the betel, smokes his cigar or pipe, and addresses whom he pleases; sometimes holding conversation with almost all who are present, though ordinarily his conversations are specially addressed to the ministers on the business of their several departments. But no mandarin dares to speak until the King opens the conversation. At one o'clock his Majesty rises, and all the nobles lift their hands above their heads and bow themselves to the ground. The mandarins withdraw to a separate hall, and discuss the mode of giving effect to the orders they have received. There is another reception at seven o'clock P.M., but it is principally attended by the princes and the ministers, and often lasts till after midnight. The affairs of the palace are arranged by the King, without the intervention of the mandarins.

Within the Palace of the First King there are said to be three thousand soldiers, and two thousand in that of the Second King. They are under the charge of a military commandant; they are grouped round the different gates; they form lines, through which visitors pass to the presence of the monarch, and they are scattered about the alleys and precincts. Some have muskets; but the majority carry swords, spears, bows and arrows, while some have only bamboo-staves. There is a still lower order of military, more resembling police, not clad in uniform, but who are sent forth to arrest misdoers, and to enforce the orders of the King.

Attached to the Royal presence are one hundred personal attendants, who serve the King with tea, tobacco, the betel-nut, read to him, write for him, and bear his messages on all sides. Two of these pages,— one of whom the King introduced to me as his adopted son, and who was obviously a great favourite,—were my more than daily visitors, conveying to me the King's wishes, and taking back any communications I might desire to make. I observed the adopted son was more familiar with the Sovereign than any other of the attendants, and not unfrequently was the conveyer of intelligence or the asker of favours, with which no other courtier ventured to trouble the King.

On the death of the King, according to Pallegoix, a

quantity of quicksilver is introduced by the mouth into the body; a golden mask is placed on the face, and he is seated on a pierced throne, beneath which is a large golden vase: the mercury drains the body, and with great ceremonials the depositions from the golden vase are conveyed to the river. When the corpse is sufficiently dried, the hands are joined, and it is placed in a sitting posture within an urn of gold, where it is kept for a year, until all the funeral preparations are made.

The forests are stripped of their largest trees; the whole people are put under requisition to build an enormous pyramidical catafalque, three hundred feet high, which is raised in a vast square in the centre of the city. The columns, timbers, and roof of this immense pavilion are covered with sheets of lead, silver, and gold. It is surrounded by representations, in wood and paper, of giants, angels, fabulous animals, monsters, dragons, and unnatural landscapes. Tents are erected for the King, the nobles, and the priests. The urn containing the royal remains is brought in great pomp on a gilded chair, and placed on an elevated platform. The public festivities begin, and last during seven days,—theatricals, combats, and a variety of sports and amusements. The new King scatters about promissory notes, and wooden limes, which contain gold and silver money. The notes represent a specified value,—such as a house, a garden, a boat; and these notes presented at the treasury are regularly paid. At night, artificial fireworks and lugubrious theatricals for the people. On the last day, the King, with his own hand, sets fire to the funeral pyre, which is made of sandal and other odoriferous woods. It is understood that the fire is produced by lightning, and not from common combustion. The bones which are not consumed are gathered together and reduced to powder, which is mixed with clay; and out of the amalgam small statues are moulded, which are placed in a temple specially dedicated to their reception. When the funeral rites are over, every vestige is destroyed, and the place left as vacant as before.*

On the day following the coronation, the Princes and great and petty nobles present their offerings to the King. His Majesty gives to each a small scarlet silk purse, containing newly-coined gold and silver money; the largest value being 80 ticals (10*l.*); the smallest, 4 ticals.

A few days afterwards, the King goes the round of the city in great pomp, once by land, and once by water. The ceremonial is called the *Liebmuang*. The streets are all lined with gaily-adorned altars, vases of flowers, pictures, incense-burners, and other marks of festivity. A body of archers heads the procession; then the army,—every regiment, having its distinguishing uniform and particular weapons, led by the mandarin who commands it, mounted on an elephant. The artillery form the rear, dressed in European style; a prodigious quantity of flags are borne aloft; bands of music accompany the troops; the King follows on a throne, richly ornamented with gold and precious stones, and wearing the pyramidical

---

* Pallegoix, i. 247—9.

crown of state. He is clad in a flowing vest, a waist-robe, and *langouti*,—all of rich silk, with golden flowers, and wearing shoes adorned with stones of various colours. In one hand he carries his scimitar, and with the other he scatters among the prostrate people money from a golden vase. He again distributes promissory notes, representing the value of an elephant, a house, a boat, a garden, and other possessions,—all of which are recognised when presented at the treasury. The members of the Royal family follow, somewhat fantastically dressed in rich costumes, and with large hats bearing plumes and panaches: this cavalcade closes the procession.

That by water is far more splendid. It is composed of more than sixty thousand persons, distributed in magnificent barges from forty to eighty cubits long, each having from sixty to a hundred rowers. The prow of each barge represents some monster of fable, splendidly gilded. They are dragons, crocodiles, serpents, fishes, unicorns, elephants, tigers, lions, eagles, giants, monkeys, the *garuda, jak,* and *hanuman* (which are the vulture, monster, and ape of Siamese tradition). The splendour of the decorations, the variety of costume, the stately and orderly movement of the bonzes, the crowds of richly-dressed spectators, the noise of the oars, and the shouts of the rowers, added to the music of innumerable instruments, produce a whole which it would be difficult to parallel elsewhere.[*]

On great occasions there is a distribution of the Royal bounty, of which the following is a correct description:—

---

[*] Pallegoix, i. 266—7.

"In five or six different points of the large area before and to the right and left of the throne were erected little platforms, on each of which was fixed something much resembling a small tree. On the lower limbs of these trees were suspended an enormous quantity of wooden limes, green and yellow. In each of these limes was deposited a piece of money, of greater or less value. In some was a silver salung (15 cts.), in some a gold salung (worth $1 20 cts.), and in some a silver half tical (worth 30 cts.) At a given signal, four men clothed in white (an emblem of purity among the Siamese as well as other people) ascended each of these platforms, and prostrated themselves three times, with their faces towards the throne. Then the King commenced the distribution of the silver and gold limes with his own hands, which he had before him in two large golden vessels. Whereupon those who were stationed at the several platforms began to pluck the limes from the trees by handfuls, and throw them to the eager thousands, whose uplifted heads and hands indicated, in a striking manner, the strong hold the love of money has upon the hearts of this people. In the mean time, the King was wholly occupied in throwing his presents to those round about the throne. He first served the male members of his own family, next his officers highest in rank, and then the females of the Royal family, and our wives."*

When the King leaves his palace, which is seldom, he is generally conveyed in a royal barge; and as it is prohibited to touch his sacred person, there is a

---

* *Missionary Herald*, p. 139: Boston, 1839.

long chain of cocoa-nuts, tied together, to be used as life-preservers should the King have the misfortune to fall into the water. On shore, he either rides a gorgeously-caparisoned elephant, or is carried by twelve bearers in a rich palanquin with curtains of cloth of gold, but is always accompanied by some hundreds of armed attendants.*

Not only is there a universal prostration in the King's presence, but his palace must not be passed without marks of reverence, such as kneeling, shutting up umbrellas, and uncovering the head. Severe punishments follow any inattention to these requirements, which are enforced by a number of archers who shoot earthen balls at those who neglect the required duty. To the bonzes alone is the King required to show any mark of respect, and this is confined to raising the left hand to the level of the eyes.

But, combined with the exercise of the most absolute power, there frequently exists a despotism even more powerful than that of the Sovereign, and which is imposed on him either by the restraints of traditional usages, religious dogmas, the teachings of sacred books, or other influences, which make the autocrat a vassal even in the midst of all the insignia of omnipotence. The *Phra raxa monthieraban* lays down the laws which the Sovereign is bound to obey, prescribes the hours for rising and for bathing, the manner of offering and the alms to be offered to the bonzes, the hours of audience for nobles and for princes, the time to be devoted to public affairs and to study, the hours for repasts, and when audiences shall be allowed to the

* Pallegoix, i. 268.

Queen and the ladies of the palace. It awards the punishment for all offences committed within the palace walls.

Pallegoix says:—" I was especially struck with this; that if, during an audience, the King becomes exasperated with any of the mandarins, and orders the sword-bearer to deliver his sword into his hands, there is the penalty of death attached to the sword-bearer should he obey his Sovereign; because he is not to be the instrument of the King's anger, but, at any risk, must refuse to place in his master's hands the means of gratifying his passion.

"The King's sons dwell in the palace till they are twelve or thirteen years old, when they are delivered to the charge of governors, and, with some hundreds of slaves and a monthly stipend, have their separate establishments. The daughters remain in the palace: they are condemned to celibacy, on the ground that a son-in-law might, by his high position, become dangerous to the Sovereign.

"Infidelity on the part of the Queen or the concubines, or unchastity on that of the princesses, are deemed crimes of *lèse-majesté*. The male criminal is punished by impalement and spearing to death; the woman is sewed up in a hide, to which a large stone is attached, and she is thrown alive into the stream. If the offender be of princely blood, he is conveyed to a pagoda, stretched on the ground, and his neck broken with two sandal-wood clubs; after which the body is dealt with as in the case of females, and flung into the Meinam by the executioners."

Though the wives, or handmaids, or odalisques, or

concubines, or by whatever names may be called the ladies of the King's family, must be reckoned by hundreds, and their attendants by thousands, the King has generally one wife who takes far higher rank than the rest, and who specially bears the title of Queen. She is selected from princesses of Royal blood, has her separate palace close to that of the King, and has, under the surveillance of an ancient dame, a body of attendants specially devoted to her service. The chief directress exercises extraordinary authority over all the female race, and reports to the King the proceedings of Queen and concubines. The concubines are gathered from all sides, and are frequently the daughters of the nobles of Siam and of adjacent countries, offered by their fathers to the King's acceptance. The directress is also charged with the control over the princesses, who are mostly condemned to celibacy, and the solitude of an almost cloistral life; seldom leaving their thrice-walled palace, except to visit the temples, or to enjoy the yet more rare privilege of a row upon the waters of the Meinam. They are liberally supplied by the King with money and fine garments, and other appliances, to make life tolerable; and it is said they have access within the palace to a beautiful garden which is the miniature of the outer world,—that it has its artificial mountains, woods, lakes, rivers, barges, bazaars, pagodas, pavilions, belvideres, statuary, and a large collection of exotic fruits and flowers.

This garden is richly illuminated at night; and Pallegoix says, the ladies deliver themselves over to the luxuries of bathing, and find consolation in a variety of amusements for their separation from the world.

In all the processions within the palace, I observed two Chinese female children dressed in the highest style of mandarin costume. The King told me that of the ladies in the palace, a hundred were trained to dramatic representations—which was only one-third of the number his father was accustomed to exercise in this manner.

There is nothing peculiar in the King's repasts, except in the richness of the table services, and the variety of the food. His meals are solitary. A dignitary attached to the kitchen seals the dishes, and accompanies them to the King's presence: the King unseals them with his own hands, and they are tasted by some of the courtiers before they are allowed to approach the Royal mouth.

As in some of the Courts of Europe, there seems always to have prevailed in Siam a passion for foreign troops as a personal guard to the King; in Spain, the Valones (Walloons), and in France and Rome the Swiss. There were formerly six hundred Japanese in the palace of Siam, and at the present time there are troops of more than one foreign nation. There seems to prevail among the army the same division which runs through many of the departments: there are the armies of the right and the left, as there are sinister and dexter functionaries in the various offices. A body of mounted Moors (Arabs) is spoken of by travellers as attached to the King's person, but I imagine they are no longer in existence. Both French and Portuguese soldiery have at various times been in the special service of the King, but of these there remain no vestiges. In ancient times, a corps of Japanese soldiers formed the body-guard of the Kings of Siam. There are no Japanese now in the country; but the traditions and recollections are many and vivid, and the subject of our commercial and political prospects in Japan was frequently discussed. The prime minister requested that I would allow him to send a Siamese noble to accompany me whenever I should visit Japan, and was particularly anxious I should bring him a couple of Japanese swords— than which there is nothing more difficult to obtain in Japan.

The King has seven principal official seals; but he has one which is specially personal, and when a change was made in the Treaty, at the King's particular request, he sent his private seal, desiring that the change might be verified by the impression of that seal. The first seal represents a three-headed elephant, carrying a palace on his back, having two seven-storied umbrellas by the sides; the second has a fabulous beast, called the "king of the lions;" the third, a fabulous bird—the garuda, a monstrous eagle; the fourth, an image of Buddha, seated, having in one hand the expanded flower, and in the other a leaf of the lotus; the fifth has an angel mounted on a demon; the sixth, an angel holding a sword, and seated on a dragon; the seventh, an angel bearing a spear, and mounted on a lion. The seals are all carved or engraved in relief; prepared vermilion is passed over the surface; and the impression is far more durable than wax, which is, indeed, ill suited for tropical usage.

The accession of the present Kings was hailed as promising important changes and useful reforms. The late King was taken ill on the 7th January, 1851, and on the 9th February he summoned his nobles, desiring they would consider who was best qualified to succeed him. But, probably in the expectation that he might recover, and the fear their choice might not be acceptable, as they had determined not to elect the King's son, no decision took place till the 17th March, when the state of the King's health had become desperate. They then designated the legitimate brothers of the King, the Princes Chau Fa Mong Kut and Chau Fa Noi, as heirs to the throne. The King died on the 3rd April, aged sixty-three, having reigned twenty-seven years; and the present First King was conducted from the Buddhist temple, which he had long inhabited, to the palace, and was fully invested with the royal dignities, on the 15th May.

The grandfather of the present Sovereign, and founder of the dynasty, was the Commander-in-Chief of the Siamese army, and was called to the throne in 1782, in consequence of a popular commotion which demanded the deposition of the reigning monarch, on the ground of his being insane. He reigned twenty-nine years, and was succeeded by his eldest son, who reigned thirteen years, and died in 1824, leaving many children, but only two by his Queen—1st, Chau Fa Yai, or T. Y. Chau Fa Mongkut (Crown Prince), and 2nd, Chau Fa Noi, the present First and Second Kings of Siam.

But their elder brother, Kromcluat, the son of their father by an inferior wife—an able, energetic, and intriguing man—managed to get the sovereignty conferred on him by the highest dignitaries, and the nomination was confirmed by a general council of princes and nobles.

Chau Fa Yai withdrew from contesting the throne, and, availing himself of the custom of the Siamese to devote themselves for a certain time to the priesthood, entered a *wat*, and thus avoided any necessity for prostration before his brother, and entitled himself to receive homage in his sacred character from the King himself. He remained nearly twenty-seven years in this political obscurity, but acquired a great religious reputation. He devoted his time to the most laborious studies, became a learned Pali scholar, and the president of the board of examiners into the proficiency of the priesthood in this sacred language; he acquired the Sanscrit, the Cingalese, and the Peguan, and associated his name with the literary honours of the priestly hierarchy. He became to some extent a religious reformer, and, like the Vedanters in Bengal with reference to Brahminism, sought to purify the Buddhist faith by rejecting the enormous masses of tradition and fable, clinging to the moral instructions of Buddhism, and recognising the principles of sound natural philosophy as regards the cosmogony of the universe.

The King was taught Latin by the French Catholic missionaries, principally by Bishop Pallegoix. English he began to study in 1845, principally availing himself of the United States' missionaries. Mr. Carswell devoted a year and a half to instructing him four times a week, one hour each lesson. He occupied himself with astronomical investigations, and is able to calculate an eclipse, and the degrees of latitude and longitude. He has introduced a press, with both Siamese and English types. He was born October 18, 1804, is of middle height, thin, with a somewhat austere countenance: his conversation is highly intelligent, but is carried on in the language of books rather than of ordinary colloquy.

The late King had seven hundred wives: he appointed no successor, but it was believed one of his sons had determined to be a candidate for the crown. The energy of the Praklang (the present Kalahom) saved the nation from the miseries of disputed succession. The Praklang's eldest son, Phya Sisuriwong, held the fortresses of Paknam, and, with the aid of his powerful family, placed Chau Fa Yai upon the throne, and was made Kalahom, being at once advanced ten steps, and to the position the most influential in the kingdom, that of prime minister. On the 18th March, 1851, the Praklang proposed to the council of nobles the nomination of Chau Fa Yai: he held bold language, carried his point, and the next day communicated the proceedings to the elected Sovereign in his *wat*, everybody, even rival candidates, having given in their adhesion. By general consent, Chau Fa Noi was raised to the rank of Wangna, or Second King, having, it is said, one-third of the revenues, with a separate palace and establishment.

The First King took the names of Somdetch Phra Paramendr Maha Mongkut. It is scarcely needful to add, that his reign constitutes one of the most remarkable epochs in the history of Siam, and that the acts of his government are likely to exert the happiest influence on the future well-being of that country.

Of the present King the following account was published in 1837:—

"The Prince Chow Fa, who is one of the royal family, appeared anxious to know how Europeans managed to print, and wished much to be taught the art. He produced a copy of Captain Low's 'Phra Bat,' and pointed out several errors: he says the impression (type) is too short, and in more than one place the Siamese characters are written wrong.

"Chow Fa is likewise very desirous of learning the English language; he speaks it a little, but writes and prints well with the pen. Of this part of his education he is very proud, and his handiwork may be seen all over his palace. On one side of his punkah is written, or rather printed, 'The House of Pleasure,' with his name, 'T. C. Momfanoi;' and on every door he has written something. He has a kind of enclosed pond, with about two dozen alligators in it, though not of a large size, which on one occasion he fed with prawns for the amusement of the writer. The alligator, in order to eat the prawns, is obliged to turn his head round, and take them up with the side of his mouth. The prince offered three or four of these animals; but the writer declined them, preferring to have a Khon Paa (orang-utan) if the prince could obtain one for him. He said he had seen but one himself, and they were not now to be procured."[*]

[*] Moor's *Notices of Ind. Arch.*, p. 232.

Mr. Robbins, an American missionary, bears the following favourable testimony to the King's character:—

"Chow Fali is probably the most intelligent man among the nobility. He has obtained a sufficient knowledge of the English language to enable him to read, write, and speak it with fluency. He has adopted European customs to a considerable extent, and may with propriety be termed a scientific man. Not a man in the kingdom, the King excepted, will attempt to come into his presence without prostrating himself before him. He is very friendly and familiar with the missionaries, and fond of getting our books; and at his house we walk perfectly erect before him. At the time of our visit, he was seated on a velvet cushion, with a gilded covering to the pillow at his back. His only article of dress consisted of a silk sarang, figured with gold and silver, extending from his waist nearly to his feet. The ladies were invited to visit his wives in the inner apartments. They saw twelve of them. He probably has as many more. They seemed happy, and treated our ladies with much attention. Both males and females keep their hair closely shorn, with the exception of a round tuft in front. At this time, however, every female in the kingdom is commanded to shave her head. Their dress is like that of the men, with the addition of a crape scarf or shawl, thrown over one shoulder and passing under the other arm. They are exceedingly desirous of obtaining everything which is European, and which their countrymen do not possess."

I have now before me a curious tract of forty pages, printed at Bangkok in 1850, and which consists of a series of communications from the present King (then H. R. H. T. Y. Chau Fa Mongkut) to the Bangkok Calendar. They give the calculations of the eclipses of the year; and the prince says he prints them, that his foreign friends " may know that he can project and calculate eclipses of the sun and moon, occultations of planets, and some fixed stars of first and second magnitude, of which the immersion in and emersion from the limb of the illuminated moon can be seen by the naked eye, for every place of which the longitude and latitude are certainly known by him."

On more than one occasion the King has written and spoken to me on the subject of polygamy, wishing I should explain to those who might be disposed to censure him, that the habit was Oriental, that it was sanctioned by Siamese laws and usages, and by the Buddhist religion. During the King's seclusion as a bonze, he religiously kept the vow of chastity. He had eleven children when he retired to the temple. He has had fourteen (royal) children born since he ascended the throne in 1851. He wrote to me that in the three months after I left Bangkok, the Royal family had been increased by the birth of *four* children.

On one occasion he pointed out his kitchen with pride, saying, " That is my cook-house; I built the first chimneys in Siam."

He frequently, in conversation, refers to the history of Siam, and on one occasion said: " There have been only two cases of abdication in Siamese history. One was unfortunate; for the King having left the throne, confusion and tumult followed, and he was obliged to resume it." I cannot fancy that the ascetic and secluded life which he led for more than twenty-six years could have much attraction for one obviously fond of pleasure, and whose habits have easily conformed themselves to the luxurious existence so strangely contrasted with the retired and meditative years passed in the convent he so long occupied.

Siam, like all other countries, though preserving many of its ancient forms, has, under the influence of the present King, accommodated itself in many of its Court usages to changes which will place his Majesty in a reasonable position as regards foreign sovereigns. The ambassador of Louis XIV. was not allowed "to represent" his master, and all the honours done were to the King's letter, of which he was the bearer. This distinction was rigidly observed, and great care was taken to show that the ambassador was not invested with any personal dignity. The King of Siam, in those days, returned an answer by messengers of his own; and the ambassador was not allowed to enter the capital until the time for the audience was fixed, nor to remain in the capital after he took leave of the King.* La Loubère seems to have embellished his discourse with figures, introducing sun, moon, stars, and other ornaments; whereupon the King told him he was a "great contriver of words;" thinking that the more the ambassador said, the less the prince was honoured—for "harangues pleased him not at all."

---

* La Loubère, p. 108, 109.

The Second King.

The institution of a Second King is one of the peculiarities of the Siamese usages. He is not charged, as in the case of Japan, with the religious as distinguished from the civil functions of government, but exercises a species of secondary or reflected authority, the limits of which did not appear to me to be at all clearly defined. His title was formerly *Uparat*, but it is now *Wangna*,—literally meaning the junior king. He is said to dispose of one-third of the state revenue, and to have at his command an army of about 2000 men. He is generally a brother or near relation of the King. The present *Wangna*, as I have before mentioned, is a legitimate brother of the First King, a cultivated and intelligent gentleman, writing and speaking English with great accuracy, and living much in the style of a courteous and opulent European noble, fond of books and scientific inquiry, interested in all that marks the course of civilization. His palace is of nearly the same extent as that of the First King. In it is a building which he makes his principal abode, and which has the accommodation and adornings of a handsome European edifice. He is surrounded with the same royal insignia as the First King, though somewhat less ostentatiously displayed; and the same marks of honour and prostration are paid to his person. He has his ministers, corresponding to those of the First King, and is supposed to take a more active part in the wars of the country than does the First King. It is usual to consult him on all important affairs of state. He signed the full powers which were given to the Commissioners who negotiated the Treaty with me; and I was told by the First King that before the final approval of its conditions, he must hold a conference with his Royal brother. He is expected to pay visits of ceremony to the First King, and his salutation consists in elevating his hands; but the brothers sit together on terms of equality. There would seem some danger in the adjacency of sovereignties so likely to clash; and the late King abolished the *Wangna*-ship, which was, however, restored by the present King and the whole body of nobles. The Second King appeared to me more occupied with philosophical pursuits than with state affairs; and probably such a course of abstention is both wise and prudent. The demands of the Second King on the exchequer must be submitted to the First King for approval, and on being sealed by him, are paid by the great treasurer.

Of the present Second King, Mr. Malcom, an American missionary who visited Siam in 1837, writes—

"Chow Fa Noi is the probable successor to the throne, and in fact is now entitled to it, rather than the present monarch, who is an illegitimate son. Should he assume the government, Siam must advance from her present lowliness and semi-civilization. No man in the kingdom is so qualified to govern well. His naturally fine mind is enlarged and improved by intercourse with foreigners, by the perusal of English works, by studying Euclid and Newton, by freeing himself from a bigoted attachment to Buddhism, by candidly recognising our superiority and a readiness to adopt our arts. He understands the use of the sextant and chronometer, and was anxious for the latest Nautical Almanac, which I promised to send him. His little daughters, accustomed to the sight of foreigners, so far from showing any signs of fear, always came to sit upon my lap, though the yellow cosmetic on their limbs was sure to be transferred in part to my dress. One of them took pride in repeating to me a few words of English, and the other took care to display her power of projecting the elbow forward."

In 1830, Mr. Abeel speaks of "the curiosity and covetousness of the princes" who visited him; but of the prince, who is now the Second King, he says, " that if divested of the fear of Royal displeasure, and rightly guided in his fondness for foreign customs, he would become a blessing to the nation. His title is the Lord of Heaven, his age about twenty-three. He has acquired a smattering of English, and is one of the most intelligent, manly, and improvable characters in the kingdom." (P. 234.)

My intercourse with the Second King was in all respects most agreeable. I found him a gentleman of very cultivated understanding,—quiet, even modest in manners,—willing to communicate knowledge, and earnest in the search of instruction. His table was spread with all the neatness and order that are found in a well-regulated English household. A favourite child sat on his knee, whose mother remained crouched at the door of the apartment, but took part in the conversation. The King played to his guests very prettily on the pipes of the Laos portable organ. He had a variety of music; and there was an exhibi-

PRINCE IN FULL DRESS

London, John W. Parker & Son, West Strand, 1857.
M & N HANHART, LITH

tion of national sports and pastimes, equestrian feats, elephant combats, and other amusements. But what seemed most to interest the King, was his museum of models, nautical and philosophical instruments, and a variety of scientific and other curiosities.

The Court.

Princes, Nobles, &c.—Next in authority to the two Kings is one of the princes, upon whom is conferred the title of Wanglang, or Viceroy. He is specially charged with the principal affairs of the State, has a direct jurisdiction over the princes of the blood and the high officers, has the general police of the palace under his direction, and is deemed the governor of the capital city. He is the first of the four princes of the highest rank, called *Krom a luang*; the princes of the second and third rank, who bear respectively the titles of *Krom a khun* and *Krom a mun*, each consist of four persons. These are the only officials of the Royal family; the remaining princes receive allowances from the King, but are represented by Pallegoix as often countenancing and committing abominable acts of tyranny and oppression, and being compelled to engage even in humble labour to maintain their families. Of the twelve official princely dignities, the duties and titles are,—1st, Master of the royal elephants and horses; 2nd, Head of the royal *corvées* (the exemptions from these are represented by Pallegoix as giving in money 12 millions of ticals= $1\frac{1}{2}$ million sterling, to the King); 3rd, The grand chief of foreign nations; 4th, Inspector of agriculture; 5th,

Minister of justice; 6th, President of the royal tribunal; 7th, Second superintendent of elephants and horses; 8th, Head of the medical department, or physicians; 9th, Intendant of arsenals; 10th, Superintendent of workmen, especially of metal founders; 11th, Superintendent of the fine arts, particularly painting; 12th, Inspector of the talapoins, or bonzes.

Among the nobility not of royal blood, there are five classes:—

    1. The *Somdetch chao phaja*.
    2. The *Chao phaja*.
    3. The *Phaja*.
    4. The *Phra*.
    5. The *Luang*.

And the first three divisions are thus classified:—

I.—1. *Somdetch Chao phaja chakri*, Generalissimo and Superintendent of the Northern Provinces.
    2. *Somdetch Chao phaja Kalahom*, Generalissimo and Superintendent of the Marine and Southern Provinces.

II.—3. *Chao phaja tharama*, Governor of the Palace.
    4. *Chao phaja Phra Klang*, Grand Treasurer.
    5. *Chao phaja Pholla tep*, Minister of Agriculture.
    6. *Chao phaja Jomarat*, Head of Functionaries.
    7. *Chao phaja Maha jota*, Chief of the Peguans.

III.—8. *Phaja aphai norit*, First Lieutenant to the Chao phaja Jomarat.
    9. *Phaja nuxit raxa*, Second Lieutenant to ditto:

and so on, there being in all twenty-six officers belonging to the third class of official nobility; those of the fourth and fifth class are the subordinates of the *Phajas*. A sort of prefect, called *Chao-Krom*, is charged with local administration. The prefect has two officers, called *balat-krom*, the lieutenants of the right and the left; who have two assistants called *phu-xuai*, and these again have subordinates named *nai muet*, upon whom from twenty to thirty functionaries depend.

The cities and towns of Siam are classed under four divisions. The capital, and every city in which a tributary prince resides, are *Muang ek*. The provincial capitals are denominated *Muang to*, and are governed by a *phaja*. The towns of the third order, called *Muang tri*, have a *phra* for ruler; and those of the fourth class, called *Muang chatava*, are governed by a *luang*. Every village has a mayor, called a *kamnan*.

The provincial governments are composed of the governor, his *balat* and *jokabat*, *i. e.*, lieutenant and deputy lieutenant. A dozen of the principal people form a council, called *Kromakan*, which meets daily, and settles all important affairs. Great complaints are heard of the exactions of the governors; and it is said they purchase impunity by bribing those on whom they depend.

Authority is for the most part hereditary in Siam, and children succeed to the offices of their parents. Twice a year all functionaries drink the lustral water, which is supposed to secure their loyalty and obedience to the Sovereign. At the end of November the principal officers receive their pay. The princes and ministers are paid each 20lb. of silver (200*l.*); the phajas, from 12lb. to 2lb., according to their rank, *i.e.*, from 120*l.* to 20*l.*; the *phra* and the *luang*, from 120 to 60 ticals (15*l.* to 7*l.* 10*s.*); subaltern officers, 40 to 16 ticals (5*l.* to 2*l.*); while the pay of soldiers, workmen, and others, is only from 10 to 12 ticals. The King has a claim for service on all his subjects; and the statute labour is called *raxa kan*. The Chinese generally pay a capitation tax of 5 ticals, and are compelled to wear a cord round their wrist, with a seal justifying the payment; the richer merchants pay a treble amount, and are relieved from the badge.

The *Khao-duan* is the forced service which the Siamese are bound to pay to the King. It is represented by their bodily labour for three months of the year, during which they are engaged in public works. They may redeem themselves by the annual payment of 16 ticals (40*s.* sterling). Their masters often levy the redemption money, but deprive the State of the service. It is an abuse sanctioned to some extent on the ground that the pay of public functionaries is inadequate to their support; and the abuse has passed into a proverb, which says, *tam na bon láng-phrai*— "they cultivate the backs of the people."

There are many forms of taxation by which the people escape the *corvée*, not only by direct composition for money, but by tribute of various kinds, which long usage has accepted as a proper compensation; but in case of war the King does not exempt any of his subjects from personal military service.

Whole clans are directly dependent on the princes and nobles. There are two forms of subjection,—one of which is limited, the other absolute, slavery. For example, some are bound to furnish rowers for the boats of their masters. When the composition tax is collected for the King, the master frequently comes to the assistance of his vassal, who, if he be unable to pay back the principal and interest, may be sold as a slave; but many of the nobles are satisfied with receiving tribute in the shape of presents and offerings to themselves and their families.

The shaving the tuft of a young prince is a most important ceremony. An artificial mountain is constructed, with a pathway leading to a pavilion at the top. A vast procession of nobles, soldiers, and children of all nations, is in attendance, gaily clad, each bearing a lotus flower. The prince, covered with golden ornaments, is carried on a chair, accompanied by music, and conducted to the presence of the King. He prostrates himself before his father, who leads him to the hall where the ashes of his progenitors are deposited. Here the prince performs acts of adoration during three days. On the fourth his hair is shaven; he is invested with a white instead of red *langouti* (the garment which girds the waist); the procession marches towards the mountain, at the foot of which the prince washes himself, and then ascends to the top with four of the nobles, where, it is said, mysterious communications are made to the future probable occupant of the throne.

Father Bruguière says—" When a prince of the Royal family attains to the age of thirteen or fourteen years, he is removed from the palace, puts on a new dress, and a talapoin cuts his hair. On this occasion, men of the highest rank and intelligence among the four nations in Siam come to the Court in the costume of their respective countries. A kind of mountain, with a pathway to the top, is made, where a tent is erected, and a little below it the figure of one or two elephants, which furnish water that falls into a basin at the base of this artificial mountain. When all is ready, the civil and military officers place themselves in two files, and the procession in this order leaves the palace. The prince who is the object of the ceremony is seated on a chair, which is borne upon the shoulders of the officers. He has on his head a high bonnet, not peaked, and slippers on his feet, and gold bracelets on his arm; a kind of rattle is shaken before him, to signify that he is yet in his infancy;—they also play on the flute, tambourine, and trumpet. The princess who is to be his future wife goes before with her hands joined, holding a plume of peacock's feathers. When the *cortège* returns to the palace, the prince prostrates himself before his father, and the King takes him by the hand and leads him into the temple, where the ashes of their ancestors are deposited, when he adores them.

"This ceremony is repeated for three consecutive days. On the fourth day the talapoins cut his hair in the ancestral temple, and he receives a white dress, instead of the red one he wore during the ceremony. The same day, he goes to the artificial mountain, accompanied by a great retinue, where he washes his hands in the basin, and then ascends with three or four lords to the top of the mountain, into the pavilion, where he is supposed to go through with some superstitious ceremony. There is some resemblance between this

Siamese ceremony and that of the ancient Romans, when their young men took the *toga virilis*."*

One-third of the population of Siam are in the condition of slaves; these are divided into three classes, as explained previously:†—1. Prisoners of war; 2. Redeemable, and 3. Unredeemable slaves. When a foreign country is invaded, the captives are distributed among the nobles, according to the King's pleasure: these captives are transferable at a ransom of 48 ticals (6*l*.) each. Redeemable slaves consist principally of those whose persons are in pawn for debt, and whose services are supposed to pay the interest of the debt. They may be ransomed by the discharge of the debt for which their persons are held in pledge. Unredeemable slaves are children sold by their parents under written contract, and are at the absolute disposal of the purchaser. The price of a slave varies according to age and sex: from twelve to sixteen, the ordinary value is from 40 to 60 ticals; a full-grown man is worth from 80 to 160 ticals. The slavery to which they are subjected is not that of field labour; and on the whole, Pallegoix says they are treated kindly, and better off than domestic servants in Europe.

The funeral ceremonies associated with the burning of the bodies of the high nobility in Siam are of a very costly and ostentatious character. The first Somdetch, who was the senior minister of the Commission charged with the negotiation of the Treaty with England, died a few days after our departure from Bangkok; and I have received from a spectator the following account of the funeral rites:—

* *Annales de la Foi*, xxv.   † See *ante*, p. 189 *et seq.*

"The building of the '*men*,' or temple, in which the burning was to take place, occupied four months; during the whole of which time between three and four hundred men were constantly engaged. The whole of it was executed under the personal superintendence of the 'Kralahome.'

"It would be difficult to imagine a more beautiful object than this temple was, when seen from the opposite side of the river. The style of architecture was similar to that of the other temples in Siam; the roof rising in the centre, and thence running down in a series of gables, terminating in curved points. The roof was covered entirely with scarlet and gold, whilst the lower part of the building was blue, with stars of gold. Below, the temple had four entrances leading directly to the pyre; upon each side, as you entered, were placed magnificent mirrors, which reflected the whole interior of the building, which was decorated with blue and gold, in the same manner as the exterior. From the roof depended immense chandeliers, which at night increased the effect beyond description. Sixteen large columns, running from north to south, supported the roof. The entire height of the building must have been 120 feet, its length about 50 feet, and breadth 40 feet. In the centre was a raised platform about seven feet high, which was the place upon which the urn containing the body was to be placed: upon each side of this were stairs covered with scarlet and gold cloth.

"This building stood in the centre of a piece of ground of about two acres extent, the whole of which ground was covered over with close rattan-work, in

PAGODA OF THE LATE SOMDETCH CHAO PHAJA

order that visitors might not wet their feet, the ground being very muddy.

"This ground was enclosed by a wall, along the inside of which myriads of lamps were disposed, rendering the night as light as the day. The whole of the grounds belonging to the adjoining temple contained nothing but tents, under which Siamese plays were performed by dancing-girls during the day: during the night, transparencies were in vogue. Along the bank of the river, Chinese and Siamese plays (performed by men) were in great force; and to judge by the frequent cheering of the populace, no small talent was shown by the performers, which talent in Siam consists entirely in obscenity and vulgarity.

"All approaches were blocked up long before daylight each morning, by hundreds—nay, thousands of boats of every description in Siam, *sanpans, mapet, ma k'êng, ma guen,* &c. &c.: these were filled with presents of white cloth, no other presents being accepted or offered during a funeral. How many shiploads of fine shirting were presented during those few days, it is impossible to say. Some conception of the number of boats may be had from the fact, that in front of my floating house I counted seventy-two large boats, all of which had brought cloth.

"The concourse of people night and day was quite as large as at any large fair in England; and the whole scene, with the drums and shows, the illuminations and the fireworks, strongly reminded me of Greenwich Fair at night. The varieties in national costume were considerable, from the long flowing dresses of the Mussulman to the scanty *panhung* of the Siamese.

"Upon the first day of the ceremonies, when I rose at daylight, I was quite surprised at the number and elegance of the large boats that were dashing about the river in every direction; some of them with elegantly-formed little spires (two in each boat) of a snowy-white, picked out with gold; others with magnificent scarlet canopies, with curtains of gold; others filled with soldiers dressed in red, blue, or green, according to their respective regiments; the whole making a most effective *tableau*, far superior to any we had during the time the Embassy was here.

"Whilst I was admiring this scene, I heard the cry of '*Sedet*' (the name of the King when he goes out), and turning round, beheld the fleet of the King's boats sweeping down. His Majesty stopped at the '*men*,' where an apartment had been provided for him. The moment the King left his boat, the most intense stillness prevailed,—a silence that was absolutely painful: this was, after the lapse of a few seconds, broken by a slight stroke of a tom-tom. At that sound, every one on shore and in the boats fell on their knees, and silently and imperceptibly the barge containing the high priest parted from the shore at the Somdet's palace, and floated with the tide towards the '*men*.' This barge was immediately followed by that containing the urn, which was placed upon a throne in the centre of the boat. One priest knelt upon the lower part of the urn in front, and one at the back. (It had been constantly watched since his death.) Nothing could exceed the silence and *immoveability* of the spectators: the tales I used to read of nations being turned to statues were here realized, with the exception that all had the same attitude. It was splendid, but it was fearful. During the whole of the next day, the urn stayed in the '*men*,' in order that the people might come and pay their last respects.

"The urn, or rather its exterior cover, was composed of the finest gold, elegantly carved and studded with innumerable diamonds. It was about five feet high, and two feet in diameter.

"Upon the day of the burning, the two Kings arrived about four P.M. The golden cover was taken off, and an interior urn of brass now contained the body, which rested upon cross-bars at the bottom of the urn. Beneath were all kinds of odoriferous gums.

"The First King, having distributed yellow cloths to an indefinite quantity of priests, ascended the steps which led to the pyre, holding in his hand a lighted candle, and set fire to the inflammable materials beneath the body. After him came the Second King, who placed a bundle of candles in the flames; then followed the priests, then the princes, and lastly the relations and friends of the deceased. The flames rose constantly above the vase, but there was no unpleasant smell.

"His Majesty, after all had thrown in their candles, returned to his seat, where he distributed to the Europeans a certain number of limes, each containing a gold ring or a small piece of money; then he commenced *scrambling* the limes, and seemed to take particular pleasure in just throwing them between the princes and the missionaries, in order that they might meet together in the ' tug of war.'

" The next day, the bones were taken out, and distributed amongst his relations; and this closed the ceremonies. During the whole time, the river each night was covered with fireworks; and in Siam the pyrotechnic art is far from being despicable."

The King sent me a long account of the burning of the body of the senior Somdetch. He died in the beginning of April; but the funeral pile was not kindled until the 28th October, in consequence of the many arrangements needed in order to show respect to the dignified position of the dead. The King says—

" His Excellency's funeral hall was erected on the eastern side of your Excellency's residence or landing-house. His remains were kept in a golden coffin, and brought in a suitable procession and retinue. There was the religious condoling of the Buddhist priests, and the last visitation of kindred and friends, native and foreign, during three days,—English and American missionaries, French priests, Portuguese consul. According to Siamese custom, a portion of gold and silver which belonged to the dead was cut in pieces and placed in balls, or wooden fruits (oranges and lemons), and distributed among the kindred and friends of the dead, and at sunset flung among the people in every direction round the funeral hall during every evening of the religious service. This is our Siamese custom; it is not a religious precept or discipline of Buddhism.

" Many boxes were also prepared of artificial flowers,

with pieces of gold and silver belonging to the dead. These are for noble visitors and noble friends—and I send two in a black bag to your Excellency, thinking that, as an intimate friend of his late Lordship, you, our most respected friend in foreign countries, will deem it suitable to accept such token of our and his late Lordship's remembrance. Also another black bag with 20 balls, containing pieces of gold and silver, which gift is like those thrown to the assembled people. I think much of your Excellency on such occasions, and wish you were present now."

The letter is dated from the spot where the ceremonial had taken place.

The Siamese, like all Oriental nations, attach the greatest importance to official seals, and none whatever to signatures. On one occasion, the Second King showed me a large collection—some of them engraved in London—of seals which he used on various occasions and for different purposes. The number employed by the First King is still greater.

Ministers.

Prime Minister.—Of the present Prime Minister, Mr. Abeel says—" He is an intelligent and crafty youth, who exerts a powerful influence for one of his age, and is probably destined to make a conspicuous figure on the political arena of Siam." (P. 235.)

He has well justified this prognostication. His sagacity, his activity, his boldness, his directness of purpose and consistency of action, excited my admiration from my first intercourse, and that feeling was only strengthened by more intimate acquaintance. Whether called by the name of craft or cunning—but, after all, what is the highest wisdom but the best craft and cunning?—whether the object was selfish or patriotic, whether motives unworthy were concealed under conduct the most praiseworthy, I know not, and care not to know; but I deemed it a great privilege to have found such a Prime Minister at Bangkok, and I wish many a civilized nation were as well off for such public servants.

He is one of the most candid persons in an argument, readily and frankly admitting the removal of a difficulty when he sees it has been explained. " I remarked to him," said an American missionary, " that if all the Siamese believed in the omnipresence of God, there would be few acts of theft, whereas they are now alarmingly frequent." " Are there no thieves in your country?" he retorted. " They are few," was the reply; and the missionary said that in the population of his native town an act of theft was almost unknown. The Prime Minister replied, that the Americans took great pains to teach religion to their children and to everybody, but in Siam it was never done. Upon which the missionary reminded him of the multitudes of priests in Siam. " Yes!" said he, " but they do not teach the people, and are often exceedingly vile themselves." He said he could understand the spherical form of the earth, but not (the mysteries of) religion. He accounted the different degree of happiness among men as the result of merit and demerit in previous stages of existence; but he could not see how this distribution of good and evil could be accounted for on the theory of the existence of an all-wise, all-powerful, and benevolent Deity. He asked the missionary to account for the revelation of true religious doctrines to Western nations so many centuries before they were communicated to the East, and was answered that a king does many things without giving his reasons, with which he professed to be satisfied.*

The American missionaries again and again speak of the great intelligence of the present Prime Minister. He invited them and their wives, and introduced them to his own family in his palace, over which is inscribed in large Roman characters, " This is Luang nai Sit's house.—Welcome, friends." They eulogize his acute and capacious mind, and say he encouraged them to teach and distribute tracts among the multitudinous Chinese. On one occasion, when the devotions of the missionaries were disturbed by the noise of Siamese musicians, he told them to remove to a place where he had prepared seats for them:—" Go up yonder, and bless God undisturbed; there is too much confusion for you to stay here:" and he escorted them about on a fine vessel of his building, constructed on a European model, saying (of course in reference to the Chinese)—" They greatly need the labours of missionaries; they have no God, no religion."†

When it was known that I had determined to visit Siam, many discussions took place among the princes and principal nobility as to the manner in which I ought to be received. The old party strenuously

---

* *Missionary Herald* for 1845, p. 274.   † *Ib.*, 1836, p. 327.

advocated a stern and stout resistance, a continuation of the policy which had been exhibited towards Sir James Brooke and Mr. Ballestier; and it was urged that this policy had been pursued with safety, and that whatever may have been the hostile thoughts and wishes of the disappointed envoys, their respective governments had exhibited no ill-will towards Siam, which might still persist in that system of repulsion which had brought with it no real molestation or inconvenience, and was not likely to do so. I have reason to know that at this period the mind of the Prime Minister was in a state of indecision. Many of his confidential conversations have been reported to me, which give evidence of marvellous sagacity, and which show how carefully he weighed the various considerations which presented themselves or were suggested to his mind, and how wisely he decided on a course of action.

Among other curious evidences of the state of his mind, I learnt that on one occasion he sent for a foreign gentleman whose opinion he greatly valued, and in the presence of many persons said to his adviser—

Q. Now *you* must make yourself Sir John Bowring: answer me—Why do you come to Siam?

A. We are become your neighbours—we wish to be your friends. Let us be friendly neighbours. We want to buy and to sell; we have things you would like, you have those we want. Don't shut the door.

Q. The door is not shut!

A. Is there no boom to stop the passage of the river at Paklat?

Q. Well! in a large house with many servants, the door may safely be left open; in a small house with few servants, the doors must be shut. Don't you shut *your* door?

A. Yes! against thieves and robbers.

Q. But we don't shut the door! Anybody may come to Siam.

A. True! but you make us pay too much for passing.

Q. Did we not reduce the payment when you complained?

A. You did; but you farm the articles that we want to buy. You make the prices too high; the ships can realize no profit: so many people take the profits between the labourer who grows and the merchant who sells, that the foreigner can get nothing.

Q. How can we do without taxes?

A. You cannot do without taxes; they should be moderate, not excessive. Besides, there are articles you will not let us buy at all—rice, for instance, and teak-wood.

Q. Teak-wood! we have none to spare. We want it. I wish anybody would find more.

A. There is abundance in the jungle.

Q. No! it is a great way off, far from the river. We have buffaloes and elephants—see how little they bring!

A. You do not encourage those who come to buy.

Q. Talk of rice! Why, in China they have two crops a year. They have mountains and valleys, and can irrigate as they will. As for Siam, it is level. We have too much water, no rice! too little water, no rice! But when we have more than we want, we export.

A. But if you allowed it to be exported, more persons would cultivate. Why is Bangkok, which was once in the midst of jungle, now surrounded with gardens — beautiful, productive gardens? Because there is a market. Open new markets, you won't want produce—rice and sugar. See what a soil you have!

Q. Yes, a soil, but no people. A soil without a people is but a wilderness; and the people we have are so lazy, not like *your* people. Your people might and would cultivate the soil. And then, you have engines and capital, and do everything by machinery. Did not the English once weave their cloth in their own houses? And now the engines make it so cheap, that no one in Siam can live by making thread for cloth.

A. Some suffer, but far more are benefited by cheaper and better clothes.

Q. I don't know that they are better clothed. Now, tell me, if rice costs fifty ticals here, and sells for sixty at Shanghae, is that a profit?

A. But where there is trade, there is a mutual benefit; a better price for what you sell, a lower price for what you buy.

Q. What can we consume? We are a small country. An alliance with England is the intimacy of a poor man with a great prince: the prince gets all the benefits, the poor man makes all the sacrifices. What can England get from Siam? Why, I have heard that there are men in England rich enough to buy all the country.

A. The riches of England grow from the trade of England: that trade is made up from many regions, every one of which will help. Siam will help, Japan will help, Cochin China will help.

Q. We have no wants; we have a hot sun. A gentleman here only requires a waistcoat or so; but with you, how many wants!

A. But you have wants; or why all these clocks, and looking-glasses, and ornaments, and a hundred things?

Q. Well, if we have wants, we have no money.

A. We don't want money—you have what is money to us.

Q. No, no! but we cannot help it. We have got what we have got. You have a parliament, you have laws, you have—[impatiently.]

A. Pray for the blessing you don't possess.

Q. Pray! pray! You have been long praying; have you obtained your prayers?

In conversations like these, who can fail to observe the workings of intelligence of a very high order?

Phra Klang.—I cannot better convey an accurate notion of the intellectual powers and extent of reading of the Phra Klang, than by reporting a conversation which took place a short time ago between this minister and an English gentleman then on a visit to him (in July, 1855).

"His Excellency commenced the conversation by asking 'the reasons and object of the present war between the English and Russians.' This I explained at great length, and his Excellency expressed himself as perfectly satisfied both as to the propriety and justice of the war.

"His Excellency then asked, 'how the English, who inhabit such a small part of the surface of the earth, have conquered the whole of India, and have made themselves feared and respected in every part of the globe?' I assigned as the reason—'1st, their insular position, which, rendering them less liable to invasion at home, permitted them to undertake greater enterprises abroad;—2ndly, that the English are descendants of Saxons, Normans, and Celts; and that while we have inherited many of their bad qualities, we have also inherited and amalgamated the various styles of valour for which those nations were so famous, viz., the Norman impetuosity, the Celtic enthusiasm, and the Saxon solidity.'

"Having, as I thought, given a very sufficient reason, I was much surprised to hear his Excellency burst out indignantly, and with a fluency that gave me the greatest difficulty in following him; and although, in general, neither his form nor features appear calculated to express much feeling, yet, as he warmed with the subject, he really seemed to become another man. I give his general meaning, as far as either Mr. Hunter or myself can recollect: 'No; it is neither their position, advantageous as it doubtless is, nor the men, though brave as lions, that has raised them to their present position. Other nations have had the same opportunities in situation, and have had brave soldiers; yet they never held their ground like the English. It is their government,—that admirable form of administration which is held in equal balance by the king, by the nobles, by the people,—that government in which every man feels that he has a certain share—that country in which he feels that his interest is cared for: these are the things that enable a man to fight— the man with a free spirit will dare things that would appal a slave. Can it be good that a few should legislate for all? Look at the Laos country: there, each district chooses one man to become a member of the Council of Six. These are the advisers of the king, and without their sanction the king can do nothing; but still he is entitled to dissent. Consider the consequences. The king and council vote for war: every man hastens to be the first to show his faith in the opinions of the council. There you can sleep without thinking of shutting or barring a door; whilst here you must watch everything with the greatest care, and even then you are not safe. We have hitherto given all the power to the nobles, and what are we? Let us give a little to the people, and try whether we shall not improve. Let us not have our ministers appointed for life; let them be elected for a term of years, and let their election depend upon the voice of the people. The more we mix with the English, the sooner will our people feel that they have a right to have some voice in the framing of laws by which they are to be governed. And if they do assert that right, who would oppose them? We have no regular army; a few slaves of the King take that name, but they would not fight against their fellows.'

" His Excellency continued to speak, with but few interruptions, for nearly two hours; but I think I have given the substance of his discourse."

The *Phra Klang*, or minister for foreign affairs, is generally spoken of by travellers as the Barcalan, or Barcalâo; a Portuguese corruption of the Siamese title, which means " lord of the factories or magazines." He is the regular channel for correspondence with foreign nations or governments, though, on all grave matters, he acts under the guidance of the Phra Kalahom, as the Kalahom is immediately controlled by the King.

There was in La Loubère's time, he says, one noble who had the privilege of not prostrating himself in the presence of the King, and he was held in high honour; but he did not discover this dignitary on the great reception, nor could he learn what were his functions. I observed no case of exception to the universal prostration, and am disposed to think so remarkable a personage (if such there be) could not have escaped notice, and that his privilege (if there had been any such) would have been reverted to in some of my many conversations and interviews with the King and the nobles.

The White Elephant.

The extraordinary reverence for white elephants is a superstition of ancient date, and their capture forms an important portion of Siamese records. In the year 908 (A.D. 1546), the annals state that a white elephant seven feet high was taken, and called " the gem of the sky." " The glory of the land," " the radiance of the world," " the earth-leveller," are among the titles—for every white elephant has a title—given to the honoured animals. This era was deemed most auspicious, for in the following year, 1547, three white elephants were captured, and in 1548 two more. The King then possessed seven, and all nations came to traffic and to pay honour. The King of Pegu asked for two of the elephants to be given him from the King of Siam's superfluity; but the Siamese Monarch refusing to surrender his treasure, was invaded by a Peguan army of 900,000 men, 7000 war elephants, and 15,000 horses, which, marching upon the Siamese capital, extracted four white elephants instead of two.

The real cause of the reverence in which the white elephant is held, is that he is supposed to be the incarnation of some future Buddha, and will therefore bring blessings on the country which possesses so great a treasure.* Hence the white elephant is sought with intense ardour, the fortunate finder rewarded with honours, and he is treated with attention almost reverential. This prejudice is traditional, and dates from the earliest times. When a tributary king, or governor of a province, has captured a white elephant, he is directed to open a road through the forest for the comfortable transit of the sacred animal; and when he reaches the Meinam, he is received on a magnificent raft, with a chintz canopy, and garlanded with flowers. He occupies the centre of the raft, and is pampered with cakes and sugar. A noble of high rank, sometimes a prince of royal blood (and on the last occasion

---

* The Indians (Hindoos) report that Buddha, under the form of a white elephant, glided into the body of a chaste and virtuous queen, named Mayé, and came forth, after ten months, from her right side.—*Histoire Générale de la Chine*, v. 53.

both the First and Second Kings), accompanied by a great concourse of barges, with music and bands of musicians, go forth to welcome his arrival. Every barge has a rope attached to the raft, and perpetual shouts of joy attend the progress of the white elephant to the capital, where, on his arrival, he is met by the great dignitaries of the State, and by the Monarch himself, who gives the honoured visitor some sonorous name, and confers on him the rank of nobility. He is conducted to a palace which is prepared for him, where a numerous court awaits him, and a number of officers and slaves are appointed to administer to his wants in vessels of gold and silver.

A superabundance of delicacies is provided for his repast; if his tusks are grown, they are enriched with rings; a sort of diadem is placed on his head; and his attendants prostrate themselves, as in the presence of the great nobles. When conducted to the bath, a huge red parasol is held over him; music and a *cortège* of slaves accompany him on his march. In case of illness, he is attended by a court physician; the priests wait upon him, offer up prayers for his recovery, and sprinkle him with consecrated water; and on his death there is a universal mourning, and distinguished funeral honours are paid to his remains.

Of the white elephant, Van Schouten says: " This country is the only one in which there are white elephants. The people say that the white elephant is a prince among the rest: the Kings of Siam have long possessed some which they treat as if they were indeed royal princes, causing them to be served with much pomp and magnificence. The King himself often visits them, and they are fed from vessels of gold. Sixty years ago, the King of Siam waged war against the Sovereign of Pegu to get one of these white elephants; Siam was conquered, and made tributary.

" During the period of my residence, the King was so fortunate as to possess two white elephants, who, however, shortly after died of grief. The people believe there is something divine in these animals, and adduce many proofs of it; so that they esteem them not only on account of the services they render, but for the intelligence they admire in these creatures. They believe that they rejoice in being treated according to their merit, when other elephants show them the respect they deserve; but that they are sad and melancholy when slighted or disrespectfully treated." (P. 32.)

Father Bruguière, speaking of the reverence of the Siamese for the white elephant, says:* " Nothing can equal their veneration for the white elephant; the King, at least, must have one as a palladium for his own life, and the prosperity of the empire.

" If the elephant dies, the King loses all the merit acquired in nourishing him; he is himself likely to die the same year: hence the great pains taken for his health. This elephant has the title of Chau p'aja, answering to grandees of the first class among the Spaniards; they take rank immediately after princes of the blood. One who should call him by his proper name would be severely punished: he lives in a kind of palace, with a numerous court of officers, guards,

---

* *Annales de la Foi,* xxv.

valets, &c.; he wears a kind of diadem on his head, and gold rings on his tusks; he is served in golden vessels, and fed on sugar-cane and delicious fruits.

"When he goes to bathe, a numerous *cortège* accompanies him; one keeps time with music, and another holds over him the red parasol of state, used only by high dignitaries. His officers may not withdraw from his presence without a profound salutation; when sick, the King's physicians attend him, and talapoins visit him, to pray for his cure and sprinkle him with holy water. In spite of all these attentions, the white elephant is often in bad humour, and many a time would have killed the talapoins if they had not kept a respectful distance from the trunk and tusks of his lordship. The one kept at present is so intractable, that they have been obliged to cut off his tusks. Every evening he is entertained with music until his excellency goes to sleep. When he dies, the King and Court are in great affliction, and give him funeral honours according to his rank. It is said that sometimes he has public audiences, when presents are made to him, which if he accepts, proves that the donor has much merit; if he refuses them, it is evidence that he is not favoured of Heaven: but I do not guarantee the certainty of this statement. He who captures one of these animals is ever after exempt, with his posterity, from all taxation and vassal service. It is difficult to assign a cause for this extravagant adulation. I think I have seen somewhere that the ancient Kings of Siam called themselves the sons of the white elephant: some among these people think differently, saying that the soul of a defunct King enters the body of an elephant; others own that they know nothing of the reason; among whom, for the present, I range myself, while waiting further information."

The white monkeys enjoy almost the same privileges as the white elephant; they are called *pája*, have household and other officers, but must yield precedency to the elephant. The Siamese say that "the monkey is a man,—not very handsome, to be sure; but no matter, he is not less our brother." If he does not speak, it is from prudence, dreading lest the King should compel him to labour for him without pay: nevertheless, it seems he has spoken, for he was once sent in the quality of generalissimo to fight, if I mistake not, an army of giants. With one kick, he split a mountain in two; and report goes that he finished the war with honour.

The Siamese have more respect for white animals than for those of any other colour. They say that when a talapoin meets a white cock, he salutes him,— an honour he will not pay a prince.

Immediately after the Royal reception at the palace, we were conducted to the domicile of the white elephant, the possession of which formed a frequent topic of self-congratulation in the conversation of the King. Amidst the most valued presents sent by his Majesty to the Queen Victoria, was a tuft of the white elephant's hairs; and of the various marks of kindness I received from the King, I was bound to appreciate most highly a few hairs from the tail, which his Majesty presented to me. He caused portraits of the elephant to be drawn, some of which were distributed among the principal gentlemen of my *suite*.

The accompanying engraving is a reduced fac-simile of the honoured animal, the account of which was furnished in Siamese and English by the King himself.

The white elephant died on the 8th of September, 1855. Her loss was a source of deep sorrow at Court. The King sent me, as a mark of Royal favour " from a beloved and faithful friend," a portion of her white skin, " with beautiful body-hairs preserved in spirits," which I transferred to the museum of the Zoological Society of London.

The Army.

One of the probable consequences of the communications now established between Siam and civilized Western nations will be the re-organization of her army, by which, no doubt, her relative position as regards surrounding nations will be mightily strengthened. Neither Cochin China, nor Tong King, nor the unconquered parts of Cambodia,—nor, indeed, any of the circumjacent regions,—could resist the power of Siam, if her military means were placed under the guidance of European skill.

Military science, judged of by any European standard, has not made much progress among the Siamese; nor, though so frequently engaged in contests with their neighbours, can they be called in any respect a warlike nation. A few officers have been engaged in the attempt to introduce the discipline of Western nations, but their numbers have been too few to produce any considerable change; and though some of the troops wear the uniform of sepoys and of foot

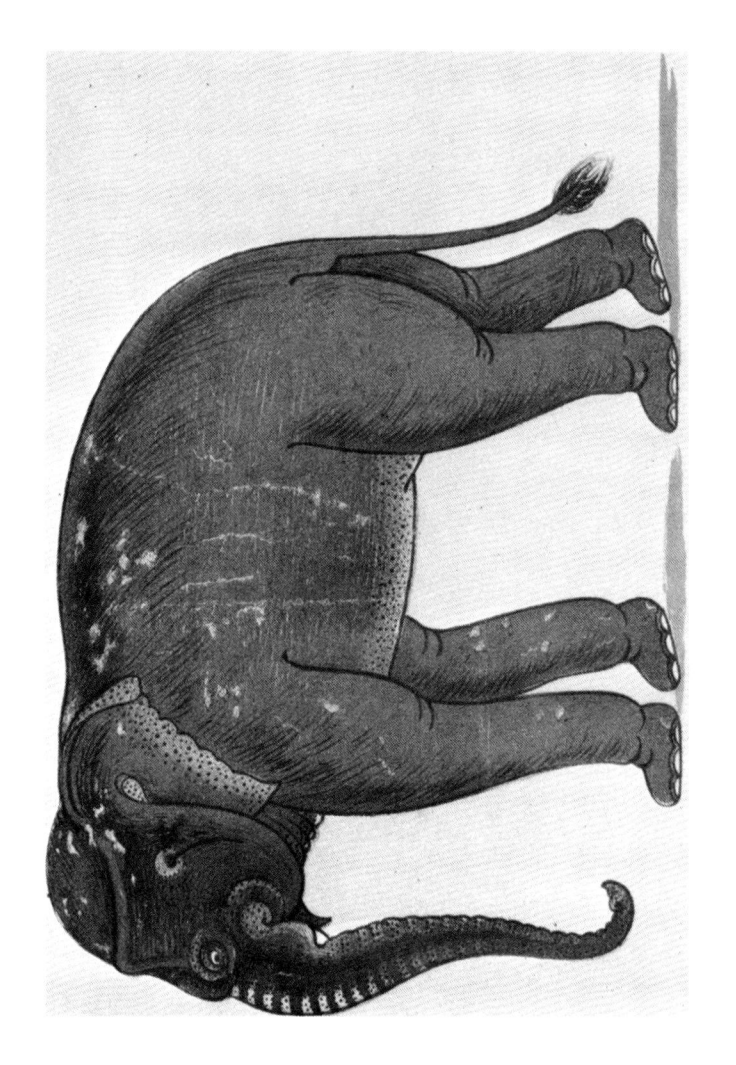

THE SACRED ELEPHANT OF SIAM

artillery, it can hardly be said that the object of the Government has been effected, or that there are any regiments which could cope with even the worst disciplined troops of the West.

When the people are summoned to war, a month's rations are provided by the Government, which undertakes to arm the population. There is no species of weapon, from a knife to a rifle, which is not called into service,—swords and spears in every possible variety, bows of all shapes and sizes; and though I have been told there is a military uniform, consisting of a red, blue, or green vest, with many-coloured loose cotton trousers, I observed among the so-called soldiery costumes as multifarious as the tribes and tongues of their wearers. A small body of Catholic soldiers, consisting of those mingled races which are found in all the localities where the foreigner has at any time left the record of his presence, are dressed almost in the European style.

The departure of the army is always appointed for some auspicious day, fixed by the official Brahmins or soothsayers, who are consulted by the King. Holy water is sprinkled by the bonzes over the soldiers, and an effigy of the prince or rebel who is about to be attacked is introduced. The public executioner strikes a heavy blow on the head of the image; and if it fall down, it is deemed a happy augury; if not, disastrous results are anticipated. The general-in-chief then draws his sword, to the sound of gongs and amidst the shouts of the soldiers, and the whole body march towards the river. There is a superstition, that if a boat should cross the stream above the spot where the troops are embarked, the campaign will be unfortunate. Public criers are, however, sent along the shores to announce the coming of the troops; but Pallegoix says the persons on board any boat which should traverse the river against the proclamation would be pitilessly massacred.*

On quitting the river, elephants are brought to carry the artillery and ammunition, and the principal chief. Each division of the army has its silk or cloth banner, generally decorated with lions, dragons, or fabulous monsters. The royal flag has a white elephant on a scarlet ground, surrounded by a white edge. Every soldier has a piece of bamboo suspended from his neck, which he fills with water whenever he finds the opportunity; and he replenishes his sack and supplies his wants by indiscriminate pillage whenever his small provision of rice is exhausted.

It is said that the Siamese have been able to gather together armies of from two to three hundred thousand men, with some thousands of horses and a thousand elephants, to act against the Cambodians, Birmans, and other neighbouring enemies. But the last campaign which was undertaken against the Laos tribes was by no means fortunate; and, as far as I could learn from an English officer who accompanied it, the war was carried on in utter disregard of all intelligent strategy,† and rather resembled the maraudings of wild tribes than any well-planned purpose. The country itself was little known to the invaders; the

---

* Pallegoix, i. 315.
† The King's account of this war is given in the Appendix.

maps furnished to the chiefs, rude, imperfect, and incorrect; the loss of life great; and, from the want of forage, elephants and horses perished in great numbers.

Every form of superstition accompanies the progress of the army; every trifle becomes an augury of good or evil; the non-observance of some usage, such as the wearing a wrong-coloured garment on a particular day, is deemed sufficient to decide the fate of a battle. Nothing but a long course of severe discipline can raise the *morale* of such a *matériel* as constitutes the main elements of the Siamese army; but its character will change by the adjacency of the Indian forces, and the growing intercourse which is likely to be established between Siam and more advanced countries; for it cannot be doubted that the commercial relations which will grow out of the Treaty of 1855 will give to Siam a new importance in the eyes of statesmen, and that the position of the country in reference to Birmah and the Tenasserim provinces will make it a valuable ally and auxiliary, should the conduct of the rulers of Ava be such as to give anxiety to the Government of India.

The retreat of a Siamese soldier before the enemy without the orders of his chief is punishable with death. The position of a general is understood to be behind, and not in front of his troops. A story is told of a late commander-in-chief who had a long lance, with which he was in the habit of " pricking" his troops in their hinder parts, shouting loudly, " Forward, my children! forward!"

The arsenals of the Siamese are generally well supplied, and the provision of military stores is not neglected.

Ordinary prisoners are not treated with inhumanity; but captive princes are carried about in iron cages and exposed to much insult, and are generally condemned to end their days fettered in dungeons.

The Siamese marine consists of five hundred war-junks, and twenty square-rigged vessels: the latter are mostly under the command of Europeans. In the course of a few years, the nautical habits of the Siamese, encouraged by the presence of foreigners, will probably lead to the creation of a powerful navy—powerful as compared with any possessed by their neighbours.*

Miscellanea.

The officer charged with the superintendence of the Christian races in Bangkok informed me that their number was between three and four thousand; and this statement was confirmed to me by the Catholic missionaries. They are mostly composed of the descendants, by native women, of the Portuguese settlers who, from the days of their ancient Oriental glories, have been from time to time poured out upon the various countries of the East. Few of these mixed races have retained the language of their forefathers: of those who are still able to speak Portuguese with tolerable correctness, several were retained for my service by the Court. We were welcomed at Paknam

---

* Pallegoix, i. 320.

by a functionary of Portuguese blood, clad in a European Court dress, which he said had been presented to him by Sir James Brooke: it was somewhat tarnished, and his cocked-hat had more of a rusty than a raven hue. His name was Alvergarias. At Paklat he was the master of the ceremonies.

Siam has obtained a world-wide fame by the production of the Siamese twins (children, however, of a Chinese father), and I conclude this chapter with the following account, as given by Mr. Abeel, of another strange phenomenon—a child whose aquatic virtues naturally excited much attention in Siam.

"Mr. Hunter sent for us to witness a sight which in more enlightened countries than Siam would be considered equally strange. It was a young child sporting in the water as in its native element, with all the buoyancy and playfulness of a fish. Its evolutions are astonishing, sometimes rolling over with a rapid motion and apparently no exertion, then turning round like a hoop by bending its face under, as it lies on its back, and throwing its feet over its head. It floats like a cork, with no apparent motion of any of the muscles; occasionally allows itself to sink till only half of the head is seen, dives, holds its face under water enough to alarm those who are ignorant of its powers, and yet appears to breathe as easily as though it had suffered no suspension of respiration. From its actions and countenance it is evidently delighted with the exercise, evinces no fatigue nor the least apprehension, and often cries when taken up. It is a singular object, both in and out of the water. It is three years old, very small, can neither speak nor walk, is very defective in sight, will take nothing but its earliest provision,—in fact, appears quite idiotic, and has exhibited the same fondness for the water, and peculiar feats in it, from the first year of its age, the first time that it was tried." (P. 296—7.)

END OF VOL. I.